COVID-19 AND FOREIGN AID

This book provides a timely, critical, and thought-provoking analysis of the implications of the disruption of COVID-19 to the foreign aid and development system, and the extent to which the system is retaining a level of relevance, legitimacy, or coherence.

Drawing on the expertise of key scholars from around the world in the fields of international development, political science, socioeconomics, history, and international relations, the book explores the impact of the COVID-19 pandemic on development aid within an environment of shifting national and regional priorities and interactions. The response is specifically focused on the interrelated themes of political analysis and soft power, the legitimation crisis, poverty, inequality, foreign aid, and the disruption and re-making of the world order. The book argues that complex and multidirectional linkages between politics, economics, society, and the environment are driving changes in the extant development aid system. *COVID-19 and Foreign Aid* provides a range of critical reflections to shifts in the world order, the rise of nationalism, the strange non-death of neoliberalism, shifts in globalisation, and the evolving impact of COVID as a cross-cutting crisis in the development aid system.

This book will be of interest to researchers and students in the field of health and development studies, decision-makers at government level as well as to those working in or consulting to international aid institutions, regional and bilateral aid agencies, and non-governmental organisations.

Viktor Jakupec is an Honorary Professor at Deakin University and the University of Potsdam. He is an international development aid consultant and a member of the Leibniz Sozietät der Wissenschaften, Berlin.

Max Kelly is Associate Professor of International and Community Development, and Research Associate at the Centre for Humanitarian Leadership, Deakin University.

Michael de Percy is a Senior Lecturer in Political Science at the University of Canberra. He was appointed to the Australian Research Council's College of Experts in 2022.

COVID-19 AND FOREIGN AID

Nationalism and Global Development in a New World Order

Edited by
Viktor Jakupec, Max Kelly, and Michael de Percy

Routledge
Taylor & Francis Group
LONDON AND NEW YORK

Cover image: © Getty Images

First published 2023
by Routledge
4 Park Square, Milton Park, Abingdon, Oxon OX14 4RN

and by Routledge
605 Third Avenue, New York, NY 10158

Routledge is an imprint of the Taylor & Francis Group, an informa business

British Library Cataloguing-in-Publication Data
A catalogue record for this book is available from the British Library

Library of Congress Cataloging-in-Publication Data
Names: Jakupec, Viktor, 1945- editor.
Title: Covid-19 and foreign aid : nationalism and global development in a new world order / edited by Viktor Jakupec, Max Kelly and Michael de Percy.
Description: New York, NY : Routledge, 2023. | Series: Rethinking development | Includes bibliographical references and index. |
Identifiers: LCCN 2022025505 (print) | LCCN 2022025506 (ebook) | ISBN 9781032227146 (hardback) | ISBN 9781032227115 (paperback) | ISBN 9781003273844 (ebook)
Subjects: LCSH: Economic assistance—Social aspects. | Economic assistance—Political aspects. | COVID-19 (Disease)—Social aspects. | Nationalism.
Classification: LCC HC60 .C6668 2023 (print) | LCC HC60 (ebook) | DDC 362.1962/4144—dc23/eng/20220826
LC record available at https://lccn.loc.gov/2022025505
LC ebook record available at https://lccn.loc.gov/2022025506

ISBN: 978-1-032-22714-6 (hbk)
ISBN: 978-1-032-22711-5 (pbk)
ISBN: 978-1-003-27384-4 (ebk)

DOI: 10.4324/9781003273844

Typeset in Bembo
by codeMantra

CONTENTS

FIGURES

TABLES

CONTRIBUTORS

Yan Bennett is an Attorney at Law and Assistant Director of the Paul and Marcia Wythes Center on Contemporary China at Princeton University and Adjunct Professor of International Affairs at George Washington University.

Stephen Brown is a Professor at the School of Political Studies, the University of Ottawa, where he is also affiliated with the School of International Development and Global Studies.

Tom Christensen is a Professor Emeritus at the Department of Political Science, University of Oslo; Visiting Professor at the School of Public Administration and Policy, Renmin University; and Distinguished Visiting Professor at the School of Public Policy and Administration, Tsinghua University.

Qun Cui is an Associate Professor at the Qingdao Institute of Administration, Shandong Province, China, in eastern coastal China.

Tobias Debiel is Professor of International Relations and Development Policy at the University of Duisburg-Essen (UDE), Deputy Director of the Institute for Development and Peace (INEF), as well as Co-Director of the Käte Hamburger Kolleg/Centre for Global Cooperation Research.

Michael de Percy is a Senior Lecturer in Political Science at the Canberra School of Politics, Economics, and Society, University of Canberra. He was appointed to the Australian Research Council's College of Experts in 2022.

Lisheng Dong is a Professor at the School of Government, University of Chinese Academy of Social Sciences (UCASS).

Leonid Grigoryev is a Tenured Professor and Academic Supervisor at the Department of World Economy, Faculty of World Economy and International Affairs, Higher School of Economics University, Russia.

Viktor Jakupec is an Honorary Professor at Deakin University and the University of Potsdam. He is an international development aid consultant and a member of the Leibniz Sozietät der Wissenschaften, Berlin.

Max Kelly is Associate Professor of International and Community Development and Research Associate at the Centre for Humanitarian Leadership, Deakin University.

Andrey Kortunov is the Director General of the Russian International Affairs Council. He is a member of expert and supervisory committees and boards of trustees of several Russian and international organisations.

Anthea McCarthy-Jones is a Senior Lecturer and Higher Degree by Research Coordinator in the School of Business at University of New South Wales, Canberra.

Mark McGillivray is an Honorary Professor at the Australian National University Poverty and Inequality Research Centre.

Mary Ana McGlasson is an Associate Professor and Director at the Centre for Humanitarian Leadership, Deakin University.

Nadja Meisterhans is a Guest Professor at the Institute for International Development, University of Vienna, and an Associate Professor at the Karlshochschule/International University in Karlsruhe.

Alexandra Morozkina is an Associate Professor at the Higher School of Economics University, Russia; Head of the Structural Reforms Division at the economic expert group; and Senior Research Fellow at the Financial Research Institute of the Ministry of Finance of the Russian Federation.

Japhace Poncian is a Lecturer in Development Studies at Mkwawa University College of Education, Tanzania.

Matthias Rompel is Honorary Professor of Development Studies at the Justus-Liebig-Universität Giessen, Germany, and the Head of the Southern Africa Division of Deutsche Gesellschaft für Internationale Zusammenarbeit (GIZ).

Morgane Rosier is a PhD candidate at the School of International Development and Global Studies, University of Ottawa.

Mathieu Rousselin is a Lecturer in Political Education at the German Federal Office for Family and Civil Society, Germany, and an independent researcher.

Angeles Sánchez is an Associate Professor in the Department of Applied Economics at the University of Granada.

Lama Tawakkol is a PhD candidate at Queen's University. Her research is primarily related to Critical Political Economy and Critical Theory.

1

TOWARDS A POST-COVID WORLD ORDER

A critical analysis

Viktor Jakupec, Max Kelly, and Michael de Percy

Introduction

Two years into the COVID-19 pandemic, addressing COVID-19 is still at the forefront of collective action in most countries. The Omicron variant has produced a significant increase in cases, globally, particularly in Europe and North America (in early 2022). Simultaneously, preventing, testing, and treating for SARS-CoV-2, the virus that causes COVID-19, is a global priority for medical and pharmaceutical research and development. The development and rollout of vaccines have been the most prominent causes for optimism in managing the impact of COVID-19. However, the multiple impacts of COVID-19 and access to vaccines are driven by a complex array of political, economic, and social factors, particularly at the global level, with repercussions at the national and local levels that are divergent within and between countries. The complex interactions of the pandemic, economically, socially, and politically, within and between countries, are impacted by, as well as impact, human development and well-being. The political and economic framing of the 'crisis' and discourses around what a post-pandemic or post-crisis world may look like are as much political and ideological as pragmatic.

Since the beginning of the 21st century, the world has experienced multiple crises, ranging from the Global Financial Crisis (GFC) to the European Monetary Crisis to the climate and environmental crisis and, more recently, the COVID-19 crisis. Some of the effects of these crises are rising inequality, stagnant economic growth globally (albeit both effects have some notable exceptions), and degradation of the natural environment. There are increased calls among academics, politicians, civil society organisations, non-government organisations (NGOs), multilateral aid institutions, and supranational organisations for socio-political and economic changes. Political push and pull, from the left and the right, debate

DOI: 10.4324/9781003273844-1

the role of the individual versus the state and market in enacting desired change, the role of supranational bodies versus the state, and whether and how global solidarity retains relevance. Populism, nationalism, illiberal democracies, and deglobalisation are under the spotlight. Economically, neoliberalism is structurally entrenched, conceptually slippery, and widely reviled (Rodrik, 2017). The political economy of aid and development is bounded by the institutions that structure its delivery (cf. Gibson *et al.*, 2005). Arguably, the COVID-19 pandemic has exposed significant fractures in the existing global foreign aid system couched in the liberal rules-based world order ideology. Global change in governance, relative powers of nations, and world order is inevitable, yet the nature or direction of change is highly uncertain, with reference to economics, politics, and society. There is, however, a sense of inertia in how change is to happen, and driven by whom, particularly regarding global affairs.

The World Economic Forum's (2022, p. 7) *Global Risks Report 2022* begins with a dire summary of the contemporary context:

> The immediate human and economic cost of COVID-19 is severe. It threatens to scale back years of progress on reducing poverty and inequality and to further weaken social cohesion and global cooperation.

The report identifies the challenges to national policy making during the pandemic, noting that the responses caused new political tensions to institutions (and policies) that threatened the collapse of multilateralism.

Further, multilateral institutions and policies to support international coordination were already in decline, and responses to the pandemic have caused new geopolitical tensions. With new stalemates and flashpoints in view, Global Risks Perception Survey respondents rated 'state collapse' and 'multilateralism collapse' as critical threats over the next five to ten years (World Economic Forum, 2022, p. 24).

Finally, the chapter turns to notions of legitimacy, the current context of the pandemic, drawing on notions of world order, and the evolving positioning of the multilateral development system. The discussion addresses the impact of COVID-19 on foreign aid under the umbrella of political analysis and the use of soft power; disruption and re-making, based on the impact the COVID-19 pandemic on foreign aid and the potential demise of multilateral institutions of the rules-based world order; poverty and inequality as far as foreign aid is concerned; and tactical vantage points taken by multilateral, bilateral, and unilateral foreign aid agencies, in COVID-19 pandemic settings and the rise of the 'vaccine nationalism' and 'climate coalition'.

Problematics

Considering the various critical threats and crises, the fundamental nature of the contemporary 'world order' is increasingly in flux. The liberal international order promulgated through 70 years of US-led discourse and practice, enacted through a development sector ideologically and practically driven by 'Western' interests and institutions, is under stress, internally and externally. Challenges from within the bastions of the Western liberal order include populism, nationalism, illiberal democracy, and deglobalisation, among others. External challenges incorporate significant shifts in the global political economy, the rising powers of China and India, and the complexities of the global role of Russia in the 21st century, among others. In essence, there is a geographical shift in development, from a northern version of modernity driven by a free-market neoliberal model to be transposed to the Global South, to a global context of unequal growth and development.

Against this background and in an atmosphere of the COVID-19 pandemic and its impact on the rules-based world order and foreign aid, the overarching aim of the book therefore is to address the key research question, 'what are the implications of the disruption of the foreign aid and development system from COVID-19?'. This raises the secondary question of 'to what extent is the development aid system retaining a level of relevance, legitimacy, or coherence?'. In order to address this question, combinations and intersections of perspectives and discourses frame this collection from disciplines including international development, political science, socioeconomics, history, and international relations. The response is specifically focused on the following interrelated themes: political analysis and soft power; the legitimation crisis, disruption, and re-making of the world order; and poverty, inequality, and foreign aid.

From this vantage point, this chapter critically unpacks the frames within which the contributions fit. Subsequently, an analysis of key concepts is provided. These include the concepts of 'world order', global distribution of power, the potential disruptors of global powers and the shifting roles of USA and China, and 'middle powers' in determining economic and political shifts. The focal point of this analysis is development aid and multilateral and bilateral development systems, which have evolved alongside a predominantly liberal Western world order but have shifted significantly both leading up to the COVID-19 pandemic and since.

From a problematic's vantage point, a cautionary note is in place, namely, the mid- and long-term impacts of COVID-19 pandemic on the world order of whichever kind one ascribes to remain unknown. One may, however, advance the idea that this catastrophe will enable governments and multilateral international organisations, including aid agencies, to utilise the emerging global COVID-19 crisis as an expedient self-justification for regressive intrusions on governance, financialisation, aid conditionalities, human rights, and other aspects of social, economic, and political lives.

World order

The pre-COVID-19 world order, be it prefixed as 'new' or 'international' or 'liberal' or 'neoliberal', has ideally one central purpose, namely, to bring all nations – developed and developing – in line with the specific socioeconomic and socio-political values, norms, and ideologies. In order to achieve this, the guardians of the world order use multilateral, global, and bilateral organisations as hegemonic instruments of governability, thereby aspired to ensure and maintain global governance of multilateral organisations, including international foreign aid agencies over sovereign states. In pursuit of expanding their own values, norms, and ideologies across the globe, the 'Western' origins of agencies such as the World Bank, International Monetary Fund (IMF), the World Trade Organization (WTO), and many others became anarchic. That means that they took on the role of the highest authority above member countries, whereby the latter lose their sovereignty in many political, economic, and social aspects. Today, in the COVID-19 era, however, there is a tendency emerging in which populaces are told that the health crisis requires obedience to bureaucratic authority (Stückelberger, 2020). This, so the argument goes, is necessary to enable economic recovery and national economic prosperity (Furman *et al.*, 2020). In other words, governments are reclaiming their anarchic status, moving away from the various forms of existing world order towards COVID-19 nationalism or COVID-19 national illiberalism, or anywhere in between.

Haass and Kupchan (2021) argue that we are in an evolving space of multiple power centres, a space which could lead to increased competition and conflict:

> A big part of the problem is that the existing international governance architecture, much of it erected soon after World War II, is outdated and not up to the task of preserving global stability. The US-centered alliance system is a club of democracies, poorly suited to fostering cooperation across ideological lines. Fly-in, fly-out G7 or G20 summits are episodic and spend too much time haggling over *communiqués*. The United Nations provides a standing global forum, but its Security Council invites grandstanding and paralysis among veto-wielding permanent members.
>
> *(p. 1)*

The notion of an unruly world, managed by no one, stands in contrast to the dream of a liberal world order.

There is a plethora of complex terminology and concepts embedded in the contested notion of a 'world order'. Scholars of international relations and world politics have debated for decades the existence of an international (or global) order, including what sustains or changes it and whether change is within the order or of the order (cf. Eilstrup-Sangiovanni and Hofmann, 2020).

Although an in-depth analysis of notions and understandings of world order is beyond the scope of this chapter, it is helpful to consider where the locus of discussions on world order may be relevant to debates concerning COVID-19 and development. As indicated above, the primary locus of this chapter, as well as this volume, refers to power, globally, among and between states and the resulting impact on economic and political ideology, values, and norms, which are formed by the society and which, at the same time, form societies; for example, the international order, established by 'Western' post–World War II (WWII) allies, encompassing liberal political and economic rules, a network of international organisations, and enforced by powerful nations. These nations ensure the world order maintenance at a systemic level, which itself is problematic.

For example, the Royal Institute of International Affairs (RIIA, 2015) conference raised three interconnected problems (in relation to system maintenance but relevant to this debate in terms of system disruption): legitimacy (the adherence to rules underpinning the system, by the principals), equity (rules-based order must work for the majority), and self-confidence (in the immutability of a system that breeds complacency). Global governance echoes historic hegemonic and rising powers, embracing in the post-war era the dominance of the liberal world order of the US or 'Western' powers, versus the rise and fall of the USSR, and, more recently, the shifts and transitions of polarities between the USA, China, and other powers.

These transitions are felt in supranational institutions, and particularly the multilateral development system incorporating the Bretton Woods institutions (World Bank, IMF), and associated development banks, as well as the United Nations, specifically of relevance to COVID-19 pandemic, of course, the World Health Organization (WHO). The emergence of non-'Western-led' multilateral finance and development institutions, specifically the Asian Infrastructure Investment Bank (AIIB), New development Bank (NDB), and the related Belt and Road Initiative (BRI), has significant impacts on countries' infrastructure investment and development decisions.

Amid the COVID-19 pandemic, neoliberal-oriented politicians and academics are set to return to the pre-pandemic social, political, and economic 'normal' as soon as possible. One may observe a naïve assumption among some Western political establishments that such a return is both desirable and inevitable. Such expectations are based on the Thatcherite (by now) infamous claim that there is no alternative to the neoliberal rules-based world order. The argument advanced is that when the COVID-19 pandemic becomes endemic, the world will return to its pre-COVID-19 pandemic self (cf. Harris, 2021; Martin, 2022).

A competing narrative of 'build back better', although more palatable to many (Kenward and Brick, 2021; OECD, 2021), raises substantial challenges to the tensions inherent between the role of government versus individual responsibility, and the motions of progressive (equitable and environmentally sound world) versus a return to normal (Lewandowsky and Ecker, 2022). As Pabst (2021) muses, early narratives of transitions from 'polarised politics' to national unity are demonstrated through acts of community generosity, applauding of health care workers, and discussions on reduced carbon emissions from reduced travel. This was overtaken by the mid-game of the pandemic, where economic impacts have been highly unequal, where hyper-capitalism returned to record profits for Apple, Amazon, and their like, while the World Bank projects that more than 160 million people had been pushed into poverty by the pandemic (Burgess, 2022).

The COVID-19 pandemic has, in fact, exacerbated existing and new forces impacting on the rules-based world order, including the rise of vaccine nationalism, a continuing and sustained advance of national populism and illiberalism, redrawing the boundaries of the geopolitical spheres of interests through soft power diplomacy,[1] and the geopolitical disruptions of the Western neoliberal rules-based world order through soft power diplomacy enacted globally by People's Republic of China (PRC) and Russia. Finally, the existing Western neoliberal rules-based world order is being weakened by the partial retreat of the USA from the leadership role of the Western world. It seems as if the world is increasingly disordered at the current time.

Global distribution of power and polarity

The above-stated problematics have a significant follow-on effect on global power 'polarities'. The existing rules-based world order has, since the demise of the USSR and until recently, been firmly couched in a unipolar power relation. To explain, following the Bretton Woods Conference in 1944 and the subsequent establishment of the World Bank, the IMF, and General Agreement on Tariffs and Trade, which became the WTO, the world was subject to bipolarity. The USA wrote the rules governing the Bretton Woods institutions, and the USSR countered with the establishment of the Communist Information Bureau and Council for Mutual Economic Assistance, which, in 1949, became Organization for International Economic Cooperation. The bipolar rules-based world order emerged and lasted throughout the Cold War era (Jakupec, 2020). Both the USA and the USSR wrote the respective rulebooks in a way to secure their hegemonic position, each within their geopolitical sphere of interest.

With the demise of the USSR in 1991, the USA was the only global political, economic, and military superpower left. However, with the rise of PRC as an economic and, lately, military power, a new rules-based world order is arguably emerging (Hamid Kwarteng and Atuahene, 2018). However, to see the world emerging from the COVID-19 pandemic as a bipolar rules-based world order may be somewhat simplistic.

For example, India is designated by some as a disruptor (Passi and Pant 2018), but this argument is difficult to sustain as India is a founding member of the PRC-led NDB and, at the same time, being part of the US-led quadrilateral security dialogue countries, namely, Australia, India, Japan, and the USA, supporting the neoliberal international economic order in the Indo-Pacific arena. Being with one foot in the PRC-led camp and with the other in the US-led camp does not support India as an economic and political disruptor.

Furthermore, we should not dismiss the regional disruptors, such as Turkey, which is emerging, through its national populist ideology, as a potential disruptor of the rules-based world order focusing on Turkic countries through the

Organization of Turkic States (OTS). OTS has two basic aims: first, it endeavours to strengthen the Turkic political, economic, cultural, and social influences in Central Asia, and second, to strengthen economic development in less-developed member states for which an investment fund was established (Organization of Turkic States, 2021).

Arguably, OTS is, to some extent, a response to and disruptor of PRC's Shanghai Cooperation Organisation and the Russia's Eurasian Economic Union (EAEU) trading block (Devonshire-Ellis, 2021). In short, as Devonshire-Ellis (2021) points out, if Turkey strengthens its trade alliance with EAEU at the expanse of its economic cooperation with the European Union (EU), it may initiate a tripartite coalition between Turkey, Russia, and PRC – a coalition that may be in a strong position to better impact on the Western EU and US-governed rules-based world order. To summarise, there are global as well as regional 'disruptors' at work.

Following the 'disruptor' phenomenon, there are two schools of thought. One argues that the PRC's rise will transform the world and thus the rules-based world order by ushering in the Asian Century, which, apart from other Asian countries, will also benefit India (Mahbubani, 2020). Another school of thought proclaims that the policy the USA has followed since the end of the Cold War is destined to fail (Mearsheimer, 2018). However, both schools of thought concur that PRC is intending to change the existing rules-based world order and is thus not a supporter of the status quo. If this stands to reason, then PRC is ready to rewrite the rules for a new world order. But to do so, it would need the support of other countries, especially Russia and organisations such as the EAEU. This means that Russia would become increasingly the 'kingmaker' in the race for (re-)writing the post-COVID pandemic rules-based world order.

Setting aside the regional disruptors, Russia as the global 'kingmaker', and thus disruptor, had a number of options. It may align itself with the West. This is, however, a highly unlikely scenario, especially in light of the Ukraine crisis. Alternatively, Russia may side with PRC forming a political, economic, and military block, disrupting the existing Western rules-based world order. Again, given Russia's war on Ukraine, this is the emerging scenario. Of course, Russia may pursue isolationism, which again is unlikely. In essence, Russia has made its choice; it is becoming a satellite of PRC.

The above-identified and other disruptors may serve as catalysts for a rise of multipolar rules-based world order or even a simple economic multipolar world order, which may not be soft power rules-based as it is understood today. It may be smart power-based, namely combining soft and hard powers (Nye, 2011), leading to multipolarity, which is a complex and contested term. As Kortunov (2018) argued, multipolarity is 'like a distant horizon that keeps receding as we move towards it' (n.p.). However, Cox (1992) argued that there is a need to recognise multilateralism as a subordinate concept within the structure of the world order and also as 'an active force shaping world order' (p. 161). Thus, from the above, however broad outline of problematics, it may be argued that

COVID-19 pandemic has not only created a health crisis but has also enhanced a pre-COVID-19 pandemic political crisis through vaccine nationalism and economic crisis through trade disruptions. In doing so, it created a legitimation crisis of the neoliberal rules-based world order underpinned by late capitalist economics, which, by extension, impacts on global development and aid.

Global development and aid

The supranational context, of global governance, multilateralism, and global political economy, is conceptually and traditionally dealt with within international relations. The context of this volume, however, is the space currently conceptualised as the Global North and Global South, or high-, middle-, and low-income countries. That is, global aid architecture provides contested spaces within which declarations and actions of support for sustainability, equality, development, and humanitarian responsibility are framed within political and economic systems that have demonstrated increases in inequality. Inequality is framed by the UN as 'an issue that will define our time' (UN, undated, n.p.). Although total global inequality has declined, mostly due to strong economic performance in China and other Asian countries, income inequality within countries has risen. Some 71% of the global population live in countries where income inequality has grown (UN, 2020).

Inequality is much more complex than the basic metric of income inequality. Inequality, opportunity is driven by a range of intersecting factors of gender, age, origin, ethnicity, disability, sexual orientation, class, and religion (UN, undated). The compounding impact of COVID is yet to be fully understood, despite the radical shifts in the impact of a global pandemic, from being a 'high-class import' impacting the wealthier and travelling elites to a global pandemic with differing impacts but concentrated in those less able to isolate. The historical space where the poor have been 'walled in' to allow disease to run its course was never an option for the poor to do in reverse (Bengali *et al.*, 2020). The global spread of COVID-19 through high-speed international travel set the scene for the current context.

Maestripieri (2021) argues that COVID-19 is a social disease and demonstrates the importance of understanding multiple and interrelating structures of inequality, in assessing the impact of COVID-19. From its early evolution, through to the current context, driven by debates around new variants and vaccines, COVID has fundamentally altered global focus, in aid, development, global public health, and in political rhetoric and economic realities. There are complex linkages between inequality, economic ideology, polarising political debates, and the behaviour of states and supranational organisations in determining the impact of COVID-19 on human well-being and development. The development and the distributional effects of the negative impacts of COVID-19 are clearly tied to the behaviour of nations and the power relationships that these factors reflect.

There is an underlying rationale that global development and aid are arguably cornerstones of the Western rules-based world order and, until 1991, were in direct competition with the USSR-led, socialist-based global development and aid order. In other words, without the existence of global development and aid, developing countries would not be able to participate in a rules-based world order of any kind. Let's not forget, it was the recognition of the need for global development and aid in the post-WWII era which acted as a catalyst for the rules-based world order emerging from the Bretton Woods Conference and the establishment of the Marshall Plan, followed by the competing Molotov Plan (Jakupec, 2020).

Following the demise of the USSR, the world shifted towards a US-led unipolar, and subsequently to a USA-PRC bipolar, and, more recently, to a multipolar world order. One of the reasons for the potential shifts in the global development and aid arena may be arguably ascribed to the impact of the COVID-19 pandemic. Even a fleeting analysis shows that in many countries of the developing world, COVID-19 pandemic has undone years of social, political, and economic progress, thus disadvantaging the poor strata of the population. The low-income nations in Central Asia, South Pacific, sub-Saharan Africa, and South America and beyond are suffering from COVID-19 pandemic disruptions to their economic activities, such as direct and other foreign investment, trade, and remittances, all of which have triggered a decline in international sources of development finance (Brown, 2021; Organization of Turkic States, 2021). Notwithstanding that multilateral development aid institutions have responded to the new COVID-19 crisis at the local, national, and international levels, the impact of this aid remains at a global level thus far unclear (Brown, 2021).

Addressing this issue, Brown (2021) argues that:

> [a]cross the Global South, the COVID-19 pandemic has reversed years of socioeconomic progress, disproportionally harming poor people. Low- and lower-middle-income countries in particular are struggling more than ever to find the resources to support their citizens' health and wellbeing at this time of crisis. Moreover, disruptions to trade, investment and remittances have caused a drop in international sources of development finance.
> *(n.p.)*

However, when one investigates the official figures, the following picture emerges. According to Organisation for Economic Cooperation and Development (OECD) in 2020, a total of USD 161.2 billion in aid money has been reached. This is in real terms a 3.5% increase from 2019, which reflects increased spending on supporting developing countries to address the COVID-19 pandemic. As far as COVID-19 stimulus is concerned, donor governments have allocated USD 16 trillion in 2020. However, Organisation for Economic Cooperation and Development (OECD) has only been able to mobilise 1% of the allocation, to assist developing countries to deal with the COVID-19 pandemic

(OECD cited in Marchant, 2021). This, according to OECD, is insufficient to adequately respond to the vaccine rollout and to address the social, economic, and political fallout of the COVID-19 pandemic.

To summarise, in addition to providing support to the income and livelihoods of the most vulnerable in developing countries, multilateral donor agencies need to help developing countries with vaccine dissemination and to support the health services. The willingness or capacity of nation states to provide an equitable response to a global pandemic, globally, is questioned, and the impact of political and economic interests of existing power polarities regarding global solidarity is in need of various analyses. One possible point of departure for a deeper analysis is to proceed from the role of multilateralism to its legitimation and legitimation crisis.

The emerging legitimacy crisis

Historically, the world is always in some form of social, political, economic, or cultural crisis, or a combination thereof. This includes the above-stated more recent GFC, the subsequent European sovereign debt crisis (ESDC), and other various humanitarian and health crises. The difference between these crises and the COVID-19 crisis is that the latter is causing a combination of crises. These include (1) a political crisis through vaccine nationalism (Reinert, 2021); (2) an economic crisis through the 'global collapse in activity and loss of jobs that is probably unprecedented in its scale and speed' (Giese and Haldane, 2020, p. 200); (3) a sociocultural crisis through the effects of social distancing and intercultural dialogue (Mansouri, 2020); and (4) an internal and international migration crisis caused by disruptions to public transport services and movement restrictions (World Bank Group, 2020). Given the interplay and combination of these crises, the COVID-19 pandemic crisis has made the above-cited crises pale in comparison (Mac Amhlaigh, 2020).

It may be useful to point out that the COVID-19 pandemic emerged in 2020 at a time of increased combined political, economic, social, and cultural disorders and crises exemplified by the rise of illiberalism, national populism, Trumponomics, polarisation, and a question of legitimacy by governments and institutions with reference to the rules-based world orders such as the WHO, UNESCO, other UN organisations, and North Atlantic Treaty Organization (NATO). These 'disorders' *cum* crises affect the reaction of populace, governments, and global institutions to the pandemic in different ways (Cornelson and Miloucheva, 2020). One of the most significant impacts of the COVID-19 pandemic on governments and international and multilateral institutions such as the aid and development institutions *cum* International Financial Institutions (IFIs) is the emerging legitimation crisis, exemplified by the diminishing legitimacy of the WHO by the Trump administration and other governments.

From the above discussion, it could be advanced that the legitimation crises may emerge due to an absence of beliefs in or acceptance of legitimation by the population into its government policies and actions and a rejection of the existing rules-based world order by a government on a basis of its anarchic status.

The main themes and structure of the book

Having identified the main problematics, it is evident that the importance of global cooperation has seldom been greater, yet never so seriously challenged. From this vantage point, this book explores the impact of the COVID-19 pandemic on development aid within an environment of shifting national and regional priorities and interactions. From a critical perspective, this volume's contributors respond to the impacts of COVID-19 as a disruptor of development discourses. This brings to the fore varied multilateral responses as experienced through COVAX, as well as the disproportionate impact of COVID-19 on those already experiencing marginalisation, poverty, and inequality. Complex and multidirectional linkages between politics, economics, society, and the culture are driving changes in the extant development aid system. From this perspective, the book provides a range of critical reflections to shifts in the world order, the rise of nationalism, the strange non-death of neoliberalism, shifts in globalisation, and the evolving impact of COVID as a cross-cutting crisis.

The book is organised around two key approaches. The first part considers the impact of the COVID-19 pandemic on the rules-based world order and the multilateral system of foreign aid and development. The second part considers the impact of the COVID-19 pandemic on regions and individual countries and how these parts of the global system navigated the rules-based world order while also addressing key regional and local issues.

Chapter 2 sets the scene with a discussion by Kortunov where he reimagines globalisation as being more than the single system of ideologically consistent multilateral arrangements that have suffered from US disinterest and hence 'institutional fatigue', to a more diverse arrangement of regional multilateralism and a denser bilateralism that does not necessarily rely on US leadership. In Chapter 3, Debiel and Rousselin consider the continued decline of the neoliberal paradigm in light of the COVID-19 pandemic. Beginning with the US-led post–Cold War global order that saw the rapid integration of market economies into a globally competitive marketplace, the extant system was readily upset by the GFC of 2008. Nation states responded with various attempts to stimulate their respective domestic markets with interventions such as stimulus spending, thus challenging neoliberalism's laissez-faire orthodoxy. Nevertheless, collective problems such as the current pandemic require collective solutions, and the tension between whether multilateralism in its current neoliberal form can be the basis for cooperation and the tendency towards nationalism in responding to global crises including the GFC, global warming, and the COVID-19 pandemic has fractured along sectoral lines that Debiel and Rousselin suggest may see the end of neoliberalism's hegemony, at least in many global policy trends.

Meisterhans continues the examination of global governance in Chapter 4 by suggesting that the COVID-19 pandemic was a consequence of nation state politics that has effectively withdrawn from the utopian ideal of human rights and evolved into a latent authoritarianism that determines how global citizens live and die. Yet out of this bleak assessment emerges the reinvigoration of progressive social movements from the feminist, anti-racist, ecological, indigenous, or workers' spheres if current ideological hegemonies can be undone by the narratives of art and protest.

In Chapter 5, Jakupec brings the discussion of the world order back to our focus on foreign aid and development. While the ideological, social, economic, cultural, and structural crises that exist in the existing foreign aid world order predicated by the challenges to the neoliberal world order, the emerging post-COVID world order produces and contributes to the creation and continuance of asymmetries of wealth and power. Jakupec advances the idea that megatrends based on an emerging bipolar North-South economic divide amid the impact of COVID-19 present competing legitimation claims on the manner in which multilateral foreign aid and development programmes are presented and delivered amid re-emerging bipolarism. In Chapter 6, Grigoryev and Morozkina explore the problems and challenges of official development assistance as an anti-crisis tool and the effect of the COVID-19 pandemic on progress towards the UN Sustainable Development Goals. In this context, social inequality hinders the steps taken to counter the crises, through, for example, COVAX as an initiative of the WHO to pool procurement and enable an equitable distribution of vaccines. However, a vast majority of people in lower-income countries are unvaccinated, and wealthier countries have effectively bought and hoarded available vaccine doses. Indeed, geopolitics, not equity, has driven access to vaccines. In Chapter 7, Kelly and McGlasson explore the political economy of vaccines, focusing on soft power and vaccine diplomacy, and the impacts of vaccine diplomacy on global cooperation. Lama Tawakkol extends the discussion in Chapter 8 by focusing on multilateral development banks and international financial institutions, which were among the first responders to COVID-19 in the Global South. She frames the COVID challenges in economic terms and encourages the state to increase private sector participation, without providing adequate social protection.

The first part finishes where we began: de Percy examines the temporal challenges to the rules-based global world order in Chapter 9 by incorporating the historical events leading up to and including the decline of the neoliberal rules-based world order by bringing in the idea of institutional change through exhaustion, where global institutions effectively run out of steam in their ability to govern during crises that exceed their original design principles.

The second part of the volume shifts from high-level global ideas and agendas to what may be regarded as the engine room of COVID-related global change: regional and nation state responses to citizens' lived reality in the post-COVID world order. To be sure, any settled idea of a post-COVID world order remains elusive, but the responses of regional multilateral agreements and individual nation states have not aligned with the neoliberal ideological hegemony.

Rather, the responses from the various regional and national jurisdictions discussed in this second part of the volume reflect regional and national interests that have typically focused on the humanitarian aspects of the COVID-19 pandemic response, providing both opportunities and challenges for any semblance of a global rules-based world order. The chapters in the second part consider global challenges, from a case study perspective of specific regions and nation states to provide a diverse perspective on COVID-19 responses as these impact on both health-related and an ageing world order.

The second part, therefore, begins with Chapter 10 and an analysis of the impact of COVID-19 on the Global South, where Rompel outlines the epidemiological and health impacts of COVID-19 in sub-Saharan Africa. He suggests that the low-income countries of the Global South are being left behind, and China and Russia are actively using the space to increase their spheres of influence through 'vaccine diplomacy' (i.e. provision of vaccines to exert influence on receiving countries). At the same time, the EU and member states like Germany are aiming to establish a manufacturing capacity for pharmaceuticals in Africa, to strengthen African economies in the long term. In Chapter 11, Sánchez analyses the connection between poverty and income inequality within the economic cycle and the public policies carried out by the 27 Member States of the EU in 2019 to deal with the negative effects of the COVID-19 pandemic. In doing so, Sánchez constructs a composite human development index to analyse the connection between poverty, income inequality, and human development with the economic cycle and the public policies carried out to address poverty within the EU.

In Chapter 12, McGillivray shifts the regional focus to the Pacific Islands, which includes some of the most economically vulnerable countries in the world, exploring the impact of COVID-19 on Pacific Island countries and the response of two of the major foreign aid donors to the region, Australia and New Zealand. McGillivray examines income poverty and other well-being indicators to assess the impact of endogenous shocks, such as behavioural responses owing to public and private aversion due to fear of infection versus exogenous shocks on the region, and argues that almost all of the impacts of COVID-19 have been transmitted through existing and well-known vulnerabilities to exogenous shocks rather than endogenous factors. In Chapter 13, Brown and Rosier compare the relative engagement with multilateralism of Canada and France on the issue of COVID-19 vaccines. Although the two countries have a history of global health diplomacy through verbal and some financial support for multilateral responses, the Canadian government took a strong 'Canada First' position to the detriment of its global 'soft power'. France, on the other hand, acted more multilaterally and strategically from the perspective of 'soft power', but Brown and Rosier argue that France's achievements will be undermined by its self-interested position on intellectual property rights, which impede the increase in global vaccine production and therefore will – like Canadian actions – prolong the pandemic at the global level. Brown and Rosier conclude that by doing so, both countries are undermining their own global health diplomacy efforts and ultimately acting against their own interests.

In Chapter 14, Qun Cui, Lisheng Dong, and Tom Christensen survey Chinese civil servants to assess their perception of the efficacy of China's management of the crisis. Dong and Qun found that Chinese civil servants generally have a very high level of trust in the state's governance capability to handle and prevent crises, especially when comparing China's response with the Western world's handling of the COVID-19 pandemic. The authors argue that China's crisis management experiences have facilitated the increasing legitimacy of the ruling party and reinforced pre-existing nationalism among public administrators.

In Chapter 15, Bennett examines the apparent dichotomy of China's UN and other peacekeeping and foreign aid efforts, in the context of its own domestic control of civil and political rights. Bennett asks how the domestic and international – inward- and outward-facing – identities of the PRC have shaped (and have been shaped by) the complex geopolitical backdrop that includes the COVID-19 pandemic. Further, the chapter examines the potential implications of China's authoritarian model for global governance, including achieving dominant narratives around foreign aid distribution and control of key multilateral organisations in the midst of a dearth of cooperation and leadership among the democratic nations.

Chapter 16, by McCarthy-Jones, looks at the impact of Chinese and Russian soft power on Venezuela, a country that was once lauded as a regional exemplar of democracy and a leading proponent of the rules-based world order in Latin America. However, Jones argues that increasing nationalism and the undermining of the rules-based world order by the USA facilitated the exercise of soft power by China and Russia in the region and in Venezuela. Further, the chapter examines the case of foreign aid and development in Venezuela from the perspective of an alternative rules-based world order created by emerging US nationalism, shifting global political rivalries, and the use of soft power by emerging powers in the region.

This theme is continued in Chapter 17, where Poncian draws on nationalist politics to examine the limits of a rules-based world order as it relates to national responses to the COVID-19 pandemic in Tanzania. Drawing on the Tanzanian case, the chapter argues that COVID-19 has helped show that the 'rules-based' world order remains in an age of reinvigorated nationalism illusive.

To conclude the volume, Kelly, Jakupec, and de Percy examine the key themes emerging from the contributions and assess their impact on the world order. They focus the discussions on global development within a context of a crisis and the negative impacts the crisis has on the gains made under pre-COVID conditions in poverty, health, education, and many other areas.

Conclusion

Despite the impact of COVID-19 pandemic on the looming legitimation crises, the steadfast belief of proponents of neoliberalism is that a key strategic measure of the global community is, following the pandemic, the need to enhance the existing rules-based world order, to strengthen multilateralism and augment existing governance capacities of aid and development hegemons. This may well be an exercise in wishful thinking, for the COVID-19 pandemic is not only inflicting destruction on public health but also the neoliberal economy globally. The pandemic is further disrupting liberal democracy by strengthening the forces of illiberalism and national populism.

At the same time, the COVID-19 pandemic is creating an epistemological and ontological schism between the existing and emerging world order polarities. Broadly speaking, there are three schools of thought addressing the question of world order polarities. One argues that the US-based unipolarity will be retained. This proposition is based on a belief of 'American exceptionalism' and the containment of PRC. Second, there is the school of thought of an emergence of a bipolar world order dividing the world into US- and PRC-led world orders. Third, there is a multipolar school of thought which perceives a rise of a multipolar world order, which includes, in addition to bipolarity, the rise of disruptors. Which of these three basic schools of thought will prevail remains an unanswered question. However, it is likely that there will be competition between the emergence of a new bipolar world and a multipolar world, each of which will have significant impacts on multilateralism. If this stands to reason, multilateralism will emerge as a dominant world order polarity and will have a significant corresponding impact, especially on lower-income and fragile states and foreign aid.

As the COVID-19 pandemic makes its way into lower-income and fragile states, it will most likely have an increasingly acute problematic effects than those which were observable thus far. We are already witnessing that with the aim of containing the pandemic, the world's largest economies are slowing down, and subsequently, the global economy is experiencing a downturn, which, in turn, will further affect the allocation and distribution of development aid.

Note

1 Terminology used throughout the volume is contextual. Drawing on Horner (2019), Global South is used to denote countries that were the geographic and economic focus of a 'northern'-centric development project. However, the increasing global interconnectedness and the blurring of a North-South divide with shared challenges and the rising power of China, as well as India and other 'southern' nations, require some clarification of terms. 'Western' is equally used in relation to discourse and practice associated with a sense of assumed universalisation of 'Western' scholarship, underpinning development (rather than endogenous development) intentions.

References

Bengali, S., Linthicum, K. and Kim, V. (2020). How Coronavirus—A 'Rich Man's Disease'—Infected the Poor. *Los Angeles Times* (8 May 2020). https://www.latimes.com/world-nation/story/2020-05-08/how-the-coronavirus-began-as-a-disease-of-the-rich

Brown, S. (2021). The Impact of COVID-19 on Foreign Aid. *Devpolicyblog* (1 April 2021). https://devpolicy.org/the-impact-of-covid-19-on-foreign-aid-20210401-2/

Burgess, A. (2022). Oxfam Report Says Australian Billionaires and World's Richest Men Have Doubled Wealth during Pandemic. *ABC* (Posted Monday, 17 January 2022). https://www.abc.net.au/news/2022-01-17/oxfam-report-covid-pandemic-billionaires-increase-fortune/100760968

Cornelson, K. and Miloucheva, B. (2020). *Political Polarization, Social Fragmentation, and Cooperation during a Pandemic*. Working Paper No. 663. Toronto: Department of Economics, University of Toronto.

Cox, R.W. (1992). Multilateralism and World Order. *Review of International Studies*, 18(2), pp. 161–180.

Devonshire-Ellis, C. (2021). Organisation of Turkic States Rebranded with Intention to Balance Central Asian Politics. *Silk Road Briefing* (30 November 2021). https://www.silkroadbriefing.com/news/2021/11/30/organisation-of-turkic-states-rebranded-with-intention-to-balance-central-asian-politics/

Eilstrup-Sangiovanni, M. and Hofmann, S.C. (2020). Of the Contemporary Global Order, Crisis, and Change. *Journal of European Public Policy*, 27(7), pp. 1077–1089.

Furman, J., Geithner, T., Hubbard, G. and Kearney, M.S. (2020). Promoting Economic Recovery after COVID-19 2020. Report of the Economic Strategy Group of the Aspen Institute. June 2020. https://www.economicstrategygroup.org/wp-content/uploads/2020/11/Promoting-Economic-Recovery-After-COVID-0615-FINAL.pdf

Gibson, C., Andersson, K., Ostrom, E. and Shivakumar, S. (2005). *The Samaritan's Dilemma: The Political Economy of Development Aid*. Oxford: Oxford University Press.

Giese, J. and Haldane, A. (2020). COVID-19 and the Financial System: A Tale of Two Crises. *Oxford Review of Economic Policy*, 36(Issue Supplement_1), pp. S200–S214.

Hamid Kwarteng, A. and Atuahene, E. (2018). The Rise of China: The Emergence of a Bipolar Superpower and the Implication for the Future of International Law. *Asian Research Journal of Arts and Social Sciences*, 6(3), pp. 1–12.

Harris, J. (2021). How Will post-Covid Britain Look? For Many, Like It Did in the Brutal 19th Century . *The Guardian* (29 November 2021). https://www.theguardian.com/commentisfree/2021/nov/28/covid-britain-boris-johnson-poverty-hunger

Haass, R. and Kupchan, C.A. (2021). A Concert of Powers for a Global Era. *Project Syndicate* (25 March 2021). https://www.project-syndicate.org/commentary/concert-of-powers-for-global-era-by-richard-haass-and-charles-a-kupchan-2021-03

Horner, R. (2019). Towards a New Paradigm of Global Development? Beyond the Limits of International Development. *Progress in Human Geography*, 44(3), pp. 415–436.

Jakupec, V. (2020). Multilateral Foreign Aid and the Shadow of Cold War II. In Jakupec, V., Kelly, M., and Makuwira, J. (eds.), *Rethinking Multilateralism in Foreign Aid: Beyond the Neoliberal Hegemony*. Oxford/New York: Routledge, pp. 195–214.

Kenward, B. and Brick, C. (2021). Even Conservative Voters Want the Environment to Be at the Heart of Post-COVID-19 Economic Reconstruction in the UK. *Journal of Social and Political Psychology*, 9(1), pp. 321–333.

Kortunov, A. (2018). Why the World is Not Becoming Multipolar. *Russian International Affairs Council* (27 June 2018). https://russiancouncil.ru/en/analytics-and-comments/analytics/why-the-world-is-not-becoming-multipolar/

Lewandowsky, S. and Ecker, U. (2022). Life after COVID: Most People Don't Want a Return to Normal – They Want a Fairer, More Sustainable Future. *The Conversation* (2 January 2022). https://theconversation.com/life-after-covid-most-people-dont-want-a-return-to-normal-they-want-a-fairer-more-sustainable-future-173290

Mac Amhlaigh, C. (2020). Legitimacy in the Time of Coronavirus. *VerfBlog* (17 April 2020). https://verfassungsblog.de/legitimacy-in-the-time-of-coronavirus/

Maestripieri, L. (2021). The Covid-19 Pandemics: Why Intersectionality Matters. *Frontiers in Sociology*, 6, 642662.

Mahbubani, K. (2020). *Has China Won?: The Chinese Challenge to American Primacy*. New York: PublicAffairs.

Mansouri, F. (2020). The Socio-Cultural Implications of COVID-19. *UNESCO* (29 May 2020). https://en.unesco.org/news/socio-cultural-implications-covid-19

Marchant, N. (2021). Foreign Aid Hit a Record High Last Year. Here's What It Means for the Global Recovery from COVID. *World Economic Forum* (23 April 2021). https://www.weforum.org/agenda/2021/04/foreign-aid-2020-covid-19-oecd/

Martin, S. (2022). 'Living with Covid' Has Turned Scott Morrison's Promise Sour before the Summer Is Out. *The Guardian* (8 January 2022). https://www.theguardian.com/australia-news/2022/jan/08/living-with-covid-has-turned-scott-morrisons-promise-sour-before-the-summer-is-out

Mearsheimer, J. (2018). *The Great Delusion: Liberal Dreams and International Realities*. New Haven, CT/London: Yale University Press.

Nye, J. (2011). *The Future of Power*. New York: Public Affairs.

OECD (2021). *COVID-19 and Well-being: Life in the Pandemic*. Paris: OECD Publishing.

Organization of Turkic States (2021). Turkic Council reforms into Organization of Turkic States. *TRTWORLD* https://cms.trtworld.com/turkey/turkic-council-reforms-into-organization-of-turkic-states-51608

Pabst, A. (2021). Politics after the Pandemic: Post-liberalism and the Renewal of Our Common Life. *ABC Ethics and Religion Opinion* (17 November 2021). https://www.abc.net.au/religion/adrian-pabst-promise-of-post-liberal-politics/13635960

Passi, R. and Pant, H.V. (2018). Debating Disruption: Change and Continuity. In Passi, R. and Pant, H.V. (Eds.), *Debating Disruption in the World Order*. Raisina Files. Delhi: Observer Research Foundation, pp. 3–9.

Reinert, K.A. (2021). Vaccine Nationalism and the WTO. *The Hill* (13 December 2021). https://thehill.com/opinion/international/585533-vaccine-nationalism-and-the-wto.

Rodrik, D. (2017). The Fatal Flaw of Neoliberalism: It's Bad Economics. *The Guardian* (14 November 2017). https://www.theguardian.com/news/2017/nov/14/the-fatal-flaw-of-neoliberalism-its-bad-economics

Stückelberger, C. (2020). Post-corona World: Balancing International Cooperation and National Sovereignty. *World Health*, 11(2), p. 55.

The Royal Institute of International Affairs (RIIA) (2015). *Challenges to the Rules-Based International Order*. London: Chatham House. https://www.chathamhouse.org/sites/default/files/London%20Conference%202015%20-%20Background%20Papers.pdf

United Nations (2020). *World Social Report 2020: Inequality in a Rapidly Changing World*. Rome: Department of Economic And Social Affairs, United Nations. https://www.un.org/development/desa/dspd/wp-content/uploads/sites/22/2020/01/World-Social-Report-2020-FullReport.pdf

United Nations (undated). Inequality – Bridging the Divide. *UN Website* (8 December 2021). https://www.un.org/en/un75/inequality-bridging-divide

World Bank Group (2020). *COVID-19 Crisis through a Migration Lens: Migration and Development Brief 32*. Washington: World Bank. https://openknowledge.worldbank.org/bitstream/handle/10986/33634/COVID-19-Crisis-Through-a-Migration-Lens.pdf?sequence=5

World Economic Forum (2022). *The Global Risks Report 2021*. 16th ed. Geneva: World Economic Forum.

2

INTERNATIONAL MULTILATERALISM IN A NON-HEGEMONIC WORLD

Andrey Kortunov

Introduction

The term "multilateralism" is not well developed in Russian theories of international relations. For some time, this term remained in the shadow of the much more popular term "multipolarity" (as well as gradually replacing "multipolarity" and "polycentrism"). Sometimes it seems that "multilateralism" and "multipolarity" are used in Russian academic and political discourses as synonyms that reflect the long-term processes of democratization of the international system after the end of the era of the "unipolar world" (Lavrov, 2009).

However, multipolarity is not the same as multilateralism. If the first fixes the presence of pluralism in the distribution of power in an international system where there are three or more independent centers of decision-making, the second describes one of the options for the interaction of these centers with each other. Without multipolarity (polycentrism) at least in the embryonic state, there cannot be meaningful multilateralism, since in a unipolar or bipolar system, there are not enough actors for a full-fledged multilateral interaction (although, as will be shown below, certain elements of multilateralism were present in both bipolar and unipolar systems of world politics).

But multipolarity, even a "mature" multipolarity, does not include multilateralism, since relations within a multipolar system can theoretically be reduced to a set of bilateral ties between individual centers of power or to the unilateral actions of these centers. Supporters of "political realism" refer to multipolarity, not multilateralism when they compare world politics to a chaotic collision of balls on a billiard table: there can be a lot of balls on that table, but they interact with each other in bilateral and unilateral formats, without creating a stable multilateral system. If the coordination of the actions of individual authors does occur, then it is not horizontal but vertical in nature – weak international

DOI: 10.4324/9781003273844-2

actors follow foreign policy priorities of their stronger patrons. Multilateralism sets much higher standards for international behavior than multipolarity; it puts more emphasis on cooperation between states than on competition.

With some reservations, it is fair to note that multipolarity (polycentrism) reflects a certain objective balance of power between the main participants in world politics, while multilateralism fixes their subjective readiness to interact with each other in a certain regime and according to certain rules. In international relations theory, multipolarity refers to basic foundations, and multilateralism is attributed to political superstructure. In international practice, multilateralism looks less stable and a more flexible phenomenon than multipolarity. For example, US President Joe Biden is not able to change the movement of the world toward multipolarity, but he is quite capable of giving impetus to international multilateralism by abandoning the unilateral actions of his predecessor.

It is conceivable that, under certain conditions, the development of multilateral negotiating practices and institutions can not only follow the processes of forming a "mature" multipolarity but also overtake these processes, thereby reducing the risks associated with the transition of that international system to a polycentric world. On the contrary, a significant lag in multilateral practices from the development of multipolarity will increase these risks, as well as a variety of transit costs. The important task of international players, in theory, should not only be to keep the development of multilateralism ahead of the transition of the international system to multipolarity but also not to allow the separation of advanced multilateralism from the still-unformed multipolarity.

Multilateralism: old and new

Today, the once-clear horizons of international multilateralism are clouded. Many authors deny prospects for meaningful multilateralism in the future world order, arguing that it will be based on the balance of power of the great powers. But today we are witnessing a crisis of one specific format of multilateralism that developed in the middle of the last century that served the peculiar and unique model of international relations of that time. Further, it sequentially served two models: the bipolar model that existed until the beginning of the 1990s and the model of the unipolar world that replaced it for one or two decades. Since these two models, with minor modifications, have existed for three-quarters of a century, it is not surprising that they now look somewhat outdated. Moreover, in a bipolar and unipolar world, multilateralism was deformed and not quite full-fledged.

Many features of the old format of multilateralism today appear as archaic.

First, the old multilateralism was based on hegemony and hierarchy. The post–World War II world order was established by a small group of great powers and reflected their interests and aspirations. The number of active subjects of world politics also remained small until the 1960s, and hierarchical relations, understood by all, developed between these subjects and the associated objects of confrontation between the great powers. The US created North Atlantic Treaty Organization (NATO) as a multilateral defense alliance, but it never occurred to anyone to challenge the American leadership in this alliance, insisting on the actual and not only the formal equality of the participants. The security interests of the US and its European allies were not represented equally in NATO: it was the territory of Europe, not the US, that was considered by American strategists as the main theater in the event of a military clash between the West and the Soviet Union.

Soviet hegemony in the Warsaw Pact (WP, as well as in the Council for Mutual Economic Assistance – COMECON) would have been more explicit and indisputable, the WP being a more "pseudo-multilateral" structure than NATO. The asymmetry of military, economic and other capabilities within the Soviet bloc was greater than within the US bloc. History has shown that in a bipolar system, multilateralism remains relative and incomplete; it may be more correct to speak of the existence of quasi-multilateralism or embryonic multilateralism in this system, which has the potential to grow over time into mature multilateralism. The first examples of mature multilateralism (European Commission and Association of Southeast Asian Nations [ASEAN]) arose in the economic sphere, where the postwar Soviet-American bipolarity was the first to undergo noticeable erosion.

Moreover, old multilateralism rested on a rigid institutional framework. It assumed that a large number of well-developed organizational structures with multilevel bureaucratic apparatuses, complex decision-making mechanisms and systems of a variety of explicit and implicit linkages allowed participants to balance their concessions in some areas with compensation in other areas. Such a device was an ideal solution in the conditions of a static system of world politics when systemic shifts occurred slowly and had limited influence on the global balance of power as a whole. One can question the effectiveness of the multilateral institutions of the Cold War, but at least they supported the stability of the existing system of world politics. Periodic corrections of the global balance of power took place in the format of local wars (Korea, Vietnam, Afghanistan) and did not affect the foundations of the existing system.

The old multilateralism of the second half of the last century appealed to values in one way or another. In a world divided into two opposing blocs, most of the multilateral mechanisms and procedures assumed a unity of values between the members of each of the blocs. In most cases, the picture of the world was built as a confrontation between "us" and "them", and multilateralism within the groups of "us" (NATO and the WP, the European Union [EU] and COMECON) was in rare cases complemented by multilateralism between "us" and "them" (the system of United Nations [UN], multilateral arms control treaties, the Helsinki Final Act). Even the notion of "global public goods", in a divided world, was spread to narrow spheres of international relations. The main sources and guardians of values of opposing systems were the world hegemons – the Soviet Union and the US. The formation of genuine global multilateralism was postponed for the future, considered possible after the victory of one system of values over the other.

Since the two socioeconomic systems developed in isolation from each other, multilateralism in the bipolar world was reduced to the sphere of security to prevent nuclear war, the proliferation of nuclear weapons, or a major military conflict using conventional weapons in Europe. Multilateralism also affected problems of preventing regional crises outside Europe, although bilateral Soviet-American relations played a major role here. But in the sphere of development, multilateralism was almost not manifested in any way – the countries of the so-called Eastern bloc did not participate in the implementation of Western economic and financial projects; Western and Eastern programs of assistance to the developing world were not complementary but competitive.

Further, the old multilateralism perceived sovereign states as full-fledged subjects of world politics. Nation-states remained exclusive participants in the most important multilateral institutions and regimes, while non-state actors, except some large transnational corporations, were content to be observers and/or executors of relevant decisions of "their" state.

After the Cold War, the West tried to extend "its" multilateralism to the rest of the world in order to unite humanity under the banner of political liberalism. In some areas, such as international trade, this has almost succeeded: the EU made impressive progress under the General Agreement on Tariffs and Trade and, more recently, within the World Trade Organization.

But in the financial sphere, internal European multilateralism became more difficult and contradictory. Some EU countries have not entered the "euro area", thereby weakening European currency in world financial markets. The EU also failed to take full advantage of its positions in the International Monetary Fund and the International Bank for Reconstruction and Development, often failing to achieve a consolidated European position on the most important issues of the functioning of these institutions. The situation was worse with external multilateralism, especially attempts to extend European models of multilateralism to the international system. For example, numerous attempts by Brussels to create a universal multilateral regime of foreign direct investment were unsuccessful; as a result, the EU had to sign many bilateral agreements with its partners.

At the end of last century, many multilateral institutions and regimes were created, and many spheres of public life that were previously under the jurisdiction of nation-states fell under multilateral control. The practice of multilateral peacekeeping operations under the UN developed, the number of victims of armed conflicts decreased and global indicators of human development (Human Development Index) and social equality (Gini Index) improved on average. However, these positive trends were not typical for all regions; for example, in the post-Soviet space and the Western Balkans, the opposite dynamics were observed.

It became clear that "old" multilateralism was ill-suited to the new reality. American hegemony was fragile; a short "unipolar moment" turned into imperial overstrain and the subsequent geopolitical retreat of the US. The "old" multilateral institutions of the West reached their geographical and functional limits; both NATO and the EU face numerous challenges not only to their effectiveness but also to their unity. Political liberalism has not become a universal system of values. Over time, nation-states have proven less able to solve global problems without interaction with a variety of non-state actors in international relations amid talk of a "crisis of multilateralism", resulting in a return to a traditional balance of power.

The legitimacy of "old" Western multilateralism has been undermined, yet it seems doubtful that in the future it will be possible to reach an acceptable level of global governance using exclusively unilateral and bilateral instruments of foreign policy. The rejection of multilateralism would make it impossible to agree on universal rules of the game in those spheres of world politics where the tasks of such coordination are not burdened with the challenges of geopolitical confrontation. Such an unmanageable world in an era of resource scarcity, rapid climate change, unprecedented cross-border migration flows and the uncontrolled development of new technologies cannot exist for long. Proponents of a multipolar (polycentric) world cannot fail to take into account that the increase in the number of actors in world politics (multipolarity without multilateralism) does not bring the world any closer to solving common problems. Imagine India, Brazil or Japan becoming a permanent member of the UN Security Council. In practice, this means that the task of reaching consensus in the Security Council will be more difficult than today. The same applies to regional organizations. For example, the entry into the Shanghai Cooperation Organisation of India and Pakistan as full members without changing the nature of relations between these two countries has given rise to many problems in terms of the effectiveness of this organization.

Without a fundamental change in the nature of relations between the great powers, the multiplication of the number of poles of world politics will mean a proportional multiplication of the number of political and security risks. To avoid ungovernability and chaos, the expansion of the spectrum and the increase in the number of participants in world politics and the economy must be accompanied by an increase in the density of the existing network of multilateral agreements, regimes and organizations. This network creates the regulatory framework, control tools and horizontal connections that prevent world politics from falling into anarchism. Multilateral organizations also form what can be designated as the "political credit history" of individual states (as well as non-state participants in world politics), the reputation of reliable or unreliable partners and allies. Other mechanisms are less effective at this task.

In principle, most modern politicians and experts in one way or another recognize the main advantage of multilateral diplomacy, its inclusive nature. Only multilateralism makes it possible to form the broad coalitions necessary to solve complex problems affecting the interests of more than two international players. Moreover, multilateralism in many cases enhances the international legitimacy and sustainability of agreements reached (Chatham House, 2021).

Legitimacy and multilateralism

The demonstrative rejection of multilateralism, in some cases, can lead to negative consequences. In the autumn of 2013, Brussels rejected the proposal of Ukrainian President V. Yanukovych to hold trilateral negotiations between the EU, Ukraine and Russia regarding the consequences of the signing of the Association Agreement between Ukraine and EU for Ukrainian-Russian economic cooperation. After aggravation of the situation in Ukraine and around it, the EU still had to go to trilateral negotiations, which ended with an agreement to postpone the creation of a free trade zone between Ukraine and the EU until December 31, 2015.

Additional legitimacy arises in situations where the formed multilateral coalitions are representative, that is, when the positions and interests of all significant players are represented in the work on solving the problem. In that sense, it is interesting to compare multilateral international operations under the auspices of the US in Afghanistan (2001) and Iraq (2003). In both cases, the main organizer of military interventions was Washington. However, there was a broad international consensus on the operation in Afghanistan, which made it possible to adopt a corresponding UN Security Council resolution and ensure the legitimacy of a foreign military presence in this country. In the case of Iraq, a number of leading powers (including Russia, France and Germany) raised serious objections, which prevented the Bush administration from using either the UN Security Council or NATO to legitimize the operation.

However, politicians cannot fail to realize that the specific features of multilateral diplomacy are in some cases its weak point. Multilateral negotiations can be difficult to focus, as each participant has its own priorities. Multilateral negotiations tend to require more time and resources than bilateral negotiations, let alone unilateral actions. Procedural issues in a multilateral format are also much more difficult to agree on than in a bilateral one. In cases where multilateral coalitions are formed by joining members to an unconditional leader or to a group of leaders, such coalitions are difficult to categorize as full-fledged multilateral structures.

Further, the decisions taken as a result of multilateral negotiations can turn out to be half-hearted, fuzzy and declarative, since negotiators have to focus on the search for the lowest common denominator to maintain the support of the maximum number of contracting parties. Sometimes multilateral negotiations can be blocked by any of the participants under even the most far-fetched pretext (Turk, 2020). A textbook example is the discussion in the EU in September 2020 of the issue of sanctions against Belarus, when the decision was blocked by representatives of Cyprus, who linked sanctions against Minsk with sanctions against Ankara and made their agreement on the "Belarusian issue" dependent on measures that would force Turkey to stop exploration and production of gas in the Mediterranean Sea.

In most cases, there is an inversely proportional relationship between legitimacy and efficiency. High legitimacy is achieved through low efficiency and vice versa. The same relationship can be traced between the timing of reaching agreements and the sustainability of the latter: rapidly concluded agreements tend to be less stable and reliable than agreements that have resulted from lengthy negotiations. As a general rule, it can be assumed that multilateral and representative formats have no alternative when it comes to fundamental systemic problems of world politics or economics. However, when it comes to the need to respond quickly to a sudden problem, the actions of small groups of players who are more interested in solving the problem may be more effective. For example, the achievement of an agreement on the cessation of hostilities in the territory of Nagorno-Karabakh in November 2020 was reached in the trilateral Russian-Armenian-Azerbaijani format, bypassing the paralyzed OSCE Minsk Group. There is a part of legitimacy to pay for efficiency. The speed and efficiency of closed formats for solving specific problems can turn into difficulties at a time when longer-term or more complex, strategic issues come to replace these tasks.

Multilateralism is associated with many other problems and difficulties. For example, it is not clear how it is "fair" to divide between all participants in multilateral negotiations the areas of responsibility and burden associated with the implementation of the agreements reached, when the agreements involve significant costs and their participants are not comparable in their resource capabilities. There are no definitive answers to questions of fairness; any answer will be subjective and vulnerable to criticism. Nor is it easy to decide what measures should be taken against those who approach multilateral agreements selectively or sabotage their implementation. Multilateralism à la carte is becoming a serious problem of world politics and the economy, contributing to the growth of instability and the decline in the quality of global governance. Thus, in cases where their serious economic interests are threatened, states that advocate freedom of world trade often switch to positions of protectionism, accusing their competitors of dumping or manipulation of exchange rates.

In multilateral negotiations, the problem of trust of the participants in relation to each other is more acute than in bilateral negotiations, since multilateralism comes with fear of behind-the-scenes coordination of negotiating positions by separate groups of participants promoting their own interests. This problem is acute when a new actor is included in an already established multilateral structure that differs from its other members in one way or another. Despite many weaknesses of multilateral formats, none of them is fatal. In any case, any proposed unilateral or bilateral alternatives are burdened with no smaller number of vulnerabilities and imperfections. The question is about the conditions and criteria for effective multilateralism, about those models of multilateralism that could maximize its comparative advantages and minimize its organic shortcomings.

Considering common problems with multilateralism, several preconditions can be formulated, which allow for success of multilateral negotiating and institutional formats. These conditions relate to approaches and expectations of negotiators and relevant multilateral regimes and institutions. They are of a general nature and need to be clarified and specified in relation to individual dimensions of international life.

First, multilateral negotiators should be interested in achieving sustainable results (in solving the problem) and not in a diplomatic or strategic "victory" over partners. A "victory" of this kind can undermine the agreement and result in a final defeat. The benefits of one or another option of "solving the problem" can be distributed differently among the parties to the agreement, but the interest in the solution should be the main incentive for all participants in multilateral formats. If in bilateral formats negotiations on the principle of a "zero-sum game" are possible, albeit undesirable, then in multilateral formats it is impossible to identify a "zero amount" due to the fact of the presence of a number of participants exceeding two. The binary negotiating system in a multilateral context does not work, if only the negotiators are not grouped into two opposing coalitions.

Second, the participants should be focused on finding a compromise, including their own concessions. Practice shows that the violation of a reasonable balance between the concessions of the participants undermines the stability of the agreement, even when such a violation is tactically justified. An asymmetry in the scale of concessions between participants is not only possible but almost inevitable. The more participants, the greater the asymmetry. But such an asymmetry should be conscious and not perceived as a defeat by those who gave more than they received. Unlike the classical postulates of "political realism", multilateralism involves achieving not only a stable balance of power but also a balance of interests of participants belonging to different weight categories in world politics.

Third, negotiators should proceed from the principle of "diffuse reciprocity", that is, be ready in difficult situations to demonstrate solidarity with partners, if necessary, sacrificing their immediate interests for the sake of a longer-term gain. "Diffusion" (uncertainty) in this case means that, in the exercise of its goodwill, a multilateral negotiator is unable to determine when and in what form it will receive adequate "compensation" from its negotiating partners. Nevertheless, negotiators can be sure that such "compensation" will follow one way or another. Multilateral arrangements should be long-term and stable so that the prospects for "compensation" in the future are realistic.

Fourth, negotiators must have "internal legitimacy" – that is, be able to commit themselves on behalf of those they represent. Only strong leaders with broad political support in their own countries are able to act as successful negotiators. In both Western liberal and Eastern authoritarian political systems, problems can arise with "internal legitimacy". In the first case, any shift in the internal political balance of power calls into question the consistency of foreign policy; in the second case, the multilateral agreements reached look like those imposed on society by autocrat leaders. However, "internal legitimacy" is necessary for bilateral negotiation formats.

Fifth, mechanisms for the enforcement of the agreements reached should be defined. If these mechanisms are not in place, multilateral negotiations will be useless at best and harmful at worst, serving to mask the unilateral actions of certain players. The problem of enforcement remains one of the most difficult in multilateral agreements. As a rule, the problems of verifying the implementation of concluded agreements in multilateral formats are more difficult to solve than in bilateral agreements. In the first case, it is necessary to create special international organizations that have a significant degree of autonomy in relation to individual parties to the agreements; in the second case, such a need does not arise.

It is worth noting that success of multilateral diplomacy paradoxically depends on the willingness of the participants to unilateral and bilateral actions. Practice shows that behind any success of multilateral efforts, there is always a leader or a group of leaders who take the initiative in determining the agenda and priority of the issues under consideration, in maintaining the schedules of the negotiation process, acting as a mediator in reaching compromises. The multilateral format does not cancel and does not replace the bilateral format but is a necessary addition or prerequisite of the latter. An example of this combination is the bilateral German-French negotiations on the alliance for multilateralism.

Multilateralism and globalization

The current crisis of multilateralism is a reflection of the broader crisis of globalization. Presently, humanity is going through a painful period of deglobalization, affecting all participants in world politics together and individually. This is not limited to the immediate social or economic consequences of the COVID-19 pandemic. Failures in usual mechanisms for the growth of interconnectedness and interdependence of countries and peoples did not begin yesterday, and they will not end tomorrow. We are witnessing a global response to the multiple costs of the model of globalization that took shape at the turn of the century. Multilateralism as one of the formats in which global processes are implemented is also under attack.

Globalization does not have to be implemented in a multisided format: an increase in the level of connectivity and interdependence of states and societies can go through an increase in the density of the network of bilateral agreements and treaties of various kinds. However, multilateralism does not exist only at the global level. In the context of deglobalization, regional multilateralism is of particular importance. The agreement signed at the end of 2020 to establish a Regional Comprehensive Economic Partnership (RCEP) in Asia illustrates the success of regional multilateralism. On the European continent, multilateralism remains the fundamental principle of EU institutions (Cossa and Glosserman, 2020). But the crisis of multilateralism at the global level has a negative impact on many regional multilateral projects, limiting the number of participants and the depth of cooperation between them. India refused to participate in the RCEP at the last moment, and within the EU, the principles of multilateralism are disputed by nationalist-minded populist leaders (Poland, Hungary). Geopolitical confrontation between the great powers leads to attempts on their part to prevent the success of the integration projects of their competitors such as US opposition to China's "Belt and Road Initiative" and the EU not helping the formation and development of the Eurasian Economic Union.

If multilateralism today is linked to globalization, the future of multilateralism depends to a large extent on the future of globalization. One can argue about the extent to which deglobalization was inevitable and, if not, who exactly is responsible for its arrival. In any case, the global financial crisis of 2008–2009 and the postcrisis period of 2010–2013 have shown that the linear, exponential development of globalization can still be forgotten (Altman and Bastian, 2020). Today, centrifugal processes have already accumulated enormous inertia, and it would be naïve to expect that an event such as the coming to power of the Biden administration in the US can stop or reverse them. The ongoing deglobalization is serious and long-lasting.

Multilateralism will face challenges and opposition in the coming years. It can be assumed that in the context of deglobalization, multilateral regimes and formats will often lose out to available unilateral or bilateral alternatives. The increased volatility of world politics and the economy is problematic, hindering long-term investment in multilateral structures and regimes. Unilateral steps in the face of increased volatility often look like successful speculation, while multilateral efforts are presented as long-term investments with not always clear prospects. The increase in the level of international tension and geopolitical confrontation between great powers makes it difficult to implement the principle of "diffuse reciprocity" both at the global and the regional levels, encouraging transactional, situational approaches. The Biden administration's attempts to revive multilateralism among US allies often boil down to restoring the transatlantic pseudo-multilateralism that characterized the Cold War period.

However, as the current crisis of globalization is overcome, the demand for multilateralism is likely to increase again, albeit slowly, with stops and retreats; humanity is moving forward along the thorny path to future unity. Proceeding from the experience of the crisis of 2008–2009 and assuming that we are approaching the lowest point of the new "deglobalization stage" of the globalization cycle, the next change in the vector of world development is likely to occur by the middle of this decade. Adjusting for the more complex nature of the world cataclysms of 2020–2021, the moment of change of vector will have to be shifted forward, at least for another two to three years, toward the end of the third decade of the 21st century that has just begun. In this direction, the world is pushed by two powerful factors, which over the years are becoming stronger, no matter what triumphant anti-globalists may claim. First, the pressure of common problems such as climate change and global pandemics affects everyone and requires the combined efforts of global society in the interests of common survival. Some of the global challenges, ranging from possible environmental catastrophe to uncontrolled development of new technologies and the threat of global nuclear war, call into question the continued existence of humanity. The instinct of self-preservation of the human population must manifest itself one way or another (Solana, 2021).

Many of these challenges place high demands on the quality of global governance, including cooperation between states and the involvement of private business, international organizations and civil society. Constructive interaction between large states like China and the US will not be sufficient to solve problems. The current Westphalian international system is incapable of ensuring a new quality of global governance. The coronavirus pandemic has highlighted the existence of broad public demand for reforms not only of global health but also of global models of socioeconomic development (Kadakia and Thoumi, 2020).

Second, technological progress is creating new opportunities for remote communications of various kinds. The physical space and resource potential of the planet are shrinking; the possibilities for geographically distributed models of work, study and socialization are expanding; and Napoleon's old aphorism about geography as destiny is losing its former axiomaticity. Paradoxically, the COVID-19 pandemic has become a catalyst for the unification of humankind by accelerating the development and diffusion of new information and communication technologies, which, in turn, helped to accelerate the movement toward global markets for labor, education, science and entertainment. Recalling Thomas Friedman's famous turn-of-the-century bestseller, the world is emerging from the pandemic as a whole flatter than it was at the entrance to it.

The processes of deglobalization taking place in the world today could not be stopped and, in some ways, accelerated the tendency to diffusion of power in world politics, which will continue. Consolidation of peace on the basis of the revival of a unipolar or rigid bipolar system seems unlikely. Nation-states will remain key players in world politics, with the preservation of the principles of sovereignty and territorial integrity. Further, the number and international activity of non-state actors will continue to grow, undermining the hierarchy in world politics and the economy. With traditional formats of international cooperation demonstrating low efficiency, the need for new complex multilateral and multilevel formats will increase. In international relations, many variants of multilateral constructions arise, which theoretically did not exist throughout the previous history of mankind.

Humanity may have five to eight years in reserve to prepare a new historical cycle of globalization and to establish new algorithms for multilateral interaction that could underpin the coming globalization cycle. This will require a radical renewal of political elites in most countries of the world, learning how to resist right- and left-wing populists and prevent a world war, global environmental catastrophe, a new pandemic, or other unfortunate delays during transit to these algorithms. The main issues of the new agenda will be different not only from current issues but also from the issues of the era of "Globalization 1.0". For example, if the victorious march of globalization at the beginning of the century was under the sign of the strengthening of the aggregate East and the weakening of the aggregate West (Kortunov, 2021b), then the fundamental issue of "Globalization 2.0" will be the question of a large-scale redistribution of resources between the North and the South in favor of the latter.

If the "old" globalization was associated with an acceleration of economic growth and increase in personal and public consumption, then in the course of the "new" globalization, most likely, the main criterion for success will be to ensure a transition to sustainable development models, both at the national and the global levels. If the global processes of the turn of the century reflected the universal public demand for freedom, then in the second quarter of the century, we are likely to see a more articulated and more persistent demand for justice. Many of the usual algorithms of foreign policy activities will also change. The main international organizations by the end of this decade will still be preserved. But a significant part of international activity will be bubbling not around or within rigid bureaucratic institutions but around specific problems. To solve these specific problems, mobile situational coalitions of participants will be formed, from among nation-states, the private sector, civil society institutions and other participants in international life. The old hierarchies will lose their meaning, and the terms "superpower" and "great power" will be perceived as archaic and explaining little in modern life.

Toward a new world order

The urgent task of the present is not to resurrect the old format of multilateralism of the Cold War era or the period of the unipolar world but to invent a new format by adapting its general principles to changing reality. First, state leaders must be prepared to promote multilateralism without counting on the leadership of a multilateralist hegemon. It would be wonderful if the US again became an active supporter of multilateralism under the Biden administration. We should all welcome Washington's desire to return to WHO, the Paris climate agreements and the Joint Comprehensive Plan of Action on Iran. Nevertheless, one of the lessons of the Trump administration is that we can no longer rely on unconditional American support for multilateralism as a given. A critical attitude toward international multilateralism remains an important part of American political culture and will continue throughout the foreseeable future, meaning that some multilateral structures will have to be built without Washington's active involvement (Kortunov, 2021b).

Second, diplomats and experts must learn to use multilateral formats in the face of the relative weakness of international organizations and the erosion of international hierarchies. There is a widespread "institutional fatigue" in the world that is unlikely to disappear in the near future. Old unions lose their former cohesion, and new ones often remain unions only on paper. Therefore, the realism of proposals to revive multilateralism using formats similar to the Conference on Security and Cooperation in Europe in the first half of the 1970s is questionable (Gardener, 2021). Flexible multilateral regimes have more promise than rigid multilateral organizations. Voluntary commitments by states may become more practical than traditional, legally binding, international agreements requiring lengthy harmonization and ratification procedures.

The selective use of multilateralism, with a focus on the least toxic dimensions of international engagement, would facilitate agreements but, at the same time, create additional challenges. Given the deep interdependence of individual dimensions of world politics and the economy, it is easy to predict that agreements in one area will affect the relations of the parties to such agreements in other spheres. For example, any multilateral climate-related agreements will affect global trade regimes in one way or another through the imposition of borderline carbon taxes. In turn, multilateral trade agreements will influence international information transfer regimes through the harmonization of common digital trade standards. It is likely that any future multilateral arrangements relating to international trade will have to include environmental protection, social protection of the labor force and foreign direct investment. Otherwise, in addition to unilateral taxes, the world will face similar environmental social taxes, which will become a serious obstacle to the development of world trade. Linking security and development issues will be more challenging. Presently, the two main areas of multilateralism are loosely linked, which reduces the effectiveness of work in both areas. Closer interaction between major multilateral mechanisms, such as the UN Security Council and the G20, is likely to be required to achieve synergies in conflict resolution and in ensuring regional and global stability. Taking into account the mutual influence of different multilateral regimes with different sets of actors is difficult.

Third, a new type of multilateralism should not see common values as a *sine qua non* for reaching agreements. A necessary and sufficient condition is only the coincidence of interests. The old mantra that multilateralism and the liberal world order as a whole are nothing more than derivatives of political liberalism as the dominant ideology of major international players should be rejected as irrelevant and impractical. The multilateralism of the 21st century can only become universal if it is suitable for a world of value pluralism (Tarpaulin, 2020). At the same time, multilateralism should become a tool for overcoming the value conflicts that exist in the modern world. In other words, common values should not be the starting point in moving toward multilateralism but the end point to which multilateralism can lead. Since geopolitical confrontation will continue for some time, new formats of multilateralism should be based on the principle of "competitive cooperation" or "competitive multilateralism", when relations of competition and confrontation between powers, as well as non-state actors, should not prevent them from working together. Developing specific parameters and adopting the practice of "competitive cooperation" is one of the greatest challenges for future global politics (Jones and Malcorra, 2021).

Fourth, multilateralism should become as inclusive as possible in the overall representativeness of multilateral formats. This applies to the representation of states representing particular interest groups that are currently underestimated or ignored altogether. For example, current discussions on global Internet governance involve countries with significant technological potential to develop new information and communication technologies (supply side). At the same time, countries that, due to global demographic shifts before our eyes, are becoming the main users of the Internet (demand side) are almost absent from these discussions. Multilateral agreements between states are insufficient if they do not involve the private sector, civil society and other private and public actors. The most important international issues, the future of arms control, climate change, managing technological progress and regulating migration, require the creation of broad and flexible coalitions of a variety of players to address them (Chatham House, 2021). It is no coincidence that Microsoft has opened a separate office in New York to interact with UN entities. It is conceivable to assume that most of the new generation of multilateral coalitions will be built on the principle of public–private partnerships (PPPs). In this case, it is important to ensure clarity and transparency of the process of involving various types of stakeholders such as PPP.

The expansion of the circle of active participants in multilateral agreements complicates the process of negotiation and monitoring of compliance with the agreements reached. After all, non-state actors, whether private companies, municipalities, regional authorities or non-profit organizations, can no longer be seen as convenient tools that states arbitrarily use to achieve their goals. These players form their own interests, priorities and values that differ from those operated by states. And imposing the state will on non-state actors in multilateral formats will not be easy for liberal democracies (Fernandez and Galceran-Vercher, 2021).

Thus, if multilateral practices survive in the near future, it will be in the format of ad hoc or project (problem) multilateralism. Project multilateralism will become as common in international relations as the project-based construction of the educational process is today in leading universities. Such examples of multilateralism exist at the regional level (cf. Arctic Council) and in individual functional areas (cf. International Civil Aviation Organization). This format of multilateralism has many drawbacks and limitations; they are mobile, unstable, selective and fragile. Nevertheless, it remains the best option for the near future given the lack of conditions for the implementation of more complex and more advanced formats.

It would be logical to assume that multilateral coalitions with a limited number of participants and a narrow mandate, which have already demonstrated their effectiveness and sustainability, could develop, involving new members and expanding the range of activities. However, experience suggests that this logic does not always work. The founders of "closed clubs", be it the UN Security Council, the G7 or the G20, often fear the erosion of existing formats, the complication of the negotiation process and the loss of part of their influence when expanding this format. The expansion of the mandate is also a matter of concern, as it can bring new complex and contentious issues to the agenda and undermine confidence in areas where its existence was not previously questioned.

Another important feature of new multilateralism should be the simplification of multilateral mechanisms, overcoming bureaucratic inertia and combating duplication of functions. Most public opinion polls show that there is still broad support for multilateralism in the world, but, at the same time, there is a growing critical attitude to many specific practices at the global and regional levels. Such criticisms include bureaucracy, slowness, isolation from ordinary people, lack of transparency and excessive administrative costs (Davis, 2020).

Global multilateralism should focus on a small number of problems and challenges that cannot be addressed at the regional or national levels with everything else delegated to structures and mechanisms closer to the problems and tasks to be addressed. Otherwise, global multilateral institutions will be blamed for problems for which others should be held responsible such as deepening socioeconomic inequalities within individual countries.

It is unlikely that leaders in the development of a new format of multilateralism will be great powers such as the US, China or Russia. All of these powers are too accustomed to asymmetric interdependence relations with their weaker partners and therefore tend to pursue a path of maximizing their comparative advantages in bilateral relations. Moreover, isolationist sentiments will likely gain strength in these countries in the near future, limiting their involvement in multilateral structures and regimes (Kortunov, 2021a). However, countries like the members of the EU or ASEAN have already accumulated a great deal of experience in various multilateral formats (Jones and Malcorra, 2021). It can be assumed the role of small and medium-sized countries in promoting multilateralism will increase not only in new areas of climate, international governance in cyberspace or in the development of biotechnology but also in traditional security issues, including arms control (Meier, 2020).

While in many cases multilateral structures have evolved and will continue to emerge on a regional basis, other principles for the formation of multilateral coalitions are likely to become common. For example, the common interests of the international Alliance of Small Island States have successfully influenced the global climate agenda despite their different political systems and diverse geographic locations. Further, multilateral coalitions of medium and small countries are forming around specific issues of governance such as the 2019 amendments to the Basel Convention on the Control of Transboundary Movements of Hazardous Wastes and their Disposal (the so-called Basel Plastics Ban), made possible by concerted action by Norway, Vietnam and Indonesia (Kumar and Sridhar, 2019).

Prospects for multilateral formats depend on the formation of a global culture of multilateralism, which at the moment is only in an embryonic state. The task of promoting norms and values of multilateralism should be solved at different levels, from the introduction of personal practices in diplomatic departments to educational programs in secondary schools. Conditions must be created for the emergence of a broad public demand for multilateralism, as well as for effective counteraction to popular sentiments of isolationism and unilateralism.

At present, opponents of multilateral international cooperation use modern information and communication technologies to promote their positions, often using the methods of information warfare. It is necessary to find formats of constant dialogue between leading multilateral organizations and owners of the largest social networks acceptable to both sides in order to counter the spread of misinformation and the destructive impact on public consciousness.

Conclusion

Only the first steps have been taken in the study of the complex issues of multilateralism, and the number of questions that arise far exceeds the available answers. The same conclusion arises from the experience of the new type of multilateral political practice accumulated since the turn of the century. This experience is still insufficient and too contradictory to make reasonable and convincing generalizations. In any case, multilateralism (including multipolarity or polycentrism) cannot be considered a universal mechanism for solving all international problems. The multilateral format is cumbersome, complex, slow and often leads to disappointing results. Multilateralism cannot and will not replace a two-pronged approach and a willingness to take unilateral foreign policy action, especially when it comes to major powers claiming to preserve their state sovereignty as fully as possible. Nor can multilateralism lead to a balance of interests prevailing in global or regional affairs and the balance of power factor becoming a thing of the past.

In the medium term, multilateralism is one of several options for developing the international system, perhaps not the most likely. Today, many are talking about the revival of the bipolar model in the form of a long-term confrontation between the US and China. Another quite possible option would be to continue the fragmentation of the international system with a tendency to "atomize" world politics and increase isolationism in the leading world powers. An independent alternative is the model of regionalization, where leading powers do not abandon foreign policy but concentrate their resources and efforts on their "natural" spheres of their strategic interests. Theoretically, a new rise of the West, led by the US, is possible, including a return to many traditional quasi-multilateral formats characteristic of the period of the unipolar world.

However, multilateralism has its comparative advantages. It would be a mistake to ignore or downplay such features of multilateralism as democracy, representativeness, legitimacy and the sustainability of the results achieved by the multilateral negotiation process. None of these alternatives to multilateralism offers any hope of progress toward uniting the efforts of humankind to meet the challenges they face.

In summary, multilateralism is:

- a chance for weak players to ensure that their voices are heard and their interests taken into account.
- an opportunity for strong players to make their leadership more civilized, less burdensome and less intrusive for all other participants in international life.

- a format that allows international organizations and regimes to maintain an acceptable level of autonomy from their founders and participants and to pursue an independent course in world politics and the economy.
- a prospect for non-state actors to take a direct part in discussing and solving problems on which the future of these players depends.
- a mechanism that contributes to the establishment of greater openness and transparency in the practice of international relations, improving the quality of publicly available information on the activities of governments, the private sector and international organizations.
- a means of building trust among a wide variety of participants in international communication, pursuing common and sometimes divergent interests.

Multilateralism is, as far as can be judged, the only democratic mechanism to prevent the final collapse of the ailing international system and the means of expanding the reproduction of much-needed global public goods. As the pressure of common problems on the participants of world politics increases, the objective prerequisites for the establishment of the practice of many externalities will manifest themselves more actively.

Multilateralism, like any other format of political and diplomatic activity, will always be as effective or ineffective as the players practicing these formats themselves want. So far, most of these players remain in positions of narrowly understood national interest. Selective multilateralism is becoming increasingly widespread, reflecting the current priorities of certain leaders and power groups. Closed multilateral formats created by some participants in world politics and the economy to confront other players are becoming popular. Multilateralism, with rare exceptions, is not considered as an independent value but is utilitarian and used only when it is impossible to do without it.

In order to reverse this negative trend and begin to move toward strategic multilateralism, it is necessary to revise many well-established stereotypes about foreign policy priorities, threats to national security and the content of state sovereignty. Moreover, such a transition will be required not only on the part of the leaders of major powers but also on the part of the societies represented by these leaders. Today, one can only wonder under what circumstances and in what time frame such a transition is possible. It is to be hoped that the time frame for the transition would be rather short.

References

Altman, S.A. and Bastian, C.R. (2020). DHL Global Connectedness Index 2020. The State of Globalization in a Distancing World. URL: https://www.logistics.dhl.ru/content/dam/dhl/global/dhl-spotlight/documents/pdf/spotlight-g04-global-connectedness-index-2020.pdf.

Chatham House. (2021). Reflections on building more inclusive global governance. *Chatham House*. URL: https://www.chathamhouse.org/2021/04/reflections-building-more-inclusive-global-governance/03-ten-insights-reflections-building.

Cossa, R.A. and Glosserman, B. (2020). Multilateralism (Still) Matters in/to Asia. *Comparative Connections*. URL: http://cc.pacforum.org/2021/01/multilateralism-still-matters-in-to-asia/.

Davis, E. (2020). Survey: Advanced Countries Favorable of U.N., but 'Doubts Persist'. *US News & World Report*. URL: https://www.usnews.com/news/best-countries/articles/2020-09-21/on-75th-anniversary-of-the-un-some-countries-question-its-effectiveness?mc_cid=bca2ed9c2e&mc_eid=[6f24f55c06].

Fernandez of Losada, A. and Galceran-Vercher, M. (Eds.) (2021). Cities in global governance: From multilateralism to multistakeholderism? Barcelona Centre for International Affairs. URL: https://www.cidob.org/en/publications/publication_series/monographs/monographs/cities_in_global_governance_from_multilateralism_to_multistakeholderism.

Gardener, H. (2021). Does Biden's Presidency mean for multilateralism? *Defence Horizon Journal*, Special Edition 1/21. Geopolitics. https://ca9d3787-8643-4d85-9af7-d052377ac9b8.filesusr.com/ugd/0d3ede_730a5ba77e0c40fb9637da417752d0eb.pdf.

Jones, B. and Malcorra, S. (2021). It is now time to focus on multilateral order. *Brookings Institution*. URL: https://www.brookings.edu/blog/order-from-chaos/2021/04/19/it-is-now-time-to-focus-on-multilateral-order/?utm_source=feedblitz&utm_medium=FeedBlitzRss&utm_campaign=brookingsrss/programs/foreignpolicy

Kadakia, K. and Thoumi, A. (2020). The coronavirus is a siren for the health-related sustainable development goals. *Brookings Institution*. URL: https://www.brookings.edu/blog/future-development/2020/05/13/the-coronavirus-is-a-siren-for-the-health-related-sustainable-development-goals/?mc_cid=cc5adcff70&mc_eid=[6f24f55c06].

Kortunov, A. (2021a). To leave or to stay? Seven Russian claims against the OSCE. *RIAC*. URL: https://russiancouncil.ru/analytics-and-comments/analytics/uyti-ili-ostatsya-sem-rossiyskikh-pretenziy-k-obse/.

Kortunov, A. (2021b). What will Globalization 2.0 look like? *RIAC*. URL: https://russiancouncil.ru/analytics-and-comments/analytics/kakoy-budet-globalizatsiya-2-0/.

Kumar, H. and Sridhar, L. (2019). Basel convention's plastic ban amendment a new step against waste colonialism. *Wire*. URL: https://thewire.in/environment/basel-conventions-plastic-ban-amendment-is-a-new-step-against-waste-colonialism.

Lavrov, S.V. (2009). Potential for change. International relations in a new coordinate system. *Rossiyskaya Gazeta*. URL: https://rg.ru/2009/09/08/lavrov.html.

Meier, O. (2020). Yes, we can? Europe responds to the crisis of multilateral arms control. *ELN Policy Brief*. URL: https://www.europeanleadershipnetwork.org/policy-brief/yes-we-can-europe-responds-to-the-crisis-of-multilateral-arms-control/.

Solana, J. (2021). Multilateralism or bust. *Project Syndicate*. URL: https://www.project-syndicate.org/commentary/more-multilateralism-on-climate-change-covid19-cyberspace-by-javier-solana-2021-05.

Tarpaulin, M. (Ed.). (2020). Reforming multilateralism in post-COVID times. For a more regionalised, binding and legitimate UN. Brussels: Foundation for European Progressive Studies. URL: https://www.iai.it/en/pubblicazioni/reforming-multilateralism-post-covid-times.

Turk, D. (2020). Multilateralism must deliver. The Robert Bosch Stiftung. *Quarterly Perspectives* 4. URL: https://www.robertboschacademy.de/en/perspectives/multilateralism-must-deliver.

3

COVID-19 AND THE DECLINE OF THE NEOLIBERAL PARADIGM

On the erosion of hegemony in times of crises

Tobias Debiel and Mathieu Rousselin

Introduction

The COVID-19 pandemic sent global shock waves through economy and politics – and it will most likely continue to do so for many years to come. Concerns about a slowdown in growth, a collapse in healthcare and political instability triggered state interventions in numerous countries around the world, reminiscent of the global financial crisis of 2008. A flurry of commentators had already interpreted the 2008 crisis as a challenge to the neoliberal hegemony; wasn't the market all too obviously unable to respond adequately to excessive risk-taking by lending institutions such as Lehman Brothers? The pandemic also saw a proliferation of calls predicting the end of the neoliberal hegemony in global economic relations (Bello, 2021; Saxer, 2020) or announcing the "twilight of the gods of neoliberalism" (Brandt and Windels, 2020: 26–27, *translation by the authors*).

And these analysts did put forth convincing reasons for their prophecies. Indeed, one of the basic tenants of the neoliberal doctrine, namely the kind of financial deregulation that culminated with the repel of the Glass-Steagall legislation in 1999, was widely seen as one of the root causes for the development of highly speculative financial products (so-called derivatives) loosely tied with mortgage-backed securities that ultimately lead to the financial collapse of the North American real estate market before spreading to the entire global financial system. In a similar fashion, the current pandemic has also been described as yet another proof of the outdatedness of the neoliberal toolkit, with state interventions to manage the global health crisis possibly bringing about the end of the neoliberal era (Kilic, 2021; Saad-Filho, 2020; Tooze, 2021). Yet, to this day no death certificate has been produced so that obituary notices for the neoliberal world order would seem very much premature.

DOI: 10.4324/9781003273844-3

Will neoliberalism remain the eternal patient, resolutely clinging on to its deathbed? Or will the COVID-19 pandemic eventually pave the way for a post-neoliberal world order? We claim in the following contribution with a focus on the Global Northwest that the neoliberal paradigm may have been eroded as a political project and even possibly as an economic doctrine as a result of the two "global macro events" (Leisering, 2021: 399) but that it proved surprisingly resilient as a cultural formation and a subtle technology of power.[1] Rather than giving way to alternative paradigms, neoliberalism in many regions of the world skilfully changed its shape and developed new variants adapted to new economic and political circumstances. At the same time, however, the pandemic in contrast to the world financial crisis from 2008 has fostered a renaissance of the "caring state" that is concerned not only with the bailout of banks but also with the welfare of its citizens. It indicates a new form of governmentality that might foreshadow the emergence a post-neoliberal model.

Our contribution is divided into four parts. First, we look at an astonishing paradox: although the neoliberal ideology has steadily lost support over the past 15 years, its prescriptions are so institutionally entrenched that they continue to determine socioeconomic policies. This was clearly demonstrated, we secondly argue, in the world financial crisis. It could have been an oath of revelation for neoliberalism, but the latter recovered quickly with the help of state intervention in favour of banks and capital markets. Although the first major crisis of the 21st century did fuel social polarisation and dissatisfaction with technocratic governance by political elites, the authoritarian-reactionary right-wing populism did not lead to questioning core economic elements of neoliberalism. Rather, it establishes a new, authoritarian-national phase of neoliberalism, which was most clearly demonstrated by the Brexit and Trump's election as US president in 2016.

The next major crisis of the 21st century, the COVID-19 pandemic, according to our third argument, brought about a state interventionism that went beyond the measures of the 2018 global financial crisis and led to the renaissance of the "caring state". This undermined the legitimacy of neoliberalism not only among the "globalisation losers" but also among broad segments of the population. In many of the Western industrialised countries, the state gained new scope for action that went well beyond the basic neoliberal mission of ensuring free and fair competition. Yet, we maintain that state intervention does not mark the end of the neoliberal era and the return to a cherished Keynesian world order. The neoliberal project is characterised by its impressive flexibility and capacity to adapt to various crises, rendering it highly resilient even in the face of state intervention. A closer look at macroeconomic and fiscal policies during the COVID-19 pandemic reveals that the core ideological assumptions and structural asymmetries that are constitutive of the neoliberal world order largely remain untouched.

Zooming in on the sectoral level, we show in the fourth section that the COVID-19 pandemic did shatter some of neoliberalism's most dearly held assumptions, for instance, in the field of global health cooperation. Promising initiatives such as COVID-19 Vaccines Global Access (COVAX) and Global Initiative on Sharing All Influenza Data (GISAID) provide cooperative templates that emphasise a rhetoric of global solidarity and in very practical terms break with key ideological tenants of the neoliberal orthodoxy such as market allocation and intellectual property rights. At the same time, the disappointing results in the implementation of COVAX illustrate once more the limitations of voluntary commitments and highlight the need for an internationally binding treaty on the global management of pandemics.

In our concluding remarks, we discuss, finally, the impact of a possible paradigm shift in the Global Northwest on the conditions in the Global South and the redesign of development cooperation.

The neoliberal paradox: a widely contested model with no clear expiry date

It has become rare to find anybody in a prominent political position openly jumping to rescue neoliberalism. As early as 2006, Dani Rodrik (2006: 974) stated that "nobody really believes in the Washington Consensus anymore". Gone are the days when outspoken neoliberal figures such as Margaret Thatcher could taunt their political opponents with sentences like: "There is no alternative". The ranks of explicitly professed neoliberals have now shrunk considerably while the opposing side is becoming louder. A simple Google search with the keywords "end of neoliberalism" brings up more than 15 million results, including quite a few that declare neoliberalism clinically "dead". Joseph Stiglitz, former chief economist of the World Bank, among others, for instance, did so very prominently, declaring "neoliberalism must be pronounced dead and buried" (Stiglitz, 2019). At the same time, however, concrete policies remain deeply shaped and informed by neoliberalism. Stated otherwise, while the ideology may be on the defensive, neoliberal policy prescriptions are still very much present (Aalbers, 2013: 1083).

Since the 1970s, the hard-fought ideological counterpart, Keynesianism, had been intellectually defeated and gradually substituted. This was achieved paradigmatically and brutally by the Chicago boys, disciples of Milton Friedman's work (e.g. Friedman 1962), in Pinochet's Chile. The neoliberal mantra became globally effective via the Washington Consensus (Williamson, 1990). The macroeconomic doctrine of Keynesianism, which found its expression in the model of the welfare state, was replaced by two basic principles (Halimi, 2006; Klein, 2014): the emphasis on individual freedoms (first and foremost, the almost unconditional protection of private property) and the notion of the state as promoter of virtuous competition between private economic actors through four main governance instruments (privatisation, deregulation, tax cuts and free trade).

There may well be no uniform, so to speak lexical definition of neoliberalism that could be convincing. Rather, neoliberalism comes with its various shades and forms. A first approach to the term is offered by Mitchell Dean's (2014: 151) distinction. According to this analysis, neoliberalism can be understood in terms of a historical reconstruction as a "thought collective" (Mirowski, 2018) that developed from Friedrich Hayek's Mont Pèlerin Society. It has found its adversary in the macroeconomic theory of Keynesianism, which shaped *les trente glorieuses*, the three golden decades after the end of World War II, and then came into crisis. Neoliberalism became hegemonic in the 1990s (Beckert, 2020: 321), after the Kuhnian paradigm shift (Kuhn, 1962) away from Keynesianism. It promised to solve the crisis problems of the 1970s/80s (stagflation, unemployment, public debt, weak growth) better than its predecessor.

In a Gramscian move, advocates of neoliberalism achieved this feat by progressively undermining the public trust in the ability of state bureaucracies to effectively allocate resources. Instead, they argued that the highest mission for the public hand ought to consist in "levelling the playing field", merely ensuring "the conditions necessary for the free operation of the market" (Dean, 2014: 154). It would thus be short-sighted to equate neoliberalism with the disappearance of the state. Rather, Friedrich Hayek (2006: 194, quoted by Kiely, 2020: 404) already said that "it is the character rather than the volume of government activity that is important".

The various schools of neoliberal thought share unequivocal foundations but also diverge significantly from one another.E.g., Davies and McGoey (2012) argue that Friedrich Hayek attributed scientific authority to markets under conditions of uncertainty and complexity and, in his sceptical epistemology, distrusted centralised knowledge. In contrast, the Chicago School placed its faith in mathematic economic models of neoclassical provenance. Furthermore, it sees the concentration of bureaucratic and computing capacities within the market as a possible basis for better decision-making and distinguishes itself from the Freiburg and Vienna Schools, which are rather known for being particularly dismissive of monopolies:

> Where Hayek had questioned the possibility of any authoritative economic knowledge claims on a priori grounds, the Chicago School opened up the possibility that concentrations of bureaucratic and calculative capacity within the market might be a basis for better and more efficient decision-making.
>
> *(Davis and McGoey, 2012: 71)*

Thus, the neoliberal model is not merely deregulation but its own model of regulation, which strives for a "certain regime of government" (Dean, 2014: 156). In doing so, neoliberalism must certainly strive for social integration. However, this is done through money and markets, supplemented and enforced by bureaucratic power; thus, governance takes on an "elite-technocratic form" (Condon, 2021: 809) that came under heavy fire during the management of the 2008 financial crisis.

The world financial crisis 2008: a pledge of reform with little consequences

If the oil price and debt crises of the 1970s were an oath of revelation for Keynesianism, neoliberalism apparently met a similar fate with the world financial crisis of 2008. Banks collapsed, economic output shrank and unemployment and social dislocation were the global consequences. Accordingly, it was expected that there could be a shift to a post-neoliberal regime "that would be actively concerned with system-level risk and impose restrictive regulations on financial institutions and markets" (Konings, 2016: 268). Indeed, with the bailout of several major banks, the principle of deregulation had to be reversed, at least temporarily. However, the neoliberal model proved remarkably resilient in the face of its adversaries and its inherent weaknesses. This soon became apparent when the structural adjustment programmes for Portugal and Greece were launched, which were both characterised by strict austerity ideology (Cahill, 2011: 480). Even the derivatives market, almost universally acknowledged as one of the root causes of the 2008 global financial crisis, had already returned to its pre-crisis level by December 2013 (Charrel, 2013).

A quick reading may take these developments as a sign of state capture by omnipotent financial elites. But this falls short and runs the risk of following "an instrumentalist or even conspirational character understanding of institutional power" (Konings, 2016: 269). It is probably more convincing to argue that neoliberalism is a thoroughly historical project that has become firmly embedded in "ideological norms, class relations, and institutional rules" (Cahill, 2011:479). Beyond its structural entrenchment, moreover, the permanence of neoliberalism can be explained by its impressive flexibility and adaptability, at least as long as its essential core features remain untouched. This impressive plasticity has made it possible, e.g., for neoliberal approaches to spread under different names relatively independently of the political colouring or even of the religious orientation of the regime. It could even be linked to political Islam, as has been shown for the Muslim Brothers in Egypt, the AKP (Turkey Justice and Development Party) in Turkey or for the Ennahda in Tunisia (Rousselin, 2016).

The question of how neoliberalism relates to populist protest, which experienced a global upsurge in the 2010s, seems particularly relevant to us. Here we focus on the right-wing authoritarian variant that has the upper hand in Western industrialised countries. These populist protests are indicative of a certain "loss of legitimacy" on the part of the regulatory institutions. According to the considerations developed by Max Weber (1978), in the context of the modern state, a relationship of authority can be deemed "legitimate" when the governed grant the governors a right to impose binding regulations and follow them themselves largely independently of their content. Yet, popular protests can largely be attributed to the erosion of output-oriented legitimacy as defined by Scharpf (1997, 2004). The dismantling of the welfare state has caused, among other things, an increase in social inequality, economic marginalisation and fears of social decline. It is often underestimated in analyses that not only the industrial workforce or the urban poor are affected by these trends but also significantly the rural areas (using the example of Europe Mamonova and Franquesa, 2020). A serious factor in the perception of output failure is that neoliberalism was unable to deliver what Beckert calls "promissory legitimacy", i.e. the legitimacy that results from promises about the future. This leads to disenchantment regarding the "expectations followers have regarding future effects of the actions pursued" (Beckert, 2020: 319). The consequence is an alienation of significant strata of the population from the socio-political system.

The right-wing populist protest shows that the social legitimacy of neoliberalism was already eroding before the COVID-19 pandemic, i.e. it was not previously in a kind of normal state of aggregation (Condon, 2021: 805). In this context, the social protest against the neoliberal economic and social model is somewhat related to the 2008 world financial crisis (Beckert, 2020: 323). However, the loss of political legitimacy only became irrefutably clear later, when the Brexit shock combined with Trump's election as US president in 2016 (Condon, 2021: 810) showed that populism can be understood as resistance to technocratic elites (de la Torre, 2019: 64) and relies on an adversarial counterpart, vis-à-vis which a homogenised "us, the people" becomes the frame of reference (Mamonova and Franquesa, 2020: 712).

The "reactionary-populist" protest is ambivalent in its relationship to neoliberalism. On the one hand, it can be seen as an antagonist, insofar as it sees the globalisation pursued by the competitive state as a threat to identity and social status. In addition, this protest explicitly opposes socially liberal variants of neoliberalism, such as those developed by Tony Blair in the sense of the so-called Third Way in Great Britain (Kiely, 2020: 399). At the same time, on the other hand, a coalition of right-wing conservative and reactionary-populist forces can emerge that ideologically links the neoliberal economic model with an authoritarian nationalism. By referring to nation or even racist stereotypes, it creates a recruitment base that opposes a mobilisation based on the categories of class or cash (Fischer, 2020: 380–381). In addition, this type of right-wing populism differentiates social policy with regard to the "deserving and undeserving poor" (Kiely, 2020: 409). Moreover, many political measures differed significantly from nationalist rhetoric, e.g. the deregulation of financial capital under Trump (Kelleher, 2019; Rodriguez Valladares, 2019).

We follow Sumonja's argument that neoliberalism entered an "authoritarian" phase in an appreciable number of countries after 2008 (Sumonja, 2020: 7–8). Examples can be found around the world, such as more recently with Hungary under Viktor Orbán in East-Central Europe, Brazil (Jair Bolsonaro) in South America, India (Narendra Modi) in South Asia or the Philippines (Rodrigo Duterte) in Southeast Asia. The aforementioned connectivity to authoritarian ideologies, as expressed particularly drastically since 1973 in Chile, thus does not remain alien to the nature of neoliberalism (Brown, 2019; Bruff and Tansel,

2021). It is the always potentially present political shadow side of the model that has become increasingly apparent since the 2010s.

Will the COVID-19 pandemic seal the doom of the neoliberal hegemony?

The second major crisis of the 21st century was associated with the COVID-19 pandemic, which triggered a genuine recession in 2020. Similar to the global financial crisis, there was massive government intervention. But there was one key difference, as Saad-Filho points out: neoliberal beliefs such as "fiscal austerity" were challenged at breakneck speed, and they "vanished faster than one could spell 'bankruptcy'" (Saad-Filho, 2020: 477). Moreover, the state intervened as problems in global supply chains loomed and health care was threatened. The surprising speed of this doctrinal U-turn in the wake of the pandemic revealed the devastating consequences of four decades of neoliberal hegemony:

> The pandemic hit after four decades of neoliberalism had depleted state capacities in the name of the "superior efficiency" of the market, fostered deindustrialization through the "globalization" of production and built fragile financial structures secured by magical thinking and state guarantees, all in the name of short-term profitability.
>
> *(Saad-Filho, 2020: 478)*

The "Renaissance of the State" versus...

The global financial crisis of 2008 had already resulted in a "legitimacy crisis" of the neoliberal model, increasingly perceived as threatening social stability by failing to address capital accumulation (Bonanno, 2017). This ongoing legitimacy crisis was notoriously deepened by the COVID-19 pandemic, which further illustrated the limits of "market competition as a mechanism of coordination and development" (Condon, 2021). Interestingly, the COVID-19 pandemic also led to a "renaissance of the state" (Brandt and Windels, 2020: 27) and initiated a trend towards the concomitant re-legitimisation of the public hand that went beyond the flash in the pan that followed government interventions to manage the global financial crisis. In addition, the role of the state has changed: while it confined itself to the bailout of banks during the world financial crisis, it has been concerned with the welfare of its citizens during the pandemic.

To address the global health crisis, methods were resorted to that were not part of or even frankly run against the neoliberal repertoire (Kilic, 2021: 610). On the one hand, and as already mentioned, austerity policies were quickly abandoned and unprecedented public expenditures were tolerated if not openly encouraged by international financial institutions that were formerly guardians of the neoliberal orthodoxy, with public debt ratios (arguably fuelled by the perspective of virtually interest-free borrowing) breaking historic records in many advanced countries.[2]

On the other hand, state authorities restricted the scope of a number of individual freedoms and civil liberties that were historically a cornerstone of the liberal school of thought such as the freedom of movement, the freedom of peaceful assembly and of association or the right to worship or assemble in connection with a religion. In many cases, states did not issue mere recommendations while pledging voluntary compliance by responsible and virtuous private actors – rather, public authorities enacted legally binding legislation that foresaw fines and even imprisonment for violations (e.g. of up to two years in Germany for breaching lockdown). This signifies a reassertion of the state that was welcome by a majority of citizens. Opinion polls have shown that these restrictive measures are well understood and even enjoy a fairly large public support within the population,[3] which may be indicative of the erosion of the neoliberal paradigm. Even intellectual property rights, one of the core mechanisms of neoliberalism, was questioned by none other than US President Joe Biden, who threatened to revoke the patent protection on COVID vaccines enjoyed by major pharmaceutical companies under the World Trade Organization's law so as to allow for the mass production of cheaper generic medicine (Shalal et al., 2021).

Finally, the "caring" state has led to many people experiencing a form of "corona solidarity community", as the German economist Bert Rürup, former chairman of the German Council of Economic Experts, noted (Rürup, 2020, *translation by the authors*). An example of these communities are, for instance, solidarity networks at the level of neighbourhoods with countless initiatives to provide support for children during home-schooling or to help people with disabilities or elderly people purchase food, medicine, clothing or essential household equipment. This has created a social capital that can also be used for future crises.

... *the remarkable resilience of the neoliberal order*

Is this return of the state and the claim to enforce binding rules for the greater common good a first indication of a counter-model to neoliberal ideology? Is a revived Keynesianism on the horizon, with investment programmes and infrastructure projects oriented towards the major crises of the 21st century? Does the emerging narrative of global solidarity point to a shift in ideological norms?

Until the COVID-19 pandemic, it could be argued that major crises, including the 2008 world financial crisis, failed to seriously threaten the primacy of neoliberal principles. Crises may cause economic disruption and undermine trust in political institutions; they may destroy people's jobs and lives – but they do not shake the overall logic. The various crises that appeared to plague the normal functioning of the neoliberal world order somehow counter-intuitively helped strengthen its predominant position and rule out alternative models. In particular, these crises repeatedly served as a justification for massive state interventions that consolidated the neoliberal system by rescuing and recrediting its main actors (Aalbers, 2013). In other words, neoliberals have succeeded in maintaining the ideological primacy of the market through the seemingly paradoxical recourse to state interventionism (Mirowski, 2018).

This impressive persistence of neoliberalism thanks to its radical, almost constitutive flexibility is a prime example of resilience. The somehow vague and malleable notion of "resilience" was initially borrowed from individual psychology and systems ecology and subsequently translated into political strategy documents by some of the institutions serving as the armed wing of the Washington Consensus (such as the World Bank) in order to denote the capacity of individuals or of ecosystems to recover from recurring stresses or perturbances and to "bounce back" to their previous state of normalcy or possibly to "bounce forward" to a new state of normalcy that is more sustainable than the previous one (Vuori, 2021). Since resilience emphasises individual responsibility and personal adaptability in times of complex systemic crises, it has been argued in the critical literature that it constitutes a key instrument of "neoliberal governmentality" (Joseph, 2013; Mavelli, 2019). Given our analysis of the 2008 financial crisis, it can also convincingly be argued that resilience has become a defining feature of the neoliberal accumulation model itself, a model that prospers thanks to its remarkable ability to adapt to a wide array of crises in a large variety of national and regional contexts (Madariaga, 2017; Schmidt and Thatcher, 2013; Syrovatka, 2020).

The COVID-19 pandemic, however, may well have shattered the ideological supremacy long enjoyed by the neoliberal intellectual project in the Global Northwest. Yet, as a fundamentally asymmetrical system of power, neoliberalism remains very much alive, at least at the level of macroeconomic structures. Furthermore, in many parts of the Global South, state interventions were primarily to protect markets (see, e.g., India and other export-oriented countries). Let us now turn our attention to the micro-level of practices in the field of global health cooperation to see whether we can detect a sectoral weakening of the neoliberal paradigm.

Zooming in on global health governance: a sectoral weakening of neoliberalism?

The coronavirus pandemic has been a crucial test for the global health system and its governance. Following Hoffman and Cole (2018), the global health system can be defined as "the transnational actors that have a primary intent to improve health and the polylateral arrangements for governance, finance, and delivery within which these actors operate". The network of global health actors is characterised by "the overwhelming presence of global civil society organizations and non-governmental organizations" as well as a number of public–private partnerships and private industrial and pharmaceutical groups revolving around one major UN entity – the World Health Organization (WHO).

When it comes to the management of the coronavirus pandemic, two major features of the global health governance system may be highlighted that further strengthen our analysis on the decline of the neoliberal paradigm and the concomitant re-emergence of the state as a legitimate regulatory actor. First, coordination mechanisms at the UN level were primarily based on so-called Centres of Government that performed a variety of functions from policy-setting and decision-making to operational coordination and from information gathering to external communication (Kunicova, 2020; OECD, 2020). This illustrates the preeminent role of state authorities in the management of the pandemic, which is yet another example of the re-legitimation of the state we discussed above. Second, it is interesting to notice that health norms and response procedures were not forced upon passive or reluctant states as a result of some top-down, hierarchical diffusion process initiated at WHO level. Stated otherwise, national policies were not the mere translations of some international consensus, with governments acting as "norm conciliators". Rather, in the words of Biswas (2021), "The national actors have adopted, modified, and established the various lockdown measures to contain the health risk, according to their own political structures and local socioeconomic conditions".

Our sectoral analysis on the decline of neoliberalism in the wake of the COVID-19 pandemic and the emergence of more solidarity-based mechanisms for resource allocation (COVAX) and information sharing (GISAID) echoes previous analyses that call for a reframing of global health narratives away from security discourses towards issues of shared vulnerabilities that are to be addressed through the provision of global public goods (Sondermann and Ulbert, 2020).

The COVAX initiative: more than a rhetoric of global solidarity?

The use of safe and effective vaccines remains the cornerstone of any serious policy aiming to address the COVID-19 pandemic. Yet, vaccines are still scarce commodities, which begs the question of the mechanism that ought to be implemented for effective and fair resource allocation. In the neoclassical doctrine, the market allocates resources through the formation of prices, which is considered a natural outcome of supply and demand. We saw plenty of examples of this logic over the last months, as unfortunately publicised through the tweet of a Belgian minister revealing the prices of all COVID vaccines covered by confidentiality clauses in ongoing commercial negotiations between the European Union (EU) and pharmaceutical companies (Boseley, 2020). The price list evidenced differences in the purchasing costs of medicines between the EU, the UK and the US that can only partly be attributed to initial differences in public funding schemes for various medical research projects.

Though the UK and EU approaches to vaccine procurement are readily contrasted as instances of "vaccine nationalism" (UK) versus "multilateral commitment" (EU), both mechanisms of resources allocation are identical at their core. Through the use of Advance Purchase Agreements (APAs), the EU and UK strike bilateral deals with pharmaceutical companies during the development phase. The buying side commits to purchase an agreed number of doses at a fixed price, while the selling side commits to deliver the said number of doses of the unfinished product after due authorisation by the competent regulatory instance. Given the uncertainties of medical research and the authorisation process, APAs entail a significant degree of risk – yet, they are also a prime instrument of "vaccine nationalism" for governments willing and able to pay the hard price to secure a significant share of vaccines to protect their population. As argued by Phelan et al. (2020):

> Governments of countries that disagree with the ethics and effectiveness of APAs or that do not have the financial resources to purchase vaccines at comparable prices or engage in commercial negotiations are at risk of not having access to vaccines when they first become available and of having access delays while manufacturing capacity is fulfilled first by wealthy countries' orders. This was the case during the 2009 influenza A H1N1 pandemic when many APAs held by high-income countries (HICs) were used to secure their priority access to vaccine, making procurement in other countries more difficult.

It is precisely to avoid this oligopolistic allocation mechanism of vaccines to the highest bidder that COVAX was established. Under the leadership of the WHO, the Access to COVID-19 Tools Accelerator (ACT-A) was founded in April 2020 as a multilateral response to the pandemic with the aim of promoting a fair access to COVID-19 vaccines, diagnostics and treatments. As the "vaccines pillar" of the ACT-A, COVAX seeks to establish COVID-19 vaccines as global public goods that ought to be accessible and affordable for all countries. By adhering to the COVAX Facility (a sort of global procurement platform), national governments can mandate Global Alliance for Vaccines and Immunisation to sign collective agreements with pharmaceutical companies in their names, much the way the UK or EU sign their own bilateral agreements. Upon delivery of the vaccines, COVAX members receive their share as a proportion of their population. The COVAX Facility is a form of pooling of sovereignty that runs against the principle of oligopolistic market allocation by preventing mutual competition among COVAX parties, with states potentially attempting to outperform one another (e.g. by negotiating higher numbers of doses or faster deliveries in exchange for higher selling prices).

GISAID: overcoming the logic of secretive competition

Although it is not the focus of quite as much media or public attention as the vaccines, there is another important instrument to fight the pandemic – the patient gathering, sharing and processing of scientific data on the coronavirus. Decoding the genetic sequences of deadly pathogens is often the first step towards the production of effective medication. Yet, the world of medical research mirrors the neoliberal institutional framework within which it takes place: fiercely competitive and secretive, with large pharmaceutical companies using direct private funding or public–private partnerships to collect epidemiological and experimental data, assess the effectiveness of potential new medicines and carefully scrutinise viral mutations. Given the enormous economic profits at stake, the collected information remains in the duly protected property of the funding companies and may often not be freely shared among scientists, hindering scientific cooperation.

Yet, there have been attempts to break with the neoliberal logic of secretive competition. Back in 2008, GISAID was established as a global science initiative to provide open access to genomic data of influenza viruses and of the coronavirus, thus providing researchers worldwide with an alternative to the flurry of conventional but notoriously inconvenient public-domain archives. In January 2020, the SARS-CoV-2 genetic sequence was released by the Chinese Center for Disease Control and Prevention and subsequently disseminated globally through the GISAID network, prompting the development of the first vaccines as well as of the first diagnostic kits (Polack, 2020). In the words of the WHO's chief scientist, Soumya Swaminathan (2020):

> The data-science initiative GISAID has been a game changer. It was launched in 2008 to overcome access restrictions to avian-influenza data by creating a transparent sharing mechanism that permits providers to retain their rights to virus data. Since January, GISAID's data-sharing platform has been the primary source of genomic and associated data from SARS-CoV-2 cases.

Challenging neoliberalism from within: taking stock of the sectoral analysis

Despite its initial promises, the COVAX initiative is partly failing to live up to expectations, with critical voices pointing to repeated delays in vaccines' delivery for developing countries. On the one hand, and as noted above, COVAX's global approach is being undermined by the tendency of richer states to negotiate more favourable bilateral (US, UK) or multilateral (EU) agreements with pharmaceutical companies. In addition, high- and middle-income countries that are a part of the COVAX Facility are only expected to cover the costs of the vaccine doses they effectively receive. This means that vaccine doses for 92 lower-income countries are formally procured via the Facility but separately financed through the COVAX Advanced Market Commitment, which is largely funded through Official Development Assistance as well as through contributions from the private sector and philanthropy (Berkley, 2021; Bliss, 2021). As a result, higher-income countries are under no obligation to finance the participation of the lowest-income economies, whose access to the life-saving medicine is thus dependent on the goodwill, the foreign policy priorities and the domestic political situation of richer donors. In this regard, the decision of the extraordinary session of the World Health Assembly in December 2021 to launch negotiations for a global treaty on pandemic prevention, preparedness and response may initiate a welcome shift away from a "charity approach" towards a more legally binding instrument to manage global solidarity.

On the other hand, the domestic production and international supply of vaccines have become major instruments of power politics. Countries such as China, Russia and India have been shown to rely on their national COVID-19 vaccines (Sinovac, Sputnik and Covaxin, respectively) for the consolidation as their domestic power base (India) or as part of a new "vaccine diplomacy" to strengthen their position beyond their historical spheres of influence. In addition to Belarus, Russia has, for instance, actively promoted Sputnik-V in Southeast Asia through the Association of Southeast Asian Nations countries (Murphy, 2021). Similarly, only around 16% of Chinese vaccines' exports or donations did come multilaterally through COVAX. The bulk of Chinese aid did take place on a bilateral basis and was targeted towards countries or regions with which Beijing wishes to strengthen economic relationships, particularly Africa, and usually flanked by information campaigns with ostensible displays of gratitude being orchestrated for the benefit of Chinese leadership (Lin et al., 2021).

Somehow relatedly, a closer examination at the inner workings of GISAID network reveals a number of features that do not match the network's professed openness and transparency. There is indeed an important difference between GISAID and truly open-access, public-domain databases such as the GenBank or the European Molecular Biology Laboratory: GISAID users must undergo a process of registration with identity confirmation and may only access the Epi-Flu Database after agreeing to GISAID's Database Access Agreement (DAA). The DAA not only grants all authorised users "a non-exclusive, worldwide, royalty-free, and irrevocable license to collect, store, reproduce, access, modify, display, distribute, coordinate, arrange, and otherwise use the Data" but also forbids authorised users to distribute data "to any third party other than Authorized Users as contemplated by this Agreement". In addition, the DAA also institutes an interesting cooperative mechanism whereby database users (1) are required to acknowledge the original source of the data ("originating laboratory") and (2) agree to "make best efforts to collaborate with representatives of the Originating Laboratory" and involve them in analyses and further research.[4]

A number of scientists have complained about the possibly unintended and yet perverse effects of GISAID's constraints on access and especially of its prohibition on the resharing of data. For instance, the DAA requires all users to use exclusively GISAID data for their websites and tools and to comply with GISAID-approved strain names. This makes external communication with non-GISAID users and with the interested public more difficult, causing some scientists to voluntarily abandon GISAID so as to be able to communicate more freely through their personal or institutional websites. The failure of GISAID to follow the basic principles of open access was directly addressed in an open letter[5] signed by over 800 epidemiologists urging their fellow scientists to deposit sequences in GenBank, the European Nucleotide Archive (ENA), and Japan's DNA Data Bank of Japan (DDBJ), on the grounds that open-access databases allow users to both access sequences anonymously and share data freely and without restrictions. As expressed by Guy Cochrane, head of the ENA: "The ideal setup is completely open access … Having a limited group controlling [access] would never be a good thing" (Wadman, 2021).

Conclusion

The COVID-19 pandemic poses a challenge to the neoliberal competitive state in several respects. It can no longer deliver on the promise of continued economic growth, the burden of the pandemic is unevenly distributed and significant government intervention is needed to contain the pandemic and its consequences. The pandemic could therefore have a collateral benefit: the end of the hegemony of the neoliberal paradigm, which has either instrumentalised or marginalised the state and public institutions since the 1980s. Neoliberalism was already on the defensive after the 2008 global financial crisis, but it managed to outlast the oath of revelation at that time. The chapter has argued that responses to the pandemic have fundamentally shattered the ideological supremacy enjoyed by neoliberalism as an intellectual doctrine that can no longer present itself as the latest expression of modernity.

Against this background, the COVID-19 crisis offers an opportunity to formulate more solidarity-based counter-models for "The World after Coronavirus" that are characterised by civic trust in scientific expertise, by a re-legitimisation of state control and by combating international injustices thanks to global cooperation or at least by pooling national resources (Harari, 2020) – developments for which COVAX and GISAID are, despite of their shortcomings, prime and promising examples. In this regard, the COVID-19 pandemic has shown that neoliberal norms can be overcome and institutional rules renegotiated that ascribe a proactive role to the state while engaging civil society. However, there is little evidence so far that such a counter-model also takes the social question and class relations into account. Rather, the costs of the crises threaten to be distributed very unequally with the effect of boosting right-wing populist movements. The transformation into a post-neoliberal model will thus only be possible if it is also about a social transformation.

The focus of this chapter was mainly on the Western industrialised countries. Its scope, insofar, is limited – as the dominance of the West is increasingly being challenged by the authoritarian model of China with its authoritarian-communist state capitalism. It is also obvious that the hegemony of neoliberalism is not likely to be broken by developments in the centre alone, insofar as the semi-periphery of rising countries such as Brazil, Turkey or India has been able to partially emancipate themselves from political, economic and ideological developments in the Global Northwest. They have also sometimes reacted differently to the pandemic, e.g., India with a supply-oriented policy in which exporting factories were allowed to resume production very quickly while at the same time severely restricting fundamental labour rights, i.e. with an authoritarian-neoliberal justification narrative.

At the same time, it is clear that due to the dominance of the Global North-west in the global financial institutions, such as World Bank and International Monetary Fund, a break with the neoliberal paradigm would also be reflected in the periphery and semi-periphery. The programmes to strengthen the public good of health in the shadow of the COVID-19 pandemic could already be a foretaste of this. Central to their success is the quality of state institutions in terms of information gathering, service delivery and the design and implementation of assistance programmes. Furthermore, COVAX and GISAID have established models that provide alternatives to neoliberal logics regarding the allocation of vaccinations and scientific cooperation in sharing virus data. Though particularly COVAX's success so far was limited, it shows that post-neoliberal models are on the horizon. And it provides an important insight: in a system of polycentric governance (Abbott, 2017), challenges to neoliberal hegemony will not only be relevant on the macroeconomic level but also come from sectoral fields of overarching importance, such as global health governance.

It is probably too early to tell whether these cooperative developments at the sectoral level constitute a genuine and irreversible departure from the neoliberal model. On the one hand, there are still powerful interest groups in each policy area that keep advocating for neoliberal solutions and continue the ideological struggle. In consequence, the answer to the question "is neoliberalism still alive and kicking?" may depend on the policy sector considered, reflecting power dynamics and *rapports de force* at the sectoral level. On the other hand, it is not yet possible to speak of a paradigm shift at the system level, because the counter-models still aren't fully fleshed out. Yet, what matters is that the neoliberal system of production is changing from within and losing some of its most essential constitutive features, as evidenced by our analysis of global health policy. Eventually, neoliberalism may quietly cease to be, without noise or revolution, simply overcome by a more effective system based on solidarity and joint ownership that is better able to cope with the most pressing crises of our times.

Notes

1 In this paragraph, we follow Prügl (2015) who differentiates between neoliberalism as "a political project" most prominently carried out by Thatcher, Reagan and the Bretton Woods institutions; neoliberalism as "an economic doctrine or ideology" as expressed by Hayek, Friedman and the Chicago School; and neoliberalism as "a cultural formation, a 'rationality' in the Foucauldian sense" characterised by specific mechanisms of government such as the reliance on private market forces for the organisation of public governance. See also Larner (2000) and Ferguson (2009) on which Prügl's categories rely.

2 It is estimated that OECD governments had issued a combined $11 trillion in new debt by the end of 2020 (Levitz, 2021). Large-scale deficit spending was facilitated by most central banks, which started buying up their own governments' bonds, a decision that long constituted a neoliberal heresy due to the risk of fuelling inflation.

3 According to a poll of the Eurobarometer (2020), 68% of EU citizens considered that "the fight against the corona virus pandemic fully justifies recent limitations to my individual freedoms" (28% opposed), with an absolute majority of respondents (56%) being satisfied with the measures their national government had taken so far against the coronavirus pandemic.
4 GISAID's Terms of Use: https://www.gisaid.org/registration/terms-of-use/.
5 Text of the Open Letter: https://www.covid19dataportal.org/support-data-sharing-covid19.

References

Aalbers, Manuel B. (2013). Neoliberalism is Dead… Long Live Neoliberalism! *International Journal of Urban and Regional Research, 37(3),* 1083–1090.

Abbott, Kenneth Wayne. (2017, June 8). Orchestration: Strategic Ordering in Polycentric Climate Governance (June 8, 2017). https://papers.ssrn.com/sol3/papers.cfm?abstract_id=2983512

Beckert, Jens. (2020). The Exhausted Futures of Neoliberalism: Form Promissory Legitimacy to Social Anomy. *Journal of Cultural 'Economy, 13(3),* 318–330.

Bello, Walden. (2021, April 15). After Neoliberalism... What? *Transform Network.* https://www.transform-network.net/blog/article/after-neoliberalism-what/

Berkley, Seth. (2021). The Gavi COVAX AMC Explained. *Gavi.* https://www.gavi.org/vaccineswork/gavi-covax-amc-explained

Biswas, Shreejita. (2021). The Coronavirus Pandemic and Global Governance: The Domestic Diffusion of Health Norms in Global Health Security Crises. *Jadavpur Journal of International Relations, 25(2),* 208–234

Bliss, Katherine. (2021, April 27). The COVAX Advance Market Commitment 'One World Protected' Investment Opportunity Launch. *Center for Strategic and International Studies.* https://www.csis.org/analysis/covax-advance-market-commitment-one-world-protected-investment-opportunity-launch

Bonanno, Alessandro. (2017). *The Legitimation Crisis of Neoliberalism. The State, Will-Formation, and Resistance.* Palgrave Macmillan.

Boseley, Sarah. (2020). Belgian minister tweets EU's Covid vaccine price list to anger of manufacturers. *The Guardian,* Sat 19 Dec 2020 04.53. https://www.theguardian.com/world/2020/dec/18/belgian-minister-accidentally-tweets-eus-covid-vaccine-price-list?fbclid=IwAR1694Yhd5eZALbwMLh5QUO4JtMqUssoElIA3oMd9mhyQCSOO3om3vnribo

Brandt, Arno and Windels, Torsten. (2020). Zur politischen Ökonomie der Corona-Krise. *SPW, 4,* 22–28 (*On the Political Economy of the Corona Crisis*).

Brown, Wendy. (2019). *In the Ruins of Neoliberalism: The Rise of Antidemocratic Politics in the West.* Columbia University Press.

Bruff, Ian and Cemal Burak Transel. (2021). Authoritarian Neoliberalism: Trajectories of Knowledge Production and Praxis. In: Ian Bruff and Cemal Burak Tansel (Eds.), *Authoritarian Neoliberalism: Philosophies, Practices, Contestations.* Abingdon-on-Thames Routledge.

Cahill, Damien. (2011). Beyond Neoliberalism? Crisis and the Prospects for Progressive Alternatives. *New Political Science, 33(4),* 479–492.

Charrel, Marie. (2013, December 17). Les Produits D*érivés* D*épassent leur* Niveau d'avant-Crise. *Le Monde.* https://www.lemonde.fr/economie/article/2013/12/17/les-produits-derives-depassent-leur-niveau-d-avant-crise_4335868_3234.html

Condon, Roderick. (2021). The Coronavirus Crisis and the Legitimation Crisis of Neoliberalism. *European Societies, 23(Supppl. 1),* S805–S816.

Davies, William and McGoey, Linsey. (2012). Rationalities of Ignorance: On Financial Crisis and the Ambivalence of Neo-Liberal Epistemology. *Economy and Society, 41(1)*, 64–83.

de la Torre, Carlos. (2019). Is Left Populism the Radical Answer? *Irish Journal of Sociology, 27(1)*, 64–71.

Dean, Mitchell. (2014). Rethinking Neoliberalism. *Journal of Sociology, 50(2)*, 150–163.

Eurobarometer. (2020, October 7). *Uncertainty/EU/Hope. Public Opinion in Times of COVID-19.* Public opinion survey commissioned by the European Parliament. A Public Opinion Monitoring Study. Brussels: European Union. https://op.europa.eu/de/publication-detail/-/publication/d98bae75-0c32-11eb-bc07-01aa75ed71a1

Ferguson, James. (2009). The Uses of Neoliberalism. *Antipode, 41(S1)*, 166–184.

Fischer, Andrew M. (2020). The Dark Sides of Social Policy: From Neoliberalism to Resurgent Right-wing Populism. *Development and Change, 51(2)*, 371–397.

Friedman, Milton (1962). *Capitalism and Freedom.* The University of Chicago Press.

Halimi, Serge. (2006). *Le Grand Bond en Arrière.* Éd. Fayard.

Harari, Yuval Noah. (2020, March 30). The World After Coronavirus. *Financial Times.* https://www.ft.com/content/19d90308-6858-11ea-a3c9-1fe6fedcca75

Hayek, Friedrich. (2006). *The Constitution of Liberty.* Oxford: Routledge (Original published 1960).

Hoffman, Steven and Cole, Clarke. (2018). Defining the Global Health System and Systematically Mapping Its Network of Actors. *Global Health, 14*, 38. https://globalizationandhealth.biomedcentral.com/articles/10.1186/s12992-018-0340-2#citeas

Joseph, Jonathan (2013). Resilience as Embedded Neoliberalism: A Governmentality Approach. *Resilience: International Policies, Practices and Discourses, 1(1)*, 38–52.

Kelleher, Dennis. (2019, June 12). Trump's Assault on Financial Reform. *The American Prospect.* https://prospect.org/economy/trump-s-assault-financial-reform/

Kiely, Ray. (2020). Assessing Conservative Populism: A New Double Movement or Neoliberal Populism? *Development and Change, 51(2)*, 398–417.

Kilic, Sadik. (2021). Does COVID-19 as a Long Wave Turning Point mean the End of Neoliberalism? *Critical Sociology, 47(4–5)*, 609–623.

Klein, Naomi. (2014). *This Changes Everything: Capitalism vs the Climate.* New York: Simon and Schuster.

Konings, Martijn. (2016). Governing the System: Risk, Finance, and Neoliberal Reason. *European Journal of International Relations, 22(2)*, 268–288.

Kuhn, Thomas M. (1962). *The Structure of Scientific Revolutions.* Chicago, IL: University of Chicago Press.

Kunicova, Jana. (2020). Driving the COVID-19 Response from the Center: Institutional Mechanisms to Ensure Whole-of-Government Coordination. *World Bank.* Working Paper 154217. November. https://documents.worldbank.org/en/publication/documents-reports/documentdetail/944721604613856580/driving-the-COVID-19-response-from-the-center-institutional-mechanisms-to-ensure-whole-of-government-coordination

Larner, Wendy. (2000). Neo-liberalism: Policy, Ideology, Governmentality. *Studies in Political Economy, 63 (Autumn)*, 5–25.

Leisering, Lutz. (2021). Social Protection Responses by States and International Organisations to the COVID-19 Crisis in the Global South: Stopgap or new Departure? *Global Social Policy, 2(3)*, 396–420.

Levitz, Eric. (2021, October 14). Neoliberalism Died of COVID. Long Live Neoliberalism! How the Predominant Ideology of Our Time Survived the Pandemic. *Intelligencer.*

Nymag. https://nymag.com/intelligencer/2021/10/neoliberalism-died-of-covid-long-live-neoliberalism.html

Lin, Bonny, Matthew Funaiole, Brian hart and Hannah Price. (2021, September 30). China Is Exploiting the Pandemic to Advance Its Interests, with Mixed Results. *Center for Strategic and International Studies.* https://www.csis.org/analysis/china-exploiting-pandemic-advance-its-interests-mixed-results

Madariaga, Aldo. (2017). The Astonishing Resilience of Neoliberalism: Capitalism, Democracy and Development in Latin America and Eastern Europe. MPIfG Yearbook 2017–2018, *Max Planck Institute for the Study of Societies*, 75–80.

Mamonova, Natalia and Jaume Franquesa. (2020). Populism, Neoliberalism and Agrarian Movements in Europe. Understanding Rural Support for Right-Wing Politics and Looking for Progressive Solutions. *Sociologia Ruralis, 60(4)*, 710–731.

Mavelli, Luca. (2019). Resilience Beyond Neoliberalism? Mystique of Complexity, Financial Crises, and the Reproduction of Neoliberal Life. *Resilience: International Policies, Practices and Discourses, 7(3)*, 224–239.

Mirowski, Philip. (2018). Neoliberalism: The Movement That Dare Not Speak Its Name. *American Affairs, 2(1)*, 118–141. https://americanaffairsjournal.org/2018/02/neoliberalism-movement-dare-not-speak-name/

Murphy, Meghan. (2021, September 21). Russia's New Frontier in Southeast Asia: Vaccine Diplomacy. *Center for Strategic and International Studies.* https://www.csis.org/blogs/new-perspectives-asia/russias-new-frontier-southeast-asia-vaccine-diplomacy

OECD. (2020). Building Resilience to the COVID-19 Pandemic: The Role of Centres of Government. 2 September. https://www.oecd.org/coronavirus/policy-responses/building-resilience-to-the-COVID-19-pandemic-the-role-of-centres-of-government-883d2961/

Phelan, Alexandra, Mark Eccleston-Turner, Michelle Rourke, Allan Maleche and Chenguang Wang. (2020, September 19). Legal Agreements: Barriers and Enablers to Global Equitable COVID-19 Vaccine Access. *The Lancet, 396.* https://www.thelancet.com/article/S0140-6736(20)31873-0/fulltext

Polack, Fernando. (2020). Safety and Efficacy of the mRNA COVID-19 Vaccine. New England *Journal of Medicine, 383(27)*, 2603–2615.

Prügl, Elisabeth. (2015). Neoliberalising Feminism. *New Political Economy, 20(4)*, 614–631.

Rodriguez Valladares, Mayra. (2019, May 22). The Weakening of Big Bank Regulations Under Trump Is the Seed for the Next Financial Crisis. *Forbes.* https://www.forbes.com/sites/mayrarodriguezvalladares/2019/05/22/the-weakening-of-big-bank-regulations-under-trump-is-the-seed-for-the-next-financial-crisis/?sh=228e28f54f4c

Rodrik, Dani. (2006). Goodbye Washington Consensus, Hello Washington Confusion? A Review of the World Bank's Economic Growth in the 1990s: Learning from a Decade of Reform. *Journal of Economic Literature, 44(4)*, 973–987.

Rousselin, Mathieu. (2016). In the Name of Allah and of the Market: The Capitalist Leanings of Tunisian Islamists. *Science and Society, 80(2)*, 196–220.

Rürup, Bert. (2020, April 16). Corona und das Ende der neoliberalen Weltordnung. *Handelsblatt* (*Corona and the End of the Neoliberal World Order*). https://www.handelsblatt.com/politik/international/analyse-serie-global-challenges-corona-und-das-ende-der-neoliberalen-weltordnung/25742458.html

Saad-Filho, Alfredo. (2020). From COVID-19 to the End of Neoliberalism. *Critical Sociology, 46(4–5)*, 477–485.

Saxer, Marc. (2020, March 18). Epochenbruch: Die Corona-Krise sendet Schockwellen durch alle Systeme. Das eröffnet aber auch Chancen. *IPG Journal* (International

Politics and Society) (*Epochal Rupture: The Corona Crisis Sends Shockwaves Through all Systems. But it also opens up opportunities*). https://wwww.ipg-journal.de/regionen/global/artikel/epochenbruch-4170/

Scharpf, Fritz W. (1997). Economic Integration, Democracy and the Welfare State. *Journal of European Public Policy, 4*, 18–36.

Scharpf, Fritz W. (2004). Legitimationskonzepte jenseits des Nationalstaats. MPlfG [Working Paper] 05/06. Max Planck Institute for the Study of Societies (*Legitimation Concepts beyond the Nation State*).

Schmidt, Vivien and Mark Thatcher. (2013). *Resilient Liberalism in Europe's Political Economy*. Cambridge University Press.

Shalal, Andrea, Jeff Mason and David Lawder. (2021, May 5).U.S. Reverses Stance, Backs Giving Poorer Countries Access to COVID Vaccine Patents. *Reuters*. https://www.reuters.com/business/healthcare-pharmaceuticals/biden-says-plans-back-wto-waiver-vaccines-2021-05-05/

Sondermann, Elena and Cornelia Ulbert. (2020). The Threat of Thinking in Threats: Reframing Global Health during and after COVID-19. *Zeitschrift für Friedens- und Konfliktforschung, 9*, 309–320 (ZeFKo Studies in Peace and Conflict).

Stiglitz, Joseph. (2019, May 30). Neoliberalism Must Be Pronounced dead and Buried. Where Next? *The Guardian*. https://www.theguardian.com/business/2019/may/30/neoliberalism-must-be-pronouced-dead-and-buried-where-next)

Sumonja, Milos. (2020). Neoliberalism is not Dead – On Political Implications of COVID-19. *Capital and Class, 00(0)*, 1–13.

Swaminathan, Soumya. (2020, December 17). The WHO's Chief Scientist on a Year of Loss and Learning. *Nature*. https://www.nature.com/articles/d41586-020-03556-y

Syrovatka, Felix. (2020, June 25). Resilience: Europe's latest Neoliberal Fashionable Term. *Jacobin*. https://jacobin.de/artikel/resilienz-neoliberalismus-eu-hoekstra-wettbewerbsfaehigkeit/

Tooze, Adam. (2021, September 2). Has Covid Ended the Neoliberal Era? *The Guardian*.. https://www.theguardian.com/news/2021/sep/02/covid-and-the-crisis-of-neoliberalism

Vuori, Juha (2021). Politics of Resilience. *Oxford Bibliographies*. https://www.oxfordbibliographies.com/view/document/obo-9780199743292/obo-9780199743292-0297.xml (30.11.2021)

Wadman, Meredith. (2021, March 10). Critics Decry Access, Transparency Issues with Key Trove of Coronavirus Sequences. *Science*. https://www.science.org/content/article/critics-decry-access-transparency-issues-key-trove-coronavirus-sequences

Weber, Max. (1978). *Economy and Society: An Outline of Interpretive Sociology*. Oakland: University of California Press.

Williamson, John. (1990). What Washington Means by Policy Reform. Chapter 2 from *Latin American Adjustment: How Much Has Happened?* Edited by John Williamson. Published. https://www.piie.com/commentary/speeches-papers/what-washington-means-policy-reform

4

THE GLOBAL DIALECTICS OF A PANDEMIC

Between necropolitics and utopian imagination

Nadja Meisterhans

Introduction

The world is infected. Not only by COVID-19 but also by an authoritarian turn that could have a dramatic impact on global commitment to human rights and global governance. The COVID-19 outbreak is not an isolated example that diseases do not stop at national borders. Health crises with a global format have a long history, for example, the bubonic plague, Spanish flu, HIV, or Ebola. And yet the current pandemic has revealed that little has been learned from past health crises (Holst, 2019, 2020, 2021; Holst and Razum, 2018; Meier and Gostin, 2018; Meisterhans, 2016a, 2016b, 2020; Pas and Belle, 2015; Razum *et al.*, 2014). In the first part of this chapter, it will be argued that the pandemic is not a natural but rather a politically made disaster. The starting point is thus to elaborate in what sense the spread of COVID-19 demonstrates that states have been neglecting global responsibilities that stem from human rights in a context of multiple crises (Brand, 2012, 2016; Demirović, 2013; Volkmer and Werner, 2020).

Considering that health narratives in the context of disease control always entail a risk of authoritarian abuse, this chapter problematizes, with reference to the postcolonial concept of necropolitics and through the perspective of the psychoanalytically informed ideology critique of the early Frankfurt School (Adorno and Horkheimer, 2008), in what sense the global health crisis has become instrumentalized by authoritarian populists. From a dialectical perspective, the global health crisis could nevertheless provide an opportunity for political and societal learning processes in a global context. Therefore, in a final step, it will be outlined theoretically under what conditions the pandemic could reopen spheres of utopian imagination, based on societal critiques that could serve to critically rethink global transformation in a post-pandemic world order. The basic idea

DOI: 10.4324/9781003273844-4

to be unfolded is that civil societies and social movements form a fundament for political progress.

Worldwide, feminist as well as anti-racist, ecological, indigenous, or workers' movements have had great impact improving the political, social, and also legal situation of the structurally marginalized, by not only creatively resisting but also envisioning another better world. Against this background, this chapter relates to contemporary utopian-theoretical debates in the (queer)feminist context (Chrostowska and Ingram, 2016; Daniels and Klapeer, 2019; Jones, 2013; Meisterhans, 2019) and argues that under certain conditions, ideological interpellations can be subverted by dystopian storytelling and performances. The latter is to explicate under what conditions art-based narratives and protest actions can challenge hegemonical constellations. Therefore, it is argued that reworking the trauma of political dis-recognition depends on specific solidarity-based practices that allow to mourn the suffering and dying of those societal groups who are made invisible in necropolitical contexts.

Structural origins of the contemporary health crisis

Since the founding of the World Health Organization (WHO) in 1948, equal access to health has been a normative goal based on human rights. Human right to health is a fundamental right, enshrined in the Universal Declaration of Human Rights (1948) and later sealed in the International Covenant on Economic, Social and Cultural Rights (1966). Globally, governments, not just since the onset of the pandemic, failed to fulfil their obligations under international law (Meier and Gostin, 2018; Meisterhans, 2020). Despite an impressive rate of scientific progress and massive economic growth since the ending of two horrific world wars and the establishment of the UN system, global inequalities have remained, and in some regions even amplified. This leads, within a context of the pandemic, to the erosion of public health services and lack of medicines. Half of the world's population is excluded from all healthcare due to poverty, political and social discrimination, migration, war, unfair economic and trade structures, and precarious statehood (WHO, 2017). Under current political and economic patterns worldwide, an extremely unequal distribution of resources and global burdens, such as poverty, climate change, and war, is one of the biggest obstacles for realizing health as a human right. Many states lack adequate resources to establish a welfare system capable of providing effective social protection (Global Health Watch 4, 2014, p. 5, 2017; Transform, 2017).

In the past few decades, in particular, neoliberal globalization processes[1] have been generating and deepening multiple crises involving finance, food security, and global environmental change, constantly producing social inequalities and structural and intersectional discriminations (Brand, 2012, 2016; Demirović, 2013), consequently weakening already precarious health systems, not only in the Global South (Holst and Razum, 2018; Razum *et al.*, 2014). From this perspective, capitalism and neoliberalism are major causes of the lack of resources to fund the public sector in the Global South and, also, in the Global North (Holst and Razum, 2018; McCoy, 2017; Razum *et al.*, 2014). Against this backdrop, it is not surprising that, as the current Oxfam report (Berkhout *et al.*, 2021) and, also the UN report on Sustainable Development Goals reveals (United Nations, 2020, pp. 28–31), the ongoing COVID-19 crisis is massively exacerbating these existing social and economic inequalities and does not affect everyone equally (Wachtler *et al.*, 2020; Žižek, 2020).

In the first phase of the pandemic, even in high-income countries, health systems were close to collapse. The recent pandemic also shows that the existing structures for combating global and national health crises have major deficits and inadequacies (Meisterhans, 2016b; Pas and Belle, 2015; Sanders *et al.*, 2015).

In other words, in recent decades, a debate emerged that was pushed by a variety of transnational civil society and critical scientific networks, dealing with human rights-based perspectives of global governance for health. Four main actions were identified: (1) strengthen national health systems on the basis of human rights and equity (Global Health Watch 4, 2014, p. 5, 2017; Meier and Gostin, 2018); (2) recognize the political as well as social determinants of health (McCoy, 2014); (3) focus on the power-structural origins and intersectional interdependencies of global crises; and (4) acknowledge local, national, and transnational non-profit civil society-based activities and their counter-hegemonic expertise in knowledge production and problem solving in the horizon of multi-level governance (Global Health Watch 4, 2014, p. 5, 2017).[2] It follows that the global health crisis is both a 'social disaster' (Connell, 2020, p. 747) and a political disaster, as outlined above.

Addressing the structural causes of the global health crisis would mean that government leaders worldwide take a holistic, human rights-based view. This would imply the linking of the ongoing health crisis to other crises in the areas of war, environment, economy, trade, migration, food, and developing policies to overcome them in the spirit of sustainable global governance (Brand, 2012, 2016; Demirović, 2013; Volkmer and Werner, 2020).

There is another crucial insight we can take from these developments, namely that, 'global health inequality is driven … by a state of chronic acceptance that some have poorer health than others' (Sandset, 2021, p. 1411). This brings us to the question of whether the ongoing global health crisis can be interpreted in logics of necropolitics, as outlined by Achille Mbembe (2003, 2019). In doing so, there is also another aspect that must be considered; in recent decades, various democracies have been confronted by a growing authoritarian backlash and reactionary populism in both national and global contexts (Katsambekis and Stavrakakis, 2020; Moffitt, 2016; Sauer, 2017, 2019), and this rollback has obviously solidified in the current conditions of contemporary biopolitical crisis management of the COVID-19 pandemic.

Numerous democratic governments are currently inclined to demonstrate their capacity to act, falling into a pattern of populist hyperactivity, as, for example, in the context of vaccination-nationalism, which deals with the symptoms of the current health crisis, but not with their own failures to prevent the wider global health crisis (Gostin *et al.*, 2020; Katsambekis and Stavrakakis, 2020). From this perspective, it is no coincidence that the WHO was made a scapegoat, not only by neo-fascist populists such as former US President Donald Trump[3] (Gostin *et al.*, 2020; Meisterhans, 2020) but also by governmental leaders in Australia, Denmark, Canada, and Japan (doubting scientific studies analysing the origins of the coronavirus in China).[4]

Before delving into the concept of necropolitics, it seems relevant to assess if and in what sense current crisis management has contributed to an intensification of authoritarian populism. In answering this question, one may relate to contemporary debates that address the global rise of authoritarian populism. While doing so, reference may be made to some ideas of psychoanalysis, which have also inspired the critical theory of the Frankfurt School's first generation (Adorno and Horkheimer, 2008). This is done in order to shed light on the affectual dimension not only of authoritarian populism but also of necropower, especially by focusing on the relationship between ideological interpellation and subjectification. This line in argumentation is motivated by the attempt to close a research gap in the current debate not only on authoritarian populism but also on necropolitics in the context of the pandemic (Sandset, 2021).

Why do people identify with authoritarian populism in the context of crises?

What is still missing in the context of research not only on authoritarian populism but also on necropolitics is a systematic psychoanalytic analysis of the affectual dimension. In order to get a more complete picture, one may like to concentrate on the structural relationship between ideological interpellations and the formation of partly *unconscious structures of desire* in the context of crises.

The aim of this section is to exert some crucial insights from not only Freudian and Lacanian psychoanalysis (Freud, 2000a–c; Lacan, 2005) but also critical theory of the Frankfurt School (Adorno, 1966, 1970, 1974, 1995; Adorno and Horkheimer, 2008) as an ideology critique. What is addressed here is a critique of ideology that can explain the emergence of authoritarian desires but can also be made, as shown in the last section of this chapter, fruitful for utopian-theoretical considerations in the context of the pandemic. The expectation that is central at this point is that a psychoanalytically informed critical theory can, like no other social theory, inform us about affectual and partly unconscious societal dynamics triggered by COVID-19.

Therefore, in the following, processes of political subjectification will be addressed, theorizing the partly unconscious effects of ideological interpellations (this idea is inspired by Althusser [1977] and Lacan [2005]) on the formation of desires for recognition and its inherent fantasies and affects [this idea is inspired by Hegel {1986, p. 149} and Lacan {2005, pp. 35, 50}]). What is special about this perspective is that it looks for our understanding of the relationship between governmentality and ideology deeply inscribed in the psyche. In this sense, a psychoanalytic-inspired critique of ideology can serve to comprehend not only the underlying affectual dynamics that explain the growing societal support for authoritarian governmental populism but also the emergence of social movements and forms of civic resistance that can be both emancipatory and in line with authoritarian populism and therefore regressive.

Thus, the task is to understand 'the ways in which the populists construct and propagate their narratives' (Yilmaz and Erturk, 2021, p. 1524) and to take up an important insight of research on populism and how populists have mediated the pandemic through spectacularization (Moffitt, 2014).

> One of the most obvious ways that populist actors promote and perform a sense of crisis is through media events, designed as spectacles to attract wide attention, garner salience for the particular threat, and identify the enemies of the people.
>
> *(Moffitt, 2014, p. 203)*

This not only includes clarification of how they manage to tie in with latent ressentiment and aggression in society but also manifests anxieties of people in the context of the pandemic.

In doing so, a first step should be to recognize that authoritarian desires have deep roots in society (Adorno and Horkheimer, 2008), insofar as they are the consequence of an ideologically conditioned concealment, i.e., a power-technological mythologization of the structural causes of crises and of societal discomfort (Adorno and Horkheimer, 2008; Freud, 2000a). In other words, why do people in various societies identify with authoritarian politics, authoritarian leaders, and authoritarian ideas about law and order?

As noted above, this means reflecting partly unconscious structures of political desires for recognition and their inherent affects (Lacan, 2005). My central claim is that there is general but *diffuse* (Bieber, 2012) and *partly unconscious* societal discomfort with neoliberal ideologies, which had been instrumentalized already *before* the pandemic by right-wing movements and parties. And now during the pandemic, this diffuse and societal discomfort increases due to specific anxieties that are caused by growing unemployment, a general fear of death, and also political, economic, and social transformations inherent in the global health crisis, such as a global pandemic, and has traumatic effects. Hence, it seems plausible that this experience can cause destructive societal and psychoanalytical reactions.

The reference to a psychoanalytically informed critique of ideology is thus of interest insofar as asymmetrical power constellations are often based on discourses (Althusser, 1977) that render profound social and ideological conflicts of recognition invisible and thus unconscious (Erdheim, 1984; Meisterhans, 2019). This also includes the problematization that the neoliberal appeal is based on *ideological illusions*, suggesting manifold chances for self-realization, which, at the same time, are regularly and necessarily disappointed – for example, with regard to phenomena of precarization in the world of work (Bröckling, 2016; Ehrenberg, 2008).

Up to this point, it seems plausible that those deep structural changes in democratic societies, caused by processes of neoliberal globalization, give grounds for collective regressions (Geiselberger, 2017; Heitmeyer, 2018). Thus, a psychoanalytically informed ideology's critical perspective can help to understand why people identify with conspiracy theories and authoritarian leadership. With this in mind, it also has to be considered that neoliberal ideologies, and neoliberal culture techniques in particular, negate the social as a sphere of political action, and, by declaring themselves as post-ideological, they put counter-hegemonic interventions from civil society, which aim to scandalize the impact of neoliberalism in a solidarity-oriented way, potentially into a subaltern position (Žižek, 2009, 2010).

However, if we take a lesson from Freud's (2000a) psychoanalysis, then it could be argued that as long as these ideological conflicts for social, cultural, and political recognition are suppressed, it is likely that these effects will turn back in a destructive manner. Furthermore, as delineated in the context of the early Frankfurt School (Adorno, 1966, 1970; Adorno and Horkheimer, 2008), this fortifies political feelings of failure, powerlessness, guilt, and shame at the centre of societies and builds the fundament of what Theodor W. Adorno once described as pitiless anger towards structurally marginalized groups (Adorno, 1970, p. 94). In other words, this anger, caused by real *and* conceited precarization, through a potential loss of economic and social status, and by the effects of repressive subjectification, is directed towards the most vulnerable populations, such as deprived persons, refugees, and migrants (Haubl, 2008; Hövermann *et al.*, 2015; Krause *et al.*, 2016).

One could even argue that neoliberal thought is already grounded in a *latent* necropolitical rationality in which certain groups, as outlined in the next section, are condemned to live a shadow life and are therefore forced to exist as the walking dead or as living zombies (Dima, 2014; Goldberg, 2011). We will return to this point in the "An Obscene Enjoyment of Death?" section of this chapter.

Seen in this light, it is likely that collective desires for rigid leadership, and punishment towards the subalternized, find fertile soil in the impact of socio-economic and political transformations inherent in the neoliberal project, which have caused a variety of experiences of collective deprivation and anxieties (Brähler and Decker, 2016; Heitmeyer, 2018; Manow, 2018). It also causes collective forms of alienation due to the loss of cultural orientation (Inglehart and Norris, 2019) and a general crisis of political representation (Mouffe, 2018). Consequently, the question of why necropolitics in the pandemic work on a global scale could find an answer in debates that point to an internal connection between neoliberalism and authoritarian populism (Demirović, 2018; Heitmeyer, 2018; Jessop, 2019) and stress that authoritarian populism is also part of neoliberal crisis management (Demirović, 2018; Hall, 2014).

Furthermore, the dramatic socio-economic outcomes of the present health crisis management reinforce existing social inequalities and asymmetrical power constellations, causing new societal frustration (Schels, 2020). Hence, it is hardly surprising that these frustrations have been instrumentalized, not only by populist parties but also by reactionary social and political movements (Müller, 2020). It is noteworthy that right-wing movements and parties often arbitrarily relate to a set of contradictory normative positions, such as ideas on democracy and on constitutional rights, in order to empty or reverse their original meaning and to find acceptance with the democratic public (Sauer, 2017). Right-wingers in the US, and other countries, have scandalized the lockdown measures by relating them in a conspiratorial and strategic manner to (the loss of) constitutional freedoms rights (Jakob and Wahmkow, 2020; Kreil, 2020; Stöber, 2020; Wilson, 2020).[5]

Observing these developments, the question is if this ideological flexibility expresses a mode of arbitrariness that is already inherent in neoliberal ideologies and that is now pushed by right-wingers to establish a new cultural hegemony (Gramsci, 1971), legitimizing a non-democratic social order. This assumption seems at least plausible if one follows debates that point to an internal connection between neoliberalism and authoritarian populism (Demirović, 2018; Heitmeyer, 2018; Jessop, 2019).

Considering an important insight from contemporary populism research, the pandemic has also been (mis)used by right-wing populists to stage health crises in the mode of 'spectacularization' (Moffitt, 2014, p. 190) while conspiratorially mythologizing the complex origins and effects of the current global health crisis. This brings us to the interesting twist of how the structural failure of the international community of states to establish robust global governance arrangements has been exploited by populists, not only in the context of governmental action but also on the basis of right-wing-oriented social and political movements. Interpellations in the pandemic have often been based on the conspiratorial mythologization of death and dying.

The populist mythologizing of death and dying

When observing how governmental leaders, for example, in some Central European countries, have framed the public health discourse, one may argue that a disciplinary rhetoric has been established, in order to ensure societal compliance. Although the authoritarian abuse of health crises is historically not a new phenomenon (Aït-Touati, 2020; Gehrlach, 2020; Lucci, 2020), it seems alarming that legal measures by governments, for example, France, have been accompanied by warlike rhetoric (Mudde, 2020; Wiegel, 2020) or, as in Austria, have been linked to the rhetoric of terror prevention. Those who do not comply with their obligations are branded as a mortal danger to society (Gigler, 2020; Tóth, 2020).

These mythological 'politization of death' (Yilmaz and Erturk, 2021, p. 1526) and the populist attempt to associate the pandemic with war and terror have been used *to create a historical momentum* (Connell, 2020). An essential feature of this narrative was that the pandemic revealed a 'moment of truth' (Moffitt, 2014,

p. 196). In typical populist agitation, this moment of truth served to establish various apocalyptic scenarios, including, for example, presenting 'the foreign virus as a great threat' or migrants and refugees as virus-spreaders (Agamben, 1998), as zombies (Crofts and Vogl, 2019) who endanger one's own population. Simultaneously, the supposed national (white) superiority was used to demonstrate one's own defensibility as historical momentum (Wondreys and Mudde, 2020).

Thus, as before, the pandemic combined 'anti-elitism' with 'anti-globalism' (Löfflmann, 2019, p. 119) and pointed to corrupt political and economic elites who were allegedly abusing the health crisis to increase their own privileges. Concurrently, populists have been quite flexible in what has been played up by right-wing parties and movements have been scandalizing the lockdown measures as unwarranted interference with personal liberty and vaccination programmes as unnecessary interventions that are harmful to health and perhaps even lethal (Brunner *et al.*, 2021; Katsambekis and Stavrakakis, 2020). Despite different populist response patterns, it seems plausible that since the pandemic, democratic societies are confronted with a *new quality of destructive populism that frames the discourse on death in a certain way but is also 'centered on power over death'* (Lee, 2020). Therefore, the question now to be discussed is if this new quality of populism can be qualified as necropower, which is based on 'contemporary forms of subjugation of life to the power' and also tends to generate 'death-worlds' (Mbembe, 2003, pp. 39–40) and 'death zones' (Mbembe, 2011, pp. 75–76), where the structurally marginalized 'experience a permanent condition of being in pain' (Mbembe, 2003, p. 39) and subaltern groups become criminalized and dehumanized (Burman, 2010). So far it seems that we are confronted with a paradox: On the one hand, references to the dead and dying are used to discipline the living, and on the other, the suffering and dying of the structurally marginalized and the subalternized are made invisible.

The suffering and dying of the marginalized

In the context of the present global health crisis, it has become obvious that vulnerable groups, refugees, migrants and internally displaced people, informal workers, and the poor are not at the centre of democratic crisis management. In contrast, lockdown measures, for example, in the context of the European Union (EU), have had especially dramatic effects on the situation of structurally marginalized people, who lack access to healthcare, accurate health information, and preventative services, such as proper sanitation facilities (Shah *et al.*, 2020). Worldwide, precarious workers in low-income jobs, who have been shouldering the brunt of the crisis by working during the lockdown, were at particularly high risk of infection.

The picture is even more drastic in consideration of how intersectional gender and class relations play out in the context of the gendered division of labour in the COVID-19 crisis in the Global South (Löw, 2020; Shah *et al.*, 2020). For example, women in the Global South often rely on jobs in the informal economy, which means that lockdown-related restrictions on mobility result in a loss of income, and, due to the very nature of informal employment, there is no access to public healthcare or social security. It also fits into the picture that large parts of the population in the Global South can still not be vaccinated and that in the wealthier countries, vaccine doses are now going to waste due to declining demand (Cohen and Kupferschmidt, 2021).

At the same time, the pandemic has given politicians in many countries a strong argument for turning away migrants and refugees at their borders and thus preventing them from coming to Europe at all. And since the UN Refugee Agency and the International Organization for Migration have temporarily had to suspend their resettlement programmes due to the COVID-19 pandemic, even the weakest and most vulnerable have had to wait at Europe's gates and are put into camps inside the EU, without access to health services (Nossem, 2020).

The dire situation in these camps during the pandemic has been illustrated through an open letter from refugees who have had to endure in Moria, Greece:

> We know you are tired of hearing this, but since hardly anyone is writing anything about this then we feel like it is our duty to make it clear that the threatening covid-19 situation in the camp is not passing, it is in fact escalating: everything we warned about for one year ago now seems to become reality! People are of course very scared about that. The last time we had many cases of covid-19 in the camp, the camp burnt down, and everything that happened in the night of the fire, and the weeks after too, placed us in an even worse situation in all ways. … Covid-19 comes with many bad effects. It is not only about people getting sick and possibly dying from it, or even the lack of hospital beds and staff and equipment for treatment. In December last year, a report was published saying that every third refugee in Lesvos had suicidal thoughts, and every fifth refugee had attempted to end their own life.[6]

In line with the de facto suspension of the right to asylum, and also the human right to health, it seems that in various democracies, a general contempt, or at least ignorance, regarding certain forms of suffering is becoming increasingly rationalized and normalized. Viewed from a global perspective, populists differ in their reactions to the pandemic, and at first glance, there is no coherent pattern of how to respond to the global health crisis (Katsambekis and Stavrakakis, 2020). It is, however, significant that populist politics declare certain societal groups as disposable and certain lives as worthy of protection, while others are at the mercy of death (Agamben, 1998; Bauman, 2004; Foucault, 2004; Mbembe, 2003, 2011).

An obscene enjoyment of death?

As mentioned above, in the first wave of the COVID-19 pandemic, a central figure of various government speeches was regular references to the (potential) dead and the use of a warlike rhetoric (Mudde, 2020). At the same time, populist leaders such as Donald Trump or Jair Bolsonaro denied the threat of COVID-19, cynically edging that the economy is more important than disease control (Kremer, 2020).

Although populists differ in their strategies to cope with the crisis, regarded from a psychoanalytic perspective, there seems to be an *obscene populist enjoyment* (Hook, 2017; Lacan, 1992; Žižek, 1993) of disease, death, and punishment. It became apparent that the crisis has been used cynically as a populist strategy to increase national narcissism and to delegitimize any form of global cooperation or basic healthcare and health promotion based on international solidarity, outlined, for example, in the 'Declaration of Alma-Ata' (WHO, 1978).

Against this backdrop, it seems plausible that we are confronted with a new form of populism that can be categorized as necropolitical (Braidotti, 2007; Gržinić and Tatlić, 2014; Mbembe, 2003, 2019), which has serious effects on global governance arrangements based on the legacy of human rights. This is to outline a concept of populism that is based on a 'generalized instrumentalization of human existence and the material destruction of human bodies' (Mbembe, 2003, p. 14). Mbembe defines necropolitics as a scenario in which governments have a right to decide not only who will live and who will die but also how humans will live and die (Mbembe, 2003, p. 12). In conjunction with this, the necropolitical character of populist crisis management can also be traced back to the 'fact that the virus does not affect everyone equally' and that the will to sacrifice certain lives and to save others is a typical feature in the context of neoliberal crisis management (Gržinić and Tatlić, 2014). In this sense, structurally marginalized people are forced to live a life as the living dead (zombies), or at least as shadows (Mbembe, 2003), which appear only as a projection foil for societal ressentiments that become manifest due to the current health crisis.

Following Sandset (2021), let us now return to the affectual dimension of necropolitics. This includes addressing the relationship between the state of emergency, which, according to Mbembe, is a central feature of necropolitics, and the question of why the suffering and dying of the structurally marginalized find acceptance in the long run:

> If the exceptional state of emergency that Mbembe draws upon to elaborate on the necropolitics of the war on terror or the colonial plantation, then this conjecture states that the necropolitics of global health inequality is driven not by a perpetual state of emergency, but by a state of chronic acceptance.
>
> *(Sandset, 2021, p. 1412)*

In other words, regarding the ongoing health crises, as outlined in the first section of this chapter, the question is in what sense the present state of emergency relates to a 'state of acceptance' (Sandset, 2021, p. 1412). This includes recognition that '[n]ecropolitics is often "chronic" and slow yet its influence on people's lives often comes to the fore when an abrupt crisis emerges such as COVID-19' (Sandset, 2021, p. 1412). Arguably the answer lies in what has been outlined in the previous sections, namely that *before* the pandemic, various societies were already confronted with authoritarian interpellations with the intention of preventing solidarity in society with the structurally marginalized. So, the acceptance of necropower has obviously one root in normalizing authoritarian populism and national narcissism.

A further consideration is that the necropolitical threat of COVID-19 crisis management also stems from the inability, or even unwillingness, of democratic leaders to clearly distinguish communication practices and political agenda-setting from right-wing populist discourses in the context of crisis solutions (Heitmeyer, 2018; Salzborn, 2018). Right-wing populists may thus encounter enabling conditions that are inherent in (neo)liberal democracy itself. In the previous section, it was argued that we are confronted with a populism that works with interpellations that intend to prevent societal sympathy and solidarity with the structurally marginalized (Gržinić, 2020). In this sense, it is possible to relate to psychoanalytic debates in conjunction with the concept of necropolitics (Gržinić and Tatlić, 2014; Ritchie, 2017). With reference to these debates, another point can be addressed, and that is the relation between ideology and political sadism[7] (Adorno, 1974, 1995).

The global health crisis – an opportunity for societal learning processes?

Seen from a dialectical perspective (Adorno and Horkheimer, 2008), the global health crisis could nevertheless provide an opportunity for political and societal learning processes. All the more, critical sciences, civil societies, and social movements are now called upon to remind politics – on the local, national, as well as supranational levels – of their global responsibility, not only in the field of health. From the perspective of critical theory, these are certainly not new insights, and yet the critical negation of the status Quo (Adorno, 1966, 1974) remains the decisive moment for learning from current and past crises. Accordingly, in a last step, it may be opportune to outline theoretically, in what sense and under what conditions the COVID-19 pandemic could reopen spheres of utopian imagination based on societal critiques (cf. Žižek, 2020). Referring to Adorno's concept of negative dialectics (Adorno, 1966), the question is if and in what conditions social movements and civil society could subvert necropolitical populism.

My thesis is that the subversion of ideological interpellations, which have specific effects on processes of collective subjectification, can take place if human abyss and the inescapable destructiveness of human activity are not denied but are taken as a starting point for concrete utopian thinking (Bloch, 1985), based on radical negation (Adorno, 1985). Simply put, imagining and creating a better world depend on recognizing potentially destructive social dynamics by reflecting on past man-made horrors and processing them through social mourning.

This also involves reflecting on the social psychological origins of collective loss of sympathy with the subalternized and negating those power structures and practices that lead to societal excess (Adorno and Horkheimer, 2008). At the same time, I argue that these power-critical considerations form the basis for a 'realist utopia' (Brown, 2020, p. 7) and concrete utopian thinking.

Accordingly, my claim is that civil society-based scandalizations can be emancipatory, if they take the form of performative negation practices, which follow a strategy of self-empowerment and transnational solidarity. This is to address societal practices that enable collectively reworking the trauma of ideological and structural violence that have led to subaltern subject positions (Spivak, 1994). In this light, the question is whether necropolitical populism can be subverted through dystopian storytelling (Heller, 2016).

To illustrate in what sense this could happen, I now want to point to corona-related (queer-)feminist protests, which take an art-based form and are based on dystopian storytelling, such as Margaret Atwood's novel *The Handmaid's Tale* (Meisterhans, 2019). The interesting point is that feminist protests currently form a transnational movement (Lorey, 2018), offering not only a visible counterpart to authoritarianism and right-wing radicalism but also scandalization of the global health crisis as a symptom of complex structural power asymmetries in the context of national and global governance, which have been increased by neoliberal austerity policies (Couto *et al.*, 2019; Germain, 2018). A good example is the protest performances of the Chilean feminist theatre troupe and feminist collective *Las Tesis*. This collective had its starting point in the scandalization of sexual violence and inspired feminist protests not only in Argentina and Mexico but also in Austria, France, the US, Spain, and Germany and was also transformed into a call for comprehensive health, education, and pension reform and a critique of neoliberal politics (Ripp, 2021).

Accordingly, my claim is that dystopian narratives and performances, which are based on different science fiction genres, such as pandemic films (Robnik, 2020),[8] or novels like Sam J. Miller's *Blackfish City* (2018) (Palm, 2020), can stimulate public discourses, i.e. if they enable perspectives of immanent transgression in a context of death and life. This means addressing practices of societal transnational resistance that point to the intersectional and complex interdependencies of the global health crisis, highlighting the political determinants not only of health but also of living and dying taking the form of art-based performances. Referring to contemporary utopian-theoretical debates in the (queer-)feminist context (Ashcroft, 2009; Chrostowska and Ingram, 2016; Daniels and Klapeer, 2019; Jones, 2013; Meisterhans, 2019), my argument is that these civic interventions can be distinguished from populist interpellations that work with the figure of death in order to create apocalyptic scenarios based on conspiracy theories. The essential point is that

> right-wing populism mainly serves to 'displace the weight of grief by the energies of grievance' ... it does not seek out mourning as a means of

> letting go or moving beyond certain forms of life but remains fixated on fantasies about the past. As such, populism rejects the need to sacrifice an attachment to a particular vision of flourishing, in order to work through these losses and imagine or create new futures.
>
> *(McIvor et al., 2021, p. 167)*

My final point is that reworking the trauma of ideological (dis-)recognition depends on specific solidarity-based practices and affects (Sauer, 2016). The precise twist here is to address solidarity-based practices that mourn the subaltern living and dying in the form of art-grounded protests and of performative actions (Butler, 1990; Gržinić, 2008; Meisterhans, 2019). In this sense, I would like to outline that dystopian storytelling can be part of the solidarity-based work of grieving (Butler, 2004, 2010), as it might not only allow remembering, repeating ideological interpellations that have led to structural marginalization. The point is, however, not to leave the discourse on death and dying to right-wing populists.

Conclusions

The starting point of this chapter was to outline in what sense the spread of COVID-19 demonstrates the structural failure of the international community of states to respond to multiple crises. It has therefore been argued that the current pandemic reveals that global health policies are still insufficiently oriented towards human rights standards, equity, and the social and political determinants of health and that this has a particular impact on the situation of structurally marginalized people in the Global South but also the Global North. At the same time, it was highlighted that health narratives in the context of disease control always entail a risk of authoritarian abuse. Therefore, with reference to the phenomenon of increasing nationalism and populism, it was problematized from a psychoanalytically informed ideology critique in what sense the global health crisis has become instrumentalized by authoritarian populists and how this could be qualified as *necropolitical* populism. Taking a dialectical perspective, it was outlined in what sense the global health crisis could nevertheless provide an opportunity for political and societal learning processes in a global context. In this sense it was emphasised that solidarity-based practices in the civic context that mourn the subaltern living and dying in the form of art-grounded protests and dystopian storytelling could subvert the populist spectacularizing of death and abuse of collective anxieties. These counter-hegemonical interventions could also build the fundament for concrete utopian thinking and transformation of global governance.

Notes

1 It would also certainly be an abbreviation to speak of neoliberalism as a unique political phenomenon, yet neoliberalism can be supposed to be an ideological project, in which certain core libertarian elements, such as ideas not only about the relationship between the individual and society but also on the relationship between state and

market, have a significant influence on processes of subjectification, albeit to varying degrees, depending on the phase and country (for an overview, see Ötsch and Thomasberger, 2009).

2 In the Lancet-University of Oslo Commission on Global Governance for Health, it was highlighted that the solving of global crises would need to overcome top-down governance and to upgrade bottom-up politics by including community groups and social movements on the local, national, and also transnational contexts.

3 Following Harris *et al.* (2017), I describe Trump in his presidential performance as a neo-fascist.

4 14 Länder zweifeln an Qualität von WHO-Studie zu Corona. https://www.zeit.de/news/2021-03/30/14-laender-zweifeln-an-qualitaet-von-who-studie-zu-corona.

5 See also: Protest gegen Corona-Politik. Entsetzen über Eskalation am Reichstagsgebäude. https://www.tagesschau.de/inland/corona-demo-berlin-131.html.

6 'Open letter', medico international, 17.5.2021, https://www.medico.de/en/this-is-not-disneyland-18200.

7 The concept of *political sadism* refers to the idea that ideological interpellations can be based on sadistic impulses and forms of othering, which are aimed at devaluing and degrading certain societal groups. What is addressed here is that political leaders, by constructing scapegoats, drive people, in turn, to project sadistic aggressions in pathic ways onto stigmatized populations.

8 See also: https://www.paranoia-tv.com/en/program/content/453-drehli-robnik-pandemic-cinema.

References

Adorno, Th. W. (1966). *Negative Dialektik.* Frankfurt/M.: Suhrkamp.

Adorno, Th. W. (1970). Erziehung nach Auschwitz. In G. Kadelbach and Th. W. Adorno (Eds.), *Erziehung zur Mündigkeit: Vorträge und Gespräche mit Hellmut Becker 1959–1969* (pp. 92–109). Frankfurt/M.: Suhrkamp.

Adorno, Th. W. (1974). Zur Logik der Sozialwissenschaften. In H. Maus, and F. Fürstenberg (Eds.), *Der Positivismusstreit in der deutschen Soziologie* (pp. 125–143). Nezwied: Luchterhand.

Adorno, Th. W. (1985). 'Etwas fehlt ...' Über die Widersprüche der utopischen Sehnsucht (Ein Rundfunkgespräch mit Theodor W. Adorno). In E. Bloch (Ed.), *Tendenz – Latenz – Utopie* (pp. 350–368). Frankfurt/M.: Suhrkamp.

Adorno, Th. W. (1995). *Studien zum autoritären Charakter.* Frankfurt/M.: Suhrkamp.

Adorno, Th. W., and Horkheimer, M. (2008). *Dialektik der Aufklärung. Philosophische Fragmente.* Frankfurt/M.: S. Fischer.

Agamben, G. (1998). *Homo Sacer: Sovereign power and bare life.* Stanford, CA – London, UK: Stanford University Press.

Aït-Touati, F. (2020). 1984 – 'Wir sind zahlreicher, als wir dachten'. Bruno Latours 'Pasteurisation of France' wiedergelesen. *Stay in Touch.* http://stay-in-touch.org/bruno-latours-pasteurisation-of-france-wiedergelesen/

Althusser, L. (1977). *Ideologie und ideologische Staatsapparate. Aufsätze zur marxistischen Theorie.* Hamburg: VSA.

Bauman, Z. (2004). *Wasted lives: Modernity and its outcasts.* Cambridge, UK: Polity Press.

Berkhout, E., Galasso, N., Lawson, M., Rivero Morales, P. A., Taneja, A., and Vázquez Pimentel, D. A. (2021). *The inequality virus. Bringing together a world torn apart by coronavirus through a fair, just and sustainable economy.* Oxford, UK: Oxfam. https://www.oxfam.de/system/files/documents/the_inequality_virus_-_english_full_report_-_embargoed_00_01_gmt_25_january_2021.pdf

Bieber, A. (2012). Gesellschaftliche Utopien. Oder: Wie politisch ist die Kunst? In A. Besand (Ed.), *Politik trifft Kunst. Zum Verhältnis von politischer und kultureller Bildung* (pp. 83–93). Bonn: Bundeszentrale für Politische Bildung.

Bloch, E. (1985). *Das Prinzip Hoffnung*. Vol. 5, Chapter 1–32. Frankfurt/M.: Suhrkamp

Brähler, E., and Decker, O. (Eds.) (2016). *Flucht ins Autoritäre*. Gießen: Psychosozial Verlag.

Braidotti, R. (2007). Bio-power and necro-politics. *Springerin, Hefte für Gegenwartskunst, 13*(2), 1–8.

Brand, U. (2012). Contradictions and crises of neoliberal-imperial globalization and the political opportunity structures for the Global Justice Movement. *Innovation: The European Journal of Social Science Research, 25*(3), 283–298.

Brand, U. (2016). How to get out of the multiple crisis? Towards a critical theory of social-ecological transformation. *Environmental Values, 25*(5), 503–525.

Bröckling, U. (2016). *The entrepreneurial self. Fabricating a new type of subject*. London, UK – Thousand Oaks, CA: Sage.

Brown, C. (2002, Jan.). The Construction of a "Realistic Utopia": John Rawls and International Political Theory. *Review of International Studies, 28*(1), 5–21.

Brunner, M., Daniel, A., Knasmüller, F., Maile, F., Schadauer, A., and Stern, V. (2021). Corona-protest-report. Narrative – Motive – Einstellungen.

Burman, J. (2010). *Transnational yearnings. Tourism, migration, and the diasporic city*. Vancouver, BC: University of British Columbia Press.

Butler, J. (1990). *Gender trouble. Feminism and the subversion of identity*. New York, NY – London, UK: Routledge.

Butler, J. (2004). *Precarious life: the powers of mourning and violence*. London, UK – New York, NY: Verso.

Butler, J. (2010). *Frames of war: When is life grievable*? London, UK – New York, NY: Verso.

Chrostowska, S. D., and Ingram, J. D. (Eds.) (2016). *Political use of Utopia: New Marxist, anarchist, and radical democratic perspectives*. New York, NY: Columbia University Press.

Cohen, J., and Kupferschmidt, K. (2021, May 26). Fairer shares. Rich countries cornered the marketplace for COVID-19 vaccines. *Science*. https://www.science.org/content/article/rich-countries-cornered-covid-19-vaccine-doses-four-strategies-right-scandalous

Connell, R. (2020). COVID-19/Sociology. *Journal of Sociology, 56*(4), 745–751.

Couto, M. Th., Oliveira, E. de, Alves Separavich, M. A., and Carmo Luiz, O. do (2019). The feminist perspective of intersectionality in the field of public health: A narrative review of the theoretical-methodological literature. *Salud Colectiva, 15*, e1994.

Crofts, P., and Vogl, A. (2019). Dehumanized and demonized refugees, zombies and World War Z. *Law and Humanities, 13*(1), 29–51.

Daniels, A., and Klapeer, Ch. (Eds.) (2019). Her mit der Zukunft?! Feministische und queere Utopien und die Suche nach alternativen Gesellschaftsformen. *Femina Politica, 28*(1), 1–178.

Demirović, A. (2013). Multiple Krise, autoritäre Demokratie und radikaldemokratische Erneuerung. *PROKLA Zeitschrift Für Kritische Sozialwissenschaft, 43*(2), 193–215.

Demirović, A. (2018). Autoritärer Populismus als neoliberale Krisenbewältigungsstrategie. *PROKLA. Zeitschrift Für Kritische Sozialwissenschaft, 48*(190), 27–42.

Dima, V. (2014). You only die thrice: Zombies revisited in The Walking Dead. *International Journal of Žižek Studies, 8*(2), 1–21. http://zizekstudies.org/index.php/IJZS/article/view/748

Ehrenberg, A. (2008). *Das erschöpfte Selbst. Depression und Gesellschaft in der Gegenwart*. Frankfurt/M: Suhrkamp.

Erdheim, M. (1984). *Die gesellschaftliche Produktion von Unbewußtheit. Eine Einführung in den ethnoanalytischen Prozeß*. Frankfurt/M.: Suhrkamp.

Foucault, M. (2004). *The birth of Biopolitics: Lectures at the Collège de France, 1978–1979*. New York, NY: Palgrave Macmillan.

Freud, S. (2000a). Das Unbehagen in der Kultur. In A. Mitcherlich, A. Richards, and J. Strachey (Eds.), *Studienausgabe*, vol. IX: *Fragen der Gesellschaft und Ursprünge der Religion* (pp. 193–270). Frankfurt/M.: Fischer.

Freud, S. (2000b). Warum Krieg. In A. Mitcherlich, A. Richards, and J. Strachey (Eds.), *Studienausgabe*, vol. IX: *Fragen der Gesellschaft und Ursprünge der Religion* (pp. 275–286). Frankfurt/M.: Fischer.

Freud, S. (2000c). Das ökonomische Problem des Masochismus. In A. Mitcherlich, A. Richards, and J. Strachey (Eds.), *Studienausgabe*, vol. III: *Psychologie des Unbewußten* (pp. 341–354). Frankfurt/M.: Fischer.

Gehrlach, A. (2020). 430 v. Chr. – Die Seuche von Athen. Thukydides 'Der Peloponnesische Krieg' wiedergelesen. *Stay in Touch*. http://stay-in-touch.org/thykydides-der-peloponnesische-krieg-wiedergelesen/

Geiselberger, H. (Ed.) (2017). *Die große Regression. Eine internationale Debatte über die geistige Situation der Zeit*. Berlin: Suhrkamp.

Germain, A. (2018). The global movement for sexual and reproductive health and rights. In C. O'Monique, and P. Fourie (Eds.), *Global Health and Security* (pp. 78–95). London, UK: Routledge.

Gigler, C. (2020, April 27). Corona-Politik. Opposition kritisiert Kurz: 'Ein Bundeskanzler soll nicht Angst verbreiten'. *Kleine Zeitung*. https://www.kleinezeitung.at/politik/5805859/CoronaPolitik_Opposition-kritisiert-Kurz_Ein-Bundeskanzler-soll

Global Health Watch 4. (2014). An alternative health report. In People's Health Movement, ALAMES, Health Action International, and Medico International (Eds.), *Third World Network and Medact*. London, UK: Zed Books.

Global Health Watch 5. (2017). An alternative health report. In People's Health Movement, ALAMES, Health Action International, and Medico International (Eds.), *Third World Network and Medact*. London, UK: Zed Books.

Goldberg, D. T. (2011). *The threat of race: Reflections on racial neoliberalism*. Malden, MA – Oxford, UK: John Wiley and Sons.

Gostin, L., Halabi, S., and Wilson, K. (2020). The International Health Regulations (2005), the threat of populism and the COVID-19 pandemic. *Globalization and Health, 16*(70).

Gramsci, A. (1971). *Selections from the prison notebooks of Antonio Gramsci*. New York, NY: International Publishers.

Gržinić, M. (2008). *Re-politicizing art, theory, presentation and new media technology. Publications of the Academy of Fine Arts Vienna*, Vol. 6. Vienna: Schlebrugge.

Gržinić, M. (2020). *Refugees, Europe, death and Covid-19*. Vienna: Academy ofFine Arts Vienna. https://www.akbild.ac.at/Portal/universitaet/uber-uns/corona_essays/refugees-europe-death-and-covid-19

Gržinić, M., and Tatlić, Š. (2014). *Necropolitics, racialization, and global capitalism*. Lanham, MD: Lexington Books.

Hall, St. (2014). Popular-demokratischer oder autoritärer Populismus. In St. Hall (Ed.), *Populismus, Hegemonie, Globalisierung (Ausgewählte Schriften 5)* (pp. 101–120). Hamburg: Argument.

Harris, J., Davidson, C., Fletcher, B., and Harris, P. (2017). Trump and American fascism. *International Critical Thought,* 7(4), 476–492.

Haubl, R. (2008). Die Angst, persönlich zu versagen oder sogar nutzlos zu sein. Leistungsethos und Biopolitik. *Forum der Psychoanalyse, 24*, 317–329.

Hegel, G. W. F. (1986). *Phänomenologie des Geistes, Werke 3.* Frankfurt/M.: Suhrkamp.

Heitmeyer, W. (2018). *Autoritäre Versuchungen. Signaturen der Bedrohung.* Berlin: Suhrkamp.

Heller, A. (2016). *Von der Utopie zur Dystopie. Was können wir uns wünschen?* Vienna – Hamburg: Edition Konturen.

Holst, J. (2019, April). Global health – hope oder hype? *GGW – Das Wissenschaftsforum in Gesundheit und Gesellschaft, Jg. 19*(2), 7–15.

Holst, J. (2020). Global Health – emergence, hegemonic trends and biomedical reductionism. *Global Health, 16*, Article 42.

Holst, J. (2021). Corona treibt den Globus um. *Gesundheit und Gesellschaft, 06*/2021. https://www.gg-digital.de/2021/06/thema-des-monats/corona-treibt-den-globus-um/index.html

Holst, J., and Razum, O. (2018). Globale Gesundheitspolitik ist mehr als Gefahrenabwehr. *Das Gesundheitswesen, 80*(10), 923–926.

Hook, D. (2017). What is 'Enjoyment as a political factor'? *Political Psychology, 38*(4), 605–620.

Hövermann, A., Groß, E., and Zick, A. (2015). 'Sozialschmarotzer' – der marktförmige Extremismus der Rechtspopulisten. In B. Küpper, and A. Zick (Eds.), *Wut, Verachtung, Abwertung. Rechtspopulismus in Deutschland* (pp. 95–108). Bonn: Dietz.

Inglehart, R., and Norris, P. (2019). *Cultural backlash: Trump, Brexit and Authoritarian Populism.* Cambridge, UK: Cambridge University Press.

Jakob, C., and Wahmkow, J. (2020, August 2). Coronaproteste in Berlin: Dichtgedrängt gegen 'Virokraten'. *Taz.* https://taz.de/Coronaproteste-in-Berlin/!5705179/

Jessop, B. (2019). Authoritarian neoliberalism: Periodization and critique. *South Atlantic Quarterly, 118*(2), 343–361.

Jones, A. (Ed.) (2013). *Critical Inquiry into Queer Utopias.* New York, NY: Palgrave Macmillan.

Katsambekis, G., and Stavrakakis, Y. (Eds.) (2020). *Populism and the pandemic. A collaborative report.* POPULISMUS Interventions No. 7 (special edition) in collaboration with the Populism Research Group at Loughborough University. Thessaloniki: http://populismus.gr/wp-content/uploads/2020/06/interventions-7-populism-pandemic-UPLOAD.pdf

Krause, D., Küpper, B., and Zick, A. (2016). *Gespaltene Mitte – Feindselige Zustände. Rechtsextreme Einstellungen in Deutschland.* Bonn: Dietz.

Kreil, Ch. (2020, May 11). Corona-Demos: Identitäre Impf-Taliban machen Stimmung. *Der Standard.* https://www.derstandard.at/story/2000117342095/corona-demos-identitaere-impf-taliban-macht-stimmung

Kremer, D. (2020, May 9). Wirtschaft gegen Gesundheit: Bolsonaros Spiel mit dem Virus. *Frankfurter Allgemeine Zeitung.* https://www.faz.net/aktuell/wirtschaft/bolsonaro-wirtschaft-wichtiger-als-covid-19-bekaempfung-16762055.html

Lacan, J. (1992). *The ethics of psychoanalysis. 1959–1960. The seminar of Jacques Lacan. Book 7*, ed. by J.-A. Miller, trans. D. Porter. London, UK: Routledge.

Lacan, J. (2005). *Meine Lehre.* Vienna: Turia + Kant.

Lee, Ch. J. (2020, January 1). The necropolitics of COVID-19. *Africa is a Country.* https://africasacountry.com/2020/04/the-necropolitics-of-covid-19

Löfflmann, G. (2019). America first and the populist impact on US foreign policy. *Survival, 61*(6), 115–138.

Löw, Ch. (2020, October 10). Pandemie – Corona, postkolonialer Feminismus und Necropolitics in Indien. *blog interdisziplinäre geschlechterforschung.*

Lorey, I. (2018). 8M – Der große feministische Streik. Vorwort. *Transversal Texts*. https://transversal.at/blog/8m-der-groe-feministische-streik

Lucci, A. (2020). 1998 – Als nur das tote Mikrobium ein gutes war. Hans Blumenbergs 'Infektion als absolute Metapher' wiedergelesen. *Stay in Touch*. https://www.chicagomanualofstyle.org/tools_citationguide/citation-guide-2.html#cg-journal

Manow, P. (2018). *Die Politische Ökonomie des Populismus*. Berlin: Suhrkamp.

Mbembe, A. (2003). Necropolitics. Trans. by L. Meintjes. *Public Culture, 15*(1), 11–40. https://muse.jhu.edu/article/39984

Mbembe, A. (2011). Nekropolitik. In M. Pieper, Th. Atzert, S. Karakayali, and V. Tsianos (Eds.), *Biopolitik in der Debatte* (pp. 63–93). Wiesbaden: VS Verlag für Sozialwissenschaften/Springer Fachmedien.

Mbembe, A. (2019). *Necropolitics*. Durham, NC: Duke University Press.

McCoy, D. (2017). Critical global health: Responding to poverty, inequality and climate change comment on 'Politics, power, poverty and global health: Systems and frames'. *International Journal of Health Policy and Management, 6*(9), 539–541.

McCoy, D. (2014) David McCoy on the Lancet-UiO Commission on Global Governance for Health. *Blogpost Medact*. http://www.medact.org/david-mccoy-the-lancet-commission-on-global-governance-should-scrap-its-recommendations-and-come-up-with-new-ones/

McIvor, D. W., Hooker, J., Atkins, A., Athanasiou, A., and Shulman, G. (2021). Mourning work: Death and democracy during a pandemic. *Contemporary Political Theory, 20*(1), 165–199.

Meier, B. M., and Gostin, L. O. (2018). *Human rights in global health: Rights-based governance for a globalizing world*. New York, NY: Oxford University Press.

Meisterhans, N. (2016a). Health for all: Implementing the right to health in the post-2015 agenda – Critical interventions from the global South (in English and Spanish). *Social Medicine / Medicina Social, 9*(3), 109–125.

Meisterhans, N. (2016b). WHO in crisis. Lessons learned from the Ebola outbreak and beyond. *The Chinese Journal of Global Governance, 1*(2), 1–29.

Meisterhans, N. (2019). Wider dem Tod der feministischen Utopie. Zum emanzipatorischen Potential radikalfeministischer und postkolonialer Ansätze in Zeiten des autoritären Backlashs. *Femina Politica. Zeitschrift für feministische Politikwissenschaft, 1*(2019), 72–84.

Meisterhans, N. (2020). *Globale Gesundheitspolitik: Die WHO und der Philantrokapitalismus in Zeiten von Corona*. Series of the Jahoda Bauer Institut. https://jbi.or.at/globale-gesundheitspolitik-die-who-und-der-philantrokapitalismus-in-zeiten-von-corona/

Moffitt, B. (2014). How to perform crisis: A model for understanding the key role of crisis in contemporary populism. *Government and Opposition, 50*(2), 189–217.

Moffitt, B. (2016). *The global rise of populism. Performance, political style, and representation*. Stanford, CA: Stanford University Press.

Mouffe, Ch. (2018). *Für einen linken Populismus*. Berlin: Suhrkamp.

Mudde, C. (2020, March 24). 'Wartime' coronavirus powers could hurt our democracy – without keeping us safe. *The Guardian*. https://www.theguardian.com/commentisfree/2020/mar/24/wartime-coronavirus-powers-state-of-emergency

Müller, J.-W. (2020, April 7). How populists will leverage the coronavirus pandemic. *World Politics Review*. https://www.worldpoliticsreview.com/articles/28663/how-populists-will-leverage-the-coronavirus-pandemic

Nossem, E. (2020). The pandemic of nationalism and the nationalism of pandemics. *UniGR-CBS Working Paper*. Vol. 8.

Ötsch, W. O., and Thomasberger, C. (Eds.) (2009). *Der neoliberale Markt-Diskurs. Ursprünge, Geschichte, Wirkungen.* Marburg: Metropolis.

Palm, M. (2020, May 11). Pandemics and Trumpian echoes in Miller's 'Blackfish City'. *Pop Matters.* https://www.popmatters.com/sam-j-miller-blackfish-city-2645956817.html

Pas, R. van de, and Belle, S. van (2015). Ebola, the epidemic that should never have happened. *Global Affairs, 1*(1), 95–100.

Razum, O., Zeeb, H., Mueller, O., and Jahn, A. (Eds.) (2014). *Global Health. Gesundheit und Gerechtigkeit.* Bern: Hans Huber

Ripp, A. (2021). Pandemic performances. The viral triumph of Las Tesis. *Theater, 51*(1), 1–4.

Ritchie, N. (2017). Life and Death. The Freudian roots of necropolitics and the question of 'civil' living. *Somatechniques,* 7(2), 234–249.

Robnik, D. (2020). *Ansteckkino. Eine politische Philosophie und Geschichte des Pandemie-Spielfilms von 1919 bis Covid-19.* Berlin: Neofelis.

Salzborn, S. (2018). Was ist Rechtspopulismus? Einleitung der Redaktion zum PVS-Forum. *Politische Vierteljahresschrift, 59*(2), 319–321.

Sanders, D., McCoy, D., Legge, D., Birn, A.-E., and Sengupta, A. (2015). Social and political remedies needed for the Ebola tragedy. *The Lancet, 386* (9995), P738.

Sandset, T. (2021). The necropolitics of COVID-19: Race, class and slow death in an ongoing pandemic. *Global Public Health, 16*(8–9), 1411–1423.

Sauer, B. (2016). Affektive Gouvernementalität. Eine geschlechtertheoretische Perspektive. In M. Greco, E. Mixa, S. Pritz, and M. Tumeltshammer (Eds.), *Un-Wohl-Gefühle. Eine Kulturanalyse gegenwärtiger Befindlichkeiten* (pp. 147–162). Bielefeld: transcript.

Sauer, B. (2017). Geschlechtertheoretische Überlegungen zum europäischen Rechtspopulismus. Zum Erklärungspotential der Kategorie Geschlecht. *Politische Vierteljahresschrift, 58*(1), 1–20.

Sauer, B. (2019). Anti-feministische Mobilisierung in Europa. Kampf um eine neue politische Hegemonie? *Zeitschrift für Vergleichende Politikwissenschaft, 13*(3), 339–352.

Schels, B. (2020, June 17). *Objektive Einschnitte und subjektive Wahrnehmung: Wie junge Erwachsene bislang durch die Corona-Krise gehen.* University of Vienna. Vienna Center for Electoral Research. https://viecer.univie.ac.at/corona-blog/corona-blog-beitraege/blog-59/

Shah, G. H., Shankar, P., Schwind, J. S., and Sittaramane, V. (2020, July/August). The detrimental impact of the COVID-19 crisis on health equity and social determinants of health. *Journal of Public Health Management and Practice, 26*(4), 317–319.

Spivak, G. Ch. (1994). Can the subaltern speak? In P. Williams, and L. Christman (Eds.), *Colonial discourse and post-colonial theory. A reader* (pp. 66–111). London, UK: Routledge.

Stöber, S. (2020, May 1). Jahrmarkt der kruden Ideen. *Tagesschau.de.* https://www.tagesschau.de/faktenfinder/corona-demos-101.html

Tóth, B. (2020, April 15). Unser täglich Pressebrot gib uns heute. *Falter.at.* https://www.falter.at/zeitung/20200415/unser-taeglich-pressebrot-gib-uns-heute/_0f9f3675bc

Transform (2017). *Legal frameworks for rights based social protection floors – Manual for a leadership and transformation curriculum on building and managing social protection floors in Africa.* http://socialprotection.org/institutions/transform

United Nations. (2020). *Ziele für nachhaltige Entwicklung. Bericht 2020.* https://www.un.org/depts/german/millennium/SDG%20Bericht%202020.pdf

Volkmer, M. and Werner, K. (Eds.) (2020). *Die Corona-Gesellschaft. Analysen zur Lage und Perspektiven für die Zukunft.* Bielefeld: transcript.

Wachtler, B., Michalski, N., Nowossadeck, E., Diercke, M., Wahrendorf, M., Santos-Hövener, C., Lampert, Th., and Hoebel, J. (2020). Sozioökonomische Ungleichheit und Covid-19 – Eine Übersicht über den internationalen Forschungsstand. *Journal of Health Monitoring, 5*(S7), 3–18.

WHO. (1978). *Declaration of Alma-Ata.* https://www.who.int/publications/almaata_declaration_en.pdf

WHO. (2017, December 13). *World Bank and WHO: Half the world lacks access to essential health services, 100 million still pushed into extreme poverty because of health expenses.* https://www.who.int/news/item/13-12-2017-world-bank-and-who-half-the-world-lacks-access-to-essential-health-services-100-million-still-pushed-into-extreme-poverty-because-of-health-expenses

Wiegel, M. (2020, March 17). Corona-Krise in Paris: Macron und der sechsfache Krieg. *Frankfurter Allgemeine Zeitung.* https://www.faz.net/aktuell/politik/corona-krise-in-frankreich-macron-erklaert-virus-den-krieg-16682743.html

Wilson, J. (2020, April 17). The right-wing groups behind wave of protests against Covid-19 restrictions. *The Guardian.* https://www.theguardian.com/world/2020/apr/17/far-right-coronavirus-protests-restrictions

Wondreys, J., and Mudde, C. (2020). Victims of the pandemic? European far-right parties and COVID-19. *Nationalities Papers (2020),* 1–18.

Yilmaz, I., and Erturk, O. F. (2021). Populism, violence and authoritarian stability: Necropolitics in Turkey. *Third World Quarterly, 42*(7), 1524–1543.

Žižek, S. (1993). *Tarrying with the negative: Kant, Hegel, and the critique of ideology.* Durham, NC: Duke University Press.

Žižek, S. (2009). *Auf verlorenem Posten.* Frankfurt/M.: Suhrkamp.

Žižek, S. (2010). *Die Tücke des Subjekts.* Frankfurt/M.: Suhrkamp.

Žižek, S. (2020). *Pandemie! COVID-19 erschüttert die Welt.* Wien: Passagen.

5

THE RULES-BASED WORLD ORDER AND THE NOTION OF LEGITIMACY CRISIS

Impact of the COVID-19 pandemic on foreign aid

Viktor Jakupec

Introduction

Throughout Western human history, crises were the norm rather than the exception. The 21st century is no different. The world witnessed the Global Financial Crisis (GFC), the European Sovereign Debt Crisis (ESDC), the European Refugee Crisis, an escalation of the exiting global environmental crisis, and, more recently, the COVID-19 pandemic crisis. Most earlier crises affected a limited spectrum of economic, social, and political foundations of Western rules-based world order establishment. The crises caused by the COVID-19 pandemic is different in magnitude. It contributes to and intensifies the political crises of the dominant neoliberal Western rules-based world order, the existing health crises especially in developing countries, and the ongoing environmental crises and brought about an economic crisis.

As far as foreign aid is concerned, prior to the COVID-19 crisis, funding levels and external flows of foreign aid to low- and middle-income countries were already inadequate to achieve Sustainable Development Goals (SDG). Given the high levels of sovereign debt and other socio-economic pressures brought about by the COVID-19 pandemic on major foreign aid finance sources, many low- and middle-income countries are struggling to support their economic, public health, social, and political responses to the COVID-19 pandemic.

Against the above background, the chapter provides an analysis of the impact of the COVID-19 pandemic on foreign aid amid an emerging Habermasian legitimation crisis of the existing (neo-)liberal post–World War II rules-based world order. The point of departure is the proposition the COVID-19 pandemic emerged as an unprecedented disruption to the economic, social, and political aspects of the rules-based world order, thereby generating major challenges

DOI: 10.4324/9781003273844-5

for neoliberal democracies and policymakers globally, ranging from a surge of illiberalism to emergence of national populism to anti-globalisation. Thus, it is argued that one of the greatest challenges is the resolution of the paradox between the rapid rise of vaccine nationalism and the UN rules-based world order institutions, such as the World Health Organization (WHO), which designate COVID-19 vaccine as a 'global public good', especially amongst the major Western economies and pursuant to the values and norms of the (neo-)liberal post–World War II rules-based world order.

COVID-19 pandemic as a (neo-)liberal crisis: a brief note

It is important to note that all the above-mentioned crises preceding the COVID-19 pandemic, as well as ongoing crises, have been played out within the (neo-)liberal post–World War II rules-based world order, built on values such as (hyper-)globalisation, dominance of the free market philosophy, commercialisation, and privatisation.

The situation with the COVID-19 pandemic as a crisis is different. Because of the COVID-19 pandemic, the (neo-)liberal post–World War II rules-based world order values and norms have been set aside by nation states, which turned politically, economically, and socially to vaccine nationalism (Fox, 2021). This return to nation states was fuelled by populist movements, anti-globalisation, and illiberalism. Even though COVID-19 vaccinees were designated as a 'global public good' in 2021, Vaccines Global Access (COVAX) was unable to deliver the promised vaccinees to low-income countries including agreed free COVID-19 vaccines to the poorest countries (Goldhill, 2021; Gavi, 2022). This lack of equitable global distribution of COVID-19 vaccines highlighted the partial disintegration of the (neo-)liberal post–World War II rules-based world order.

On domestic fronts the political, economic, and social popular sentiments provided a backlash against vaccination mandates and restrictions expressed through mass demonstrations, civil disobedience, blockades, disruptions to distribution of goods and provision of services, and anti-government attitudes. With this brief note, we can turn to unpacking the concept of the (neo-)liberal post–World War II rules-based world order.

The (neo-)liberal post–World War II rules-based world order

For this discussion the rules-based world order is defined as

> a shared commitment by all countries to conduct their activities in accordance with agreed rules that evolve over time, such as international law, regional security arrangements, trade agreements, immigration protocols, and cultural arrangements.
>
> *(United Nations Association of Australia, 2017, p. 4)*

However, it is useful to recall Kissinger's (2015) claim that there was never an actual world order. He argued that throughout history, civilisations established their own specific concept of order. Every hegemonic nation viewed itself as being at the world centre and projected its distinct values, norms, and beliefs to its outranked or satellite states.

From historical perspective, the post–World War II era consisted of a US-led bipolar rules-based world order, following the Bretton Woods agreement (Lamoreaux and Shapiro, 2019) and the USSR-led order. The former and its allies established Bretton Woods institutions, whereas the latter established the Council for Mutual Economic Assistance. Both aimed to provide development aid and development cooperation to and between countries they perceived as being in their sphere of influence (Jakupec, 2020). Both the USA and the USSR had their own respective 'world orders'.

Following the dissolution of the USSR, and until the establishment of the China-led New Development Bank (NDB), Asian Infrastructure Investment Bank, and the Belt and Road in the early 21st century, the USA presided over a unipolar rules-based world order and enjoyed an unquestioned legitimacy with the ideals of the Washington Consensus (Jakupec, 2020). With the rise of People's Republic of China (PRC) in the foreign aid arena and its alliance with Russia through the China-led development banks and initiatives, the question arises if the rules-based world order is at a crossroads.

Arguably with the various aforementioned crises of the 21st century, especially with the impact of the COVID-19 pandemic on the economic, political, and social aspects of both the developed and developing countries, an unprecedented changing point has been reached. PRC as a new power is rising, and the USA as an established power is declining (Allison, 2017). Yet, both, PRC supported by Russia and USA by its Western allies, are seeking to become the hegemon using COVID-19 vaccines as an instrument of soft power (Nye, 2011), which would contribute to their respective claims of legitimacy as the global hegemon and imposing their respective world order. Once legitimised, a bipolar world order will most likely emerge.

It is too early to determine which if any of the two world powers will emerge as the hegemon, using COVID-19 vaccine and other existing soft power (Nye, 2011) instruments as catalyst for expansion or strengthening geo-political spheres of interest. Much will depend how the rest of the world perceives and legitimises the competing rules of the world order. Much will also depend on the impact of the national populist, illiberal democratic, and deglobalisation movements as far as the political, economic, and societal legitimation aspects are concerned.

Legitimation crisis as a theoretical framework: a Habermasian vantage point

The theoretical framework of this chapter is informed by the social-critical school of thought, generally, and the Habermasian (1973a,b) concept of *legitimation crisis*.

The concepts of *legitimation* and *legitimation crisis* are complex phenomena, for both are subject to the political and economic circumstances of the times. For example, at a basic level, a legitimation crisis emerges when a government or an international or multilateral organisation is close to failing. However, this does not say anything about the type of failure needed to reach a *legitimation crisis* of the neoliberal rules-based world order, affected by the COVID-19 pandemic with a view on foreign aid. Thus, it is useful to unpack the concepts called *legitimation* and *crisis*, respectively and subsequently, to address the Habermas' (1973a,b) idea of legitimation crisis in a context of this chapter.

Legitimation

Legitimation is defined as a catalyst for the sustainability of any system of political rule (cf. Riedmüller and McElheny, 1977; Tallberg and Zürn, 2019). Legitimation, according to Dahl (1998), promotes agreed ideologies, which attempt to explain and justify the control of the political, economic, social, or cultural system by the dominant powers, claiming legitimacy by converting their influence into authority. Thus, legitimation grants an entity (e.g. institution or a government) the authority and political power to enact certain codified rules. Thus, legitimation is associated with acceptance and obedience of rules, regulations, values, and norms imposed by a legitimate entity on the subordinate actors. That is, prior to obeying certain codified rules, a subordinate entity will ascertain the legitimacy of the superior political system or authority. From this vantage point, legitimation and obedience are two concepts that are linked to the stability of a political system or authority. However, if a constituent actor perceives political basis with its rules, regulations, values, and norms as having no legitimacy, such an entity can withdraw from or refuse to obey the political system. Such a withdrawal or refusal may lead either to a political and economic instability or to a legitimation crisis.

'Crisis'

Notwithstanding that the COVID-19 pandemic has provoked political, economic, social and health crises, all rolled into one, it may not be seen as an 'exceptional' crisis. Arguably, the COVID-19 pandemic as a crisis, like other crises, is a part of 'normal' world affairs or 'stasis' rather than an 'exceptional' disruption to the rules-based world order.

To view the COVID-19 pandemic as an exceptional crisis contradicts the general assumptions that crises are the norm or a stasis (Habermas in Held, 1982). In short, there is no 'normal' global social-political-economic state of affairs, which is free of crises (Carr, 2001; Tooze, 2020). Thus, there is a perpetual state of albeit different and at times interrelated economic, political, humanitarian, ecological, and social crises. For example, in the 21st century, there were the aforesaid GFC, ESDC, and European Refugee Crisis, each causing different forms of crises and challenging the rules-based world order (cf. Paul, 2021). All these crises caused unstable epochs and challenged, in various ways, the Western neoliberal rules-based world order (Rajan and Zingales, 2004; Reinhart and Rogoff, 2011).

The short catalogue of crises should suffice to substantiate the claim that political, social, and economic crises are the 'normal' – a normal punctuated by scrambled improvisational solutions (Wolf, 1981). Crises are defined as a continuum challenging confidence in polity (the form or process of civil government or constitution), institutions, functions, or political, economic, social, and moral leadership (Marcuse, 2002). Having unpacked both, the concept of legitimation and crisis, we can now turn to the main concept, namely *legitimation crisis*.

Legitimation crisis

Legitimation crisis as a scholarly term was initially coined by Habermas (1973a,b) and Offe (1984) denoting a decline in confidence of administrative functions, organisations, or governance.

According to Habermas (1973b), a legitimation crisis arises when normative principles, values, and beliefs are diminished, and the confidence in social, political, economic, or cultural institutions and systems is lost amongst their respective constituency. According to Habermas (1973a,b), this means that a *legitimation crisis* arises when an entity such as a government, a supranational, or an international organisation, such as the International Financial Institutions (IFIs), does not have the administrative capacity to sustain or establish social, political, moral, and rational structures required to achieve their objectives. Thus, a legitimation crisis arises when the political, economic, cultural, or social structures established by authorities are no longer perceived as fulfilling the practical and ideological functions for which they have been established and legitimised. In other words, and putting this within a contemporary context, the outcome of popular dissatisfaction with the neoliberal rules-based world order and its instrumentalities led to the rise of illiberal democracies, nationalism, and populism causing a political, social, cultural, and an economic legitimation crisis affecting Western liberal democracies.

Returning to the question of COVID-19 pandemic as a stasis or an exception, there is a general perception amongst the academe that a pre-COVID-19 pandemic notion of 'normality' has been suddenly broken. From this vantage point, the socio-political transformation caused by the pandemic is seen from a limited viewpoint and as a form of contemporary life. Thus, the contemporary life becomes part of the COVID-19 pandemic as a crisis. By treating COVID-19 pandemic crisis as an exception, rather than a 'stasis', within a realm of other interrelated crises militates against the broader apprehension of socio-political, economic, and cultural subtleties, which are linked to the existing COVID-19 crisis (Condon, 2020). In other words, the impact of the COVID-19 pandemic as an economic, political, and societal crisis will continue beyond the pandemic into an epidemic stage, establishing a 'new normal'.

If one accepts the argument that due to the COVID-19 pandemic, the world is experiencing a continuing neoliberal rules-based world order legitimation crisis, the prospect of a return to a hegemonic 'normal' bilateral (USA-PRC) world order after the pandemic may be wishful thinking. The point is that the neoliberal rules-based world order has, since 2016 with the USA presidential election, BREXIT, and the rise of populist and illiberal movements, been in decline. In other words, at least since 2016, a political transformation of the neoliberal rules-based world order has been taking place, and it has been augmented by the COVID-19 pandemic, leading to an extension and a continuation of the already-existing crises of the rules-based world order with corresponding asymmetries of wealth and power in foreign aid (Condon, 2020, S.814–815).

Foreign aid and the COVID-19 pandemic: asymmetries of wealth and power

The COVID-19 pandemic has the capacity cause significant social, political, and economic damage to low- and middle-income counties. The pandemic has the potential to disrupt humanitarian and foreign aid flows. But even if one projects to post-COVID-19, it is uncertain what foreign aid strategies and policies will look like. However, it is possible to imagine that whatever type of world order will emerge following the COVID-19 pandemic, it will affect all areas of humanity including politics, economics, governance, polity, trade, and foreign aid and development. We need to remember that the severity of the COVID-19 pandemic crisis follows an already-existing crisis of neoliberalism and its rules-based world order. The pandemic has, on the one hand, exacerbated the asymmetries of wealth and power between the wealthy and poor nations and, on the other hand, with the rise of PRC and various 'disruptors' (see Chapter 1 in this volume), accelerated the potential emergence of a new world order, which needs to address the question of asymmetries of wealth and power concerning low- and middle-income countries.

At a basic level, imbalances between the wealthy developed nations and the low- and middle-income economies are evident by the fact the former can open up their economies because they have extensive access to vaccines and corresponding high vaccination rates, vast testing capacities, a well-developed health infrastructure, and a sophisticated health data organisation. The COVID-19 pandemic has made the global health care infrastructure increasingly fragile and is causing asymmetries between the wealthy donor and the poor foreign aid recipient countries. Notwithstanding the increased commitment of foreign aid contributions, the distribution of COVID-19 vaccines allocated to developing nations lags far behind (Abdellatif and Graeden, 2020). Such asymmetries of wealth and power between low- and middle-income countries and the wealthy high-income economies have potential consequences on the stability of the rules-based world order and the epistemic and ontological assessments of COVID-19 pandemic as a systemic legitimation crisis.

The COVID-19 pandemic as a systemic legitimation crisis: epistemic and ontological perspectives

Given that the COVID-19 crisis affects political, social, economic, cultural, and health events of the existing neoliberal rules-based world order, it could be argued the COVID-19 pandemic institutes an epistemic cataclysm for the existing hegemonic world order. The COVID-19 crisis is not only being impacted on but is also escalating the pre-COVID-19 legitimation crises of the rules-based world order; a legitimation crisis caused by the aforesaid rise of populism, nationalism, and illiberalism at ideological level and protectionism, mercantilism, and deglobalisation at economic practice levels. This epistemic cataclysm is a problem of knowledge, for at basic level, it pits the episteme of neoliberal ideology and late capitalism against the episteme of illiberalism and national populism, undermining the legitimation of democratic processes and eroding the societal confidence in public as well as multilateral institutions. It deepens social and economic divisions and inequalities, centrality of asymmetric polarisation, and political radicalisation.

Apart from the epistemic cataclysm, the COVID-19 pandemic (crisis) is creating a corresponding ontological cataclysm of the neoliberal-late capitalist rules-based world order and, by extension, foreign aid. From an ontological vantage point, the COVID-19 pandemic is seen as a disruptor of the pre-COVID-19 economic and political crises (OECD, 2020b), causing socio-economic shocks (Blum and Neumärker, 2021). The disruption and the socio-economic shocks are requiring epistemic and ontological behaviour changes of neoliberal rules-based world order IFIs, which use a foreign aid playbook for a neoliberal and late capitalism-centred rules-based world order that is waning.

At the ontological level, the global foreign aid environment is experiencing shifts in alliances through the provision of soft power and smart power (Nye, 2011). These shifts were, in part, influenced by the rise of PRC. This led to political and economic crises in developing countries, such as in Solomon Islands (Seneviratne, 2022) and Horn of Africa countries (The Zimbabwe Mail, 2022), and the financial legitimation crisis in Sri Lanka (The Strait Times, 2022), to name but a few.

To put this into a context of Habermas (1973a, 1985), a systemic legitimation crisis arises when the political system fails to deliver the expected outcomes. Thus, in the advent of a legitimation crisis, the societies, governments, and multilateral agencies such as IFIs may become susceptible to political, economic, and social forces that attempt to change the status quo (Habermas, 1985). This perpetuates the crisis and subsequently leads to a world order based on authoritarian populism and illiberalism, without necessarily referring to, for example, the COVID-19 pandemic and the existing foreign aid goals.

COVID-19 pandemic and the current foreign aid goals: a very brief analysis

Prior to the COVID-19 crisis, levels and trends in national revenues and international flows to low- and middle-income economies were already considered inadequate to support the SDGs (OECD, 2020a). With high sovereign debt levels and additional pressures engendered by the COVID-19 pandemic on all major IFIs and other lenders of development finance, low- and middle-income countries find it increasingly difficult to finance their public health and social and economic responses affected by the COVID-19 pandemic crisis. According to OECD (2020a), there are some indicators pointing to substantial 'debt and equity outflows from developing economies that accompany a drop in remittances, and ripple effects on domestic finance already solicited by the unfolding public health and economic crises' (OECD, 2020a, n.p.).

This raises a question about avoiding 'a development finance collapse that would send millions back into poverty, and compromise our capacity to reach the SDGs, our common blueprint for a stronger, fairer, and more sustainable world' (OECD, 2020a, n.p.).

To be sure, prior to the onset of the COVID-19 pandemic, foreign aid financing had already been reduced, due to rising public debt in developed and developing countries. Furthermore, the COVID-19 pandemic may provoke a major setback in available funding for foreign aid generally and for achievement of SDG specifically. That is, national aid funding allocated by donors for foreign aid will need to be reduced due to diminished economic activities globally. These are only two economic indicators of a legitimation crisis and should suffice to illustrate the emerging and continuing legitimisation crisis from a politico-economic vantage point.

Furthermore, if one takes into account the existing state of affairs concerning the ontology of foreign aid, the reason for a heightened legitimation becomes increasingly evident. As Brown (2022) pointed out, the developing world is experiencing a downturn from years of socio-economic development, which hurts and disadvantages especially the poor sections of population. Following the advent of the COVID-19 pandemic, low- and middle-income economies are under increased pressure to acquire resources needed to support their population's welfare at the time of the COVID-19 crisis. In addition, Brown (2022) states that the economic interruptions of trade activities, foreign investment, and remittance have contributed to a decline in international developing funding. If this stands to reason, then foreign aid is more critical than ever.

The important point here is that it is unlikely that there will be a return to 'business as usual'. More likely the world will be faced with a reset, whereby the post-COVID-19 pandemic future for foreign aid will be governed by a world order characterised by a decline in populist and illiberal forces and a renewed legitimation of (neoliberal) governance structures, or there will be an increase of illiberal and populist sentiments globally or regionally, which, in turn, will enhance a legitimation crisis of (neoliberal) multilateralism (University of Cambridge, 2022). However, it may be difficult to sustain the either-or scenario, for it may be the case that both types of foreign aid governance with its own foreign aid goal(s) will emerge. Either way, to gain a deeper understanding of the foreign aid governance of the day, it may be advantageous to theorise the nexus between COVID-19 legitimation crisis and its effects on foreign aid, from a theoretical discourse vantage point.

The COVID-19 legitimation crisis and its effects on foreign aid: a theoretical discourse

The following analysis of the COVID-19 legitimation crisis and its effects on foreign aid is the based on the proposition that the neoliberal rules-based world order is fraying. However, a cautionary note is in place, namely the full impact of COVID-19 crisis on foreign aid remains to a large extent unknown. However, there is compelling argument to be made that the COVID-19 pandemic will have a significant effect on the structure(s) and legitimacies of the existing rules-based world order, geo-political alliances, economies, and foreign aid.

Even with the most optimistic views advanced by the International Monetary Fund (IMF), the World Bank, and the Organisation for Economic Co-operation and Development (OECD), the global economy will be at the output level of 1921 (Schwab and Malleret, 2020) due to the impact of the COVID-19 pandemic. These claims are impacted by the emerging sovereign debt in developed and developing countries, which needs to be repaid over long periods of time. If these forecasts by multilateral foreign aid organisations stand to reason, it is difficult to imagine that donor nations will be able to maintain their contributions to foreign aid at pre-COVID-19 pandemic levels.

The paramount question is to what extent, if any, is the COVID-19 crisis a defining moment for 21st-century international relations and, by extension, foreign aid? That is, what type of a world order emerges at the end or following the COVID-19 crisis? From a structural vantage point, there are a number of world order options, such as a new Cold War order (Jakupec, 2020), the emergence of a bipolar world order, some form of multipolar world order, a fragmented world order, or a multipolar world order based on regional trading blocks and alliances, a mercantile, or an anarchic world order.

To reflect on what the future may look like, we could turn to two potential options. One is the establishment of increased autonomy of nation states, and the other is the increased cooperation with multinational organisations. In either case, there is the question of the anarchic status.

However, the current difficulty is to determine to which extent the COVID-19 legitimation crisis is providing the following scenarios. The neoliberal rules-based world order may become obsolete, it may continue on a life-support system, it may emerge as a phoenix from the ashes of the COVID-19 pandemic, or it may be replaced by another unclear world order. From a legitimation crisis perspective, each of these scenarios will impact differently on foreign aid.

Addressing the question of change, however tentatively, it may be argued that the Western multilateral foreign aid institutions are increasingly subjected to the impact of questions of their legitimation from developing countries. An increasing number of developing countries are seeking aid from non-Western IFIs (Eggen and Roland, 2014). This can broadly be seen as an emergence of bipolar or even multipolar foreign aid systems.

An alternative viewpoint is that the COVID-19 legitimation crisis has brought to the fore the importance of national sovereignty and state anarchism by exposing the limits of the existing rules-based world order with its multilateral IFIs. This may lead to a foreign aid structure characterised by a Westphalian system with major actors as foreign aid donors being nation states. Multilateral IFIs roles would play a much curtailed role. Thus, national sovereignty of the foreign aid recipient country would become paramount.

From a sovereignty perspective, the Habermasian legitimation crisis as a theoretical framework provides a basis for an analysis of the COVID-19 pandemic impact on foreign aid and needs to be addressed by contextualising the COVID-19 pandemic and the rules-based world order and foreign aid within the Habermasian legitimation crisis.

A Habermasian legitimation crisis contextualised: COVID-19 pandemic, the rules-based world order, and foreign aid

The Habermasian legitimation crisis is based on the politics and economics of the 1960s and 1970s. Thus, within a contemporary foreign aid architecture, legitimation crisis needs to be contextualised with a framework of the currently dominant neoliberal rules-based world order. In short, the outlines of legitimation crisis within a neoliberal politics and economics as it exists today differ from the legitimation crisis as discussed originally by Habermas in the 1970s. There is also a difference between the previously mentioned GFC, ESDC, and other crises and the COVID-19 pandemic crisis. The last mentioned goes beyond singular financial, economic, political, and humanitarian dimensions and questions not only the legitimacy of the existing neoliberal rules-based world order but also the liberal democracy-based social fabric of Western society more generally (Condon, 2020; Habermas, 2021). Thus, legitimation crisis of contemporary foreign aid architecture needs to be contextualised with a framework of neoliberal rules-based world order. In short, the outlines of legitimation crisis within a neoliberal politics and economics as it exists today differ from the legitimation crisis as discussed originally by Habermas in the 1970s.

The contemporary legitimation crisis of the neoliberal hegemony and the social, cultural, economic, and political contexts of the existing world order, which is characterised by civil disobedience and a de-legitimation of the rules-based world order-based multilateral organisations. This legitimation crisis is splitting the political fabric at domestic level in many developed countries and internationally with the challenges to the hegemonic IFIs from new foreign aid donors. In short, we are witnessing a fragmentation of the political fabric internationally and nationally in many countries.

In addition, there are divergent views by member countries of multilateral organisations as to the processes to control the COVID-19 pandemic, which brings into question the latter's legitimacy. A typical example is the attempted de-legitimation of the WHO by the Trump administration and the PRC's support of the WHO as a legitimate multilateral organisation. Together, these phenomena are challenging at different levels of the existing rules-based world order from within and without. Of course, both are interrelated and are subject to the notions of obedience and authority as discussed above.

However, a political legitimation crisis gained global traction already prior to the emergence of the COVID-19 pandemic. The existing neoliberal rules-based world order was challenged by the Trump administration and domestically. The USA became split socially, economically, and politically. BREXIT polarised the UK voters between national and international sentiments. Hungary, Poland, and some other European Union (EU) countries distanced themselves from the values and norms of the EU by embracing illiberalism. Many countries moved towards populism, abandoning the socio-political ideals of the Western democracies. These ideological changes account for an unprecedented legitimation crisis of the neoliberal rules-based world order.

In order to contextualise these ideological changes, it may be useful to recall that even before the COVID-19 pandemic, legitimation crises existed at least since the turn of the century. These crises are characterised by significant absenteeism in democratic elections in the West, rise of right-wing extremism, extensive dissatisfaction amongst voters with the neoliberal governments and the neoliberal world order, the decreasing integrity of the USA as a legitimate rational and reliable world hegemon, the virtual decline of left-wing parties in the West, the acute narrowing of economic policies between the Left and the Right, and the diminishing status of public power, which were hijacked by private and corporate interests. The above refers mainly to the Global North. The situations in Latin America, Southeast Asia, and especially China and Africa are somewhat different. Using the above characteristics as parameters, it is possible to contextualise the COVID-19 pandemic and the (neoliberal) rules-based world order in a broader context of the Habermasian legitimation crisis. In other words, a general legitimation crisis existed prior to the advent of COVID-19 pandemic. However, the COVID-19 pandemic is a game changer, caused by problematic vaccinee distribution and leading to vaccine weaponisation.

The lack of adequate access to the vaccine by low- and medium-income countries attests to the growing asymmetries of wealth and power. Given that the COVID-19 pandemic is in the foreign aid arena raises the question how to respond to asymmetries. Given that the COVID-19 pandemic and its effects on foreign aid are ongoing and its future remains unpredictable, it is nevertheless possible to advance emerging megatrends.

A megatrend: the emerging world order(s), foreign aid, and legitimation

To identify a megatrend, we need to step back and to provide an outline of the emerging political mosaic. To restate, since the advent of the COVID-19 pandemic, the political alliances have shifted, new alliances have been forged, and the boundaries between traditional bipolarity have become blurred. For example, India is a founding member of the NDB (formerly BRICS Bank) and at the same time is a member of the Quadrilateral Security Dialogue consisting of India, Japan, Australia, and the USA, with the aim to secure the rules-based world order in the Asia-Pacific region. Concerning world order in February 2022, Russia signed a pact with PRC declaring a new era in world order (Wright, 2022).

Despite the, at times, competing world order alliances, Russia and India cooperate on many diverse programmes, ranging from development of COVID-19 vaccines, to trade, to space technology, to military hardware. Russia is India's single-largest military hardware supplier. In addition to being a member of Quadrilateral Security Dialogue, India is a member of the Shanghai Cooperation Organisation. And there is the Organisation of Turkic States (OTS, 2021) and the Russia's Eurasian Economic Union trading bloc (Devonshire-Ellis, 2021).

Each of these alliances aspires to forge a world order in their own image. For example, member governments of the Quadrilateral Security Dialogue aspire to bolster the Western-led rules-based world order, based on (neo-)liberal values of and ideals of liberal democracy. The problem, of course, is that there was never a 'world' order, for neither the then USSR and now Russia nor PRC, amongst other nations were included, nor did they accept the US-led 'order'. Given the new alliances, such as the above-mentioned and recently signed Russia–PRC pact, combined with the PRC's growing economic power, the role India plays in a range of international and multilateral alliances points to a trend where the USA can no longer impose its vision of a rules-based order on the rest of the world. If this stands to reason, then the emerging megatrend is the development of new and strengthening of existing multilateralism and thus a wide range of 'orders'.

Arguably, the most likely overarching megatrend to emerge in the post-COVID-19 era is a further fragmentation of the existing 'world order' and a rise of a number of newly emerging competing regional and international 'orders'. Thus, it is unlikely that the world will return to the pre-COVID-19 pandemic 'rules-based world order' because each of the aforementioned alliances will seek to establish its 'order' within the geo-political and geo-economic spheres of interest.

If one accepts the above proposition of fragmented existing order, then it could be argued that a range of political, economic, and social orders will emerge, each being defined by various degrees of polarity, internationalism and multilateralism, and other socio-political and economic factors. At a pragmatic level, the emerging fragmented orders, irrespective of their regionality or globality, and notwithstanding their international and multilateral orientation, or their underpinning polarities, will depend, for their success or otherwise, on (1) the success of power transition between the competing interests (Acharya, 2017); (2) new 'non-one-size-fits-all' social contract between foreign aid donors and recipients (United Nations, 2022); and (3) realignment of soft power (Nye, 2011) between the PRC–Russia alliance and the Western alliances and USA-led IFI. Finally, much will depend on the recognition by all players that COVID-19 pandemic is posing a political, social, and economic risk due to the rise of illiberalism and national populism, which, in turn, challenges the legitimacy of existing and emerging 'orders' globally and regionally. To conclude, each of the identified factors deserves a separate and an in-depth analysis. This should be a different debate left to others.

Nevertheless, if we accept the above-identified megatrend with its aspects, it may be possible to articulate scenarios for the impact of the emerging world order(s) on foreign aid. Much of the academic literature concerning the impact centres around the competition and an escalating tension between the USA and PRC (Hass, 2021). Less is being said about the rise of regional alliances, yet it could be argued that the diverse geo-political and geo-economic interests will promote multidimensional foreign aid response by donor entities. Thus, multilateralism with its rules-based world order and associated foreign aid infrastructure, which is already facing challenges from forces of unilateralism, are in danger of losing relevance and legitimation. It could be argued that, for example, the World Bank, IMF, WHO, and a number of other international organisations are under pressure from various actors to retain their legitimacy on a global scale.

Conversely, regionalism is expanding into global power vacuum left behind by the US-led foreign aid and the decline of the rules-based world order. Given the impact of COVID-19 pandemic on the global social, political, and economic fabrics in developed and developing economies, the hegemonic neoliberal development models that promoted economic growth through market liberalisation, globalisation, democratisation, and reduced government interference into the economy are experiencing unprecedented challenges. These may include the need for (re-)legitimising the existing rules-based world order institutions but in a new key, and especially in the face of illiberal and national populist legitimation crisis. There are sufficient opportunities for political leaders, to take advantage of the COVID-19 pandemic and create new alliances and world orders or to pursue a world order based on, for example, illiberalism or national populism. This in itself may create another megatrend with its own legitimation crisis, but as said above, a legitimation crisis in a 'new key'.

One option to adopt a world order that ensures that foreign aid recipient countries retain their sovereignty at a policymaking level enabling them to gain from developed countries and IFIs experiences and, at the same time, adopts these know-hows in line with their own unique national economic, political, and social conditions, realities, and needs. Buttressing national interests by alleviating and reducing poverty and, at the same time, minimising inequalities of authority and power between donors and recipients could be a basis for minimising a potentially ongoing legitimation crisis.

To deduce, amid the COVID-19 pandemic, the trust in formal institutions such as IFIs and other multilateral organisations at all levels, which have been central to much foreign aid development, is facing an unexpected legitimation crisis. The above analysis of the impact of the COVID-19 pandemic on foreign aid amid an emerging Habermasian legitimation crisis of the existing rules-based world order may now be integrated in a cognate sense as shown in the conclusion.

Conclusion

The basic argument posed in the preceding discussion is that there is a worldwide legitimation crisis directed at the existing Western neoliberal rules-based world order, which impacts on the geo-political and geo-economic global infrastructures. It has been argued that this is a crisis that is questioning the legitimacy of the social-political fabric of many developed and developing countries, and by extension, there is a looming question of legitimacy of the existing global governance, polity, and politics, which is subsequently translated into a legitimation crisis of IFIs and thus to foreign aid.

Notwithstanding the existing legitimation crisis of the neoliberal rules-based world order, which is heightened by the COVID-19 pandemic, much political debates focus on the COVID-19 crisis simply through a looking glass of vaccines. It is much more than that, namely the COVID-19 pandemic is increasingly contributing to a rejection of the existing neoliberal rules-based world order, including globalisation, and the perception of the lower economic population strata in developed countries as being disenfranchised. In other words, even when the COVID-19 pandemic comes to an end and turns into an endemic, the legitimation crisis that is engulfing the existing (neo-)liberal rules-based world order will not necessarily end. Perhaps the only way out of existing legitimation crisis is to advance a new world order or to turn to state anarchism, nationalism, and populism and thus rejecting any form of 'world' order.

As stated previously, the emerging legitimation crisis has its roots in pre-COVID-19 political, economic, financial, and cultural crises, for the COVID-19 pandemic crisis has amalgamated all these crises into one. In other words, it would be naive to try to disentangle the various crises or their consequences from the COVID-19 pandemic as a stand-alone health crisis. Alternatively, it could be argued that the COVID-19 pandemic as a crisis gives rise to a Habermasian legitimation crisis, facilitating the rise of above-mentioned political, economic, humanitarian, social, and cultural crises within the neoliberal rules-based world order.

However, the legitimation crisis has blurred the boundaries between the neoliberal rules-based world order, on the one side, and nationalism, illiberalism, and populism, on the other. The forces on both sides are forming a Faustian pact or an unholy alliance at the detriment of the low- and middle-income economies. To clarify, much of the multilateral development aid is based on and administered by neoliberal rules-based world order aid agencies such as the US-led World Bank, the IMF, and other IFIs. These organisations see themselves as anarchic and are legitimised as such by their member countries. However, since the GFC and ESDC, the multilateral neoliberal rules-based world order institutions have been losing their anarchic status through a legitimation crisis caused by the rise of nationalism and national populism, the advance of illiberal democracy, and the augmentation of de- and anti-globalisation sentiments, on a global scale.

Finally, vaccine nationalism (hording of COVID-19 vaccine by wealthy nations causing an unequal distribution) provokes a legitimation crisis, which, if not addressed by governments and relevant multilateral aid agencies, will lead to a 'catastrophic moral failure' of the existing rules-based world order (Ghebreyesus, cited in Okunola, 2021, n.p.). From a Habermasian vantage point, COVAX, Global Initiative on Sharing All Influenza Data, and vaccine nationalism create a legitimation crisis of the neoliberal and late capitalist rules-based world order, caused by economic and political crises. In short, the COVID-19 legitimation crisis is a consequence of a demand for economic and political changes in the rules-based world order to meet the expectation of the populace and other relevant entities in the face of the COVID-19 pandemic.

To conclude, in broad terms, the question how the COVID-19 pandemic will be addressed by various alliances, multilateral institutions, and individual countries will most likely have a substantial impact on the format of the world order, which will emerge in the repercussion of the pandemic. After all the COVID-19 pandemic has not run its full course, and thus, it is too early to advance any factual reverberations. For the time being, however, there are two competing schools of thought discernible, each with its own competing narrative. One is that key players (countries and alliances) will form a united front to address the legitimation crisis of the existing rules-based world order. The other school of thought is that countries, even those who are members of alliances, need to stand apart, as to better shield themselves from a multilateral collective legitimation crisis on the home front. From this vantage point, the COVID-19 pandemic crisis signifies an unambiguous assessment of the competing illiberal versus (neo-) liberal values and norms at societal, political, and economic levels, and thus the impact on foreign aid. As the COVID-19 pandemic evolves, it will test not only the effectiveness of multilateral aid agencies, including the World Bank and the IMF, but also the basic assumptions underpinning the existing (neo-)liberal rules-based world order as well as the foundations of emerging world orders, comparing their underpinning social, political, and economic accords.

References

Abdellatif, Y.O. and Graeden, E. (2020). A Funding Gap Is Hurting Developing Countries' Efforts to Contain COVID-19. The European Sting, December 23, 2020, https://europeansting.com/2020/12/23/a-funding-gap-is-hurting-developing-countries-efforts-to-contain-covid-19/

Acharya, A. (2017). After Liberal Hegemony: The Advent of a Multiplex World Order. *Ethics and International Affairs*, Vol. 31(3), pp. 271–285.

Allison, G. (2017). *Destined for War: Can America and China Escape the 'Thucydides Trap'?* Boston, MA: Houghton Mifflin Harcourt.

Blum, B. and Neumärker, B. (2021). Lessons from Globalization and the COVID-19 Pandemic for Economic, Environmental and Social Policy. *World*, Vol. 2, pp. 308–333.

Brown, S. (2022). *The Impact of COVID-19 on Foreign Aid.* Devpolicyblog, Development Policy Centre, Canberra: Australian National University. https://devpolicy.org/the-impact-of-covid-19-on-foreign-aid-20210401-2/

Carr, E.H. (2001). *The Twenty Years' Crisis, 1919–1939: An Introduction to Study International Relations.* New York: Palgrave.

Chin, M. (2021). What Are Global Public Goods? Global Institutions Must Coordinate to Preserve the Goods that Benefit Us All. *Finance and Development* (December 2021), pp. 62–63.

Condon, R. (2020). The Coronavirus Crisis and the Legitimation Crisis of Neoliberalism. *European Societies*, Vol. 23, S805–S816.

Corbyn, J. and Ashton, N. (2021). G7 Leaders Are Guilty of Vaccine Nationalism – This Shameful Stance Will Prolong the Pandemic. *The Independent* (17 June 2021). https://news.yahoo.com/g7-leaders-guilty-vaccine-nationalism-093355632.html?fr=yhssrp_catchall

Dahl, R.A. (1998). *On Democracy.* New Haven, CT: Yale University Press.

Damousi, J. and Patricia O'Brien, P. (2018). *League of Nations: Histories, Legacies and Impact.* Melbourne: Melbourne University Press.

Devonshire-Ellis, C. (2021). Organisation of Turkic States Rebranded with Intention to Balance Central Asian Politics. *Silk Road Briefing* (30 November 2021). https://www.silkroadbriefing.com/news/2021/11/30/organisation-of-turkic-states-rebranded-with-intention-to-balance-central-asian-politics/

Eggen, Ø. and Roland, K. (2014). *Western Aid at a Crossroads: The End of Paternalism.* Hampshire: Palgrave MacMillan.

Fox, B. (2021). Rich Countries Fail to Agree Aid Price for COVID-19 Vaccine Donations. *Euroactive* (22 December 2021). https://www.euractiv.com/section/health-consumers/news/rich-countries-fail-to-agree-aid-price-for-covid-19-vaccine-donations/?_ga=2.88289563.147350542.1643519807-1689712008.1643519807

Gavi (the vaccine alliance) (2022). COVAX Crosses Milestone of 500 Million Donated Doses Shipped to 105 Countries. https://www.developmentaid.org/#!/news-stream/post/137528/covax-500-million-donated-doses?utm_source=Newsletter&utm_medium=Email&utm_campaign=NewsDigest&token=d95be861-06e8-11ea-8cc5-52540068df95

Gevorgyan, S. (2022). Uneven Progress Towards Covid-19 Vaccination Around the World. *Development Aid News* (27 January 2022). https://www.developmentaid.org/#!/news-stream/post/136702/covid-19-vaccination-around-the-world?utm_source=Newsletter&utm_medium=Email&utm_campaign=NewsDigest&token=d95be861-06e8-11ea-8cc5-52540068df95

Goldhill, O. (2021). 'Naively Ambitious': How COVAX Failed on Its Promise to Vaccinate the World. *Statnews* (8 October 2021). https://www.statnews.com/2021/10/08/how-covax-failed-on-its-promise-to-vaccinate-the-world/

Habermas, J. (1973a). *Legitimationsprobleme im Spätkapitalismus.* Frankfurt am Main: Suhrkamp.

Habermas, J. (1973b). *Legitimation Crisis.* Boston, MA: Beacon Press.

Habermas, J. (1985). *The Theory of Communicative Action: Lifeworld and System; A Critique of Functionalist Reason* (vol. 2). Boston, MA: Beacon Press.

Habermas, J. (2021). Corona und der Schutz des Lebens Zur Grundrechtsdebatte in der pandemischen Ausnahmesituation. [Transl. *Corona and the Protection of Life on the Fundamental Rights Debate in the Pandemic Emergency Situation*]. Blaetter (September 2021). https://www.blaetter.de/ausgabe/2021/september/corona-und-der-schutz-des-lebens

Hass, R. (2021). How China Is Responding to Escalating Strategic Competition with the US. *China Leadership Monitor.* https://www.brookings.edu/articles/how-china-is-responding-to-escalating-strategic-competition-with-the-us/

Held, D. and Koenig-Archibugi, M. (Eds.). (2005). *Global Governance and Public Accountability.* Oxford: Blackwell.

Jakupec, V. (2020). Multilateral Foreign Aid and the Shadow of Cold War II. In Jakupec, V., Kelly, M., and Makuwira, J. (Eds.), *Rethinking Multilateralism in Foreign Aid: Beyond the Neoliberal Hegemony.* Oxford/New York: Routledge, pp. 195–214.

Kissinger, H. (2015). *World Order: Reflections on the Character of Nations and the Course of History.* London: Penguin Press.

Lamoreaux, N. and Ian Shapiro, I. (Eds.) (2019). *The Bretton Woods Agreements.* New Haven, CT and London: Yale University Press.

Marcuse, H. (2002). *One-Dimensional Man: Studies in the Ideology of Advanced Industrial Society.* Milton Park and New York: Routledge.

Nye, J. (2011). *The Future of Power.* New York: PublicAffairs

OECD (2018). *Global Outlook on Financing for Sustainable Development 2019: Time to Face the Challenge.* Paris: OECD Publishing. https://doi.org/10.1787/9789264307995-en.

OECD (2020a). *The Impact of the Coronavirus (COVID-19) Crisis on Development Finance.* Paris: OECD (24 June 2020). https://oecd.org/coronavirus/policy-responses/the-impact-of-the-coronavirus-covid-19-crisis-on-development-finance-9de00b3b/

OECD (2020b). *COVID-19 and Africa: Socio-economic Implications and Policy Responses.* Paris: OECD Publishing. http://www.oecd.org/coronavirus/policy-responses/covid-19-and-africa-socio-economic-implications-and-policy-responses-96e1b282

Offe, C. (1984). *Contradictions of the Welfare State.* London: Hutchinson.

Okunola, A. (2021). COVID-19 Vaccine Nationalism Puts World on Brink of 'Catastrophic Moral Failure'. *Global Citizen* (19 January 2021). https://www.globalcitizen.org/en/content/covid-19-vaccine-nationalism-failure-tedros-who/#!

Organski, A.F.K. (1958). *World Politics.* New York: Knopf.

OTS (Organisation of Turkic States) (2021). Turkic Council Reforms into Organization of Turkic States. *TRTWORLD.* https://cms.trtworld.com/turkey/turkic-council-reforms-into-organization-of-turkic-states-51608

Paul, T.V. (2021). Globalization, deglobalization and reglobalization: adapting liberal international order. *International Affairs*, Vol. 97 (5), pp. 1599–1620. https://doi.org/10.1093/ia/iiab072

Rajan, R.G. and Zingales, L. (2004). *Saving Capitalism from the Capitalists: Unleashing the Power of Financial Markets to Create Wealth and Spread Opportunity.* Princeton, NJ: Princeton University Press.

Rectenwald, M. (2021). What Is the Great Reset? *Hillsdale College*. https://freedomlibrary.hillsdale.edu/programs/cca-ii-the-great-reset/what-is-the-great-reset

Reinhart, C.M. and Rogoff, K.S. (2011). *This Time Is Different: Eight Centuries of Financial Folly*. Princeton, NJ/Oxford: Princeton University Press.

Riedmüller, B. and Mc Elheny, G. (1977). Crisis as Crisis of Legitimation: A Critique of J. Habermas's Concept of Political Crisis Theory. *International Journal of Politics*, Vol. 7 (2), pp. 83–117.

Schwab, K. and Malleret, T. (2020). *Covid-19: The Great Reset*. Geneva: Forum Publishing.

Seneviratne, K. (2022). Geopolitical Battle In South Pacific Heats Up: China Prepares To Send Police Officers To Solomon Islands. *Eurasia Review* (7 January 2022). https://www.eurasiareview.com/04012022-geopolitical-battle-in-south-pacific-heats-up-china-prepares-to-send-police-officers-to-solomon-islands/

Sommerer, T. and Agné, H. (2018). Consequences of Legitimacy in Global Governance. In J. Tallberg, K. Bäckstrand, and J. A. Scholte (Eds.), *Legitimacy in Global Governance: Sources, Processes, and Consequences* (pp. 153–168). Oxford: Oxford University Press.

Stein, F. (2021). Risky Business: COVAX and the Financialization of Global Vaccine Equity. *Globalization and Health*, Vol. 17, 112.

Tallberg, J. and Zürn, M. (2019). The Legitimacy and Legitimation of International Organizations: Introduction and Framework. The Legitimacy and Legitimation of International Organizations: Introduction and Framework. *Review of International Organisations*, Vol. 14, pp. 581–606.

The Straits Times (2022). Top China Diplomat to Visit Sri Lanka as Forex Crisis Deepens. *The Straits Times* (7 January 2022). https://www.straitstimes.com/asia/south-asia/top-china-diplomat-to-visit-sri-lanka-as-forex-crisis-deepens\

The Zimbabwe Mail (2022). Ethiopian Crisis: China Regains Grip on Horn of Africa, as the Battered US Flees. Staff Reporter, *The Zimbabwe Mail* (7 January 2022), Harare.

Tooze, A. (2020). The COVID-19 Shock: Crisis as Usual or Something New. *Lecture Presented at Summer Academy 2020 for Pluralist Economics*. https://www.youtube.com/watch?v=yJnZGRlwf1Y

United Nations (2022). Not a Moment to Lose, in Race to Meet Sustainable Development Goals: Guterres. *Development Aid* (11 February 2022). https://www.developmentaid.org/#!/news-stream/post/137846/sustainable-development-goals-human-rights?utm_source=Newsletter&utm_medium=Email&utm_campaign=NewsDigest&token=d95be861-06e8-11ea-8cc5-52540068df95

United Nations Association of Australia (2017). *The United Nations and the Rules-based International Order*. Canberra City: UNAA.

University of Cambridge (2022). The Great Reset: Democratic Attitudes, Populism, and the Pandemic (18 January 2022). https://scitechdaily.com/the-great-reset-support-for-populist-politics-collapsed-globally-during-the-covid-pandemic/

Wadman, M. (2021). Critics Decry Access, Transparency Issues with Key Trove of Coronavirus Sequences. *Science Magazine* (10 March, 2021). https://genomics.ucsc.edu/2021/03/11/critics-decry-access-transparency-issues-with-key-trove-of-coronavirus-sequences/

Wintour, P. (2020). Covid-19 Will Devastate Poorest Nations if West Does Not Act, Warns UN. *The Guardian* (17 July 2020). https://www.theguardian.com/world/2020/jul/16/covid-19-may-devastate-poorest-nations-if-west-does-not-act-warns-un

Wright, R. (2022). Russia and China Unveil a Pact Against America and the West. *The New Yorker* (7 February 2022).

Zelli, F. (2018). Effects of Legitimacy Crises in Complex Global Governance. In J. Tallberg, K. Bäckstrand, and J.A. Scholte (Eds.), *Legitimacy in Global Governance: Sources, Processes, and Consequences* (pp. 169–188). Oxford: Oxford University Press.

6

PANDEMIC SHOCK AND RECESSION

The adequacy of anti-crisis measures and the role of development assistance

Leonid Grigoryev and Alexandra Morozkina

Introduction

The shock of the COVID-19 pandemic severely disrupted global sustainable development plans in 2020–2021 and affected all of the sustainable development goals (SDGs). Unexpected shocks of such magnitude require a fast-track analysis, decision making, and resource allocation – first of all as a 'triage' operation. Subsequently, global society needs to adjust and sometimes develop new long-term strategies and, collectively, make thoughtful financial decisions. Thus, promotion of international development cooperation as a mechanism targeting the resolution of developing countries' problems can help overcome the fallout of the COVID-19 crisis.

Assistance provided by developed countries constitutes an important source for financing of recipients' development projects, particularly for the countries that have no access to international capital markets. Sometimes donors may contribute more than a third of a small country's gross domestic product (GDP) and over US$500 per capita annually. That is why the survival of some countries hinges upon international assistance, particularly against the background of decreased remittances and foreign direct investment inflows.

However, one of the main outcomes of this crisis is increased inequality, within and between countries. As developed countries have been focusing on their own paths out of recession, and their domestic fiscal stimuli increased on a unique scale, preliminary data show that some donor countries actually reduced their aid allocations. The money was redirected toward national vaccine development funds, which is by no means important, but not directly for the developing countries.

Of course, it was hard to expect an immediately dramatic increase of funding at the same time that developed nations' domestic revenues were falling. It means that financial funds for development aid shifted down in relative terms and

DOI: 10.4324/9781003273844-6

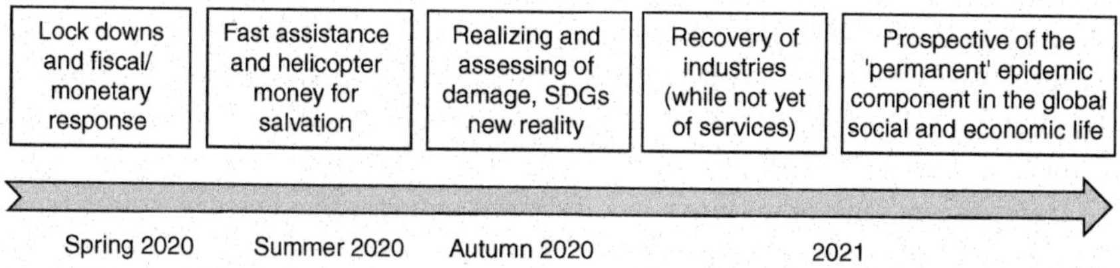

FIGURE 6.1 Timeline of the challenges for international society related to COVID-19.

were not sufficient to meet increased demand. Thus, it is important to compare increased needs and available resources to understand whether they are a part of a historical trend in the development sphere or a 'new normal' and to formulate clearer recommendations for international assistance policies.

The challenges for international society discussed above evolved from the short-term analysis and measures of deeper layers of problems for adaptation to current and possible future crises. Throughout 2021, continuous mutations of the COVID-19 virus and insufficient vaccine protection (quantitatively and qualitatively) have opened the prospect of a 'permanent' epidemic component (stream) in global social and economic life (Figure 6.1). Accordingly, changing dangers for humankind from an evolving cycle of pandemic to recession to new waves of infections, the focus of our study considers the deeper layers of problems for adapting to current and possible future crises.

The first section of this chapter explores the problems and challenges of official development assistance (ODA) as an anti-crisis tool. The second section is devoted to an analysis of the increased demand for assistance and the effect of the crisis on progress toward the SDGs. The third section considers social inequality as a hindering factor to effectiveness of the steps to counter the crises.

ODA as an anti-crisis device

In times of global macroeconomic crisis, financial aid plays an important role. At first, the major problem is to provide support for a number of affected small countries, or less developed countries with big losses of income, especially labor remittances (Bondarenko, 2020). But in the longer term, the key problem is the restoration of growth and a return to the development path.

It has been theoretically substantiated that development aid provided by developed countries may insure recipients against macroeconomic shocks (Pallage *et al.*, 2006), but empirical research indicates that real-life scenarios can vary greatly. Some studies have shown that during prior crises, 'development aid helped mitigate the outflow of private capital and alleviate the effects of economic recession' (Dang, 2009, p. 2). This opinion is illustrated by the Asian crisis of 1997–1998 when affected countries received almost US$100 billion in the shape of loans and grants provided by donors through multilateral and bilateral channels for aid distribution. Similarly, ODA facilitated Mexico's recovery after the 1994–1995 crisis. Further, other studies demonstrate the absence of counter-cyclicity in ODA, that is, the increase of ODA during shocks in recipient countries in order to counter the crisis. Thus, when recipient countries are in recession, aid volume may not increase, and in some cases, it could actually decrease. For example, Bulir and Hamann (2008) explore the correlation between GDP growth and aid volume using data from 76 recipient countries over the period of 1975–2003. They conclude that when a recipient country is experiencing a drop in its GDP, the likelihood of it obtaining additional aid is in the 5–30% range, whereas the probability of aid being reduced under similar conditions is commensurate – in the 10–20% range (Bulir and Hamann, 2008, pp. 2060–2061). According to their findings, periods of significant aid growth rarely coincide with periods characterized by a drop in GDP.

During COVID-19 recession, difficulties exhibited by recipient countries included increased demand for development assistance caused by (1) an 8% decline in export revenues (10% – in the least developed countries); (2) a drop in the volume of foreign investment, in particular, 17% decrease in the inflows without China; and (3) a decrease of the remittances to emerging economies by 1.6% (WB, 2021a).

Multiple studies analyzing economic cycles have identified various effects on donor decisions on aid distribution. Some researchers state that crises lead to a decrease in aid allocated to developing countries (Dabla-Norris *et al.*, 2015; Morozkina, 2019) because 'governments of donor countries are forced to redirect funds allocated for development assistance to the resolution of domestic issues, in particular, coverage of unemployment benefits and financing of large-scale infrastructure programs' (Dang, 2009, p. 3). Others identify how increased donor budget deficits and national debt (Faini, 2006) and output gaps (Bertoly *et al.*, 2008) adversely affect the quantity of aid provided. And most importantly, in the majority of cases, ODA tends to decline during the first year of a crisis (Hallet, 2009; Frot, 2009).

At the same time, studies analyzing assistance prior to 2000 (a period characterized by 'aid fatigue') and in the early part of the 21st century feature rising donor activities and wide inclusion of development assistance issues in the global governance framework. For example, the Organisation for Economic Co-operation and Development (OECD) (2021a, p. 4) found that '2000–2010 was the most generous decade for ODA'. During COVID-19 crisis, the first response from bilateral and multilateral donors was large compared with previous periods. In April 2020, in view of the unfolding pandemic crisis, members of the Development Assistance Committee (DAC) published a joint statement promising to 'strive to protect their [DAC members'] ODA budgets' (DAC OECD, 2020). After that, total amount of DAC aid increased by 10% in 2020 comparing to 2019, reaching US$161 billion (and by 3.5% in grant equivalent). The 0.7% goal (a long-term commitment accepted by DAC members in 1970 (UN, 1970), has been reached and even surpassed in Sweden (1.14%), Norway

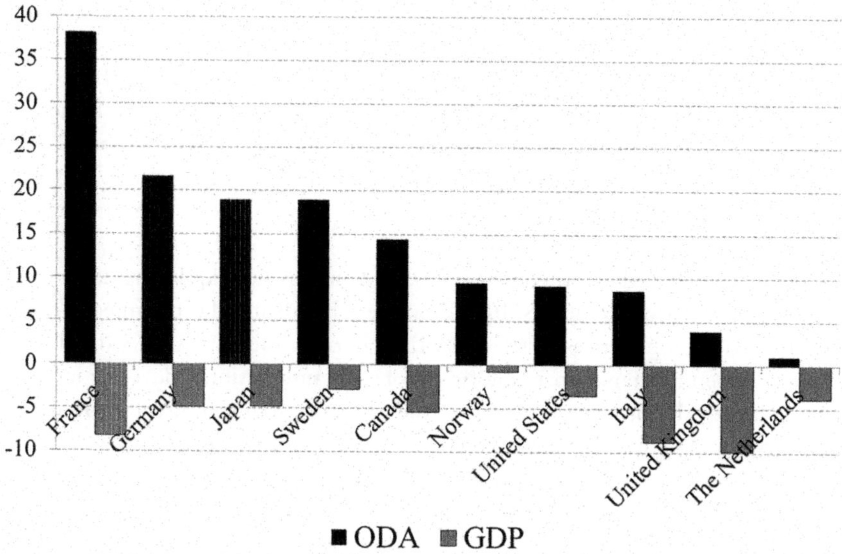

FIGURE 6.2 ODA and GDP growth (in real terms), 2020–2019, %.

(1.11%), Luxembourg (1.02%), Germany (0.73%), Denmark (0.73%), and the UK (0.7%). ODA growth at the same time was not related to the economic performance of the donor (OECD, 2021). During the pandemic, all countries experienced GDP decline, although some of them, despite unfavorable conditions, managed to increase development assistance levels (outlined in Figure 6.2).

Some of the largest donors (such as the USA and Japan) declared an increase in their ODA budgets when the recovery of their economies commenced in 2021. On the contrary, the UK announced a temporary decrease in ODA even below the psychologically important level of 0.7% of gross national income (GNI) to 0.5% of GNI in 2021. The International Monetary Fund (IMF) quickly stepped in at the beginning of the crisis. Starting from March 2020, the IMF approved loans to 84 countries with a total amount of US$109 billion and also extended the capacity of the Catastrophe Containment and Relief Trust to 29 of the fund's poorest and most vulnerable members (World Bank, 2021b). The World Bank has made available US$14 billion through the Fast-track Facility and US$20 billion to help developing countries finance the purchase and distribution of COVID-19 vaccines (World Bank, 2021c). Further, Bondarenko (2020, p. 63) highlights the strong financial aid provided by international organizations to Central Asian and South Caucasian countries to address the effects of COVID-19. Generally, the reaction of bilateral donors can be seen as usual, while multilateral organizations' reaction was much stronger as well as the needs for assistance due to the scope of the shock.

In general, we may agree on the stability of donors in their traditional obligations. However, the scope and complexity of global needs have increased dramatically during the COVID-19 pandemic: as per OECD estimates, SDGs financing gap increased up to US$3.7 trillion in 2020 (OECD, 2021a). Both these trends – small increase in assistance and large increase in development financing needs – lead to decline in the relative capacity of the ODA. Especially unfair the situation looks when paying attention to geographical distribution of assistance: share of low-income countries as recipients fell by 3.5% (to US$25 billion) (OECD, 2021b). Naturally – as one could expect – the priority of ODA had shifted to healthcare and medical needs (especially vaccination) during the pandemic (IHME, 2021).

However, it shoud be noted that the record amounts of aid during 2020 were negligible in relation to the US$16 trillion spent by advanced economies to combat domestic consequences of the COVID-19 crisis. Table 6.1 shows the differences between assistance to domestic 'poor' and international development for the ten largest donors. By comparison, the average amount of fiscal stimulus for the low-income countries (based on available data for 24 countries) was 3% of GDP. Preliminary estimates show that implementation of a 0.7% of GNI goal by all donors would have mobilized an additional US$189 billion for international assistance aimed at combating COVID-19, distributing vaccines, and addressing poverty (Rivera and Harcourt, 2021).

The extent of fiscal stimulus deployed within developed countries in 2020 demonstrates the magnitude of the possible financial mobilization. Generally, the higher the amount of inflow from monetary authorities (average of 8.2% of GDP for 13 countries with GDP per capita above US$45,000), the lower the decline of real personal consumption (Grigoryev *et al.*, 2021). Domestic fiscal stimuli had probably saved the developed countries (and the rest of the world) from a much

TABLE 6.1 Development assistance, fiscal stimulus, and decline in consumption of the developed countries, 2020

Country	*ODA, % GDP*	*ODA, %, year over year*	*Fiscal measures, % GDP*	*Final consumption, %, year over year*
France	0.6	38.1	10.7	–6.0
Germany	0.8	21.6	11.0	–3.5
Japan	0.3	18.9	20.7	–5.6
Sweden	1.2	18.9	10.9	–3.2
Canada	0.3	14.4	18.5	–4.7
Norway	1.2	9.4	4.2	–4.3
United States	0.2	9.0	25.5	–3.9
Italy	0.2	8.6	8.9	–7.8
United Kingdom	0.7	3.9	16.8	–9.9
Netherlands	0.6	1.0	6.1	–3.9
High-income countries, average	**0.35**	**9.2**	**10.6**	**–3.6**

Source: OECD (2021b), IMF (2021b), and WB (2021a).

deeper economic recession. But it is understandable that these steps had created more debts and potentially a problem in the case of reemerging inflation.

The slow and relatively insufficient response to the COVID-19 crisis by traditional donors provided an opportunity for emerging powers such as Brazil, Russia, India, China, and South Africa (BRICS) to play a bigger role in the international development assistance framework. Given that recipient structures and sectorial distribution of aid are more flexible in case of new donors (especially if operating outside the structural adjustment requirements of the World Bank and IMF), it allowed BRICS to fulfill existing agreements and simultaneously mobilize resources for combating COVID-19 in a more nuanced and timely fashion.

BRICS countries, especially China and Russia, have already shown a readiness to provide leadership on global issues and provide beneficial and well-timed international development aid. Thus, the New Development Bank (NDB), a BRICS-led development finance institution, which is often compared with the traditional Bretton Woods institutions, granted a well-timed and effective loan to its members. It approved the first NDB Emergency Assistance Program in Combating COVID-19 in March 2021 and, soon after the time of writing, is expected to have provided loans to Brazil, China, India, and South Africa, totaling US$10 billion. China and Russia have also taken some bilateral measures aimed at support for other developing countries. For example, Russia has distributed COVID-19 tests, protective and medical equipment, medicine, and medical personnel and directed funds to 46 countries around the world (Shakirov *et al.*, 2020). Apart from bilateral aid, Russia made additional contributions to international organizations such as the United Nations Development Programme, the Red Cross, and the World Health Organization. Further, in May 2020, China announced a US$2 billion aid package for other developing countries to be distributed in 2020–2021, the establishment of a cooperation mechanism of Chinese hospitals with 30 African hospitals, and a debt relief program and promised to make any vaccine developed by China a global public good. Obviously, these measures are similar to humanitarian aid actions taken by traditional donors, but to adopt a leadership position in these aspects of diplomacy, BRICS might aim to present a striking difference to other countries, including scaling up of resources, increasing effectiveness of development assistance, and in transparency.

Thus, if traditional donors follow the historical trend and decrease their ODA volumes in the post-crisis period, it will seriously challenge the world's ability to get on a sustainable development path in the near future. In this case, BRICS nations, which often position themselves as representatives of emerging countries, have an opportunity to increase their role in global governance, although it depends on their ability to develop an ambitious agenda in development assistance sphere and show an example of effective and beneficial post-crisis development aid.

Challenges to SDGs, focus on SDG 3

The conventional reaction of the donor countries and development cooperation system changed in response to the dramatic challenges of the 'new normal', and today we see the necessary realigning of the general norms of the SDGs with urgent global challenges. Until 2019, the international community appeared optimistic about the then present course of events (based on the UN National Voluntary SDG reports). Discussions relating to the achievement of the SDGs commonly focused on the expected success of the implementation of the SDG agenda by 2030, although, at the same time, achievements on the ground were not impressive in many respects.

Nevertheless, the shock caused by the COVID-19 pandemic changed the anticipated trajectory, disrupting the SDGs and creating a new checklist of problems to address and subsequently the SDGs, with special attention for the damage done to their progress by the ensuing shocks. For example, the year 2020 demonstrated the unsustainability of some of the results that had been achieved thus far (Sachs *et al.*, 2021). Further, the global average index measuring performance of countries toward the SDGs declined in 2020 for the first time since 2015, and the pandemic has already severely affected the first goal (SDG 1, end poverty in all its forms everywhere) as a number of the people living on less than US$1.90 per day increased by more than 80 million people, while at the same time their proportion of the world population grew from 8.7% in 2019 to 9.6% in 2020 (WB, 2021a). Other goals surely were also severely affected, although for most of them the data are not readily available. Nevertheless, SDG 3 (good health and well-being) seems to be no longer achievable with the decline in life expectancy during 2020 in most European countries (EC, 2021). Target 3.3, 'By 2030, end … epidemics … and communicable disease', appears to be inconsistent with present realities (UN, 2015), especially given the growing number of COVID-19 deaths from 1.8 million in 2020 to 4.8 million in 2021 (Our world in data, 2021).

SDG 4 (quality education) will also require correcting given mass school closures last year and the effects on education, which are otherwise yet to be realized. For example, in April 2020, schools in 173 countries were closed due to lockdown measures, and in 7 more countries, schools were only partially open (UNESCO, 2021). Given differences in access to digital education, severely affected inequality within and between countries was also a factor in reducing accessibility to education (SDG 10, reduced inequalities).

In addition to the above, SDG 8 (decent work and economic growth) showed a negative performance with rising global unemployment, up from 5.4% in 2019 to 6.5% in 2020 (WB, 2021a). SDG 13 (climate action), which at first was seen as a positive impact of lockdowns, also did not fare better than others in the end, with daily CO2 emissions eventually increasing and overcoming pre-crisis levels no later than the beginning of 2021, and in sum being much higher than expected. Total CO2 emissions in 2020 were only 5.4% lower than in 2019 (Liu, 2021).

The overall effect of the crisis has been described as 'catastrophic' (UN, 2021), and it has increased the financing gap for developing countries to overcome the crisis and also to achieve the SDGs by at least 50%, amounting to US$3.7 trillion in 2020 (OECD, 2021a). IMF has also demonstrated the concern about the vaccination gap (IMF, 2021c, pp. 2–3).

Given the potential for present conditions relating to COVID-19 to become endemic, and ultimately creating a 'new normal', scholars such as Bobylev and Grigoryev (2020), Grigoryev and Medzhidova (2020), and Grigoryev *et al.* (2021) have proposed some amendments to SDGs. They suggest that it is necessary to strengthen the concept of the value of human life in the SDGs and propose two options: first, transforming SDG 3 (health) to include health-related indicators from other SDGs in it, e.g. redistributive impact of fiscal policies (target 10.4), which among other means access to healthcare facilities; second, creating an additional SDG in light of the concept of the value of human life and the risk of epidemics and new diseases (Bobylev and Grigoryev, 2020).

To explain, for a long time, the differences between national healthcare systems reflected the institutional settings of societies and taxation systems. Today, at the time of the COVID-19 pandemic, it is concerning that despite uneven performance of healthcare systems in developed countries (and we are not talking about developing countries) at the time of the pandemic, there is no public call for review of the abovementioned financial and institutional settings of health care in the new environment. Of course, it is hard to start such an overhaul in the midst of the ongoing crisis. But the absence of debates on creating of more adequate systems in the future looks strange while understandable from the viewpoint of vested interests in the huge existing healthcare systems: state (state budgets), private financing, companies providing medical drugs, etc. From this viewpoint, and as seen in Table 6.2, more questions are raised than answers were provided. Huge differences in healthcare expenditures per capita among the global community have not given protection from COVID-19 infections. All countries and medical organizations are doing their best (for the moment) to combat the pandemic, while the social and financial problems look deeper than just managerial and budgeting issues. Unexpectedly, the USA and UK have also relatively high rates of deaths during these two years, which are close to the COVID-19 mortality rates reported in Brazil and Mexico. Such correlations are worthy of a call for a review of traditional views on health systems as they relate to the SDGs. At the same time, such adverse results partly explain the difference between the scale of domestic and international reaction of donor countries, as advanced economies struggled with their own difficulties.

Moreover, the shock created by the COVID-19 pandemic, including its infectious waves and the difficulties in organizing and financing effective anti-COVID medical treatment and vaccination of masses of affected people, provides an impetus to reconsider the optimal financing and institutional relations within healthcare systems. Figure 6.3 demonstrates the rather high rates of public expenditures per capita in developed countries (high-income and upper-middle-income

TABLE 6.2 Differences in healthcare systems, latest available data[a] (2018 for expenditures and October 2021 for COVID-19 effect)

	Healthcare expenditures, current USD per capita, 2018	*Cumulative number of COVID-19 deaths, % to population*	*Cumulative number of confirmed COVID-19 cases, % to population*	*Share of people fully vaccinated, % of population October 2021*
High-income countries, *incl.*	**5 665**	**0.14**	**8.4**	**63**
United States	10 624	0.22	13.7	56
United Kingdom	4 315	0.21	12.9	67
France	4 690	0.18	10.7	67
Germany	5 472	0.11	5.3	66
Upper-middle-income countries, *incl.*	**532**	**0.08**	**3.1**	**58**
Russia	609	0.15	5.6	33
China	501	0.00	0.0	80
Mexico	520	0.22	2.9	40
Brazil	848	0.28	10.2	51
Lower-middle-income countries, *incl.*	**98**	**0.03**	**1.8**	**18**
India	73	0.03	2.5	21
Ukraine	228	0.15	6.4	16
Philippines	137	0.04	2.5	23
Low-income countries, *incl.*	**35**	**0.01**	**0.2**	**1.5**
Ethiopia	24	0.01	0.3	0.9

[a] All countries in the World Bank database by income groups (and averages).

Source: World Bank (2021a) and Our World in Data (2021).

groups) in spite of the long way to private care. Figure 6.3 also shows the overall tendencies of the 21st century of decreasing public social expenditures and their 'privatization' (Sinyavskaya, 2022). At the same time, we must be cautious about the actual meaning of aggregate country-based indicators, especially in terms of social structure and inequality inside all countries, and especially of developed ones as benchmarks for developing ones. The actual access of populations with urgent needs for medical services to combat the COVID-19 pandemic depended on some important cross-national factors: the organization of the health system, coverage of households, and impact of the welfare level of the country and finally (but crucially important) on income inequality.

Currently, healthcare systems in developed and developing countries are operating close to capacity in many countries. In particular, the deficit of care can be observed with the poor and persons living in problematic housing conditions

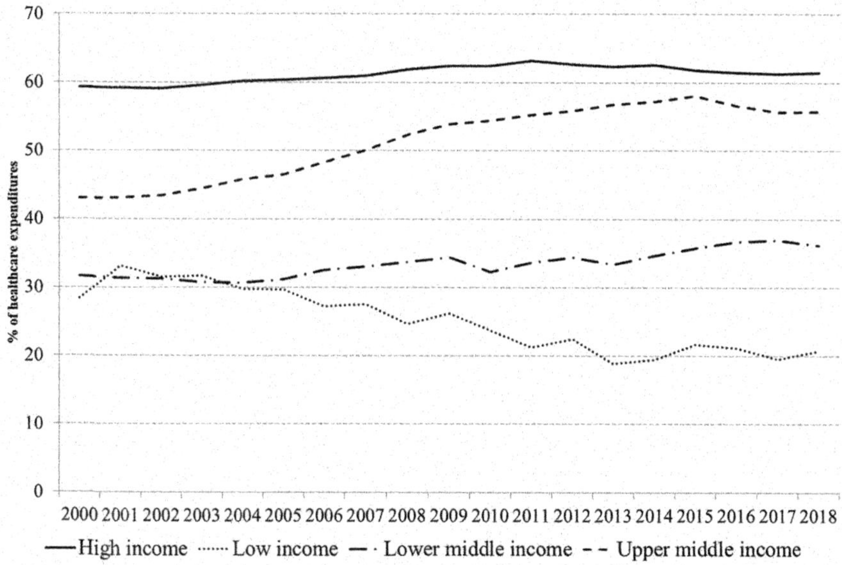

FIGURE 6.3 Public healthcare expenditures, % to total healthcare expenditures.

(with difficulty for separation of infected) (Khanijahani *et al.*, 2021). Support for those from low socio-economic backgrounds in many cases is based predominantly on vaccinations. However, as mentioned above, in current form, SDG 3 calls for elimination of all epidemics till 2030 and, thus, should be probably supplemented by at least the following points: citing pandemics as a major danger, providing more equitable access to medical services, and enhancing the global capabilities and mobility to render emergency relief to the poor domestically as well as in other countries. This choice of spending funds at home or abroad was always politically difficult, especially in the recession phases of business cycles with their tightening of budget incomes. In the current COVID-19 pandemic, competing political objectives cause particular difficulties in rationalizing aid funding. This is further magnified by issues concerning climate change, which is beginning to draw on development aid resources. Be this as it may be inevitable that global healthcare and medical systems need to be overhauled to create more reliable and equal protection against new pandemics and epidemics in the future.

Any review of healthcare systems must address at least two major obvious controversies stemming from social and business origins. First, rich strata within populations have accumulated the highest percentage of capital and thus are generally able to acquire adequate medical care and protection. Second, the entrenched interests of healthcare bureaucracies stem from business interests and the otherwise well-known interests of pharmacological companies. Most noticeable is the relative bias in the critique of the COVID-19 performances by countries based not on managerial or financial specifics but on political decision making, especially on the painful continuous process of lock-and-open (COVID restrictions and their easening).

It is beyond the scope of this chapter to evaluate healthcare systems in a significant number of countries. However, to illustrate our point, US healthcare data will be used as an *exempli gratia*. According to Table 6.2, in 2018, healthcare expenditure per capita in the USA was US$10,624. But data from the National Institute for Health Care Management (NIHCM) (2017) provide a sobering correction: 50% of the less affluent members of the population represent only 3% of all expenditures. After improving the situation for the most vulnerable after the implementation of Medicare, this level of expenditure for poor appears close to those in Russia and Brazil. Probably it tells us a lot about the actual functioning of the healthcare systems in 2020–2021. However, now we see more attention being paid to the problem of medical care in the USA, reflected in the idea that 'President Biden believes that health care is a right, not a privilege' (White House, 2021). The focus of the current US administration is on high drug prices and various ways of reducing them, especially for older people. Other than this particular policy priority, no major changes in the US system are expected any time soon.

Since it is too early to evaluate the performance of the US healthcare system in 2020–2021, the two big questions are, first, if it is possible to have a just health care above the actual national level of social equality and, second, if it is possible to secure global health stability at least for infectious diseases in spite of the actual international disparity in the level of development (Grigoryev and Pavlyushina, 2019). So far we do not have a positive answer.

Pandemic, recession, and inequality: SDG 10

The issue of the ongoing battle between governance approaches to addressing the COVID-19 pandemic and ordinary citizens' social life needs to be addressed from some traditional standpoints, in particular: the organization of health care, government–business interactions, and processes for financing needs against social inequality (SDG 10). While generally public opinion and many economists would argue against deep social inequality for economic and moral grounds, there is little discussion on the problem and the potential remedy – namely redistribution of states' funds to poor socio-economic population strata. The bold attempt of Thomas Piketty (Piketty and Saez, 2014) to suggest some steps against inequality has not created much of discussion in this respect. But it appears that the pandemic and the resulting recession of 2020–2021 may add to the research on the theme, including negative effect of crises on inequality (Bodea *et al.*, 2021).

ODA has been a major topic during discussions relating to the COVID-19 crisis, but it does not shed much light on the underlying issues affecting inequality. As previous researchers (Chong, 2009; Herzer and Nunnenkamp, 2012; Younsi, 2018) have shown, ODA has an adverse effect on inequality, mostly because of the prevailing political and economic interests of donor countries and an absence of focus on the needs of the poor. The events of 2020–2021 have highlighted the need to address the role of inequality as an important factor affecting social and economic lives. We believe that it is time to evaluate success or failure of respective anti-crisis or social programs, not by countries but by large socio-economic strata. A stabilization of wealth (mostly by stock prices revival) of affluent households in 2020 by fiscal and monetary stimuli in developed countries did not mean the same support of less prosperous households (Grigoryev, 2021). Social differentiation of the sources of income and the size of savings may create the conflict of interests between the economic and social objectives. In the 2020–2021 period, the decline of GDP negatively affected developed countries with high share of services (recreation, tourism, etc.) – like France, Italy, and Spain. But throughout the developed world, low-wage employment in service industries suffered the most.

The problem of inequality between countries was discussed in various aspects in the article by Grigoryev and Pavlyushina (2018). First, they observed divergences of GDP per capita in time between countries of different income groups. The study for the period of 1992–2019 provided a rather pessimistic conclusion of slow deviation of seven clusters from each other (groups of countries selected for 1992 by GDP per capita). No visible conversion of countries' level of development by the growth may be seen in medium term or in the time span for Energy Transition, hopefully set as 2050 by Paris Agreement of 2015 of Climate Change Prevention, and other decisions (e.g. Glasgow decisions of 2021). Actually, here is no focus on conversion of levels of development: catching up is not a part of the agenda on Energy Transition (Grigoryev and Medzhidova, 2020). Recently there were offered some indicators for monitoring success in reducing inequality between countries (Bobylev and Grigoryev, 2020), such as reducing/increasing disparity between 20 leading developed countries and other countries, calculated in 10-year increments, for example, 1990–2000–2019 (years of peaks by business cycles). The same should be measured for spans of GDP per capita levels between the less developed and middle-income countries. The suggested monitoring could give a clearer picture, configuration of issues for the SDG agenda, and also the real budget and investment constraints for countries in the complex process of pursuing multiple important objectives simultaneously in the next decades.

Second, social inequality is growing at the top of the society (10th decile, 100th percent, etc.). Redistribution of income (consumption) in favor of the lower strata may improve Gini coefficients but not the social distance between the rich and the poor. In the case of a double blow – a shock pandemic of COVID-19 in 2020 and a severe recession 2020–2021 – it creates a risk of social instability and actually delays achievement of the SDGs' objectives.

Growing social inequality in the world has been the focus of discussions in recent years (Grigoryev and Pavlyushina, 2019). The current double crisis of 2020–2021 makes social inequality especially visible and highlights that it [needs to be?] addressed at the highest international levels (Guterres, 2020, 2021).

In the respective article (Bobylev and Grigoryev, 2020), the suggestion was to use some quantitative parameters for consideration: the growing share of income (consumption) going to the 1st quintile for the same groups of countries, calculated in five-year increments, and the decreasing share of income going to the 5th quintile, calculated in five-year increments (from levels above 45%). The relative numbers (per a million of citizens) of suicides and homicides by countries may also be added and classified as unfavorable indicators related to social inequality (SDG 10). In particular, homicides are associated with poverty and countries with low and middle income per capita, while suicides with upper- and upper-middle-income countries and strata (Grigoryev and Popovets, 2019).

In the discourse of social inequality, Kuznetz (1955) established the tradition of giving names to theoretical or applied curves (Kuznetz's umbrella curve). Milanovich (2012) created an 'Elephant' for the global distribution of people by income, and Grigoryev and Pavlyushina (2019) created a 'Crocodile' in 2019, which shows the widening income gap between the 10th decile and 2nd quintile along the growing GDP per capita line of countries over time. Now we will address the issue of inequality and the impact of the recession 2020–2021 on inequality by using the abovementioned graphs as instruments.

Kuznetz (1955), in his early work, concluded that there can be an inverted U-shaped relation between income per capita and inequality. The implications of the *Umbrella* curve were brilliant and dynamic: countries were to grow and, with the income per capita growth, were to push social inequality along the umbrella. However, it was built on a limited statistical basis. Indeed, Kuznetz (1955, p. 26) acknowledged that '[t]he paper is perhaps 5 per cent empirical information and 95 per cent speculation, some of it possibly tainted by wishful thinking'. Many researchers, such as Waldenstrom (2015), find it difficult to avoid criticizing Kuznetz's (1955) work and generally come to the conclusion that it lacks a sufficient empirical basis.

Our conclusion from previous studies indicates that we do not see the actual movement of inequality (mainly – the share of 10th decile) along the *Umbrella* curve. In statistical terms, we have many developed countries with relatively low inequality. However, their position on the curve has been defined by level of development, institutions (especially taxation), and traditions. So, generally in the available period of observation, social inequality is characteristically rigid (Grigoryev and Pavlyushina, 2019). Our assessment of the actual dynamic of the share of the 10th decile in income led us to the conclusion of rigidity of the share in most countries in the past three decades. Major fluctuations did not change the general picture. Of course, shares of poor in consumption were higher than in income. It appears that the actual inequality in each country was established on an institutional level at a certain point in the past, including the type of welfare state, taxes, the system of income redistribution, social mobility, and public opinion on poverty and wealth. Formation of such set of institutions of each country some time ago had established the relative indicators, which did not change much upon a time with general welfare growth.

Of course, inequality by assets or by wealth was higher and mostly rigid – i.e. stays the same or does not change widely (Grigoryev and Pavlyushina, 2019). We would like to underline that the stock market's boom and reinvestments of forced savings (instead of services' consumption) of rich strata was a global event (Grigoryev, 2021). Those savings mostly went into shares, financial instrument, and real estate. One may call it a dual outcome: first, it was a way for recovery of financial markets and the economy in general; and second, they were reinvestments of the rich strata with the growth of wealth for rich, so natural outcome probably will be more inequality by assets after the recession.

Second, the approach to the analysis of inequality dynamics of Milanovich was a global view of inequality at the time of the UN millennium development goals and the advancement of global society into the 21st century. However, the so-called Elephant curve demonstrating unequal distribution of income growth for individuals belonging to different income groups (see Milanovic, 2012) has this form actually as a by-product of China's and India's success with high economic growth rates in 2000–2015. Both countries had achieved great success in combatting absolute poverty (Milanovic, 2012) that moved the mass of people from the low strata to the middle of global society, as it is shown in Figure 6.3. Meanwhile, domestic relative measures of inequality stayed generally the same, and the IMF published a special study pointing to the huge increase of relative inequality in China (Jain-Chandra, 2018). The difference between approaches gives the limits for the statistical analysis in this field: high growth in China probably improved the life of the Chinese population but not the indicators of inequality – as the calculated share of the 10th decile in personal income went up above 50%. During the current crisis, the real income of the rich strata was stable or growing worldwide, whereas the income of the poor inside developed countries was temporarily supported at the time of recession but not for long time. However, the poor in the developing world suffered the most. Some possible socio-political consequences were already reflected in the report of the Economist Intelligence Unit (EIU) of October 2021 on risk assessment in 2022 pointing at (see Risk scenario #6): 'Widespread social unrest weighs on the global recovery' (EIU, 2021).

This risk is well-reflected in Figure 6.4 ('Crocodile'), which displays two effects: increasing the absolute income gap between the 10th decile and the 2nd quintile upon a growth of GDP per capita by purchasing power parity (PPP) and also the widening of this gap between 2000 and 2016. For convenience, authors recalculated GDP per capita from countries to deciles and quintiles to make all of the measures comparable (Grigoryev and Salmina, 2013). Authors did not put the 10th decile numbers against the poorest 1st quintile, since these strata receive the main bulk of assistance and redistribution. Also authors could not foresee the character of the current pandemic and the recession in 2020: the rich strata (the high and upper middle strata in some countries) were prevented from consuming services, while the low middle strata and small and medium-sized enterprises (SMEs) (closely tied to the 2nd quintile) were a main source of increased unemployment.

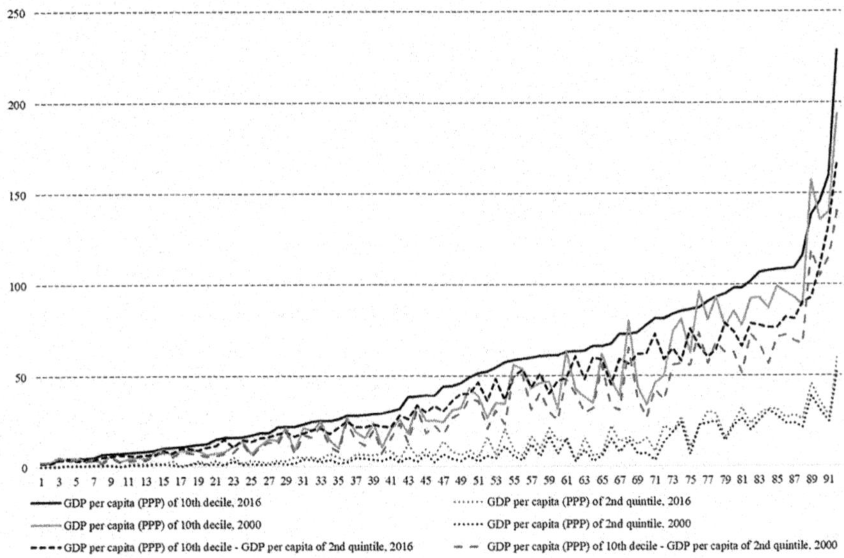

FIGURE 6.4 GDP per capita (PPP) of 10th decile and 2nd quintile, 2000 and 2016, 'Crocodile' curve.

If not for generous fiscal stimuli (respective to countries' resources and political will), the recession would be much deeper and unemployment may have increased to socially and politically unsustainable levels. Thus, we consider the unusual speed and size of the stimuli in developed countries as a positive step. However, emerging economies could not afford similar levels of spending. Given the loss of two years of global development, the consequences differ for different actors. Developed countries are turning to the issues of inflation, debt, and macroeconomic management. Rich strata are rushing to use the period of growth with low interest rates: reinvesting, enjoying capital gains, and managing real estate options. From our observational angle, we expect that some forced savings and fiscal stimuli gave the rich strata a unique opportunity to increase wealth in the phases of recession and recovery, whereas normally they would need to wait a few years before upturn. But as a general result, we may state that the *Crocodile* is opening its jaw wider.

Conclusions

Global affairs in 2020–2021 were unexpected, dangerous, and had an unpredictable character. Socio-economic institutions were taken aback with the overload, and the healthcare systems suffered most and first. Fiscal stimuli, especially those implemented by advanced economies, were in general helpful in limiting the damage and containing the recession. Recovery is ongoing, however, only as an industrial one, with limited recovery of domestic (recreation and catering, etc.) and international (travel and tourism) services. Development assistance in general was not unprecedented and of course not corresponding to the increased demand for the resources, although we cannot blame countries for focusing on their domestic affairs in the first place.

To conclude, the first reaction to the pandemic, including domestic and international support, was arguably valuable and wide. However, we highlight its inadequacy in several fields. First, international assistance to low-income countries was inadequate as the share of this country group in ODA decreased in 2020, which is especially important on the background of increased development financing needs. Second, we raised a concern that the implemented fiscal and monetary measures did less to restore the welfare of certain affected categories of poor inside countries, given the rising unemployment, and will most likely lead to higher inequality. For example, inequality by assets is definitely growing as a result of lockdown and financial stimulus. Third, the health system and long-term measures in the field were inadequate in terms of protection of the population from infectious diseases and access to adequate treatment. Generally, inequality is an obstacle for effective medical treatment and for next steps. Fourth, measures and social systems were inadequate to ensure social security nets for all population stratums.

References

Bertoly S., Cornia G.A., and Manaresi F. (2008). *Aid Effort and its Determinants.* Università degli Studi di Firenze. Working Paper N. 11/2008.

Bobylev S.N., and Grygoryev L.G. (2020). In search of the contours of the post-COVID sustainable development goals: The case of BRICS. *BRICS Journal of economics*, 1, N2. https://doi.org/10.38050/2712-7508-2020-7

Bobylev S., and Solovyeva S. (2017). Sustainable development goals for the future of Russia. *Studies on Russian Economic Development,* 28(3), 259–265.

Bodea C., Houle C., and Kim H. (2021). Do financial crises increase income inequality? *World Development,* 147. https://doi.org/10.1016/j.worlddev.2021.105635

Bondarenko K. (2020). The impact of the COVID-19 pandemic: The case of remittance recipient countries. *International Organisations Research Journal*, 15(3), 109–128 (in English). https://doi.org/10.17323/1996-7845-2020-03-04

Bulir A., and Hamann J. (2008). Volatility of development aid: from the frying pan into the fire? *World Development*, 36(10), 2048–2066.

Chong A., Gradstein M., and Calderon C. (2009). Can foreign aid reduce income inequality and poverty? *Public Choice*, 140, 59–84.

Dabla-Norris E., Minoiu C., and Zanna L.-F. (2015). Business cycle fluctuations, large macroeconomic shocks, and development aid. *World Development*, 69, 44–61.

DAC OECD (2020). *COVID-19 Global Pandemic: Joint Statement by the OECD Development Assistance Committee.* Paris: OECD. https://www.oecd.org/dac/development-assistance-committee/dac-covid-19-statement.htm

Dang H.-A., Knack S., and Rogers H. (2009). *International Aid and Financial Crises in Donor Countries.* World Bank Policy Research working paper no. 5162. Washington, DC: The World Bank Group.

EC (2021). Life expectancy decreased in 2020 across the EU. https://ec.europa.eu/eurostat/web/products-eurostat-news/product/-/asset_publisher/VWJkHuaYvLIN/content/id/12645457/pop_up

EIU (2021). *EIU Risk Outlook 2022: 10 Scenarios that Could Impact Global Growth and Inflation.* https://www.eiu.com/n/10-risk-scenarios-that-could-impact-global-growth-and-inflation-in-2022/

Faini R. (2006). *Foreign Aid and Fiscal Policy.* CEPR discussion paper no. 5721. Washington, DC: Center for Economic and Policy Research, 2006.

Frot E. (2009). Aid and the financial crisis: Shall we expect development aid to fall? *SITE/Stockholm School of Economics*, Stockholm, Sweden (Unpublished manuscript).

Grigoryev L.G., and Salmina A.A. (2013) "Structure" of inequality of the modern world: problems of measurement. *Sotsiologicheskiy Zhurnal = Sociological Journal*, 3, 5–21. (in Russian). https://doi.org/10.19181/socjour.2013.3.395

Grigoryev L.M., Elkina Z.S., Mednikova P.A., Serova D.A., Starodubtseva M.F., and Filippova E.S. (2021). The perfect storm of personal consumption. The perfect storm of personal consumption. *Voprosy Ekonomiki*, (10):27–50. (in Russian). https://doi.org/10.32609/0042-8736-2021-10-27-50

Grigoryev L.M., and Medzhidova D.D. (2020). Global energy trilemma. *Russian Journal of Economics* 6 (2020), 437–462.

Grigoryev L.M., and Pavlyushina V. (2018). Mezhstranovoe neravenstvo: Dinamika i problema stadij razvitiya. *Voprosy Ekonomiki,* 7, 5–29 [International inequality: Dynamic and the problem of stages of development. *Issues of Economics,* 7, 5–29].

Grigoryev L.M., and Pavlyushina V. (2019). Relative social inequality in the world: Rigidity against the economic growth, 1992–2016. *Russian Journal of Economics, 5*(1), 46–66. https://rujec.org/article/35485/

Grigoryev L.M., and Popovets L. (2019). Sociology of individual tragedies. Homicides and suicides: Cross-country cluster analysis. *Russian Journal of Economics, 5*(3), 251–276.

Guterres A. (2020, July 18). *Opening Remarks at Nelson Mandela Lecture: Tackling the Inequality Pandemic: A New Social Contract for a New Era.* https://www.un.org/sg/en/content/sg/speeches/2020-07-18/remarks-nelson-mandela-lecture-tackling-the-inequality-pandemic-new-social-contract-for-new-era

Guterres A. (2021, December 1). *Opening Remarks to the Press with Moussa Faki Mahamat, Chairperson of the African Union Commission, Following the AU-UN Conference.* https://www.un.org/sg/en/node/260948

Hallet M. (2009). *Economic Cycles and Development Aid: What Is the Evidence from the Past?* ECFIN Economic Brief 5, European Commission's Directorate-General for Economic and Financial Affairs, November 2009.

Herzer D., and Nunnenkamp P. (2012). The effect of foreign aid on income inequality: Evidence from panel cointegration. *Structural Change and Economic Dynamics* 23 (2012), 245–255. https://doi.org/10.1016/j.strueco.2012.04.002

IHME (2021) *Financing Global Health 2020: The Impact of COVID-19.* Seattle, WA: IHME, 2021.

IMF (2021a) *World Economic Outlook* [dataset]. IMF. https://www.imf.org/en/Publications/WEO/weo-database/2021/April

IMF (2021b) *Fiscal Monitor Database of Country Fiscal Measures in Response to the COVID-19 Pandemic* [dataset]. IMF. https://www.imf.org/en/Topics/imf-and-covid19/Fiscal-Policies-Database-in-Response-to-COVID-19

IMF (2021c) *Economic Outlook. Recovery During a Pandemic. Health Concerns, Supply, Disruptions, and Price Pressures.* Washington, DC, October. https://www.imf.org/en/Publications/WEO/Issues/2021/10/12/world-economic-outlook-october-2021

Jain-Chandra S., Khor N.M, Mano R., Schauer J., Wingender P., and Zhuang J. (2018). *Inequality in China – Trends, Drivers and Policy Remedies.* IMF Working Paper WP/18/127. https://www.imf.org/en/Publications/WP/Issues/2018/06/05/Inequality-in-China-Trends-Drivers-and-Policy-Remedies-45878

Khanijahani, A., Iezadi, S., Gholipour, K., Azami-Aghdash S., and Naghibi D. (2021). A systematic review of racial/ethnic and socioeconomic disparities in COVID-19. *International Journal for Equity in Health* 20, 248. https://doi.org/10.1186/s12939-021-01582-4

Kuznetz S. (1955). Economic growth and income inequality. *The American Economic Review,* XLV(N1), 1–28

Liu Z. (2021). *Global Daily CO_2 emissions for the year 2020.* Researchgate. https://www.researchgate.net/publication/349759072_Global_Daily_CO_2_emissions_for_the_year_2020

Milanovic B. (2012). *Global Income Inequality by the Numbers: In History and Now.* Policy Research Working Paper No. 6259. World Bank, Washington, DC. https://openknowledge.worldbank.org/handle/10986/12117

Morozkina A.K. (2019) Official Development Aid: Trends of the Last Decade. *World Economy and International Relations, 63*(9), 86–92. https://doi.org/10.20542/0131-2227-2019-63-9-86-92 (in Russian)

NIHCM Foundation (2017, July 17). *The Concentration of Health Care Spending.* https://nihcm.org/publications/the-concentration-of-u-s-health-care-spending

OECD (2021a). Development co-operation during the COVID-19 pandemic: An analysis of 2020 figures and 2021 trends to watch, in *Development Co-operation Profiles,* OECD Publishing, Paris. https://doi.org/10.1787/e4b3142a-en

OECD (2021b) *International Development Statistics (IDS) Online Databases* [dataset]. OECD. https://www.oecd.org/dac/financing-sustainable-development/development-finance-data/idsonline.htm

Our World in Data (2021) *Our World in Data Database* [dataset]. Our World in Data. https://ourworldindata.org/

Pallage, S., Robe, M.A., and Beroube, C. (2006). The potential of foreign aid as insurance. *IMF Staff Papers, 53*(3), 453–475.

Piketty T., and Saez E. (2014). *Le capital au 21e siècle.* http://piketty.pse.ens.fr/fr/capital21c

Rivera J., and Harcourt S. (2021, April 14). Global aid spending in 2020 – What did we learn? *ONE.* https://www.one.org/international/blog/global-aid-spending-2020/

Roine J., and Waldenstrom D. (2015). Long-Run Trends in the Distribution of Income and Wealth. In A. Atkinson, and F. Bourgignon (Eds.), *Handbook of Income Distribution.* Volume 2A. https://doi.org/10.1016/B978-0-444-59428-0.00008-4

Sachs J.D., Kroll C., Lafortune G., Fuller G., and Woelm F. (2021a). *Sustainable Development Report 2021.* Cambridge University Press, Cambridge. https://doi.org/10.1017/9781009106559

Sinyavskaya O. (2022) Jevoljucija roli gosudarstva vseobshhego blagosostojanija [Evolution of Welfare state]. In I. Makarov (Ed.), *Global Economy in the Time of Big Shakeouts.* Moscow: INFRA M, 2022 *(forthcoming)* (in Russian).

Shakirov O.I., Petrosjan M.K, and Solov'ev D.B. (2020) *Gumanitarnaja pomoshh' protiv koronavirusa. Komu i kak pomogala Rossija vo vremja pandemii COVID-19?* [Humanitarian Aid against coronavirus: Whom and how Russia helped during COVID-19 pandemic?] M.: CPUR, 17 pp.

The White House (2021, August 12) *President Biden Calls on Congress to Lower Prescription Drug Prices* [Press release]. https://www.whitehouse.gov/briefing-room/statements-releases/2021/08/12/fact-sheet-president-biden-calls-on-congress-to-lower-prescription-drug-prices/

UN (1970). *International Development Strategy for the 2nd United Nations Development Decade.* UN. https://digitallibrary.un.org/record/201726

UN (2015). *Transforming our world: the 2030 Agenda for Sustainable Development.* UN. https://sdgs.un.org/2030agenda

UN (2021b). *The Sustainable Development Goals Report.* New York: United Nations Publications. https://unstats.un.org/sdgs/report/2021/The-Sustainable-Development-Goals-Report-2021.pdf

UNESCO (2021). *Education: From Disruption to Recovery.* UNCESCO, 1 April. https://en.unesco.org/covid19/educationresponse

World Bank (2021a) *World Development Indicators Database* [dataset]. World Bank. https://databank.worldbank.org/source/world-development-indicators

World Bank (2021b, June 15) World Bank, IMF Launch High-Level Advisory Group on Sustainable and Inclusive Recovery and Growth [Press release]. https://www.worldbank.org/en/news/press-release/2021/06/15/world-bank-imf-launch-high-level-advisory-group-on-sustainable-and-inclusive-recovery-and-growth

World Bank (2021c). *How the World Bank Group Is Helping Countries with COVID-19.* https://www.worldbank.org/en/news/factsheet/2020/02/11/how-the-world-bank-group-is-helping-countries-with-covid-19-coronavirus

Younsi M., Khemili H., and Bechtini M. (2018). Does foreign aid help alleviate income inequality? New evidence from African countries. *International Journal of Social Economics, 46*(4), 549–556.

7

COVAX, VACCINE (INTER) NATIONALISM, AND THE IMPACT ON THE GLOBAL SOUTH EXPERIENCE OF COVID-19

Max Kelly and Mary Ana McGlasson

Introduction

Health governance is a global responsibility, traditionally the domain of World Health Organization (WHO), a specialized agency of the United Nations (UN). WHO provides norms and standards, global action, professional management, financial resource transfer, scientific research capacity, and leadership (Ruger and Yach, 2009, p. 2). Equitable global access to vaccines has been a public health concern since the 2004 H5N1influenza outbreak, where the threat of pandemic necessitated international cooperation, yet no significant progress eventuated through the 2009 H1N1 influenza pandemic. However, the scale and scope of COVID-19 generated renewed energy to create mechanisms to address vaccine access for low- and middle-income countries (LMICs), who are unable to compete economically or politically with higher-income countries (HICs) in the vaccine marketplace.

COVAX is the vaccine pillar of the Access to COVID-19 Tools (ACT) Accelerator, a global collaboration to accelerate development, production, and equitable access to tests, treatments, and vaccines for COVID-19. ACT launched in April 2020, a few weeks into the pandemic, recognizing the need for aggressive action to ensure equitable vaccine access in the certainty that wealthier countries would buy and hoard whatever vaccine doses became available (Ducharme, 2021). COVAX is a unique innovation that presents the opportunity to address a global health crisis in a coordinated, equitable way. As the COVAX slogans states, 'working together saves lives', and 'we are not safe until we are all safe'. Controlling the spread of COVID-19 not only reduces morbidity and mortality, but it also reduces economic impacts and mitigates the virus's ability to mutate and cause further harm.

COVID-19 vaccine distribution remains heavily skewed toward rich countries. As of February 2022, the global vaccination rate varies widely, with

DOI: 10.4324/9781003273844-7

38 countries having at least 75% of their populations fully vaccinated, 105 countries having less than 50%, and a staggering 27 countries with less than 10% fully vaccinated. A total of 10.42 billion vaccine doses have been administered globally, but only 10% of people in lower-income countries (LICs) have received at least one dose (Mathieu *et al.*, 2021). Meanwhile, 1.1 billion booster doses have been administered (Richie *et al.*, 2020). The greatest shortfall is in Africa, where less than 16% are fully vaccinated. As Sidibe (2022) highlights, this equals 1.2 billion people without vaccines.

Vanderslott *et al.* (2021) define vaccine nationalism as 'the pursuit of vaccines in the national interest, for example, through supply agreements or export bans, including where this might be to the detriment of other countries' (n.p.). With COVID-19, higher-income governments have procured and hoarded far more doses than needed and prioritized booster doses for their own above global equity. Moreover, vaccine manufacturers sold more doses than they could realistically produce, and they then determine which countries received vaccines (Aizenman, 2021). The result is that vaccine distribution has often been driven by power, influence, and economics, rather than equity (Fidler, 2021).

In addition, some supply chain issues were exacerbated by demand in manufacturing to protect their own population. For example, the Government of India temporarily banned vaccine export shipments in March 2021 due to a domestic COVID-19 crisis. COVAX was heavily dependent on these shipments, yet this is only one part of a complex story of vaccine distribution, driven primarily by Organisation for Economic Co-operation and Development countries.

COVAX highlights the challenges of multilateral cooperation and solidarity in a global pandemic, where risk is decreased by collective efforts to vaccinate. The success of COVAX, as one key pillar to address COVID-19, is predicated on the assumption that rich and powerful nations are incentivized to cooperate effectively. The shortcomings of COVAX may hold insights for future multilateral mechanisms.

This chapter adopts a 'critical' discourse in contrasting the donors' and recipients' positions. It explores the political economy of vaccines, focusing on soft power and vaccine diplomacy, and the impacts of vaccine diplomacy on global cooperation, specifically the COVAX facility and its ineffectiveness in ensuring vaccine equity.

The chapter commences with brief analysis of global cooperation, through reflection on soft power, diplomacy, and the role of a global pandemic in foregrounding vaccines as new tools of diplomacy. This provides the context for a brief description of COVAX and how it was envisioned, then shifting to assess successes and blockages for COVAX in meeting vaccine distribution targets. The chapter draws on a necessarily brief analysis of key players related to vaccine nationalism and diplomacy, namely US and China, and positions this within an analysis of specific country responses to COVID, including tensions between bilateral and multilateral arrangements, soft power, and the differing narratives of multilateralism inherent in diverse responses. The analysis then moves to interactions between donors, COVAX, and three case study nations, Pakistan, Vietnam, and Malawi. The chapter concludes with a review of the implications for global multistakeholder partnerships provided by the COVAX case study and the resulting impacts on the Global South.

Overall, this analysis highlights enduring power differentials, where even a global pandemic inspires calculated attempts for economic and political gain.

Power, politics, and global cooperation

Power and politics as key determinants of health have gained significant traction (cf. Ottersen *et al.*, 2014; Paxton and Youde, 2019). The 2015 Commission on Global Governance for Health emphasized that politics was a root cause of health inequality, both within and between countries. Unsurprisingly, politics and economics are dramatically shaping the specific case of COVID-19 vaccine access, with vaccine nationalism an enduring issue. The director of WHO, Dr Tedros Adhanom Ghebreyesushas, has voiced concerns about vaccine nationalism. He frequently argues that wealthy nations should be compelled by self-interest, highlighting that global cooperation to achieve high rates of vaccination globally will reduce potential mutations benefitting rich countries, a strategic but longer-term impact.

Vaccine nationalism is driven by a government prioritizing its own interests (Vanderslott *et al.*, 2021). The short-term national interest inherent in the race to hoard vaccines and other COVID-related supplies is an expected dilemma, where there are limited incentives to go against nationalist principles (Bollyky and Bown, 2021). A secondary but fundamental aspect of vaccine nationalism is the treating of public health as a market commodity rather than a public good (Katz *et al.*, 2021). Not only are wealthy nations hoarding vaccines, but they are also restricting access to the knowledge and capacity to manufacture vaccines, making clear the link between economics and politics. Rompel (this volume, Chapter 10) delves into further debate around the waiver of intellectual property rights for COVID-19 vaccines and production capacities, particularly African nations, demonstrating how dependency on vaccines produced outside the continent is an important political context for how vaccine nationalism impacts LMICs.

Vaccine nationalism is not a new discourse specific to COVID-19. Fidler (2010) narrates the evolution of global health discourse around equitable access to vaccines emerging first from the 2004 highly pathogenic avian influenza H5N1 and following 2009 H1N1 influenza pandemic. In 2004, it became evident that there was no mechanism to ensure equitable access to vaccines or research on influenza. This was exacerbated in 2009 with H1N1. Developed countries secured in advance almost all the vaccine production capacity of key vaccine manufacturers (Fidler, 2010), firmly establishing the concept of vaccine nationalism. WHO subsequently negotiated vaccine access for LMICs, but negotiations simply secured promises of vaccines beyond those required for wealthier countries. Ultimately, there was no binding agreement related to vaccine equity; WHO instead relied on 'ad hoc, reactive, and nonbinding activities that preserve national freedom of action while demonstrating some humanitarian concern' (Fidler, 2010, n.p.).

Ebola provides a second useful precursor to COVID-19 from the perspective of global cooperation. The Global Ebola Response of 2014–2016 mainly affected three West African countries (Guinea, Liberia, and Sierra Leone) and eventually infected more than 28,000 and killed 11,325 people and spread to seven additional countries. In September 2014, the Global Ebola Response Coalition was launched, along with an Ebola Response Multi-Partner Trust Fund (MPTF), administered by the UN Development Programme, which raised more than $166 million from 50 countries. Notably, the list of MPTF contributors only includes half of G20 members. The US, European Union (EU), and others were conspicuously absent from UN-led global cooperation mechanisms, although they contributed both financial and physical resources to Ebola response through their own channels (European Commission, 2019; The White House, 2015).

Although the final impact of these outbreaks was less than initially feared, they foreshadowed what eventuated with COVID-19 vaccines, proving Fidler's analysis correct that

> [t]he appearance of a more severe influenza strain will reinforce rather than overcome this pattern, because developed countries will prize their power and flexibility of action more in a severe pandemic than in a mild one, thus making hope for a crisis-sparked breakthrough misguided. The negotiating path that could lead to a new global access framework for influenza vaccines is not apparent, especially in a context in which aggregate global production capacity is woefully inadequate, the geographic location of production facilities is concentrated in developed countries, timelines for developing new vaccines create problems for rapid prevention strategies, and existing manufacturing technologies and distribution systems require improvements.
>
> *(Fidler, 2010, n.p.)*

The emergence of a novel coronavirus in 2019 (COVID-19) created the perfect storm: a completely disease naïve human population, rapid spread, significant mortality and morbidity, and highest initial impact on wealthier countries. Vaccine scarcity, overwhelming demand, and a rapidly changing context, such as India's requirements to stop exporting vaccines considering their own drastic surge of COVID-19 cases, have ensured that vaccines are intricately related to geopolitics and power dynamics. There was a precedent for vaccine nationalism, and the scale of COVID-19 enabled vaccine diplomacy. This context conspired to challenge existing multilateral arrangements, specifically COVAX.

Global cooperation is central to much of the discourse. Bollyky and Bown (2021) are among many who flag the negative repercussions of a collapse of international cooperation arising from vaccine hoarding, which imperils not only future public health initiatives but also other existential challenges like climate change and weapons of mass destruction (WEF, 2022). We turn now to COVAX to unpack the experience of this aspirational global response.

COVAX: aspirations for a multilateral COVID-19 response

> The great merit of COVAX is guaranteeing the distribution of vaccines according to the actual needs of recipient countries, and not on the basis of the economic, political, or geopolitical interests.
>
> *Mario Draghi, Prime Minister of Italy, G20 President (quoted in Gavi, 2021, p. 2)*

COVAX is co-led by the Global Alliance for Vaccines and Immunisations (Gavi), the Coalition for Epidemic Preparedness Innovations (CEPI), and WHO. The aim of COVAX is equitable access to COVID-19 vaccines. It is a multilateral approach to vaccine procurement through a complex mix of financing mechanisms, purchasing power, financial donations, and vaccine donations. The importance of COVAX from a public health perspective is spelled out clearly in its mandate:

> without [COVAX] there is a very real risk that the majority of people in the world will go unprotected against SARS-CoV-2, and this would allow the virus and its impact to continue unabated.
>
> *(https://www.gavi.org/vaccineswork/covax-explained)*

COVAX relies on critical assumptions:

- Sufficient funding for vaccine development (spearheaded by CEPI)
- Availability (production and distribution) of vaccines
- Sufficient buy-in from 'self-financing' countries as a type of insurance policy of guaranteed doses at agreed discounts (up to 50% of their populations)
- Contributions from ODA to finance advance market commitments for 'funded' countries' vaccines (up to 20% of their populations)
- Ethical bilateral procurement practices by the wealthiest countries

Gavi noted that addressing these 'pain points' was critical to equitable vaccine access. COVAX membership would enable priority access to vaccines as they emerged, as demand would certainly outstrip supply for quite some time. Participating 'self-financing' countries were guaranteed an allocation of vaccines, subject to their investment (up to 50% of their population). 'Funded' countries would commit to purchasing doses equivalent to 20% of their populations and have access to special financing mechanisms to reduce barriers to procurement. The combination of these elements aimed to create pooled purchasing power.

COVAX incentivized rapid vaccine development through contractual investments by self-financing countries 'Committed' or 'Optional' Purchase Arrangements. This up-front capital worked in two ways – first, to underwrite costs for vaccine development and second, to guarantee that manufacturers would sell a guaranteed number of future doses for profit. Effectively, COVAX assumed that sufficient countries would invest in this insurance policy rather than take their chances on the open market.

COVAX was designed to capitalize on shared interests and market forces. However, there was an underlying assumption that economically and politically powerful countries would behave within certain boundaries that would not directly compete with or undermine COVAX in its aims to ensure access for everyone. However, replicating the 2009 experience of the H1N1 pandemic, bilateral advance purchase agreements by wealthy nations left COVAX itself with insufficient access to vaccines (Eccleston-Turner and Upton, 2021), as its pooled purchasing power did not equal the collective greed of the world's wealthiest nations. The fatal flaw in COVAX is therefore that the self-interest embedded in previous pandemics was not addressed; therefore, the required shared interest required for COVAX did not eventuate. National interest is further complicated by commercial interests.

The 'partnership' foundations of COVAX

Public–private partnerships (PPPs) have become ubiquitous in global health (and development) initiatives, emerging because of increasing government austerity measures to address resource gaps in health provision. The dominance and impact of PPPs are subject to significant critiques (Ruckert and Labonté, 2014; Storeng, 2014; Torchia *et al.*, 2015). Ruckert and Labonté (2014) argue that the outsized influence of PPPs represents a reshaping of the public and private realms, resulting in a deepening of neoliberalism through further embedding of private interest in public health. They conclude that this undermines attempts to improve public health, as PPPs do not address unequal distribution of social determinants of health (poverty and social exclusion). Their influence is rationalized by the mantra of collaboration – 'instead of dominating, we are collaborating, and we create this higher unity that we couldn't have done apart', Dagfinn HØybråten former Chair, Gavi Board (cited in Gavi, 2020).

Gavi, the 'Vaccine Alliance', is itself a PPP, launched in 2000 at the World Economic Forum (WEF) in Davos as a partnership between UNICEF, the World Bank, WHO, and the private sector, predominantly the Gates Foundation. The need for Gavi is premised on a stalemate between the public health community pushing for new vaccines in LMICs and pharmaceutical companies that would not invest given that existing vaccines were not 'selling' in LMICs (Gavi, 2020). The market-based solution is to guarantee more sales overall in exchange for lower prices.

CEPI, emerging from the 2017 WEF in Davos, is variously described as an innovative global partnership (CEPI.org), an 'alliance' and a foundation and was co-founded by Norway and India, the Gates Foundation, Wellcome, and the WEF. It is therefore broader than a PPP, with a specific focus, but underpinned by the same key actors as Gavi.

WHO, which holds a mandate to lead global health initiatives and responses, is the third partner in COVAX. WHO, as the key public health multilateral institution, is the logical leader for a globally coordinated COVID-19 response. Yet the role and mandate of WHO has been politicized, underfunded, and consequently delegitimized to a certain extent, through former US president Donald Trump's attempted withdrawal, and its seemingly complicated relationship with China throughout the COVID-19 pandemic (Chan and Lee, 2021).

The Gates Foundation played a significant role in COVID-19 response funding, as the third-largest voluntary contributor to WHO, and the provider of 25% and 13% of direct contributions to Gavi and CEPI, respectively (https://www.gavi.org/investing-gavi/funding/donor-profiles/bill-melinda-gates-foundation). Stein (2021) argues that COVAX expands the scale and scope of financial instruments and thus conflates public health risk with corporate financial risk, enabling corporate concerns to compete with public health concerns.

Vaccine nationalism, diplomacy, and apartheid

> We have behaved, I am sad to say, more or less like the passengers on the Titanic: during the period of greatest scarcity, political forces did not allow us to do better, really, than sauve qui peut. COVAX struggled for most of the year to secure doses that had been locked up in advance purchase agreements by wealthy countries or restricted from export from manufacturing countries because of pressing domestic needs.
>
> *Dr Richard Hatchett, CEO of CEPI, summarizing COVAX performance at the end of 2021 (Hatchett, 2021, n.p.)*

As described, COVAX is a complex and innovative mechanism designed to mitigate the drivers of vaccine inequity. However, nearly two years into the experiment, there are major failures. COVAX has struggled to meet its targets due to its inability to compete with the world's largest economies, with vaccine nationalism noted as a key driver. Bollyky and Bown (2021) predicted in 2020 that competition would impact vaccine prices, supply bottlenecks would leave LMICs unprotected for months or more, and this would lead to intense resentment and needless humanitarian and economic hardships. They further argued that this would imperil the kind of international cooperation required for future pandemics and other global issues of concern.

Vaccine nationalism thrives in a Western-centric market-led global health system built on multilateral institutions evolving from the post-war era. The underlying driver is economic and political power, enabling control of production and distribution of scarce goods. Bump *et al.* (2021) find parallels with the political economy of colonial extraction, following long-standing patterns of gross exploitation. They argue the benefits accrue for elites, at the expense of others, with resultant division into the haves (the vaccinated or vaccine holders) and the have nots (the rest of the world). This reproduces conditions of permanent inequity, deepening ongoing conditions of racial discrimination, marginalization, and colonialism, whereby the pandemic further entrenches weak global solidarity and cooperation and causes economic disadvantage, increased vulnerabilities, and widening power imbalance between Global North and South. This is exacerbated not just by predatory vaccine nationalism (Owusu-Antwi, 2021) but also by the evolving link between vaccine nationalism and vaccine diplomacy.

Schéré (2021) notes that despite increased global integration and interdependence, nations are still drawn to asserting their sovereign power over one another and that soft power is essential. 'Soft power' is a term coined by Joseph Nye (1990) and was framed by the Cold War. Nye identified a shift whereby power is derived as much by whose story wins as whose army. Soft power is a political tool in the space where opposing ideologies interact. Nye (1990) observed three ways that power can be used to affect behaviors – coercion, inducements, or co-option – but he also noted that power depends on resources and context.

A clear example is the appeal of American liberalism in the post–Cold War era through the export of culture and society including top US universities, film, TV, and other products, all of which demonstrated growth in positive international perceptions and, therefore, influence. However, global perceptions of the US have dramatically declined (Wike *et al.*, 2020), substantiated by emerging great power discourse, and the shifting space from a unipolar world to a bipolar or multipolar world covered elsewhere in this volume. Schéré (2021) argues that declining global perceptions of the US are exacerbated by its withdrawal from global commitments, specifically WHO and the Paris Agreement.

The pandemic created space for a new kind of soft power, vaccine diplomacy. Lee (2021) positions vaccine diplomacy within Bourne's (1978) conceptual space of 'medical diplomacy'. His research analyzes China's vaccine diplomacy and argues that the competitiveness of COVID-19 vaccine access disrupted pre-COVID conceptualizations of vaccine diplomacy, particularly with reference to the interrelationship between multistakeholder diplomacy and direct diplomacy between nations (Katz *et al.*, 2011). The links between vaccine nationalism and vaccine diplomacy are not well assessed and are in many quarters discussed as mutually exclusive. Owusu-Antwi (2021) identifies a vaccine continuum, with three reinforcing but continuous phases. The first is 'predatory' vaccine nationalism, characterized by vaccine hoarding; the second is 'benign' vaccine nationalism, where domestic needs are prioritized with restrained international distribution. The final phase of the continuum is 'ultra-diplomacy', where non-domestic needs are centered. Ultra-diplomacy goes beyond donations-centered distribution and may incorporate intellectual property waivers and diversified vaccine manufacturing. COVAX can be conceptualized as benign in design but undermined by predatory vaccine nationalism.

Following September 2021's Global COVID-19 Summit, COVAX appears to have been 'recalibrated' from primarily a procurement and financing mechanism to one which is dependent on vaccine sharing. Interestingly, donating countries are now permitted to earmark excess vaccine for distribution to specific countries, thus undermining the core principle of COVAX: equitable and fair distribution. The emerging policy allowing earmarking allows soft power to be prioritized at the expense of principled vaccine equity and warrants further focus.

Earmarking: soft power and vaccine diplomacy

> Gavi figures show that 75% of donations are earmarked to specific countries and regions, further challenging COVAX in its efforts to distribute vaccines equitably. The IAVG has warned that donating countries should reduce or remove all geographical earmarking to allow COVAX the greatest flexibility to distribute based on need.
>
> *(Usher, 2021)*

Returning to Mario Draghi's quote (Gavi, 2021, p. 2) that the greatest merit of COVAX 'is guaranteeing the distribution of vaccines according to the actual needs of recipient countries, and not on the basis of the economic, political, or geopolitical interests', the chapter turns briefly to concerns raised by Independent Allocation of Vaccines Group (IAVG), a WHO-convened body validating proposals for vaccine allocation decisions. In reporting on each round of COVAX allocations, the IAVG has repeatedly raised concerns about vaccine earmarking by manufacturers (for commercialization) and donors (geopolitics). Examples include earmarking of all donations of Pfizer from the US government in November 2021 with pre-allocations to Bangladesh, Pakistan, the Philippines, and Vietnam, totaling 36 million doses. IAVG further noted concerns about 'the effects that manufacturer-specific earmarking may have on equity in COVAX-secured coverage', in response to earmarking by the Serum Institute of India and Moderna to countries where products may be commercialized (IAVG, Round 12, 2021). IAVG noted 'persisting dangers to overall equity posed by the earmarking of donated doses" (IAVG, 2021, p. 26). The power of facilities such as COVAX to withstand pressure for earmarking is limited as it is entirely reliant on donors to succeed.

The chapter now turns to the complexity of vaccines between two worlds, the 'donors' and the 'recipients', or the 'haves and the have nots' (Bump *et al.*, 2021). The focus is a critical discourse contrasting donors' and recipients' positions, delving deeper into donor power and decision-making and an overview of the impact on selected case countries. The chapter highlights actions by the biggest donors and analyzes a snapshot of geographically based recipient countries. The intent is to provide a more nuanced understanding of the issue's complexity.

A story of two worlds: vaccine donors and vaccine recipients

The vaccine development race began almost at the same time as the pandemic was declared. On 30 January 2020, WHO declared COVID-19 a Public Health Emergency of International Concern, and by 11 March 2020, the pandemic was declared. By 30 March 2020, the US Department of Health and Human Services announced 'Operation Warp Speed', a series of policies designed to invest in the fastest vaccine development in world history. Moreover, by the time WHO declared the pandemic, the Gamaleya National Center of Epidemiology and Microbiology in Moscow was already working on a prototype of Sputnik V, funded by the Russian Direct Investment Fund, the country's sovereign wealth fund. A Chinese-produced vaccine emerged by June 2020.

At an unprecedented speed, the first COVID vaccine was granted emergency use authorization by 11 December 2020, less than one year after the first case was confirmed in the US. This was, in part, due to extraordinarily favorable public policy environments, including unprecedented government investment. G7 countries have purchased over a third of the world's vaccine supply, despite making up only 13% of the global population. Of the 54 HICs, 51 had, by October 2021, secured enough vaccine to immunize 70% of their populations, and the remaining three had secured enough vaccine to immunize at least 40% of their populations by the end of 2021. In fact, 28 out of these 54 countries had secured enough to provide double dose coverage *plus a booster* to 100% of their populations, while another 14 countries had secured enough to provide at least two doses with millions of doses to spare as a buffer for boosters, expired/wasted vaccines, or other logistical and planning challenges (Kirk *et al.*, 2021; Ritchie *et al.*, 2020).

From a domestic policy standpoint, readers can likely forgive rich countries for securing enough vaccine for double dose coverage and a reasonable buffer for boosters. However, many HICs have secured millions of doses beyond their needs. The seven worst offenders in this category (New Zealand, Germany, Slovak Republic, Hungary, Italy, Canada, and Australia) have secured a staggering 1.8 billion excess doses, enough to double vaccinate nearly 12% of the global population. Given the intent of COVAX, it is also somewhat challenging to see that donors were also recipients of COVAX supplies. Statnews (2021) noted that in June, 530,000 doses of COVAX supplies were sent to the UK (population 67 million), but that Africa as a continent (population 1.35 billion) received only four times that amount in the same period, further entrenching vaccine inequity in a state of severe scarcity. At the time of writing, only four LICs have surpassed 20% vaccination rates and the remaining 22 nations (85% of LICs) have not yet reached 10% vaccination, with an average of 4.2% across them. Digging deeper, only 1% of the total population of LICs globally are vaccinated, leaving a full 99% of LICs tracking at less than 10% vaccination rates (Ritchie *et al.*, 2020).

The 900 million doses shipped by COVAX by the end of 2021 are less than half the initial 2 billion doses promised/intended. Roughly a third of these doses were shipped in December, due primarily to increased supply from donors and pharmaceutical companies. Despite the surge in vaccines, there were more boosters administered in HICs than total vaccines in LICs (Mancini and Stabe, 2021). As Dr Ghebreyesus, WHO Chief, warned in early 2021, vaccinating younger richer people ahead of more vulnerable older, poorer people, as has happened (and exacerbated by boosters), is a 'catastrophic moral failure' (WHO, 2021).

The three biggest overall vaccine donors are China, the US, and 'Team Europe', comprising the EU, Norway, and Iceland (Kiernan *et al.*, 2021). At the end of November 2021, 2.75 billion donated doses were committed, with 75% coming from the US and China (Kiernan *et al.*, 2021). We turn now to a brief analysis of China and the US focusing on political and economic factors' motivations and their impact.

The donors

US

As of December 2021, the US was the largest donor of COVID-19 vaccines. This is a dramatic shift from the early phases of vaccine development when the Trump administration was strongly signaling a withdrawal from global cooperation. The US has been heavily affected by COVID-19, with data from the Johns Hopkins locating the US globally as fourth-highest deaths per 100,000 population and 14th highest in terms of fatalities per hundred cases, both key metrics in assessing the burden of COVID-19 (JHU, 2022). Purely in number of cases, the US has counted more than 55 million cases at the end of 2021 (CDC, 2022).

Domestic politics have been a key driver in the US response to international cooperation. In the early days of the pandemic, President Donald Trump used strong rhetoric to politicize COVID-19 as the 'China Virus' and even used racist and defamatory slurs such as "Kung Flu" (Kurilla, 2021), which played well to his political base. Never a big proponent of multilateral institutions, on May 2020 (just 11 weeks into the pandemic), Trump announced that the US would withdraw from WHO and redirect its financial support to US priorities. By July 2020, this move was formalized. In May 2020, the Trump administration launched Operation Warp Speed, a PPP designed to produce and deliver vaccines for the US population, specifically. Within 24 hours, then presidential candidate Joe Biden vowed that he would revoke Trump's order if he were elected in November 2020. On his first day in office, Biden indeed revoked the order, effectively returning the US to its pre-Trump-era status as the largest single funder of WHO. The theatrics of these pronouncements obscure the impact of shifting world order and the role of the US in multilateral spaces as well as a more critical and nuanced understanding of WHO. Hopewell (2021) argues that Trump's apparent 'dismantling' of the multilateral space is somewhat of a fallacy, and a continuation of pre-Trump trends, including the decline of the US institutional power.

The impact of Trump's position regarding WHO and COVAX is less clear. The first US vaccines were made available in December 2020, after a year which saw more than 300,000 US deaths. A total of 100 million Pfizer doses were promised by March 2021, and 200 million Moderna by June 2021 (BBC, 2020). Despite the politics and uncertainty of US support for WHO, COVAX was launched in April 2020, positioning the alliance as one of the central players in vaccine development, country-level preparedness, policy, procurement, and distribution when vaccine development itself had barely started and while scientists were still clambering to understand the emerging threat.

Under the Biden administration, and despite being the country most affected by COVID-19, in June 2021, the US launched an ambitious plan to be the single-largest donor of vaccines and COVID-19 funding support. At the virtual COVID-19 Summit on the side-lines of the UN General Assembly in September 2021, Biden announced that the US will 'become the arsenal of vaccines as we were the arsenal of democracy in World War II' (The White House, 2021, n.p.). In October 2021, the US commemorated 200 million vaccines committed and delivered to more than 100 countries and additional $9.3 billion in funds committed internationally to combat COVID-19 through a mix of bilateral and multilateral mechanisms. The $9.3 billion included $4 billion for Gavi for vaccine procurement and readiness, as well as an additional $1.5 billion for vaccine procurement to be distributed through COVAX.

US donations are channeled through either COVAX (48% in February 2022, down from 53% in September 2021) or directly (52%) (Sparks et al, 2022). By far, the top recipient of US vaccines is Pakistan at 104 million doses in February 2022 (or 471,000 doses per million people) (KFF, 2022) followed by Bangladesh (38M), the Philippines (24M), Indonesia (23M), Vietnam (23M), Nigeria (21M), Egypt (21M), Uganda (11M), Mexico (10M), and Kenya (8M) (KFF, 2022).

As of September 2021, 81% of US donations were going to MICs, while only 7% were reaching LICs. Totally 28% of US donations were directed toward countries in the Western Hemisphere, but when standardized based on population size, this is more than double the next largest recipient region (sub-Saharan Africa). By January 2022, despite a huge uplift in doses shipped worldwide, LICs were still only receiving 9% of US vaccine doses (Ritchie *et al.*, 2020).

Of the top ten US-donated vaccine recipients, all are also receiving vaccines from China as sales or donations. Four of these countries are in both the US and China's top ten recipient countries: Indonesia, Pakistan, the Philippines, and Bangladesh. All but two (Guatemala and Colombia) are also participants under a memorandum of understanding with China for its Belt and Road Initiative.

Overall, US domestic politics have played a significant role in shaping external perceptions of its global commitment to vaccine equity and global solidarity, shifting from Trump's America First rhetoric on one extreme to a position of significant responsibility for global vaccinations, but with a strong focus on bilateral agreements and soft power, despite a return to WHO and COVAX commitments.

China

China has been widely debated in academic and policy circles for its considerable strategic investments across the globe. Investment in development infrastructure, expansion of trade through the BRI, and the emergence of 'non-traditional' multilateral spaces, specifically the Asian International Investment Bank and National Development Bank, are some of the most notable examples of China's global reach with foreign aid and development. How this is perceived depends on the position of the viewer (Mohan, 2014).

By January 2021, China had produced two of the early vaccines and commenced a rapid internal rollout. About 1 billion people, or 71% of Chinese population, were fully vaccinated by September 2021 (Mathieu *et al.*, 2021). Almost immediately after the vaccination drive commenced in China, the Chinese Foreign Ministry announced the provision of 10 million doses of China-made vaccine to COVAX. Once approved, Chinese vaccines became part of COVAX shipments in July 2021. By early August, President Xi Jinping announced that China aimed to supply at least 2 billion doses of vaccines worldwide, as well as \$100 million contribution to COVAX Advanced Market Commitment, deliberately positioning China as central to global public health cooperation (Reuters, 2021). Doses were allocated to 60, mostly African, countries. Indonesia was, however, the single biggest recipient, accounting for 80% of Indonesia's vaccine supply and 20% of all Chinese vaccines exported. Sino-Indonesian relations have been strengthened during the COVID pandemic, despite increasing Sinophobia (Rakhmat, 2021).

Itugbu (2021) argues that apathy and distrust from across the African continent as well as questions about Chinese vaccine efficacy and safety have challenged efforts to increase Chinese influence through vaccines. South Africa, for example, refused Chinese vaccines due to their lack of efficacy and unknown impact on recipients with HIV (Guarascio *et al.*, 2021).

Overall, China appears focused on both the economic and the political aspects of the vaccine. Ten percent (184 million) of Chinese vaccines have been donated, and 1.7 billion (February 2022) committed in commercial deals, including with COVAX.

Recipients

Vietnam

Vietnam provides an informative case study of vaccine access, given its central position geopolitically, between the US, China, and Russia.[1] Vietnam shares a large land border with China and has similarities in government and ideology. Economic and trade ties between the nations are important, yet Le Thu (2020) notes it is a 'fragile comradeship' with maritime disputes, geopolitical competition, and security concerns causing cyclical deterioration and repairing of diplomatic ties.

The global shortage of vaccines meant that Vietnam's vaccine drive really only started to gain traction in August 2021. Vincent (2021) identified a popular anti-Chinese sentiment that is impacting uptake of Chinese vaccines within Vietnam, despite government support of and access to Chinese vaccines. Vaccine diplomacy in Vietnam is based on need and existing relationships. Vietnam had significant early success controlling the pandemic. However, case numbers exploded, reaching nearly 100,000 cases per week in July 2021 (WHO, 2021). Vaccine needs suddenly spiked, as Vietnam went from having one of the lowest daily caseloads in the region to one of the highest.

In response, the Government of Vietnam set up a vaccine diplomacy working group to try and locate more vaccine supplies. Existing relationships with former soviet states,[2] and the EU, proved successful for several reasons. Vietnam supported these countries with personal protective equipment early in the pandemic, and the Government of Vietnam lobbied for support due to long-standing 'Friendship' associations dating back to communist eras. Hutt (2021) also identified trade as driving vaccine contributions from Europe. Five million Chinese vaccines for Ho Chi Minh City raised a public outcry, and the vaccines were redeployed to northern provinces. The US donated over 24 million doses to Vietnam outpacing Chinese vaccines. There appears to be a complex mix of demand for non-Chinese vaccines, amidst political maneuvering particularly over maritime issues and a multipronged commitment from the US, including direct funding for programmatic assistance and technical support for COVID. At the time of writing, 80% of Vietnam's population had received at least one vaccine dose.

Pakistan

Pakistan secured 207 million vaccine doses, around half through COVAX and the remainder through bilateral and multilateral arrangements, resulting in 41% of the population fully vaccinated (UNICEF, 2022). Most vaccines are coming from the US and China. China was the first country to ship vaccines to Pakistan, with half a million doses of Sinopharm donated in February 2021 (Hasim, 2021). In May 2021, with great fanfare, over 1 million additional doses arrived, with the British High Commissioner to Pakistan, the EU delegate, and the US Embassy Chargé D'Affaires all making public statements as to their bilateral and multilateral commitments to Pakistan. In total (February 2022), China has shipped 111 million doses to Pakistan, of which 3.7 million were donations (Bridge, 2022). COVAX shipments include 8.5 million doses earmarked by the US specifically, as well as COVAX procured vaccines. Data is sparse as to the source of the remainder.

The obvious vaccine diplomacy at play in Pakistan has hardly gone unnoticed. Nasir (2021) argued that lack of US leadership compounded increasing anti-American skepticism and cemented the role of China as key supporter of underresourced countries, thus further entrenching the China–Pakistan versus US–India divide.

Malawi

The above two countries provide a brief snapshot of recipient countries of geopolitical and economic importance and a brief look at US–China interactions. However, it is noteworthy to consider countries with significantly less strategic relevance to China or the US. Malawi (population 19 million) has reported relatively low levels of COVID-19 infections, and a slow rollout of COVID-19 vaccines with current figures showing only 7.5% of people with at least one dose and 4% fully vaccinated. Malawi only recently (2008) reestablished diplomatic ties with China due to its support of Taiwan. Malawi has not received any Chinese COVID vaccines. Of the approximately 650k US vaccine doses, about half are through COVAX (https://www.state.gov/countries-areas/malawi/#covid_map_link).

The intransigent nature of power between the Global North and South has been widely debated. Reflecting on the above brief foray into the impact of vaccine nationalism and diplomacy, incorporating the political and economic aspects of vaccine distribution, the power differential between the Global North and South is not challenged by the existing multilateral arrangements. COVAX is limping along but powerless to challenge the self-interest of the donor nations. COVAX is arguably no longer a neutral mechanism because it has been undermined and co-opted by countries aiming to exert soft power while maintaining a semblance of international cooperation.

There is a deeper narrative at play here, which links back to broader discourse and rationale for aid. Altruism and humanitarian imperatives should incentivize vaccine equality, yet the political economy of aid reveals a complex array of perverse and disincentives, including self-interest (economic and security concerns), soft power, diplomacy, ideology, and hegemonic intent. The COVID-19 pandemic response, including the race to vaccinate, is no exception.

Conclusion

The role of politics and economics within global health governance has gained significant traction as another lens through which to analyze and promote equity in global health. Previous SARS outbreaks highlighted significant issues and risks related to vaccine equity in a neoliberal world for such time as the world would face a more lethal threat. The severity of COVID-19 impacts and the subsequent emergence of beneficial, new vaccines forced a closer look at the urgency of global health system weaknesses when vaccine scarcity is at play. Vaccine equity was flagged in early 2020 as a critical but complex problem for the evolving COVID-19 pandemic. Intrinsic drive for national self-interest, early questions around the legitimacy of multilateral systems for coordination of global events, and the simultaneous politicization of WHO were several of the key drivers within a complex series of events that continue to undermine effective response to the pandemic including the COVAX mechanism itself. This analysis does not delve into critiques of WHO outside its politicization in this context.

COVAX was conceived as market-based mechanism grounded in PPP to address vaccine equity. It proved insufficient to counter the self-interests of rich nations, who hoarded vaccines and other supplies, stifled the potential for global manufacturing by controlling patents and other intellectual property, and finally, used bilateral vaccine deals for soft power. The trajectory of vaccine diplomacy, as identified by Owusu-Antwi (2021), provides a useful lens for analysis. The US moved through phases of predatory vaccine nationalism, to benign nationalism, and finally in late 2021 and early 2022, the US is showing signs of vaccine 'ultra-diplomacy', pushing for significant international vaccine distribution, and by supporting intellectual property waivers. This example does not, however, necessarily lead to or promote a fundamental change or challenge to the entrenched power structures of the global health system (and global aid system). This trajectory, while promising, does not necessarily create space for a more values-driven global solidarity to emerge, as the fundamental power dynamics remain, without binding international agreements in place. Rich nations need more incentives. And it is unlikely that moral arguments alone will override self-interest. The vaccine outcomes of COVAX are, in the words of WHO, a catastrophic moral failure.

The role of multilateral organizations in coordinating a global health response was challenged by attempts to delegitimize WHO rather than seeking to address perceived shortcomings of a multilateral system that frames WHO. The increasing power of complex partnerships encompassing nation-states, private enterprises, and a range of other stakeholders has produced a system that secures the role of wealthy and influential nations, and corporations, as well as power holders, such as Bill Gates. COVAX is driven by a 'northern' ideology of aid, where decision-making and resources are controlled by a few wealthier countries.

COVAX tested a model of market-driven approaches instead of moral arguments, which had failed in the past. The evidence suggests that the market-driven approach relied, and thus failed, on a belief that wealthy countries would cooperate, rather than compete, and that they would be driven, at least in part, by moral imperatives and collective risk reduction. COVAX has adapted to an approach that enables the embedding of soft power through vaccine diplomacy. The issue of earmarking donations, extending soft power impact, through a multilateral institute is arguably an indication of the deepening of vaccine diplomacy and nationalism and a weakening of the moral imperative and is worthy of further research.

What lessons can be learned from COVAX that will be useful for the next global health emergency, which is likely to be sooner rather than later? A shift to models of shared technology and investment in manufacturing capacity for local distribution is one alternative that appears to be gaining traction. Yet the underpinning vision of a multilateral response that is accountable to affected populations rather than the economic and political machinations of the so-called great powers, and wealthy nations, is essential yet absent. The key point of failure of COVAX is that without binding agreements or rules-based norms, to ensure that vaccine equality is enshrined as a principle, multilateral responses are held hostage to national self-interest, and vaccines become politicized and a soft power tool. Public health is secondary to politics and economics. The COVID-19 pandemic further deepened vaccine inequality, through the capture of COVAX by political and economic interests of wealthy countries, far beyond reasonable national interest fueled by public health.

The overreach of vaccine nationalism, into soft power, into protection of private enterprise and the resulting deepening of inequality, should be the cause for international outrage but remains largely unchallenged in practice. It seems likely that there will be further global health emergencies requiring a global response. COVID-19 has set back the cause of global solidarity in public health even further than it was in 2004 and 2009 flu outbreaks. There was no crisis-sparked breakthrough in global health governance, nor is there a negotiating path clear that will lead to a new framework for equitable access to vaccines for all. This is the challenge moving forward.

Notes

1 Early in the race to vaccinate, Russia heavily promoted its domestic vaccine candidate, Sputnik V, beyond its borders in a vaccine diplomacy drive. The vaccine heavily prioritized LMICs with a focus on the cost effectiveness, being the cheapest at around $10 per dose for international buyers. March 2021 reports note that Russia had reportedly reached agreements to supply 1.2 billion doses of Sputnik V across 50 LMICs (Congressional Research Service, 2021). By late 2021, Sputnik V was approved in 74 countries, yet it is still pending Emergency Use Listening (EUL) with WHO (2022).

2 Czech Republic, Hungary, Slovakia, and Poland.

References

Aizenman, N. (2021) The goal: at least 40% vaxxed in all nations by year-end. This map shows how we stand. *NPR*, December 30, 2021. https://www.npr.org/sections/goatsandsoda/2021/12/30/1068920127/the-goal-at-least-40-vaxxed-in-all-nations-by-year-end-this-map-shows-how-we-sta

BBC (2020) Covid-19: First vaccine given in US as roll-out begins. *BBC news online*, December 14, 2020, https://www.bbc.com/news/world-us-canada-55305720

Bollyky, T.J., and Bown, C.P. (2021) The tragedy of vaccine nationalism: only cooperation can end the pandemic. *Foreign Affairs* 99(5).

Bourne, P.A. (1978). Partnership for international health care. *Public Health Reports* 93(2), 114–123.

Bridge (2021) Bridge Beijing Chinese Vaccine Data tracker. https://bridgebeijing.com/our-publications/our-publications-1/china-covid-19-vaccines-tracker/

Bump, J.B., Baum, F., Sakornsin, M., Yates, R., and Hofman, K. (2021) Political economy of COVID-19: extractive, regressive, competitive. *British Medical Journal*, 372(73), 324–332.

CDC (2022) COVID case tracker website: https://covid.cdc.gov/covid-data-tracker/#trends_totalcases. Centre for Disease Control, Washington.

Chan, L. and Lee, P.K. (2021) The World Health Organization must answer these hard questions in its coronavirus inquiry. *The Conversation*, May 21, 2020.

Congressional Research Service (2021) Global COVID-19 vaccine distribution. *In Focus*, March 26, 2021, Congressional Research Service, Washington: https://crsreports.congress.gov/product/pdf/IF/IF11796/1

Ducharme, J. (2021) COVAX was a great idea, but is now 500 million doses short of its vaccine distribution goals. What exactly went wrong? *Time*, September 9, 2021. https://time.com/6096172/covax-vaccines-what-went-wrong/

Eccleston-Turner, M. and Upton, H. (2021) International collaboration to ensure equitable access to vaccines for COVID-19: The ACT-accelerator and the COVAX facility. *The Millbank Quarterly*, 99(2), 426–449.

European Commission (2019) European civil protection and humanitarian aid operations EU response to Ebola. https://reliefweb.int/sites/reliefweb.int/files/resources/wa_ebola_en_0.pdf

Fidler, D.P. (2010). The Challenges of Global Health Governance. Council on Foreign Relations Working Paper. May 24th 2010, https://www.cfr.org/report/challenges-global-health-governance

Fidler, D.P. (2021) Geopolitics drives vaccine access in Asia. *East Asia Forum*, April 13, 2021. https://www.eastasiaforum.org/2021/04/13/geopolitics-drives-vaccine-access-in-asia/

Gavi (2020) Gavi @20. https://www.gavi.org/gavi-at-20

Gavi (2021) COVAX AMC investment opportunity. *The Vaccine Alliance*, April 15, 2021, https://www.gavi.org/sites/default/files/covid/covax/Gavi-COVAX-AMC-Investment-Opportunity.pdf

Guarascio, F., Winning, A. and Widianto, S. (2021) WHO begins shipping Chinese vaccines despite some misgivings.

Hasim, A. (2021) Pakistan receives first COVID vaccine shipment from China. *AL Jazeera*, February 1, 2021. https://www.aljazeera.com/news/2021/2/1/pakistan-receives-first-shipment-of-coronavirus-vaccine

Hatchett, R. (2021) Reflections on 2021 from CEPI CEO Dr Richard Hatchett. *CEPI News*. https://cepi.net/news_cepi/reflections-on-2021-from-cepi-ceo-dr-richard-hatchett/

Hopewell, K. (2021) Trump and trade: The crisis in the multilateral trading system. *New Political Economy*, 26(2), 271–282.

Hutt, D. (2021) COVID: Why is Europe donating so many vaccines to Vietnam? *Deutshce Welle*. https://www.dw.com/en/covid-why-is-europe-donating-so-many-vaccines-to-vietnam/a-59078252

IAVG (2021) COVAX allocation round 10 vaccine allocation decision. November 9, 2021. https://www.who.int/groups/iavg

Itugbu, S. (2021) The politics of Chinas vaccine diplomacy in Africa. *Australia Institute of International Affairs*, December 10, 2021. https://www.internationalaffairs.org.au/australianoutlook/the-politics-of-chinas-vaccine-diplomacy-in-africa/

JHU (2022) Mortality analysis, mortality in the most affected countries. *Corona Virus Resource Centre*, February 2, 2022. https://coronavirus.jhu.edu/data/mortality

Katz, I.T., Weintraub, M., Bekker, L.G., and Brandt, A.M. (2021) From vaccine nationalism to vaccine equity—Finding a path forward. *New England Journal of Medicine*, 384, 1281–1283.

Katz, R., Kornblet, S., Arnold, G., Lief, E., and Fischer, J.E. (2011) Defining health diplomacy: Changing demands in the era of globalization. *Milbank Quarterly*, 89, 503–523.

Kiernan, S., Tohme, S., and Song, G. (2021) Billions committed, millions delivered, the mixed record of vaccine donations and diplomacy. *Think Global Health*, December 2, 2021. https://www.thinkglobalhealth.org/article/billions-committed-millions-delivered

Kirk, A., Sheehy, F., and Levett, C. (2021) Canada and UK among countries with most vaccine doses ordered per person. *The Guardian*, January 30, 2021. https://www.theguardian.com/world/2021/jan/29/canada-and-uk-among-countries-with-most-vaccine-doses-ordered-per-person

Kurilla, R. (2021) "Kung Flu"—The dynamics of fear, popular culture, and authenticity in the anatomy of populist communication. *Frontiers in Communication*, 6. https://www.frontiersin.org/article/10.3389/fcomm.2021.624643

Le Thu, H. (2020) Rough waters ahead for Vietnam–China relations. *Carnegie Endowment for Peace*, September 30, 2020. https://carnegieendowment.org/2020/09/30/rough-waters-ahead-for-vietnam-china-relations-pub-82826

Lee, S.T. (2021) Vaccine diplomacy: Nation branding and China's COVID-19 soft power play. *Place Branding and Public Diplomacy*, 1–15.

Mancini, D.P., and Stabe, M. (2021, December 20) Rich nations' booster rollout exceeds first jabs for world's poor: Low-income nations grapple with high vaccine prices and uneven supplies. *Financial Times*. https://www.proquest.com/newspapers/rich-nations-booster-rollout-exceeds-first-jabs/docview/2620907953/se-2?accountid=10445

Mathieu, E., Ritchie, H., Ortiz-Ospina, E., *et al.* (2021) A global database of COVID-19 vaccinations. Nature Human Behaviour, 5(7), 947–953.

Mohan, G. (2014). 'China in Africa: Impacts and prospects for accountable development', in B. Bukenya, S. Hickey, and K. Sen (eds.), *The Politics of Inclusive Development: Interrogating the Evidence* (New York: Oxford University Press).

Nasir, M.W. (2021) The great power competition of vaccine diplomacy in Pakistan. *South Asian Voices*, May 28 2021. https://southasianvoices.org/the-great-power-competition-of-vaccine-diplomacy-in-pakistan/

Nye, J.S. (1990). Soft power. *Foreign Policy*, (80), 153–171.

Ottersen, O., Dasgupta, J., Blouin, C., Buss, P., Chongsuvivatwong, V., Frenk, J., and Fukuda-Parr, S. (2014). The Lancet and University of Oslo Commission on global governance for health: The political origins of health inequity: Prospects for change. *The Lancet*, 383, 630–667.

Owusu-Antwi, S. (2021) Vaccine diplomacy versus vaccine nationalism: Synthesis or dissonance? *Carnegie Council for Ethics in International Affairs*, https://www.carnegiecouncil.org/publications/articles_papers_reports/20210519-vaccine-diplomacy-vs-vaccine-nationalism

Paxton, N., and Youde, J. (2019) Engagement or dismissiveness? Intersecting international theory and global health. *Global Public Health*, 14(4), 503–514.

Rakhmat, M.Z. (2021) Despite COVID-19, Indonesia–China relations continue to develop. *The Diplomat*, August 10, 2021. https://thediplomat.com/2021/08/despite-covid-19-indonesia-china-relations-continue-to-develop/

Reuters (2021) Xi says China aims to provide 2 bln COVID-19 vaccine doses to world in 2021. August 6, 2021. https://www.reuters.com/world/china/xi-says-china-aims-provide-2-bln-covid-19-vaccine-doses-world-2021-cctv-2021-08-05/

Ritchie, H., Mathieu, E., Rodés-Guirao, L., Appel, C., Giattino, C., Ortiz-Ospina, E., Hasell, J., Macdonald, B., Beltekian, D., and Roser, M. (2020) Coronavirus pandemic (COVID-19). *OurWorldInData.org*. https://ourworldindata.org/coronavirus [Online Resource].

Ruckert, A., and Labonté, R. (2014) Public–private partnerships (ppps) in global health: The good, the bad and the ugly. *Third World Quarterly*, 35(9), 1598–1614.

Ruger, J.P., and Yach, D. (2009). The global role of the world health organization. *Global Health Governance*, 2(2), 1–11.

Schéré, E. (2021). Soft power—The underestimated strategy for global influence. *Fletcher Forum of World Affairs*, 45(2), 41–63.

Sidibe, M. (2022) Vaccine inequity: Ensuring Africa is not left out. *Africa in Focus Blog*, Brookings Institute, January 24, 2022. https://www.brookings.edu/blog/africa-in-focus/2022/01/24/vaccine-inequity-ensuring-africa-is-not-left-out/

Sparks, G., Kirzinger, A., Kates, J., Michaud, J. and Brodie, M. (2022) KFF COVID-19 Vaccine Monitor: Views on the U.S. Role In Global COVID-19 Response, Kaiser Family Foundation, https://www.kff.org/coronavirus-covid-19/poll-finding/kff-covid-19-vaccine-monitor-global-response/

Stein, F. (2021) Risky business: COVAX and the financialization of global vaccine equity. *Global Health*, 17, 112.

Storeng, K.T. (2014) The Gavi Alliance and the 'Gates approach' to health system strengthening. *Global Public Health*, 9(8), 865–879.

The White House (2015) *FACT SHEET: Progress in Our Ebola Response at Home and Abroad*. Office of the Press Secretary, Washington DC: The White House. https://obamawhitehouse.archives.gov/the-press-office/2015/02/11/fact-sheet-progress-our-ebola-response-home-and-abroad(

The White House (2021) *Remarks by President Biden at Virtual Global COVID-19 Summit*. Washington, DC.: The White House, September 22, 2021. https://www.whitehouse.gov/briefing-room/speeches-re8marks/2021/09/22/remarks-by-president-biden-at-virtual-global-covid-19-summit/

Torchia, M., Calabrò, A., and Morner, M. (2015) Public–private partnerships in the health care sector: A systematic review of the literature. *Public Management Review*, 17(2), 236–261.

UNICEF (2022) COVID-19 vaccine market dashboard. https://www.unicef.org/supply/covid-19-vaccine-market-dashboard

Usher, A.D. (2021) Vaccine shortages prompt changes to COVAX strategy.

Vanderslott, S., Emary, K., te Water Naude, R., *et al.* (2021) Vaccine nationalism and internationalism: Perspectives of COVID-19 vaccine trial participants in the United Kingdom. *BMJ Global Health*, 6(10).

Vincent, T. (2021) From delay to desperation: The story of Sinophobia and COVID-19 vaccines in Vietnam. *The Diplomat*, October 6, 2021. https://thediplomat.com/2021/10/from-delay-to-desperation-the-story-of-sinophobia-and-covid-19-vaccines-in-vietnam/

WEF (World Economic Forum) (2022) *The Global Risks Report 2021*. 16th ed. Geneva: World Economic Forum.

WHO (2021) *WHO Director-General's Opening Remarks at 148th Session of the Executive Board.* Geneva: World Health Organisation, January 21, 2021. https://www.who.int/director-general/speeches/detail/who-director-general-s-opening-remarks-at-148th-session-of-the-executive-board

WHO (2022) *WHO's Landscape of COVID-19 Vaccine Candidates.* Rome: World Health Organisation. https://www.who.int/emergencies/diseases/novel-coronavirus-2019/covid-19-vaccines

8

HEALTH EMERGENCY OR ECONOMIC CRISIS? FAIL FORWARD AND DE-RISKING OPPORTUNITIES IN IMF COVID LOANS TO EGYPT

Lama Tawakkol

Introduction

The outbreak of the COVID-19 pandemic in late 2019 and global measures to deal with it, including nationwide lockdowns, have left a significant toll on Global South countries. Countries already suffering from high poverty levels and constrained budgets and struggling to meet basic needs have found themselves in worse positions: they have been "particularly hard hit by a lack of medical supplies, a sudden stop of the world economy, difficulties in accessing global capital markets and, for some, a sharp drop in commodity prices and a reduction in tourism" (IMF, 2021a). In response, international financial institutions (IFIs) and multilateral development banks (MDBs) have stepped up their support to address these challenges and mitigate the pandemic's ramifications (Segal and Henderson, 2021). One of the main actors has been the International Monetary Fund (IMF), whose response to COVID-19 has entailed increased financial assistance alongside policy recommendations, capacity building and debt relief (IMF, 2021a). It has since extended this support, through both emergency financing and other financial support schemes, to 86 countries to help them contain the current ramifications of the crisis and prepare a strong post-pandemic (economic) recovery (IMF, 2021a).

Egypt was among the early beneficiaries of IMF's COVID-related assistance. In May 2020, almost two months after COVID-19's outbreak and the announcement of a health emergency in Egypt, the Egyptian government requested a $2.772 billion emergency loan through the IMF's (unconditional) Rapid Financing Instrument (RFI). Approved on top of the Fund's pre-existing four-year loan to Egypt since 2016, this loan was presented as essential support for the country to cope with the stresses of COVID-19 and maintain its "hard-won macroeconomic stability" (IMF, 2020a). These additional funds would help Egypt "contain

DOI: 10.4324/9781003273844-8

the economic impact of the COVID-19 shock … [and] alleviate some of the most pressing financing needs, including for spending on health, social protection, and supporting the most impacted sectors and vulnerable groups" (IMF, 2020a). This RFI loan was shortly followed by a more substantial Stand-By Arrangement (SBA) $5.2 million loan focused on safeguarding and continuing Egypt's economic and structural reforms since 2016 (IMF, 2020b). Rather than short-term emergency funds like the RFI, the SBA supports specific reforms intended to protect (perceived) macroeconomic gains, strengthen the economy and, thus, contribute to Egypt's overall economic and social development in the medium and long term. It aims to "strike a balance between providing the crucial short-term stimulus to minimize the human and economic toll of the pandemic while avoiding buildup of imbalances in the medium term. Recalibrating policies and priorities to continue to strike this balance may be necessary as the crisis evolves" (IMF, 2020c, p. 8). A year into the SBA, IMF congratulated Egypt's response to the crisis, noting it was the only country in the MENA region to achieve positive gross domestic product (GDP) growth in 2020 (at 3.8%) (Auf, 2021).

This chapter adopts a historical materialist lens to problematize this narrative of a balanced Egyptian response to the COVID-19 crisis, aided and supported by IMF financial and technical assistance. Through the case of Egypt, I explore IFI responses to one of the worst global health emergencies in decades, highlight their underlying power relations and politics and question the extent to which they offer effective and sustainable solutions to the pandemic's social, political and economic fallouts in the medium and long term. Situating IMF's COVID-19 loans to Egypt within global capitalism and the country's historical experience with neoliberalization, I argue that the IMF's response to the crisis extends the same neoliberal structural reforms it encouraged before the pandemic, which have arguably contributed to and exacerbated the crisis, as solutions. By primarily framing the pandemic's challenges in economic terms and promoting investment-friendly policies, IMF loans roll out and consolidate neoliberalization by encouraging the state to focus on de-risking private-sector participation, without providing adequate social protection frameworks or accounting for public interests. In that sense, the IMF's approach is a typical neoliberal fail forward response to capitalism's economic and legitimacy crises, which prioritizes private gains over the public good and fails to address underlying structural challenges.

There is an established scholarship situating health governance in global capitalism before the pandemic. It highlights the politics and inequalities of neoliberal health provision (Navarro, 2007; Gill and Benatar, 2020; Schrecker, 2020; Sell and Williams, 2020; Sparke, 2020). Scholars explore how policies play out in different contexts (Nunes, 2020) and illustrate the role of IFIs in promoting them and limiting healthcare access (Rowden, 2013; Stubbs *et al.*, 2017; Forster *et al.*, 2020). Emerging scholarship has emphasized the historical inequalities underlying the pandemic and the politics of current responses to it. Scholars show how market-based health governance provided fertile ground for the pandemic (Ortiz and Stubbs, 2020; Navarro, 2020; Sonkin, 2020; Sparke and Williams, 2021), emphasizing private healthcare's shortcomings in addressing the pandemic (Williams, Yung and Grépin, 2021), in the Global South with significantly weakened public healthcare (Zhou, 2021) and Global North where the "regulatory state" has taken a backseat in public service provision (Jones and Hameiri, 2021).

Despite such failures, scholars highlight continuities in how states push for neoliberal policies against the backdrop of the pandemic (Šumonja, 2021) and IFIs promote privatized health models (Williams, 2020). They relate development responses to COVID-19 to pre-pandemic trends of harnessing finance for development and prioritizing investors' interests in public sectors (Dimakou, Romero and Van Waeyenberge, 2021), noting how the pandemic has advanced these trends to new sectors, most notably climate policy (Dafermos, Gabor and Michell, 2021). Scholars highlight how the IMF and World Bank's COVID responses do not diverge from pre-pandemic patterns and will likely entangle recipient countries in more debt (Iturralde, 2020; Kentikelenis *et al.*, 2020; Stubbs *et al.*, 2021), highlighting the financial burdens of this aid (Laskaridis, 2021).

I build on these interventions to illustrate the power and politics of COVID-related loans, their continuities and tensions and the state's role in playing them out in specific contexts. By examining IMF's loans to Egypt and public statements against the backdrop of the pandemic, I analyze how the IMF has capitalized on COVID-19 to consolidate neoliberalization, extend its structural adjustment policies in Egypt and carve out a bigger role for the private sector, amid limited social protection frameworks. In doing so, I complicate the narrative, propagated by both the IMF and the Egyptian state, that Egypt has successfully weathered the current crisis, largely because of its IMF-sponsored structural adjustment over the past five years. I highlight how this framing erases significant parts (and voices) of the story and conceals the politics underlying current and former IMF loans to Egypt. I illustrate how the IMF's approach to COVID frames the crisis in predominantly (neoliberal) economic terms, draws on the Egyptian state to prioritize private (economic) interests over the public good and thus offers no sustainable solution to COVID's health and social implications or the structural challenges underlying them.

This section introduced my case and situated my argument in existing debates. In the "Fail Forward and De-risking Responses to the Crisis" section, I elaborate on fail forward neoliberalism as a mode of governance advanced by the IMF. I highlight how IMF policies fit into emerging trends in development finance, which open up new avenues for private investment and reconfigure the state's role to facilitate these investments. The "IMF Loans to Egypt: Rolling Out Neoliberalism" section situates these trends within Egypt's longer history of neoliberalization and empirically traces how they manifest in the IMF's COVID-19 loans to the country. In the final section, I conclude, outlining avenues for future research and political praxis.

Fail forward and de-risking responses to the crisis

Since the 1970s, the global political economy has been organized along neoliberal lines, based on neoclassical economic thought that underscores the primacy of free markets, minimal state intervention and private actors' higher efficiency and productivity.[1] While neoliberal policies commonly entail a set of similar focuses, including market and labor deregulation, privatization, cuts to social spending and austerity (Peck and Tickell, 2002), they differ based on their temporal and geographic contexts (Brenner, Peck and Theodore 2010). Much like capitalism as a mode of production, neoliberal*ization* constantly changes in response to its failure to deliver on its promises and capitalism's inherent tendency for crisis, commonly understood as a disruption to the flow of capital (Marx, 1867/1976; Harvey, 2010, 2018). COVID-19 ushered in such a crisis for capitalism. It disrupted economic and financial flows in the wake of global lockdowns and exposed the frailty of healthcare models built on neoliberal ideas and promises. As early as April 2020, IMF economists warned of a worse economic fallout and declining global economic growth than those associated with the Great Depression or 2008 financial crisis (Gopinath, 2020). In addition to significant increases in unemployment, many countries, including advanced economies, have sunk into economic recession, and large global industries, such as tourism, have suffered major losses (Jones, Palumbo and Brown, 2021; UNCTAD, 2021). This is even more pronounced in Global South contexts where pandemic responses, including vaccinations, have been slower, and development challenges like poverty have been exacerbated (World Bank, 2021).

The economic crisis ushered in by COVID-19 has not been catastrophic for global capitalism, however. One of neoliberalism's "real strengths has been its capacity to capitalize on such conditions" and turn crises into opportunities (Peck and Tickell, 2002, p. 392). Disruptions are not fatal to the capitalist economy as far as they "can provide a positive spur to regulatory reinvention" (Peck and Tickell, 2002, p. 392). In response to the impacts of COVID-19 on the global economy, development actors and policymakers are rolling neoliberalization *out*, with emphasis on the "purposeful *construction and consolidation* of neoliberalised state forms, modes of governance, and regulatory relations" to address its impact on the global political economy (Peck and Tickell, 2002, p. 384, emphasis in original). IFIs have been crucial in drawing on the crisis to further advance neoliberal interests. Through their various support strategies, they have "promulgate[d] free(r) trade, free(r) markets, and increasingly unrestricted access to a wide range of markets … to transnational corporations" (Peck and Tickell, 2002, p. 391). By economically framing what is, first and foremost, a health crisis, IFIs have advanced recovery strategies comprising keeping economies afloat, maintaining capital flow and incentivizing investment. Instead of acknowledging the failures of neoliberalization, they present as solutions the same neoliberal policies that proved, at best, inadequate at delivering on the promises of prosperity for all, and, at worst, complicit in perpetuating socioeconomic inequalities (Peck, 2010; Shields, 2020; Soederberg and Tawakkol, 2020). This is not new or unique, but an inherent part of how neoliberalization has been rolled out over the past four decades, "tend[ing] to 'fail forward,' in that [its] manifest inadequacies have—so far anyway—repeatedly animated further rounds of neoliberal intervention" (Peck, 2010, p. 6). These loans are thus typical of neoliberalization's "ability to absorb or displace crisis tendencies, to ride—and capitalize on—the very economic cycles and localized policy failures that it was complicit in creating" (Peck and Tickell, 2002, p. 400).

In this current wave of neoliberalization, IMF loans have drawn on Global South states to promote fail forward policies and consolidate neoliberalization, further advance private accumulation and contribute to the salvation of global capitalism. These loans continue pre-pandemic development trends that stress the significance of (private) finance in addressing Global South countries' challenges. They build on the narrative that financially constrained countries can close their funding gap, build stronger economies and meet their populations' needs by providing better conditions for the private sector (World Bank, 2019). While these emphases are not new, the shift to what has been termed the "Wall Street Consensus" entails deeper changes and a reconfiguration of the (Global South) state's role to one of "de-risking" that is further evident in IFI responses to the pandemic (Gabor, 2021). As part of the rolling *out* of neoliberalization against the backdrop of COVID-19, IMF loans encourage the state not only to expand opportunities for private investors but also more crucially to "[protect] their profits from demand risks attached to infrastructure assets; from political risks attached to policies that would threaten cash flows, including nationalization, higher minimum wages and, critically, climate regulation; and from liquidity and currency risks" (Gabor, 2021, p. 431). This shifts the state's role to one of actively safeguarding neoliberalization (and, hence, accumulation) instead of advancing public needs.

In the context of the pandemic, this is particularly significant to ensure that state (social) spending and intervention to contain the crisis is limited, remains an exceptional emergency measure and does not persist into the future. In that sense, the loans encourage de-risking against potential public pressure. Much like post-pandemic "support from the [World] Bank's public sector arms (IBRD/IDA) has been portrayed as aiming to strengthen public health systems, [while] recipient countries are, at the same time, urged not to forego 'structural reforms' focused on liberalization and deregulation," IMF's responses to the pandemic push for structural adjustment and a strong de-risking state as a balanced response to the crisis (Dimakou, Romero and Van Waeyenberge, 2021, p. 229). As the case of Egypt highlights below, however, while these loans contain COVID-19 as an economic crisis for global capitalism, they fail to address it for what is a health emergency with massive social impacts and deep roots in previous waves of neoliberalization.

IMF loans to Egypt: rolling out neoliberalism

The IMF in Egypt: a long history

The IMF has a long history of promoting neoliberalization in Egypt at the expense of the population majority. In 1991, the Fund, alongside the World Bank, began its first structural adjustment reforms in Egypt, liberalizing finance, deregulating the labor market, privatizing state-owned companies and cutting back social spending (Harrigan and El-Said, 2009, p. 39; Ghanem, Wood and Mehdi, 2019, p. 10). These policies revolved around more deeply incorporating Egypt into the global economy and making it more attractive to global capital (Hanieh, 2013). Though the IMF hailed Egypt as "a remarkable success story" at the time, these policies disproportionately benefitted the country's capitalist class and foreign investors at the expense of the average population (qtd. in Harrigan and El-Said, 2009, p. 46; Joya, 2018). Unemployment and poverty persisted, as secure, well-paying jobs remained elusive (Harrigan and El-Said, 2009, p. 58; Ghanem, Wood and Mehdi, 2019, pp. 14–15, 18), eventually culminating in 2011 popular uprisings. The protests opposed neoliberal policies calling for a shift toward centering reforms around social justice (Hanieh, 2013). Despite this massive discontent, and the fact that neoliberal promises had not materialized, the IMF (and other IFIs) have continued to advance neoliberalization in the post-2011 period. While they have emphasized marginalized populations' concerns, their approach remains fundamentally unchanged; they have simply "attempted to utilize the post 2011 moment to maintain the essential characteristics of past practice, while employing a language that professes a new course and sympathy with the social justice goals of the uprisings" (Hanieh, 2015, p. 133). In other words, the IMF, in typical fail forward fashion, has repackaged neoliberalization and structural adjustment as new, erasing their history and presenting them as answers to protestors' demands and the country's post-2011 political and economic turbulences. While popular opposition successfully halted new loan agreements for a few years (Hanieh, 2015), political shifts in Egypt eventually saw the IMF extend a $12 billion loan in 2016 to jump-start macroeconomic reforms.

The 2016 loan provided an opportunity to roll out and consolidate neoliberalization in Egypt after the uprisings, to the detriment of the public. Among other things, the loan's policies imposed new taxes, floated the Egyptian pound, devaluing it by half overnight, and implemented austerity, which rolled back subsidies on food, more than doubled electricity and fuel prices, increased water bills and raised transportation fares (Ghoneim and El-Mahdawy, 2018; Mada Masr, 2018a, 2018c, 2018d, 2018e, 2018f; TIMEP, 2018). These measures directly contradict 2011 calls for social justice and institutionalize neoliberal dictums on decreasing state spending. Despite IMF's praise of the program as "a remarkable turnaround" in the country's economy, like previous IMF programs, this turnaround has been far from positive for most Egyptians (IMF, 2020a). Even though inflation rates decreased on paper, average Egyptians' purchasing power significantly decreased, and they have struggled to afford essential daily needs, like transportation (Mabrouk, 2020, p. 1; Mada Masr, 2017b, 2018b). In 2017–2018, the country's poverty rate, conservatively estimated at $1.45 per day, was up by almost 5% at 32.5%, and extreme poverty, set at less than one dollar per day, stood at 6.2% (Associated Press, 2019). Even when poverty rates decreased in 2019, they remained higher than they were before this most recent bout of structural adjustment (Gad, 2021).

Austerity and cuts to social spending extended to (public) healthcare, further worsening social and health conditions (TIMEP, 2018). Health spending is only 1.7% of Egypt's GDP, and public healthcare suffers from "[d]ilapidated state-run facilities, regular drug stock-outs and lack of adequate personnel" (World Bank, 2020b, p. 7; see also World Bank, 2020a). Amid a rundown and ill-equipped health sector, 68% of Egyptians opt for significantly more expensive private healthcare and 90% of them pay for it themselves (Derr, 2020; World Bank, 2020b). With austerity raising living costs, Egyptians who cannot afford private healthcare often have to forego healthcare and medication expenses (Mada Masr, 2017a).

While neoliberalization worsened living conditions for the average population, it provided more favorable opportunities for private accumulation and business interests, including the military's, than for its own population (Joya, 2018). The private sector not only steps in to fill the gap left by the state (i.e. in health) but also benefits from loosened restrictions and subsidies, including the 2019 Investment Law amendments' tax breaks and free zones (TIMEP, 2019). In fact, "[a]ccording to estimates in the Credit Suisse 2019 Global Wealth Databook, wealth concentrated in the hands of the country's richest 45000 individuals, less than 0.05 percent of the population, is more than the median wealth distributed to the entire population" (Auf, 2021).

Egypt's recent status as one of the "world's fastest growing economies" is fundamentally unequal (Egypt Today, 2021a). In addition to the celebrated growth failing to trickle down to the ground and actually exacerbating the average population's daily lived experiences, Egypt's IMF-mandated reforms are short-term and do not address structural issues (Adly, 2018). They have further rolled out neoliberalization, deepened inequalities and failed to deliver on their promises for better living conditions. Given this history, however, it is unsurprising that the IMF has responded to COVID-19 in Egypt the way it always does in crisis: with more fail forward neoliberalization.

The IMF in the age of COVID

With neoliberalization, increasing inequalities and decreasing social spending, it is unsurprising how hard COVID-19 has hit the Egyptian population. Marginalized populations and medical workers have borne the brunt of the pandemic.

Amid outbreaks across the country and overcrowded hospitals lacking essential equipment and unable to cope with surges in infections, Egypt's COVID-related death rate has been among the highest in the world (Raghavan, 2020; Mada Masr, 2021a). This is particularly significant since official figures underestimate the true extent of the crisis. Egypt has ranked fifth globally in underreporting COVID-related deaths (Mada Masr, 2021f), and public health officials have admitted that actual infection numbers could be as high as tenfold the official figures (CNN, 2020).

Meanwhile, adding to public health's pre-existing poor conditions, the health response has been severely lacking. Public testing protocols are stringent, with testing rates well below global averages, even though testing is one of the key measures in containing outbreaks (Mada Masr, 2020b). This has made polymerase chain reaction (PCR)[2] tests the purview of those who can afford them at £1,500–3,000 Egyptian pounds, the equivalent of close to $100–200 at the time of writing, and favored the accumulation of private testing centers (Madar Masr, 2020b). Similarly, state-owned pharmaceutical manufacturers have accrued massive profits producing medical supplies during the pandemic (Kassab and Seif Eddin, 2021). In contrast, medical workers have been pressured, and often arrested, for spreading "false news" when they have publicly emphasized the situation on the ground and have been unable to access treatment and vaccines for themselves (Mourad, 2020; Salem, 2020). On the vaccine front, while reports of government deals with the private sector to provide vaccines at a fee have not materialized, as of November 2021, only 11% and 7.3% of the population are partially or fully vaccinated, respectively (Mada Masr, 2021e; Ritchie *et al.*, 2021).[3] Even though the population's lived experience with the pandemic has its roots in the deterioration of healthcare and general living conditions, largely caused by neoliberal policies, the government and IMF have advanced these same policies as solutions to the current challenges.

Economic framings of the crisis

While claiming to balance both health and economic concerns, Egypt's focus has kept in line with previous phases in the country's history, measuring success in almost exclusively economic terms and prioritizing private interests. The Egyptian government's response entailed a partial, rather than complete, lockdown and a gradual reopening of the country's non-essential sectors as early as April 2020 in an attempt to "co-exist" with the virus (Egyptian Streets, 2020). Even during partial lockdown, key economic sectors, like construction (in which the state has a high economic stake), were encouraged to continue work "at maximum capacity" for economic reasons (Mada Masr, 2020a). Like pre-pandemic reforms, this push for businesses to open regardless of the health situation prioritizes financial gain. It does not account for the fact that, in a country where precautionary measures like masks and social distancing are not effectively enforced despite official regulations, and largely viewed as a luxury many cannot afford, this approach explicitly prioritizes the economic and political interests of businesses at the expense of public health (El Battouty, 2020, p. 19). This is especially significant given the state of public healthcare and health spending: in the second year of the pandemic, after the government increased it, the health budget for 2020/2021 accounted for a mere 1.55% of GDP (Mada Masr, 2021d).

In line with its reliance on economic rather than health and social indicators to assess countries' success in responding to the pandemic, the IMF has supported Egypt's response. Its repeated advice that, to transcend the current crisis, countries' need to focus on their economies is mirrored in its emphasis that "[t]he pandemic and global shock pose an immediate and severe economic disruption that could negatively impact Egypt's hard-won macroeconomic stability if not addressed" (IMF, 2020a; Egypt Today, 2021b). Accordingly, the IMF has commended the government's economic approach to the crisis as a "balanced" and successful one (IMF, 2021b). When evaluating Egypt's performance a year into the pandemic and its latest loan, the Fund highlighted economic stability and investor confidence (IMF, 2021c). In addition to being a far cry from the more immediate health concerns facing Egyptians, this framing depoliticizes Egypt's "hard-won macroeconomic stability" and conceals how its policies, implemented at the Fund's behest, have exacerbated social challenges and, in many ways, worsened the pandemic's impact (IMF, 2020c, p. 1). Framing it as such, the Fund paves the way for further rolling out neoliberalization as the way out of the crisis. Wary of global disruptions to capital flow and potential political discontent amid worsening conditions, the IMF draws on its COVID assistance to Egypt to advance private accumulation in the country and promote the state's de-risking of it.

Fail forward and de-risking solutions

By focusing on the pandemic's economic aspects in Egypt, the IMF promotes the same fail forward neoliberal policies it has always advanced. Even though its loans and neoliberal policies have previously failed to deliver on their promises of prosperity for Egypt's marginalized, and have actually limited public capacities, it presents them, again, as the necessary (and only) solutions to COVID-19's challenges. While its RFI loan strictly provided Egypt with emergency financial assistance, the 2020 SBA specifically aims to preserve Egypt's macroeconomic changes and implement additional structural (read: neoliberal) reforms. These reforms entail "strengthening the frameworks for public finances, improv[ing] governance and transparency, and reduc[ing] barriers to competition to ensure a path towards sustainable and inclusive private sector-led growth" (IMF, 2020c, p. i). In other words, they not only advance neoliberal policies to promote investment but also rely on the state to de-risk these investments. Specific policies include changes to how the state manages its budget and finances, as well as operational and financial changes to state-owned companies.

Though presented as essential for better fiscal governance, these policies translate to new governance processes modeled along private-sector management strategies that prioritize profit and reduce risks to accumulation while neglecting public concerns. This is evident in new draft bylaws for the public business sector, which establish uniform benefits and schemes, including compensation payments, across the sector and link worker benefits to company profits (Arafat, 2020). These reforms advance the state's accumulation interests by increasing revenue and lowering benefits and ensure reduced barriers to potential private accumulation. They come at the expense of employees, however. Even when public companies have fared well profit-wise, i.e. state-owned pharmaceutical companies during the pandemic, workers' annual bonuses have been significantly cut (Kassab and Seif Eddin, 2021). The Minister of Public Business himself has admitted that proposed changes stand to negatively impact 38% of the sector's employees (Fares, 2019). The new bylaws also make it easier to liquidate or merge companies without offering guarantees to employees, decrease workers' incentives and bonuses and reduce the quality of services they are offered including transportation and health insurance (Arafat, 2020). These policies build on plans to publicly trade large portions of state-owned companies, many of which have historically held political and economic value,[4] de facto privatizing them (Kassab, 2020c; Hapi Journal, 2021; Mada Masr, 2021c). To incentivize private investors, the IMF encourages the state to restructure its companies along private-sector lines to make them more profitable (Kassab, 2020c). Through these reforms, the state lowers the costs private actors have to bear should they invest in or acquire these companies. Government reforms advocated by the IMF thus place accumulation at the heart of a loan supposedly meant to address the pandemic. They advance neoliberal policies that have consistently proved not only ineffective but also complicit, in exacerbating socioeconomic struggles, and consolidate them at the state level.

The loan's emphasis on creating business-enabling environments as a fundamental component of the pandemic response similarly rolls out neoliberal interests through the Egyptian state. Key policies to incentivize private-sector participation, and proposed benchmarks for Egypt's structural reform progress, include amending the Competition and Customs Laws and reforming the National Investment Bank (NIB) (IMF, 2020c, pp. 13–14). By streamlining and accelerating customs procedures, the new law ensures businesses' timelines are not interrupted (ITA, 2021). The state lowers the risk of businesses wasting time or money on delayed shipments and, hence, delaying their accumulation. Similarly, by ensuring that all mergers and acquisitions go through the Competition Protection Agency, and so are approved and legal, amendments to the Competition Law allow businesses to circumvent potential legal, political or economic obstacles (Kassab, 2020b). Proposed reforms to the NIB adopt a similar logic. In charge of funding national development projects, the NIB has not been under the Central Bank's authority and is said to be funding losing projects and offering significantly high interest rates (Kassab, 2020b). The SBA proposes revising the bank's mandate and business and financial models, to better supervise it and ensure its outstanding loans are paid (IMF, 2020c, p. 14; Essam El-Din, 2021).

The Bank's Executive Chairman explains that "since many government institutions, economic and service organisations, were unable to repay loans, the government, in coordination with the IMF, had determined that the bank should accept assets to settle outstanding debts" (qtd. in Essam El-Din, 2021). The IMF also recommended halting NIB loans to the government until debts were settled (Essam El-Din, 2021). These reforms subordinate state institutions to financial logics, prioritizing accumulation interests (whether for the state or private actors) over public development needs. This is clear in statements by the IMF's senior resident representative in Egypt that the state should remove any regulatory or bureaucratic constraints (read: risks) to private participation (Auf, 2021). While the IMF presents these amendments as necessary "to support private-sector-led growth and job creation," and, by extension, address the population's needs, their public gain is minimal (IMF, 2020c, p. 13). They draw on COVID-19 as an economic crisis to follow in the path of previous IMF-mandated structural programs that have advanced neoliberalization and facilitated accumulation at the expense of local needs.

While the SBA briefly mentions supporting vulnerable populations and encourages the government's COVID-related social spending, these efforts are neither sufficient nor long-term enough to offset neoliberalization's favoring of private gains over public interests. The IMF has praised the government's "comprehensive package to contain the health and economic impact of the shock," but, of £100+ billion Egyptian pounds, only £5–6 billion have gone to health, while £500 billion have provided support to tourism businesses (El Akkawi, 2020; IMF, 2020c, p. 6, 2021b). More importantly, emergency funds have been partially sourced from public servants, whose salaries have been cut by 1% as an obligatory donation to the government (Kassab, 2020a). Though the IMF frames this as a tax to increase public revenue and support those hard hit by the pandemic, this policy places the burden of the response on a population already struggling socially, economically and health-wise. The most vulnerable effectively subsidize economic reforms that favor private businesses, as COVID-response packages safeguard private-sector involvement. This is particularly the case since pre-existing social support measures are not enough. The IMF emphasizes Egypt's expansion of its cash transfer assistance program, Takaful and Karama, to 3.5 million families and irregular workers, increased supplies to vulnerable communities and funding of health and social programs. These policies are band-aid solutions and do not address the root causes of socioeconomic vulnerabilities in the long term. Cash transfers are not enough to counter decades of austerity and structural adjustment (Saad-Filho, 2016). In that sense, they do not provide a basis for avoiding similar ramifications in the case of future emergencies, health-related or otherwise.

More pertinently, the government's social support policies in light of COVID, including Takaful and Karama, do not respond to people's immediate needs. Even before the pandemic, the beneficiary base was limited, and assistance barely covered basic needs, let alone provided a surplus for households to fall back on

(Ahmed, 2018; Kassab, 2019). The program's expansion to reach 3.5% of the country's population stands in stark contrast to the fact that poverty rates are at least 30% at official estimations (Gad, 2021). Moreover, cash transfers have remained at the same value, even as people's living conditions have worsened during the pandemic (Kassab, 2021). The government's continued rollout of neoliberalization also entails additional subsidy cuts, including on food, while the average population struggles to meet basic needs, let alone address the pandemic's impact (Mada Masr, 2021b). For example, in June 2020, 73.5% of Egyptian households reported a decrease in their income (Gad, 2021). Despite that, the IMF's SBA offers no concrete solutions for COVID's health and social implications. Its structural reform policies for increasing social support consist of a public expenditure review focused on "evaluating the effectiveness of social spending, identifying gaps, and providing recommendations by April 2021" (IMF, 2020c, p. 13). This vagueness on social support measures is typical of how the IMF has historically approached social issues in Egypt and the region (Mossallem, 2015). It is another instance of IMF rhetorical emphasis on social protection, with no concrete change in its approach (Kentikelenis, Stubbs and King, 2016; Diab and Hindy, 2021). In this context, the rhetorical support for social spending can be understood as a means of legitimizing this latest phase of neoliberalization in the country and appeasing an increasingly struggling population to ensure the consolidation of private accumulation.

It is worth noting that, while the IMF emphasizes the need to support businesses in the post-COVID era, its support for increased social spending is not blanket approval. In line with the government's hopes to decrease the number of the cash transfer beneficiaries (Kassab, 2021), IMF analysts have stressed the "exceptional" nature of measures to contain the crisis "including credit guarantees, liquidity facilities, loan forbearance, expanded unemployment insurance, enhanced benefits, and tax relief" and the need to roll them back as soon as possible (Gopinath, 2020). Placing social support on the same level with business subsidies, and highlighting the need to replace them with investment incentives, aptly summarizes the IMF's economic approach to the pandemic and its fail forward neoliberal solutions to one crisis after the other. This approach prompts the state to guarantee de-risking measures into the future and is evident in IMF plans for recovery in the Global South, which overwhelmingly promote fiscal consolidation (read: austerity) to counterbalance (social) spending during the pandemic (Tamale, 2021). In doing so, the IMF consistently utilizes its COVID loans to roll out neoliberalization now and in the future and to place the state in the role of private business guarantor, to the detriment of the public good.

Conclusion

The IMF's assertion that Egypt has used a balanced and successful approach to address the pandemic is fundamentally *im*balanced in the policies and interests it promotes. Despite COVID's toll on Egyptians, the Fund is primarily concerned with COVID-19's impact on global capitalism and ensuring capital growth is not disrupted. While the situation in Egypt highlights how COVID-19 is, first and foremost, a health emergency, the IMF frames it as a predominantly economic one and encourages the Egyptian state to approach it as such. The IMF rolls out neoliberalization and advances, as the crucial ingredient for overcoming COVID's impact, the same fail forward neoliberal policies it has advocated for decades. It promotes policies that reconfigure the state's role into one of limiting risks to private investment. In doing so, it safeguards private gains in Egypt at the expense of public interests, erasing the political relations underlying its policies and neglecting their historical failure in fulfilling their promise of prosperity for all. More importantly, it does not provide an adequate framework for responding to the current health crisis and offers no sustainable policies for avoiding or responding to future ones. Even when it emphasizes the pandemic's social impact on Global South countries and their populations, the IMF advances policies whose primary focus is consolidating neoliberal interests. It is thus no wonder that the IMF keeps coming back "to Egypt again and again to fix the very problems they are currently addressing" (Adly, 2018, p. 16). This is neither accident nor incompetence but a fundamental aspect of the IMF's (fail forward) neoliberal approach and (class-based) politics (Peck, 2010).

The IMF's pandemic-related assistance to Egypt exemplifies broader trends in how IFIs have drawn on the current health crisis to advance neoliberal interests. There remains a lot to study when it comes to COVID, particularly utilizing it as a lens for understanding the class relations driving the global political economy. A useful agenda for future critical research needs to be cognizant of both continuities and ruptures in global capitalism, aid and development finance, caused by the pandemic. Questions on the race to the vaccine include how vaccines are manufactured, what incentives were provided to private producers and what this means for future medical research. In terms of vaccine distribution, how vaccine aid was formulated, who was prioritized and how accessible these initiatives have been in the Global South settings are all angles for understanding vaccine politics. We need to also seriously interrogate health policies advanced in light of COVID-19, how they change or replicate pre-pandemic patterns and the extent to which they are sustainable and resilient (and what this entails). Other important questions revolve around the types of policies and development projects yet to be extended to cope with the pandemic's economic fallouts. In addition to providing a rich research agenda, these questions allow us to approach the pandemic, and responses to it, for the political issues they are and develop more progressive and equitable responses for current and future crises.

Notes

1 While neoliberalism has multiple contested definitions, I build on critical and Marxian approaches to political economy to understand it. For examples of this approach, see Peck and Tickell (2002) and Brenner, Peck and Theodore (2010).

2 PCR tests are generally considered the most reliable means of detecting the virus in patients.

3 "A person is partly vaccinated if they have received only one dose of a 2-dose vaccine protocol. A person is considered fully vaccinated if they have received a single-dose vaccine or both doses of a two-dose vaccine" (Ritchie *et al.*, 2021).

4 For example, Egyptian Iron and Steel, founded in 1958, represented postcolonial independence and national industrialization (Mada Masr, 2021c). Similarly, the Heliopolis Company for Housing and Development "was nationalized in retaliation for Belgium's role in the assassination of Congolese Prime Minister Patrice Lumumba" at a time when Egyptian foreign policy supported African independence and anti-colonialism (Kassab, 2020c).

References

Adly, A. (2018, November). *Short term fixes for long lasting troubles: Why IMF reforms won't solve Egypt's (political) economic problems.* Friedrich-Ebert-Stiftung.

Ahmed, W. (2018, April 4). Escaping the poverty cycle? 3 years of Takaful and Karama. (Khalifa, S. Trans.). *Mada Masr.* https://www.madamasr.com/en/2018/04/04/feature/economy/escaping-the-poverty-cycle-3-years-of-takaful-and-karama/

Ahram Online. (2021, July 23). Egypt's proactive policies shielded the economy against coronavirus repercussions: IMF. *Ahram Online.* https://english.ahram.org.eg/NewsContent/3/12/417576/Business/Economy/Egypt's-proactive-policies-shielded-the-economy-ag.aspx

Arafat, N. (2020, November 11). 119 companies, 1 wage structure? Unified wage bylaws spark outrage among public business sector workers. *Mada Masr.* https://www.madamasr.com/en/2020/11/11/feature/politics/119-companies-1-wage-structure-unified-wage-bylaws-spark-outrage-among-public-business-sector-workers/

Associated Press. (2019, July 30). Egypt: A third of population lives in poverty. *VOA News.* https://www.voanews.com/a/middle-east_egypt-third-population-lives-poverty/6172941.html

Auf, O. (2021, Winter). A visualization of Egypt's economic performance during COVID-19. *The Cairo Review of Global Affairs.* https://www.thecairoreview.com/midan/a-visualization-of-egypts-economic-performance-during-covid-19/

Brenner, N., Peck, J. and Theodore, N. (2010). Variegated neoliberalisation: Geographies, modalities, pathways. *Global Networks 10*(2), 182–222.

CNN. (2020, December 20). ʻuḍwu bi-lagnit muwāgahat corona fī maṣr: Raqam al-ʻĪṣābāt al-ḥaqīqī bil-bilād 10 ʻaḍ'āf al-mu'lan [Member of Egypt Coronavirus committee: The real number of cases in the country is 10 times what is declared]. *CNN.* https://arabic.cnn.com/health/article/2020/12/20/egypt-coronavirus-committee-real-number-cases-10-times-what-declared

Dafermos, Y., Gabor, D. and Michell, J. (2021). The Wall Street Consensus in pandemic times: What does it mean for climate-aligned development? *Canadian Journal of Development Studies 42*(1–2), 238–251.

Derr, J. (2020, Winter). Hepatitis C, COVID-19 and the Egyptian Regime's Approach to Health Care. *Middle East Research and Information Project, 297.* https://merip.org/2020/12/hepatitis-c-covid-19-and-the-egyptian-regimes-approach-to-health-care/

Diab, O. and Hindy, S. I. (2021). IMF's social protection between rhetoric and action: The case of Egypt. *Middle East Critique.*

Dimakou, O., Romero, M. J. and Van Waeyenberge, E. (2021). Never let a pandemic go to waste: Turbocharging the private sector for development at the World Bank. *Canadian Journal of Development Studies 42*(1–2), 221–237.

Egyptian Streets. (2020, June 23). Egypt lifts most COVID-19 restrictions, moves to 'coexist' with the virus. *Egyptian Streets.* https://egyptianstreets.com/2020/06/23/egypt-lifts-most-covid-19-restrictions-moves-to-coexist-with-the-virus/

Egypt Today. (2021a, February 14). Egypt supports economy to overcome coronavirus crisis: IMF. *Egypt Today.* https://www.egypttoday.com/Article/3/98585/Egypt-supports-economy-to-overcome-coronavirus-crisis-IMF

Egypt Today. (2021b, May 18). IMF Managing Director says Egypt became one of the fastest growing economies in the world. *Egypt Today.* https://www.egypttoday.com/Article/3/104064/IMF-Managing-Director-says-Egypt-became-one-of-the-fastest

El Akkawi, D. (2020, November 20). COVID-19 in Egypt: Between governance and flattening the curve. *The Cairo Review of Global Affairs.* https://www.thecairoreview.com/midan/covid-19-in-egypt-between-governance-and-flattening-the-curve/

El Battouty, S. (2020, October). As Egypt recovers, sustainable growth must remain at the heart of its development plans. In M. F. Mabrouk (Ed.), *Rethinking Egypt's Economy* (pp. 19–24). Middle East Institute. https://www.mei.edu/sites/default/files/2020-10/Rethinking%20Egypt%27s%20Economy.pdf

Essam El-Din, G. (2021, August 19). Egypt: National Investment Bank survives. *Ahram Online.* https://english.ahram.org.eg/NewsContent/50/1202/419300/AlAhram-Weekly/Economy/Egypt-National-Investment-Bank-survives.aspx

Fares, O. (2019, October 15). Wazīr qiṭā' al-"amāl: 62% min al-'umāl sayastafīdūn min ta'dīl lawa'iḥ al-'ugūr wa al-baqiya sayata'atharūn [Minister of Public Business Sector: 62% of workers will benefit from wage bylaw amendments and the rest will be impacted]. *Shorouk News.* https://www.shorouknews.com/news/view.aspx?cdate=15102019andid=a61f5de7-23c4-44d3-b266-ec6ea22ef4fc

Forster, T., Kentikelenis, A. E., Stubbs, T.H. and King, L.P. (2020). Globalization and health equity: The impact of structural adjustment programs on developing countries. *Social Science and Medicine 267.*

Gabor, D. (2021). The Wall Street consensus. *Development and Change 52*(3), 429–459.

Gad, M. (2021, March 30). Egypt: The pandemic experience in a time of reform. *Middle East Institute.* https://www.mei.edu/publications/egypt-pandemic-experience-time-reform#_ftnref19

Georgieva, K. (2021, March 30). Giving people a fair shot—Policies to secure the recovery. *International Monetary Fund.* https://www.imf.org/en/News/Articles/2021/03/25/sp033021-SMs2021-Curtain-Raiser

Ghanem, N., Wood, D. and Mehdi, R. (2019, July). *Socioeconomic impacts of macroeconomic reform policies in the Arab region.* United Nations ESCWA.

Ghoneim, B. and El-Mahdawy, H. (2018, May 15). Metro fare hike prompts protests and arrests, adds to the burdens of Egyptians. *Mada Masr.* https://www.madamasr.com/en/2018/05/15/feature/politics/metro-fare-hike-prompts-protests-and-arrests-adds-to-the-burdens-of-egyptians/

Gill, S. R. and Benatar, S. R. (2020). Reflections on the political economy of planetary health. *Review of International Political Economy 27*(1), 167-190.

Gopinath, G. (2020, April 14). The Great Lockdown: Worst economic downturn since the Great Depression. *IMF Blog.* https://blogs.imf.org/2020/04/14/the-great-lockdown-worst-economic-downturn-since-the-great-depression/

Hanieh, A. (2013). *Lineages of revolt: Issues of contemporary capitalism in the Middle East.* Chicago, IL: Haymarket Books.

Hanieh, A. (2015). Shifting priorities or business as usual? Continuity and change in the post-2011 IMF and World Bank engagement with Tunisia, Morocco and Egypt. *British Journal of Middle Eastern Studies 42*(1), 119–134.

Hannah, R., Mathieu, E., Rodés-Guirao, L., Appel, C., Giattino, C., Ortiz-Ospina, E., Hasell, J., Macdonald, B., Beltekian, D. and Roser, M. (2020). Coronavirus pandemic (COVID-19). Published online at OurWorldInData.org. Accessed November 12, 2021. https://ourworldindata.org/coronavirus

Hapi Journal. (2021, January 10). Hisham Tawfik: Tarshīḥ 4 sharikāt li-birnāmig al-ṭurūḥāt al-ḥukūmiya baynaha al-naṣr lil-ta'dīn [Hisham Tawfik: 4 Companies nominated for government IPO program, including Al-Nasr Mining]. *Hapi Journal.* https://hapijournal.com/2021/01/10/هشام-توفيق-ترشيح-4-شركات-لبرنامج-الطروح/

Harrigan, J. and El-Said, H. (2009). *Aid and power in the Arab world: IMF and World Bank policy-based lending in the Middle East and North Africa.* London: Palgrave Macmillan.

Harvey, D. (2010). *The enigma of capital and the crises of capitalism.* London: Profile Books.

Harvey, D. (2018). *The limits to capital.* London: Verso.

International Monetary Fund (IMF). (2020a, May 11). IMF Executive Board approves US$2.772 billion in emergency support to Egypt to address the COVID-19 pandemic. *International Monetary Fund.* https://www.imf.org/en/News/Articles/2020/05/11/pr20215-egypt-imf-executive-board-approves-us-2-772b-in-emergency-support-to-address-the-covid19

International Monetary Fund (IMF). (2020b, July 9). IMF country focus: Egypt takes proactive approach to limit the pandemic's fallout. *International Monetary Fund.* https://www.imf.org/en/News/Articles/2020/07/09/na070920-egypt-takes-proactive-approach-to-limit-the-pandemics-fallout

International Monetary Fund (IMF). (2020c, August 10). *Request for a 12-month stand-by arrangement—Press release; staff report; and statement by the executive director for the Arab Republic of Egypt.* Country report no. 2020/266. International Monetary Fund. https://www.imf.org/en/Publications/CR/Issues/2020/08/10/Arab-Republic-of-Egypt-Request-for-a-12-Month-Stand-By-Arrangement-Press-Release-Staff-49683

International Monetary Fund (IMF). (2021a, April 8). Questions and answers: The IMF's response to COVID-19. *International Monetary Fund.* https://www.imf.org/en/About/FAQ/imf-response-to-covid-19

International Monetary Fund (IMF). (2021b, July 19). Policy responses to COVID-19: Egypt, Arab Republic of. *International Monetary Fund.* https://www.imf.org/en/Topics/imf-and-covid19/Policy-Responses-to-COVID-19#E

International Monetary Fund (IMF). (2021c, June 23). IMF Executive Board completes the second review under the Stand-By Arrangement (SBA) for the Arab Republic of Egypt and Concludes 2021 Article IV Consultation. *International Monetary Fund.* https://www.imf.org/en/News/Articles/2021/06/23/pr21193-egypt-imf-execboard-completes-2ndrev-under-the-sba-concludes-2021aiv

International Trade Administration (ITA). (2021, September 5). Customs Regulations: Egypt – Country Commercial Guide. *International Trade Administration.* https://www.trade.gov/country-commercial-guides/egypt-customs-regulations

Iturralde, P. (2020, July 16). The IMF's role in the devastating impacts of COVID-19—the case ofEcuador. *Bretton Woods Project.* https://www.brettonwoodsproject.org/2020/07/the-imfs-role-in-the-devastating-impacts-of-covid-19-the-case-of-ecuador/

Jones, L. and Hameiri, S. (2021). COVID-19 and the failure of the neoliberal regulatory state. *Review of International Political Economy.*

Jones, L., Palumbo, D. and Brown, D. (2021, January 24). Coronavirus: How the pandemic has changed the world economy. *BBC News.* https://www.bbc.com/news/business-51706225

Joya, A. (2018). The military and state in Egypt: Class formation in the post-Arab uprisings. *British Journal of Middle Eastern Studies* 47(5), 681–701.

Kassab, B. (2019, October 3). Do not rest assured: People in need are still not getting their food subsidies. *Mada Masr.* https://www.madamasr.com/en/2019/10/03/feature/economy/do-not-rest-assured-people-in-need-are-still-not-getting-their-food-subsidies/

Kassab, B. (2020a, June 23). COVID-19 relief? Where is the government getting the money? *Mada Masr.* https://www.madamasr.com/en/2020/06/23/feature/economy/covid-19-relief-where-is-the-government-getting-the-money/

Kassab, B. (2020b, September 24). New IMF loan agreement – round 2, but without austerity measures. *Mada Masr.* https://www.madamasr.com/en/2020/09/24/feature/economy/the-new-imf-loan-agreement-round-two-of-the-old-agreement-but-without-the-austerity-measures/

Kassab, B. (2020c, September 29). Entering the gated compound game: A look at the plan to develop a new Heliopolis Company for Housing and Development. *Mada Masr.* https://www.madamasr.com/en/2020/09/29/feature/economy/entering-the-gated-compound-game-a-look-at-the-plan-to-develop-a-new-heliopolis-company-for-housing-and-development/

Kassab, B. (2021, May 3). Where does social protection spending stand in Egypt's 2nd COVID-19 budget? *Mada Masr.* https://www.madamasr.com/en/2021/05/03/feature/economy/where-does-social-protection-spending-stand-in-egypts-2nd-covid-19-budget/

Kassab, B. and Seif Eddin, S. (2021, October 24). Worker-management rift remains as state pharma company reopens after strike. *Mada Masr.* https://www.madamasr.com/en/2021/10/24/feature/politics/worker-management-rift-remains-as-state-pharma-company-reopens-after-strike/

Kentikelenis, A. E., Stubbs, T. H. and King, L. P. (2016). IMF conditionality and development policy space, 1985-2014. *Review of International Political Economy 23*(4), 543-582.

Kentikelenis, A., Gabor, D., Ortiz, I., Stubbs, T., Mckee, M. and Stuckler, D. (2020, April 9). Softening the blow of the pandemic: Will the International Monetary Fund and World Bank make things worse? *The Lancet 8*(6).

Laskaridis, C. (2021). When push came to shove: COVID-19 and debt crises in low-income countries. *Canadian Journal of Development Studies 42*(1-2), 200-220.

Mabrouk, M. F. (2020, October). Introduction: Evolution, adaptation, and survival. In M. F. Mabrouk (Ed.), *Rethinking Egypt's Economy* (pp. 1–4). Middle East Institute. https://www.mei.edu/sites/default/files/2020-10/Rethinking%20Egypt%27s%20Economy.pdf

Mada Masr. (2017a, February 1). Making ends meet: 6 stories of household budgeting. *Mada Masr.* https://www.madamasr.com/en/2017/02/01/feature/society/making-ends-meet-6-stories-from-egyptian-households/

Mada Masr. (2017b, October 10). Inflation eases in September but Egyptians' purchasing power continues to fall. *Mada Masr.* https://www.madamasr.com/en/2017/10/10/news/u/inflation-eases-in-september-but-egyptians-purchasing-power-continues-to-fall/

Mada Masr. (2018a, April 19). Food subsidies to increase by marginal 5% in upcoming state budget as austerity measures continue. *Mada Masr.* https://www.madamasr.com/en/2018/04/19/news/u/food-subsidies-to-increase-by-marginal-5-in-upcoming-state-budget-as-austerity-measures-continue/

Mada Masr. (2018b, August 6). An income spent on daily subsistence: Wage earners are picking up the tab of Egypt's economic 'reform' program. (M. Gad, Trans.). *Mada Masr.* https://www.madamasr.com/en/2018/08/06/opinion/economy/an-income-spent-on-daily-subsistence/

Mada Masr. (2018c, June 12). Government raises household electricity tariffs by up to 69.2%. *Mada Masr.* https://www.madamasr.com/en/2018/06/12/news/u/government-raises-household-electricity-tariffs-by-up-to-69-2/

Mada Masr. (2018d, June 16). Government hikes fuel prices by up to 66.7%. *Mada Masr.* https://www.madamasr.com/en/2018/06/16/news/economy/government-hikes-fuel-prices-by-up-to-66-7/

Mada Masr. (2018e, June 16). Live updates: Government raises transportation costs nationwide following fuel price hikes. *Mada Masr.* https://www.madamasr.com/en/2018/06/16/news/economy/live-updates-government-raises-transportation-costs-nationwide-following-fuel-price-hikes/

Mada Masr. (2018f, June 3). Government raises household water tariffs by 46.5%. *Mada Masr.* https://www.madamasr.com/en/2018/06/03/news/u/government-raises-household-water-tariffs-by-46/

Mada Masr. (2020a, April 2). Expect higher COVID-19 numbers, but don't be alarmed, PM Madbuly says. *Mada Masr.* https://www.madamasr.com/en/2020/04/02/feature/politics/expect-higher-covid-19-numbers-but-dont-be-alarmed-pm-says/

Mada Masr. (2020b, December 3). Egypt's COVID-19 contradiction: Fewer cases, higher death rate. *Mada Masr.* https://www.madamasr.com/en/2020/12/03/feature/politics/egypts-covid-19-contradiction-fewer-cases-higher-death-rate/

Mada Masr. (2021a, April 19). Doctors, officials call for urgent measures in Upper Egypt to combat surge in coronavirus cases. *Mada Masr.* https://www.madamasr.com/en/2021/04/19/news/u/doctors-officials-call-for-urgent-measures-in-upper-egypt-to-combat-surge-in-coronavirus-cases/

Mada Masr. (2021b, August 4). Sisi says bread subsidies to be cut, ministers begin price studies. *Mada Masr.* https://www.madamasr.com/en/2021/08/04/news/u/sisi-says-bread-subsidies-to-be-cut-ministers-begin-price-studies/

Mada Masr. (2021c, January 13). Public sector giant Egyptian Iron and Steel Company to be liquidated despite opposition. *Mada Masr.* https://www.madamasr.com/en/2021/01/13/feature/economy/public-sector-giant-egyptian-iron-and-steel-company-to-be-liquidated-despite-opposition/

Mada Masr. (2021d, June 16). General budget approved despite apparent shortfall in spending on health, education. *Mada Masr.* https://www.madamasr.com/en/2021/06/16/feature/economy/general-budget-approved-despite-apparent-shortfall-in-spending-on-health-education/

Mada Masr. (2021e, June 17). Government inches toward vaccine-for-fee model with private sector. *Mada Masr.* https://www.madamasr.com/en/2021/06/17/news/u/government-inches-toward-vaccine-for-fee-model-with-private-sector/

Mada Masr. (2021f, October 11). Egypt ranks 5th worldwide in underreporting COVID-19 deaths according to World Bank report. *Mada Masr.* https://www.madamasr.com/en/2021/10/11/news/u/egypt-ranks-5th-worldwide-in-underreporting-covid-19-deaths-according-to-world-bank-report/

Marx, K. (1976). *Capital: A critique of political economy, volume I.* Penguin Books. (Original work published 1867).

Mossallem, M. (2015, December). *The IMF in the Arab World: Lessons unlearnt.* Bretton Woods Project. https://www.brettonwoodsproject.org/wp-content/uploads/2015/12/final-MENA-report.pdf

Mourad, S. (2020, July 9). Egyptian doctors in the state's eyes: Rhetoric versus reality. *The Tahrir Institute for Middle East Policy.* https://timep.org/commentary/analysis/egyptian-doctors-in-the-states-eyes-rhetoric-versus-reality/

Navarro, V. (2007). Neoliberalism as a class ideology; Or, the political causes of the growth of inequalities. *International Journal of Health Services 37*(1), 47–62.

Navarro, V. (2020). The consequences of neoliberalism in the current pandemic. *International Journal of Health Services 50*(3), 271–275.

Nunes, J. (2020). The everyday political economy of health: Community health workers and the response to the 2015 Zika outbreak in Brazil. *Review of International Political Economy* 27(1), 146–166.

Ortiz, I. and Stubbs, T. (2020, March 23). Fighting coronavirus: It's time to invest in universal public health. *Inter Press Service News Agency*. http://www.ipsnews.net/2020/03/fighting-coronavirus-time-invest-universal-public-health/

Peck, J. (2010). *Constructions of neoliberal reason*. Oxford University Press.

Peck, J. and Tickell, A. (2002). Neoliberalizing Space. *Antipode 34*, 380–404.

Raghavan, S. (2020, June 17). Egypt thought it dodged the worst of the pandemic. But now hospitals are being overwhelmed. *The Washington Post*. https://www.washingtonpost.com/world/middle_east/egypt-thought-it-dodged-the-worst-of-the-pandemic-but-now-hospitals-are-being-overwhelmed/2020/06/16/36397b8e-af2c-11ea-98b5-279a6479a1e4_story.html

Rowden, R. (2013). *The deadly ideas of neoliberalism: How the IMF has undermined public health and the fight against AIDS*. Zed Books.

Salem, O. (2020, July 7). Egypt's social media discovered its coronavirus crisis. *Foreign Policy*. https://foreignpolicy.com/2020/07/07/egypts-social-media-discovered-its-coronavirus-crisis/

Schrecker, T. (2020). Globalization and health: Political grand challenges. *Review of International Political Economy* 27(1), 26–47.

Segal, S. and Henderson, J. (2021, January 25). International financial institutions' COVID-19 approvals approach $240 billion for 2020. *Center for Strategic and International Studies*. https://www.csis.org/analysis/international-financial-institutions-covid-19-approvals-approach-240-billion-2020

Sell, S. K. and Williams, O. D. (2020). Health under capitalism: A global political economy of structural pathologies. *Review of International Political Economy* 27(1), 1–25.

Shields, S. (2020). The EBRD, fail forward neoliberalism and construction of the European periphery. *The Economic and Labour Relations Review 31*(2), 230–248.

Soederberg, S. and Tawakkol, L. (2020). The Humanitarian-Development Nexus and the Jordan Compact: Tensions and trajectories in global capitalism. *Journal für Entwicklungspolitik 36*(4), 129–154.

Sonkin, F. (2020, December 14). Gambling with our lives: Emergencies expose consequences of decades of IMF and World Bank policies. *Bretton Woods Project*. https://www.brettonwoodsproject.org/2020/12/gambling-with-our-lives-global-emergencies-expose-consequences-of-decades-of-imf-and-world-bank-policies/

Sparke, M. (2020). Neoliberal regime change and the remaking of global health: From rollback disinvestment to rollout reinvestment and reterritorialization. *Review of International Political Economy* 27(1), 48–74.

Sparke, M. and Williams, O. D. (2021). Neoliberal disease: COVID-19, co-pathogenesis and global health insecurities. *Environment and Planning A: Economy and Space*.

Stubbs, T., Kentikelenis, A., Stuckler, D., McKee, M. and King, L. (2017). The impact of IMF conditionality on government health expenditure: A cross-national analysis of 16 West African nations. *Social Science and Medicine 174*, 220–227.

Stubbs, T., Kring, W., Laskaridis, C., Kentikelenis, A. and Gallagher, K. (2021). Whatever it takes? The global financial safety net, COVID-19, and developing countries. *World Development 137*.

Šumonja, M. (2021). Neoliberalism is not dead – on political implications of COVID-19. *Capital and Class 45*(2), 215–227.

Tamale, N. (2021, August). *Adding fuel to fire: How IMF demands for austerity will drive up inequality worldwide.* Oxfam. https://reliefweb.int/sites/reliefweb.int/files/resources/bp-covid-loans-imf-austerity-110821-en.pdf

The Tahrir Institute for Middle East Policy (TIMEP). (2018, October). *Egypt's Economic Trajectory: Assessing Egypt's Economic Reform.* The Tahrir Institute for Middle East Policy (TIMEP). https://timep.org/wp-content/uploads/2018/10/TIMEP-EET-report_10-29-18-mks-edits-new-1.pdf

The Tahrir Institute for Middle East Policy (TIMEP). (2019, April 5). TIMEP brief: Investment law. *The Tahrir Institute for Middle East Policy (TIMEP).* https://timep.org/reports-briefings/timep-brief-investment-law/

United Nations Conference on Trade and Development (UNCTAD). (2021, June 30). Global economy could lose over $4 trillion due to COVID-19 impact on tourism. *United Nations Conference on Trade and Development.* https://unctad.org/news/global-economy-could-lose-over-4-trillion-due-covid-19-impact-tourism

Williams, O. D. (2020). COVID-19 and private health: Market and governance failure. *Society for International Development.*

Williams, O. D., Yung, K. C. and Grépin, K. A. (2021). The failure of private health services: COVID-19 induced crises in low- and middle-income country (LMIC) health systems. *Global Public Health 16*(8-9), 1320-1333.

World Bank. (2019). *Beyond the Gap: How countries can afford the infrastructure they need while protecting the planet.* World Bank Group.

World Bank. (2020a, April 28). *Egypt COVID-19 emergency response.* Project Information Document. World Bank. https://documents.worldbank.org/en/publication/documents-reports/documentdetail/906831588109454283/project-information-document-egypt-covid-19-emergency-response-p173912

World Bank. (2020b, March 30). *Supporting Egypt's universal health insurance system.* Project Information Document. World Bank. https://documents.worldbank.org/en/publication/documents-reports/documentdetail/933491585692791089/project-information-document-supporting-egypt-s-universal-health-insurance-system-p172426

World Bank. (2021, June 8). The global economy: On track for strong but uneven growth as COVID-19 still weighs. *World Bank.* https://www.worldbank.org/en/news/feature/2021/06/08/the-global-economy-on-track-for-strong-but-uneven-growth-as-covid-19-still-weighs

Zhou, A. (2021). Limits of neoliberalism: HIV, COVID-19, and the importance of healthcare systems in Malawi. *Global Public Health 16*(8–9), 1346–1363.

9

INSTITUTIONAL EXHAUSTION AND FOREIGN AID IN THE TIME OF COVID-19

Michael de Percy

Introduction

The US-led multilateral rules-based world order was already under threat from the rise of populism, China, and instability in US politics before the COVID-19 pandemic disrupted global diplomacy and brought about far-reaching economic crises. In response, nation-states adapted to emerging nationalism amid the US–China trade war instigated by former president Donald Trump. Such multifaceted disruption forced nation-states to re-evaluate their traditional security and foreign aid partnerships, resulting in a weakened commitment to existing multilateral institutions. Such institutional exhaustion (the inability of the global rules, routines, and procedures of the past to address the realities of the present) provided opportunities for China and Russia to offer an alternative to the existing rules-based world order through foreign aid, assistance, and development programmes that were labelled as 'coercive' by the West. The result has been a parallel, albeit novel, world order for developing nations that at first glance resembles the competition-based diplomacy of the Cold War, referred to here as neo-Cold War diplomacy. But is it possible that the US-led neoliberal hegemony was only ever regional (Western Hemisphere) and not truly global (Mearsheimer, 2001), echoing Mearsheimer's (2018) thesis of the 'delusion' of a liberal order? Before examining the institutional exhaustion evidenced by contemporary global geopolitics, the discussion below outlines the fragmented nature of the 'world order' that existed before the COVID-19 pandemic became 'the straw that broke the camel's back' (Allen, et al., 2020).

While the foreign relations rhetoric of the US under Biden has softened from the Trump period, the fragile balance of competition and cooperation between the major global powers appears more pragmatic than ideological and willing to challenge the inherent neoliberal norms of the established international

DOI: 10.4324/9781003273844-9

institutions in response to COVID nationalism. At the same time, foreign aid and development took a back seat, while wealthy countries (particularly members of the Organisation for Economic Co-operation and Development (OECD)) focused on dealing with the pandemic-driven economic and health shocks. Meanwhile, Russia has been proactive in filling the strategic vacuum created by the US withdrawal in the Middle East, while China has focused its diplomatic efforts on developing nations in South Asia, such as Papua New Guinea, using a combination of soft power through foreign aid and financial incentives through the Belt and Road Initiative (BRI) to advance its logistics network. In response, a US pushback has been supported by emboldened leadership in the UK and Australia, amid the strategic interests of Japan and India, with cautious support from Germany, France, and Italy.

Coinciding with changing global geopolitics is a shift in how foreign aid is viewed. Since World War II, funds provided by developed nations to developing (or war-torn) nations were delivered through aid distribution organisations that formed part of the multilateral institutions, ranging from the Marshall Plan (which continues to this day in Germany, see KfW, 2021) and later through organisations such as the United Nations High Commissioner for Refugees (UNHCR). It is interesting that critiques of the Marshall Plan and its impacts on Western Europe are echoed in critiques of the World Bank and the International Monetary Fund (IMF). In both instances, liberal ideas about trade were required to be implemented by aid recipients as a condition of receiving aid, although in general the approach increased living standards in Western Europe after the war, as has the impact of contemporary foreign aid in the period before the COVID-19 pandemic.

Despite its critics, China's BRI, however, provides funding at commercial rates without the West's ideological baggage (Jones and Hameiri, 2020; Raja, Dayant, and Pryke, 2019; see also O'Dowd, 2018). This is significant in that China, despite long periods of cooperation with UNHCR, the World Bank, and other international institutions regarded as part of the existing neoliberal world order (including joining a G20 moratorium on debt payments), has been prevented from having a greater say in aid in the context of the neoliberal world order (for example, China is not a member of the OECD's Development Assistance Committee) and from taking on greater global responsibilities, on the basis of ideology (Dollar, 2020). While acknowledging China's extensive network of bilateral, globe-spanning relationships and involvement in regional multilateral initiatives presents an alternative to the neoliberal world order, this chapter views China's actions as a consequence, rather than a cause, of the institutional exhaustion evident in the US-led world order.

It is the perception of centralised coherence versus the fragmented nature of the practice of multilateral and bilateral foreign aid mechanisms that is a central theme of this chapter. In particular, the chapter examines foreign aid amid changing patterns of geopolitics in response to the COVID-19 pandemic and multilateral institutional exhaustion. It examines the shift in global geopolitics towards a new multipolarity that threatens to undo the much-lauded success of global capitalism and the rules-based world order upon which such success is presupposed. Yet it also argues that the perception of coherence at a grand strategic level is rarely realised at the fragmented local level in both multilateral and bilateral arrangements for delivering foreign aid, whether the extant rules-based world order or emerging alternatives presented by the realignment of global geopolitics.

This chapter has three sections. The first outlines the neoliberal world order, from its acceleration through globalisation to the time of the COVID-19 pandemic. The second section introduces a model of how international institutional responses to contain crises over time become fragmented in practice and eventually suffer from exhaustion through decreasing returns as the external geopolitical environment continues to change. Drawing on the findings from the application of the model to international institutions, the third section considers the concept of balancing and how cooperation, competition, and containment are normal processes in international relations, and that rather than the rise of China bringing about a change in the rules-based world order, the existing institutions are under pressure from all stakeholders.

The chapter concludes that while the rules-based world order that existed before the COVID-19 pandemic has faced a crisis of legitimacy, it is unlikely to disintegrate in accordance with extant popular explanations. Indeed, the chapter posits that popular explanations for global change are little more than memes that oversimplify complex geopolitical and historical processes. Much like Fukuyama's (1992) 'end of history' thesis and its overconfident celebration of the demise of alternatives to global capitalism, attempts to understand the nature of international institutions through the application of Ockham's razor, despite their ready appeal, are unlikely to yield much in the way of explanation that will stand the test of time. By drawing on the concepts of historical institutionalism, this chapter aims to provide a more rigorous and (albeit) less digestible view of how the COVID-19 pandemic has further disrupted the existing rules-based world order and the implications of this disruption for the future of foreign aid and development.

The world order before the pandemic

One of the most perplexing changes in the rules-based world order exacerbated by the COVID-19 pandemic is an apparent return to great power rivalry. Following the collapse of the Soviet Union and the hubris associated with the 'end of history' thesis (Fukuyama, 1992), the terrorist attacks of 11 September 2001 suggested the end of nation-state rivalry in geopolitics. The rise of ISIS suggested that enemies of nation-states were no longer other nation-states but fringe elements that filled the gaps between nation-states and exploited their non-state actor status for religious, ideological, or fanatical purposes. Nevertheless, numerous humanitarian crises in the Middle East and Africa saw these non-state armed groups providing humanitarian aid that was previously provided by state-sponsored institutions or formal, organised, faith-based, non-government organisations or established charities such as the Red Crescent and the Red Cross (Chatham House, 2015). Amid the rules-based world order that is often referred to as 'neoliberal' (in that it is based on the concepts of free trade between nations, private ownership of the means of production, and the role of governments and international institutions to establish and regulate competitive markets), a relative peace between developed nations ensued with a focus on trading while not focused on protecting industry but national borders from masses of refugees, asylum seekers, and illegal immigrants who posed the security risk of terrorists infiltrating the unregulated movement of people across national borders. Foreign aid in this context relied on providing aid to poorer host countries and refugees in situ, as opposed to mass resettlement, which drew the ire of many developed countries that gradually became focused on cultural, as opposed to industrial, protection. Meanwhile, non-state actors were providing aid in conflict zones that were out of bounds to most aid workers who operate under the rules of the United Nations (UN) System.

The rules-based world order had gradually shifted away from the Keynesian welfare state towards a more aggressive form of competitive capitalism (Hall & Soskice, 2001), driven by an inevitable phenomenon known in the West as globalisation that accelerated after the collapse of the Soviet Union. The neoliberal world order was only partially disrupted by the threat of terrorism, with many countries outsourcing security services in addition to their traditional government-run security services, suggesting that neoliberalism was not so much under threat but largely able to defend itself while adopting its own principles to find an efficient private-sector solution. It was the 2008 global financial crisis (GFC) that presented the first major disruption of the neoliberal status quo, with world leaders, including Australia's then Prime Minister Kevin Rudd (2009), suggesting that the 'great neo-liberal experiment' had 'failed', and that, through social democracy, the state would be brought back in to reinstate the 'Keynesian tradition' of saving in the good times and spending in the bad. But such enthusiasm for a rolling back of neoliberalism was short-lived, with many nation-states reinvigorating their industries through stimulus packages and with greater regulation of the finance industry. Global capitalism continued as it had done, most economies recovered from the GFC, and things went back to normal.

While the economies of developed nations remained open with broader and deeper multilateral and bilateral arrangements being implemented, health-related crises in the Congo, civil war in Somalia, Syria, South Sudan, and later Yemen, amid the flow-on effects of the US-led invasion of Iraq and Afghanistan and ongoing crises in Central America (see McCarthy-Jones, this volume, Chapter 16), contributed to increasing humanitarian crises affecting millions of people worldwide. With the humanitarian sector, under the institutional arrangements of the neoliberal rules-based world order, at breaking point, refugees risked their lives in various ways to escape to nearby developing host countries or to the developed countries in order to survive. The reaction to these various waves of forced migration had a flow-on effect with both developing and developed host nations. Developing host nations were exposed by pre-existing economic and infrastructural weaknesses through rapid, massive population increase (for example, Jordan hosts some 672,000 UNHCR-registered Syrian refugees with the number of unregistered refugees bringing the total to 1.3 million; see ACAPS, 2021). Further, many of these host nations are not signatories to the 1951 Refugee Convention but operate with the UNHCR system through a memorandum of understanding to deliver aid and 'process' refugee claims. The rules-based world order in relation to refugees was originally designed to address refugees from post-war Europe but has been applied to refugees more generally since then. One of the shortcomings of the system is that non-signatories are under no obligation to comply, so international bodies tend to tie aid programmes to compliance with the 1951 Refugee Convention and 1967 Protocol as a matter of course. While aid provided for humanitarian crises do not necessarily relate to the foreign aid and development initiatives provided by the World Bank and IMF systems, the normative expectations of such aid provision mirror the obligations imposed on aid recipients by the existing rules-based international institutions.

Globalisation is no longer seen as inevitable, but nation-states choose to interact with and cooperate with the rules-based world order, referred to as globalism, in ways that suit the interests of and re-prioritise the sovereignty of nation-states (Baltz, 2021; for use of the terms 'positive' and 'negative' globalism, see Morrison, 2019). The election of Trump in the US and the withdrawal of the UK from the European Union signified a change in attitude towards the established neoliberal world order: not in ways that undid 'the great neoliberal experiment' per se but in ways that re-established the primacy of the nation-state in international relations driven by national self-interest. This was not a wholesale re-adoption of Keynesianism but a reinvigorated nationalism that was more pragmatic than ideological in relation to trade policy (including the introduction of country-specific tariffs resulting in the US–China trade war) and in protecting domestic industries from international competition and stimulating domestic industries through subsidies and other policy instruments that had proven successful during the GFC. Part of the shift to nationalism, fuelled by populism in the US and the UK (and to a limited extent in other countries such as Australia), was reaction to China's growing economic and military power. Previously, the Chinese Communist Party (CCP) remained true to the long-term diplomatic strategy of modesty and 'peaceful coexistence' established by Mao Tse-Tung (Mao, 1967/2017) and continued under Deng Xiaoping as 'keep a low profile and bide your time' (Daekwon, 2017) while gradually introducing 'consumer capitalism without at the same time allowing democracy' (Brands & Gaddis, 2021). Middle powers such as Australia were adjusting to changing strategic priorities with China as a major economic partner and the US as a major security partner. For a time, it seemed that middle powers could navigate these partnerships successfully and that should US foreign policy change at the end of President Trumps' first term, the world would return to the neoliberal norms with China peacefully replacing the US as the dominant economic and military power sometime in the distant future. The BRI, part of China's aspiration for world leadership, while having geopolitical, cultural, and social goals, is helping to build much-needed infrastructure in Asia while forming logistics relationships through 'mutually beneficial' investment programmes focused on 'cooperation' (OECD, 2018). However, aggressive nationalism that propelled Trump into the White House was followed by aggressive Chinese nationalism designed to shore up support for the CCP at the beginning of the COVID-19 pandemic. In many ways, claims of China's escalating use of 'wolf warrior' diplomacy, which includes using social media to brashly 'attack foreign critics', have changed the cooperative nature of the regional trade and security relationships that China had been courting (Weiss, 2020). While competition between US-led versus Chinese-led economic and security institutional arrangements suggests a neo-Cold War that will influence future patterns of foreign aid and development, there is the possibility that the presupposed bipolarity of a Cold War will give way to a multipolarity that constrains China's ability to flex its geopolitical muscle (Brands & Gaddis, 2021).

But has it not always been the case that the rules-based world order established at the end of World War II included an uneasy stalemate between the US, the UK, France, and China and Russia as the permanent members of the UN Security Council (UNSC)? The perception that 'neoliberal' rules-based world order reassembled the bifurcated Cold War economic system for good is tenuous at best. What, then, explains the current crisis in the legitimacy of the neoliberal rules-based world order? To answer this question, the next section presents a model that explains how multilateral arrangements designed to facilitate a sense of global order suffer from institutional exhaustion when significant critical junctures (typically exogenous events) disrupt the status quo.

A model of institutional exhaustion

Institutional theory at the global level suffers from many shortcomings, exacerbated by existing theories of international relations. For example, realism, which places the nation-state at the centre of global politics, presupposes sovereign nation-states as independent and rational actors that develop alliances and relationships with other nation-states in an anarchical international system where nation-states are either perpetually at war punctuated by periods of peace or perpetually at peace punctuated by periods of war. International or multilateral institutions create a dilemma for the realist model in that there can be no higher power than the nation-state. For Mearsheimer (2001), great powers can only become regional, not global, hegemons, and institutional theories that present institutions as means of sustainable cooperation among nation-states merely hide the fact that the preeminent great powers use these institutions to 'disguise great power politics'. It is interesting in contemporary global politics that the two great powers, the US and China, are permanent members of the UNSC, and both have access to arguably the most important inner workings of the UN System. Mearsheimer (2005) agrees with Carr's (1939) thesis that nation-states are inherently self-interested in a struggle of 'all against all' but argues that allied nation-states, when under the umbrella of a regional hegemon (such as the US and North Atlantic Treaty Organization), will exhibit a sense of cooperation and cohesiveness that is mistaken for evidence to support democratic peace theory (Maoz & Russett, 1993; Small & Singer, 1976).

Neoliberal institutionalism (a revised version of liberal institutionalism) suggests nation-states can and do cooperate and can do so sustainably. This theory of international relations is in direct contrast to Mearsheimer's neorealist position (Mearsheimer, 2001). The theory posits that, through 'repeated interactions, transparency, and monitoring' (Keohane, 1984), institutions embed habits that can enable cooperation to occur in spite of the adversarial underpinnings suggested by an anarchical world order. While this chapter adopts an institutional perspective, it does not do so to argue that the realist or liberal institutionalist perspectives are right or wrong but rather to demonstrate that the institutional arrangements that are either used for 'great power' politics (Mearsheimer, 2021) or for rational cooperation (Keohane, 1984) are subjected to institutional exhaustion over time. The method adopted here forms part of the new institutionalist approach known as historical institutionalism and draws on a model of path-dependent, punctuated equilibrium (de Percy & Batainah, 2021) to provide a method of process tracing of multilateral institutions over time.

Key to the idea of historical institutionalism is the concept of a critical juncture. If institutions establish standardised or habitual behaviours that can be studied as units of analysis (Keohane, 1984, p. 56), and these habits, observed as 'fragments of political behaviour', are conducted in accordance with 'prevailing expectations and shared beliefs' that encourage the repeated behaviours that then, in turn, reinforce the formal and informal 'rules of the game' (March & Olsen, 1989), these habits can be identified as institutions. But if institutions reinforce accepted behaviours, then, theoretically, they cannot change themselves without creating the tautological position that institutions explain both institutional stasis and change.

The model presented in Figure 9.1 indicates critical junctures in international relations that have occurred over time since World War I. The model shows how international institutions are path dependent yet tend to establish longer periods of stability in the absence of exogenous or external events, typically wars. Nevertheless, there remain path dependencies that link the institutional origins of the neoliberal world order to the institutional framework established by the League of Nations. That is not to say that the League of Nations was a deliberate precursor to neoliberal institutions evident in recent times but that parts of the League of Nations were adopted into and adapted for the UN, and the origins of the UN System and the Marshall Plan (formally the Economic Recovery Programme) were focused on peacekeeping and the reconstruction of Europe (respectively) that continued during the Cold War. Once the post-war rebuilding of Europe

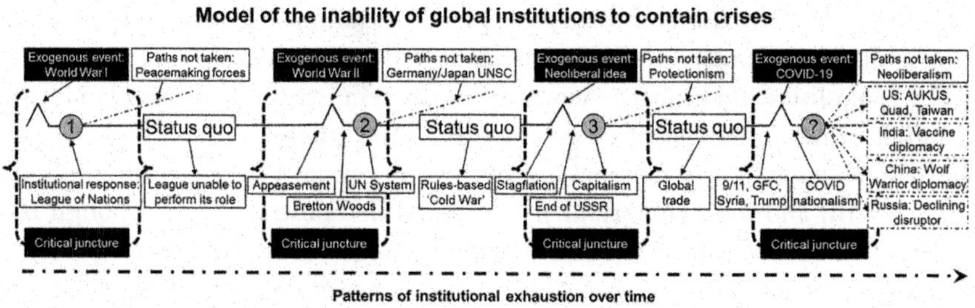

FIGURE 9.1 Path-dependent, punctuated equilibrium over time.

was complete, and following the collapse of the Soviet Union, the neoliberal rules-based world order evolved from the post-war institutions (in particular, the World Trade Organization (WTO)), and the World Bank and IMF turned from their reconstruction roles to foster development of post-Communist nations and later developing nations globally. Global trade became the norm from the collapse of the Soviet Union until the emergence of COVID nationalism in 2020.

A key feature of the model is the paths not taken and the resulting exhaustion of status quo institutions resulting from an inability to deal with the major crises presented here as critical junctures. For instance, the League of Nations faltered when the US failed to ratify the treaty in Congress. And while isolationist policies of the US restricted the League's effectiveness, combined with the lack of capacity to deploy a peacemaking force, the League was effectively a 'toothless tiger' (Rothermund, 2014, p. 841). Following the end of World War II, the five permanent members of the UNSC (importantly, those with the power of veto over UNSC decisions) do not include Japan and Germany, which, despite the devastation of war, returned to their former positions of economic power and today represent the third- and fourth-largest economies (by GDP, respectively) in the world, while the Russian Federation has been relegated to eleventh position (World Bank, 2021). While this feature alone does not make the UN ineffective, it demonstrates how, over time, the institutional arrangements established at the previous critical juncture make it difficult for the established institutions to remain relevant when the next exogenous event occurs. Similarly, the end of protectionism brought about by ideas that established the neoliberal rules-based world order were abandoned as nation-states turned inward to protect their populations from the COVID-19 pandemic. Coinciding with COVID nationalism, numerous barriers to trade have been re-established, indicating the exhaustion of the neoliberal world order.

The model above has some inherent weaknesses, particularly in relation to predicting future events; however, it provides some analytical insights into why the neoliberal rules-based world order is currently in crisis. First, exogenous events that are anticipated but not necessarily expected are difficult to build into the design of institutions, and these institutions begin with elements of the previous institutions that are carried forward over time. Second, the status quo establishes the formal and informal 'rules of the game' that nation-states function within as a framework for cooperation and competition. To be sure, ideas about geopolitics and global economics dot the temporal institutional landscape (ranging from mutually assured destruction to the efficacy of free markets), but the original flaws in international institutions are typically only obvious in hindsight. Third, and most importantly, the model demonstrates that although the rules of the world order since the end of World War I have changed as a reaction to exogenous global events, there is plenty of scope for competition and cooperation within these frameworks, and there is no evidence of the complete collapse of these enduring institutional features despite the devastation caused by exogenous events ranging from wars to ideas to pandemics.

The most recent period of institutional exhaustion has coincided with China's growth in economic and military power. While the COVID-19 pandemic represented the tipping point for the numerous crises of legitimacy that had been in play for several years, the inability of the UN to solve the numerous security and refugee crises in Africa, Asia, Latin America, the Middle East, and the Crimean Peninsula was not a new development (Solomon, 2014). Further, China's 'grand strategy' through the BRI and its Asian Infrastructure Investment Bank (AIIB) now rivals the World Bank while bringing 'desperately needed infrastructure and connectivity to Africa and Latin America' (Araya, 2019). Meanwhile, Western commentators have argued that China's 'wolf warrior' diplomacy was the catalyst for various security-related reactions to reign in China's global ambitions amid a backlash of global opinion against China's internal and external assertiveness (Martin, 2021; SIlver et al., 2021).

Some commentators suggest the 'old [world] order shaped and led by the US is over' and has been replaced by a 'new world disorder' (Raby, 2020). Such claims assume a level of peace and order in the post–Cold War period that belies the fragmentation of not only a Western-centric sense of world order but the instability that was evident in Syria and many other parts of the world (Mahapatra, 2016; Sarkees & Zunes, 1994; Stuenkel, 2016). Nevertheless, three key themes can be observed that deviate from the normative assumptions in a Western-led world order: cooperation, competition, and containment. Economic cooperation on a global scale under the WTO started to decline with Trump's 'Make America Great Again' policy that ignited a trade war with China, while, at the same time, the US threatened to withdraw from the WTO altogether (Johnson, 2020). Further, China's growing multilateral statecraft represented an alternative to the rules-based world order that the US had seemingly abandoned, deepening the legitimacy crises and adding to the existing neoliberal institutional exhaustion. Ultimately, the 'tardy' response to declaring a pandemic by the World Health Organization (WHO) hindered the ability of the existing international institutions to address the health and economic impacts of the COVID-19 pandemic. But cooperation has been occurring in security-related institutions such as AUKUS and the Quadrilateral Security Dialogue (the Quad) to contain China's expansionist ambitions. Cooperation has been occurring between China and recipients of its BRI funding, the AIIB, and the Shanghai Cooperation Organisation and other multilateral organisations such as the New Development Bank (Dollar, 2015; Stuenkel, 2016). Except for AUKUS, these examples of cooperation predate the pandemic. Yet AUKUS emerged as a form of cooperation that is designed to compete with China, particularly in the Indo-Pacific region, while at the same time attempting to contain China's 'more muscular' foreign policy approach (Raby, 2020).

COVID nationalism has undone much of the Western ideal of cooperation through open markets, with developed nations protecting their populations first before providing aid in the form of vaccines to aid partners (Lissner & Rapp-Hooper, 2020). But this approach created a vacuum that has checked an all-out nationalism. Australia, for example, had to respond to growing concerns about China's provision of regional aid and development where Australia had neglected its traditional aid relationships such as those with Papua New Guinea (Doherty, 2018) and the Solomon Islands (Smith, 2021). In the meantime, however, China and Russia have attempted to exploit the strategic vacuum by instigating 'vaccine diplomacy' by developing, amid scepticism from the West, their own vaccines and providing these to developing nations (Hill, 2021). The pandemic has provided an opportunity for China and Russia to showcase their 'soft power' credentials in the absence of Western powers, albeit China's increasingly authoritarian dealings with Hong Kong and flyovers in Taiwanese airspace, and Russia's annexation of Crimea and recent tensions with the Ukraine, make it difficult to see beyond the coercive ambitions of these two authoritarian powers (Huang, 2021; Kimmage & Kofman, 2021).

Further, the West's calls for an investigation into the origins of COVID-19, initiated by Australian Prime Minister Scott Morrison (Raby, 2020), led to an escalation in China's 'wolf warrior' diplomacy. This, in turn, encouraged the alignment of traditional Anglo alliances in the form of AUKUS (and the promise of delivering nuclear submarine technology to Australia as a strategic response to China), and the deepening of the Quad between India, Japan, Australia, and the United States, the four major democracies that geographically encompass the Indo-Pacific region.

The following section draws on the analysis presented above to consider how the concept of a world order is less a case of a unipolar, bipolar, or multipolar dominance arrangement but rather a case of actively balancing cooperation, competition, and containment strategies. The section critiques the inadequacy of popular ideas that attempt to explain the evolution of geopolitics and multilateralism and the impact on foreign aid and development.

Balancing: cooperation, competition, and containment

There is an inherent Western bias in assumptions about the efficacy of the rules-based world order that suggests any future non-Western global 'order' may be leaderless and chaotic (Stuenkel, 2016, pp. 1–9). There is a general understanding that the past three decades have been guided by a stable unipolarity with the US as the major economic and military power, albeit with some scholars suggesting that US hegemony in both power projection and leadership of international institutions was in decline as a result of the GFC (Layne, 2012). However, a more nuanced understanding of the current period in international relations is to consider the concept of 'balancing' (Parent & Rosato, 2015) between cooperation, competition, and containment (Dollar et al., 2017), on the one hand, and the concept of 'asymmetric bipolarity' (Jones, 2017), on the other. To this mix must be added the concepts of sharp power and soft power and how these relate to foreign aid and development. In terms of multilateralism, Western bias is clear in that the World Bank and the IMF and the UN System generally are considered part of the multilateral rules-based world order, while non-Western multilateral institutions are irrelevant at worst or peripheral at best. It is arguable, therefore, that it is not the nature of the world order that is changing but Western perceptions of that world order.

The concept of balancing draws on the neorealist idea that no great power can ever be a truly global power, only a regional power, and that regional powers try to contain other powers attempting to develop their own 'regional hegemony' (Mearsheimer, 2021, 2001). Great power leadership, drawing on the Western liberal ideal, utilises 'intangible power resources such as culture, ideology, and institutions' (Nye, 1990, p. 167). Nye (1990, p. 155), in developing the idea of 'soft power', suggested that the proof of possessing power 'lies not in resources but in the ability to change the behavior of states'. Soft power, then, 'occurs when one country gets other countries to *want* what it wants' (emphasis in the original), as opposed to hard power where one country orders another to do what it wants (Nye, 1990, p. 155). Soft power in this sense can be observed in the pervasiveness of American culture in movies, music, cars, architecture, art, fashion, and so on and in the multilateral institutions that shaped the post-war world when US power was at its peak (Nye, 1990, p. 153). Following the collapse of the Soviet Union in 1991, the US-led multilateral institutions were relatively unfettered, with not only China (2001) and Vietnam (2007) joining the WTO but also later Russia (2012), suggesting that global capitalism occupied the 'commanding heights' after winning 'the battle for the world economy' (Yergin & Stanislaw, 2002).

The discussion about foreign aid and development at the time of the launch of the Doha Round at the WTO's Fourth Ministerial Conference in 2001 was about providing developing countries such as Mexica, Brazil, and China access to global markets (Yergin & Stanislaw, 2002, p. 382). At the same time, against the backdrop of the terrorist attacks of 11 September 2001, an anti-globalisation protest movement was disrupting WTO negotiations (the location in Doha kept large numbers of protestors away), focused on issues ranging from anti-Americanism and anti-capitalism to poverty, debt relief, and animal rights, and focused on the WTO, the World Bank, and the IMF (the very institutions that originated from the ideas of Keynes) (Yergin & Stanislaw, 2002, pp. 381–382). China, now largely seen as disrupting the existing world order amid the decline in US power, was very much part of that same world order. The difference, then, between then and now is less about the global efficacy of US-led institutions (China and Russia had joined these voluntarily) and more about the usefulness of these very institutions to the US itself. Indeed, Mearsheimer (2021) argues that the UN *equals* China and the US and that international institutions represent the rules and the norms written by great powers, and, for the most part, international institutions help to disguise great power politics.

Yet it is difficult to disguise soft power and also difficult to develop it. If soft power is about inspiring others to follow the leader, then sharp power is about using information in coercive ways. Nye (2018) suggests that sharp power, which includes China's 'wolf warrior' diplomacy, 'helps authoritarian regimes compel behavior at home and manipulate opinion abroad'. Nye goes on to suggest that power can include a 'strong narrative' and that China's BRI can be a form of economic power drawing on soft power when things are going well but then cites the Sri Lankan port project as an example of when things go bad. Later on, Jones and Hameiri (2020) revealed in a Chatham House research report that 'many of the failed BRI projects were initiated by the recipient governments, which pursued their own domestic agendas'. Nevertheless, Nye makes it clear that sharp power begins where voluntarism has been breached. Further, Walker and Ludwig (2017) suggest that while authoritarian regimes such as those in China and Russia recognise the importance of soft power, 'the nature of these countries' political systems invariably and fundamentally color their efforts'. To be sure, the anti-globalisation protests at the turn of the century resented the influence of American culture globally, but the element of voluntarism is hardly absent in the pervasiveness of American culture and indeed in the existing world order that originated at Bretton Woods.

Although debate on whether the world order is indeed entering a new historical phase from unipolarity to bi- or multipolarity is beyond the scope of this chapter, what is clear is that, however defined, the existing powers that are able to exercise hard and sharp power are engaged in the neorealist concept of nations-states relying on their own capabilities (self-help or internal balancing) by 'arming and imitating the successful military practices of others to counter the capabilities of their rivals', whereas external balancing relies on alliances formed with other great powers (which are often viewed as risky) (Parent & Rosato, 2015). While internal balancing can be seen with the build-up of capability in China and the extension of the US's power through the AUKUS alliance and the Quad (given that the other parties to the alliances are not contemporary 'great powers'), external balancing would suggest that if China and Russia are considered to be contemporary great powers, an alliance between the two is unlikely given the territorial and historical rivalries (the US and China were formal allies in 1942, whereas Chinese and Russian forces clashed during the 1969 Sino-Soviet border conflict). Further, any internal balancing by China and Russia would not include the various voluntary middle power supporters that the US could expect to assist in any potential conflict.

The point is that great powers use international institutions to their own advantage and establish, use, or abuse the rules to suit their political aims. Raby (2020), for example, cites China's refusal to 'recognise the International Court of Arbitration's jurisdiction over the South China Sea case' and the US failure to ratify the Law of the Sea Convention: great powers violate the rules they do not like (Mearsheimer, 2021). Further, China has joined those international institutions that further its own ends (the WTO, IMF, and World Bank, for example) while insisting on being treated as a developing nation and establishing bilateral economic relations 'with other developing nations that do not always meet global standards and norms' (Dollar, 2020). While China does have a quota share (albeit below its weight) in the IMF and 'supports IMF programmes by parallel lending', China has not been offered a greater say in the institutional framework in exchange for greater responsibilities (Dollar, 2020). Similarly, the US under Trump publicly withdrew its support for the WTO, the WHO, and the UN System more broadly, thereby undermining the very system that proponents of a US-led Western hegemony argue supports a Western-centric perception of a rules-based world order. If the US is bringing about a crisis of legitimacy of the institutions that supposedly support its own hegemonic position, there is much more to the decline of the existing world order than the rise of China. Importantly, many of the issues outlined in this section were in play well before the COVID-19 pandemic struck.

Conclusion

While China has a long and positive relationship with the multilateral rules-based world order, it does not play the part of a responsible stakeholder, nor has it been given the opportunity to do so with all the privileges and responsibilities that entails (Dollar, 2020). The remnants of Cold War ideology still permeate global capitalism despite the relative consistency of global trade practices among almost all nations of the world. However, China's BRI is beset by the popular yet misleading idea of 'debt-trap diplomacy' that has become a meme – a throwaway line or oversimplified phrase that spreads like a rumour and through repetition is perceived as true without challenge – and, in effect, explains everything while explaining nothing. To be sure, China's use of sharp power in the form of 'wolf warrior' diplomacy reflects the opaque nature of increasingly authoritarian rule that reflects China's insecurities both internally and externally (Raby, 2020). Further, authoritarian rule in China and Russia hardly inspires voluntary subscription to either of these powers' values or ideas about the 'big picture of human civilization' (Hu, 2021). Yet about half of China's BRI funding is provided by private lenders in addition to state-owned banks, and the BRI is necessarily fragmented and beyond the purview of any realistic central control (O'Dowd, 2018). At the same time, if we consider the provision of foreign aid and development initiatives as normatively positive actions, China's contribution to foreign aid and development is significant and necessary. Importantly, and unlike the World

Bank and IMF, China's BRI funding has no requirement for structural readjustment or economic reform and is delivered on commercial terms at slightly higher rates than the World Bank or IMF (O'Dowd, 2018).

This chapter examined the changing world order in the context of institutional exhaustion, drawing on historical perspectives to demonstrate that institutions are designed to reinforce patterns of behaviour that make it difficult for these same institutions to change themselves. While not strong in predictive power, the examination of the major catalysts for change in the world order (albeit within the confines of a Western-centric world order that has existed since the emergence of the modern nation-state) have been exogenous events that lead to reformed or reformulated international institutions that are necessarily path dependent (they begin where the previous world order ended) and exhibit a trajectory that is punctuated by exogenous events that precipitate these changes. To be sure, ideas about a consistent unipolar world that existed from the end of the Cold War to the present fail to capture the concept of exhaustion where institutions were no longer useful to great powers amid changing circumstances. Further, the Western-centric concept of unipolarity ignores that other regional powers were engaging in an ongoing process of establishing and participating in bilateral and multilateral arrangements outside of the US-led rules-based world order until these dominant institutions ceased to suit the domestic circumstances under Trump (and consequently other US allies), giving China (in particular) the space to establish its own multilateral institutions that enabled it to create its own rules in its own sphere of influence à la Mearsheimer (2001).

The major impact of the COVID-19 pandemic on the exhausted rules-based world order that has regulated global trade and aid since at least China's ascension to WTO membership in 2001 is that the US, the originator of these same rules, has found that these no longer serve its aims in a world where China's growing economic and military power are rivalling that of the US. At the same time, China's desire to fund infrastructure to enable strategically placed developing nations to assure China's future development ambitions has a positive effect on developing nations (as did increased access to global markets at the initial Doha Round) and is providing much-needed development assistance, particularly in the Indo-Pacific region. A key driver of the institutional exhaustion of the rules-based world order has been national self-interest magnified by the impact of the COVID-19 pandemic. Nonetheless, national self-interest was already impacting upon the development effectiveness of multilateralism as donor nations were increasingly earmarking funding for specific purposes (Jones & Hameiri, 2020). The aim of multilateralism harks back to Bretton Woods and the desire to overcome the asymmetries of power inherent in bilateralism, but, much like WTO-compliant bilateral free trade agreements, the desire for earmarking aid and development funding effectively negates the first principles of multilateralism.

In many ways, the COVID-19 pandemic represents the tipping point for the change in focus that the already exhausted institutions could no longer address. The inefficacy of the rules-based world order and the apparent undoing of the inevitability of globalisation present its own problems for foreign aid and development (Yergin & Stanislaw, 2002, pp. 382–283). As China attempts to become a regional hegemon and the US-led regional hegemon attempts to contain China's ambitions, the scope for competition increases, while the scope for cooperation is likely to become polarised at the same time. But there is cause for hope. Despite the Solomon Islands riots, driven largely by citizens' growing frustration with the prime minister courting Beijing and cutting ties with Taiwan, the prime minister called on Australia to contain the civil unrest, thus averting a major strategic issue for the Indo-Pacific among growing tensions in the region. The situation suggests that China's growing influence in the region is only skin-deep and that soft power idealism and the penchant for voluntarism are alive and well.

Importantly, China's sharp power has limited capacity to win hearts and minds, and, unlike the resilience of democracies, once an authoritarian leader's time on earth expires, the potential for internal renewal is vast if not disruptive to any coordinated regional ambitions. At the same time, arrangements such as the Trans-Pacific Partnership and the AIIB demonstrate that middle powers such as Japan and Australia are willing to break ranks with the US and China when national economic interests clash with security alliances (see Parent & Rosato, 2015). These emerging and alternative institutional arrangements are less a threat to the existing world order and more an opportunity for cooler heads to prevail as the exogenous impact of the COVID-19 pandemic reveals the weaknesses inherent in a system designed for earlier times.

While the funds available for foreign aid and development programmes may increase as emerging powers compete with the US for regional influence, an obvious consequence of regional rather than global multilateralism is the potential for barriers to global trade to impact upon the wealth of developing nations. Should the change in the world order be more than a change in Western perception that results in a wholesale departure from the cooperation inherent in multilateralism, then the resulting institutions will be prone to exhaustion sooner rather than later. Like the COVID-19 pandemic, it is difficult to predict future critical junctures, but international cooperation is key to solving problems that affect the species as opposed to nation-states. Whether international institutions can prevent rational individuals from acting like collective fools will remain the next great challenge for global society.

References

ACAPS. (2021). *Jordan: Syrian Refugees*. Retrieved 4 December from https://www.acaps.org/country/jordan/crisis/syrian-refugees.

Allen, J. R., Burns, N., Garrett, L., Haass, R. N., Ikenberry, G. J., Mahbubani, K., Menon, S., Niblett, R., Nye Jr., J. S., O'Neil, S. K., Schake, K., & Walt, S. M. (2020). How the World Will Look after the Coronavirus Pandemic. *Foreign Policy*, 20 March 2020. https://foreignpolicy.com/2020/03/20/world-order-after-coroanvirus-pandemic/ (Accessed 17 February 2022).

Araya, D. (2019, 19 January). China's Grand Strategy. *Forbes*. https://www.forbes.com/sites/danielaraya/2019/01/14/chinas-grand-strategy/?sh=4ef53a981f18

Baltz, M. J. (2021). 'Americanism not Globalism Will Be Our Credo!': An analysis of the Economic Nationalism(s) of Trump's Administration and an Agenda for Further Research. *Nations and Nationalism, 27*(3), 797–815.

Brands, H., & Gaddis, J. L. (2021). The New Cold War: America, China, and the Echoes of History. *Foreign Affairs*. https://www.foreignaffairs.com/articles/united-states/2021-10-19/new-cold-war

Carr, E. H. (1939/2016). *The Twenty Years Crisis, 1919–1939: An Introduction to the Study of International Relations*. London: Palgrave Macmillan.

Chatham House. (2015). *Non-State Armed Groups, Health and Healthcare*. London: Chatham House.

Daekwon, S. (2017, 25 October). Xi Jinping Thought Vs. Deng Xiaoping Theory. *The Diplomat*. https://thediplomat.com/2017/10/xi-jinping-thought-vs-deng-xiaoping-theory/

de Percy, M. A., & Batainah, H. S. (2021). Identifying Historical Policy Regimes in the Canadian and Australian Communications Industries Using A Model of Path Dependent, Punctuated Equilibrium. *Policy Studies, 42*(1), 42–59.

Doherty, B. (2018). China's Aid to Papua New Guinea Threatens Australia's Influence. *The Guardian*. https://www.theguardian.com/world/2018/jul/02/chinas-aid-to-papua-new-guinea-threatens-australias-influence

Dollar, D. (2015). *The AIIB and the 'One Belt, One Road'*. Brookings Institution. Retrieved 5 December from https://www.brookings.edu/opinions/the-aiib-and-the-one-belt-one-road/.

Dollar, D. (2020, 14 September). *Reluctant Player: China's Approach to International Economic Institutions*. Brookings Institution. Retrieved 7 December from https://www.brookings.edu/articles/reluctant-player-chinas-approach-to-international-economic-institutions/.

Dollar, D., Hass, R., Kagan, R., Lieberthal, K. G., Li, C., Rapp-Hooper, M., Stromseth, J., Jones, B., & Chhabra, T. (2017). *Avoiding War: Containment, Competition, and Cooperation in U.S.-China Relations*. B. Institution. https://www.brookings.edu/research/avoiding-war-containment-competition-and-cooperation-in-u-s-china-relations/.

France24. (2021). *Far-Right Pundit Eric Zemmour Launches 2022 Bid for French Presidency*. Retrieved 4 December from https://www.france24.com/en/france/20211130-far-right-pundit-eric-zemmour-announces-2022-bid-for-french-presidency.

Fukuyama, F. (1992). *The End of History and the Last Man*. New York: Free Press.

Hall, P. A., & Soskice, D. (Eds.). (2001). *Varieties of Capitalism: The Institutional Foundations of Comparative Advantage*. Oxford University Press.

Hill, I. (2021, 21 September). *Russia and China's Vaccine Diplomacy: Not Quite the Geopolitical Slam Dunk*. Australian Institute of International Affairs. Retrieved 5 December from https://www.internationalaffairs.org.au/australianoutlook/russia-and-chinas-vaccine-diplomacy-not-quite-the-geopolitical-slam-dunk/

Hodge, A. (2021, 6 December). Taliban Gunmen Steal Australian Food Aid in Afghanistan. *The Australian*. https://www.theaustralian.com.au/world/taliban-gunmen-steal-australian-food-aid-in-afghanistan/news-story/6d5446f90adfb99e21e3c6df7d66a19d

Hu, X. (2021, 5 December). Whole-Process Democracy in China Is a Great Practice of Universal Significance. *Global Times*. https://www.globaltimes.cn/page/202112/1240667.shtml

Huang, Y. (2021, 11 March). Vaccine Diplomacy Is Paying Off for China. *Foreign Affairs*. https://www.foreignaffairs.com/articles/china/2021-03-11/vaccine-diplomacy-paying-china

Johnson, K. (2020, 27 May). U.S. Effort to Depart WTO Gathers Momentum. *Foreign Policy*. https://foreignpolicy.com/2020/05/27/world-trade-organization-united-states-departure-china/

Jones, B. (2017, 28 November). *The New Geopolitics*. Brookings Institution. Retrieved 7 December from https://www.brookings.edu/blog/order-from-chaos/2017/11/28/the-new-geopolitics/.

Jones, L., & Hameiri, S. (2020). *Debunking the Myth of 'Debt-trap Diplomacy': How Recipient Countries Shape China's Belt and Road Initiative*. https://www.chathamhouse.org/sites/default/files/2020-08-19-debunking-myth-debt-trap-diplomacy-jones-hameiri.pdf.

Keohane, R. O. (1984). *After Hegemony: Cooperation and Discord in the World Political Economy*. Princeton, NJ: Princeton University Press.

KfW. (2021). *Impact: A Boost from the USA*. Retrieved 4 December from https://www.kfw.de/stories/kfw/stories/society/social-cohesion/marshallplan/.

Kimmage, M., & Kofman, M. (2021, 22 November). Russia Won't Let Ukraine Go without a Fight. *Foreign Affairs*. https://www.foreignaffairs.com/articles/ukraine/2021-11-22/russia-wont-let-ukraine-go-without-fight

Layne, C. (2012). This Time It's Real: The End of Unipolarity and the Pax Americana. *International Studies Quarterly, 56*, 203–213.

Lissner, R., & Rapp-Hooper, M. (2020, 30 September). A Foreign Policy for the Day after Trump: Reimagining – not Restoring – the Liberal International Order. *Foreign Affairs*. https://www.foreignaffairs.com/articles/united-states/2020-09-30/foreign-policy-day-after-trump

Mahapatra, D. A. (2016). The Mandate and the (In)Effectiveness of the United Nations Security Council and International Peace and Security: The Contexts of Syria and Mali. *Geopolitics, 21*(1), 43–68.

Mao, T.-t. (1967/2017). *On Practice and Contradiction*. London: Verso.

Maoz, Z., & Russett, B. (1993). Normative and Structural Causes of Democratic Peace, 1946–1986. *The American Political Science Review, 87*(3), 624–638.

March, J. G., & Olsen, J. P. (1989). *Rediscovering Institutions: The Organizational Basis of Politics*. New York: The Free Press.

Martin, P. (2021, 6 October). Why China Is Alienating the World. *Foreign Affairs*. https://www.foreignaffairs.com/articles/china/2021-10-06/why-china-alienating-world

Mearsheimer, J. J. (2001). *The Tragedy of Great Power Politics*. New York: W. W. Norton.

Mearsheimer, J. J. (2005). E.H. Carr vs. Idealism: The Battle Rages On. *International Relations, 19*(2), 139–152.

Mearsheimer, J. J. (2018). *The Great Delusion: Liberal Dreams and International Realities*. New Haven, CT: Yale University Press.

Mearsheimer, J. J. (2021). *The New Cold War* [Interview]. Centre for Independent Studies.

Morrison, S. (2019, 3 October). In Our Interest. 2019 Lowy Lecture, Sydney.

Nye, J. (1990). Soft Power. *Foreign Policy*, (80), 153–171.

Nye, J. S. (2018). China's Soft and Sharp Power. *The Strategist*. https://www.aspistrategist.org.au/chinas-soft-sharp-power/

O'Dowd, S. (2018, 13 November). *Papua New Guinea and the Belt and Road Initiative: The Road to Ruins or Riches*. Coral Bell School of Asia Pacific Affairs, The Australian National University. Retrieved 8 December from https://dpa.bellschool.anu.edu.au/news-events/events/6513/papua-new-guinea-and-belt-and-road-initiative-road-ruins-or-riches.

Organisation for Economic Cooperation and Development (OECD). (2018). China's Belt and Road Initiative in the Global Trade, Investment and Finance Landscape. In *OECD Business and Finance Outlook 2018*. OECD Publishing.

Parent, J. M., & Rosato, S. (2015). Balancing in Neorealism. *International Security, 40*(2), 51–86.

Raby, G. (2020). *China's Grand Strategy and Australia's Future in the New Global Order.* Melbourne University Press Digital. Kindle Edition.

Raja, R., Dayant, A., & Pryke, J. (2019). Ocean of Debt? Belt and Road and Debt Diplomacy in the Pacific. Lowy Institute, 21 October 2019. https://www.lowyinstitute.org/publications/ocean-debt-belt-and-road-and-debt-diplomacy-pacific (Accessed 17 February 2022).

Reuters. (2021, 30 November). *India Promises More COVID-19 Shots to Omicron-hit Africa after Chinese Move.* Reuters. Retrieved 5 December from https://www.reuters.com/world/india/india-promises-more-covid-19-shots-omicron-hit-africa-after-chinese-move-2021-11-30/

Rothermund, D. (2014). War-Depression-War: The Fatal Sequence in a Global Perspective. *Diplomatic History, 38*(4), 840–851.

Rudd, K. (2009, February). The Global Financial Crisis. *The Monthly.* https://www.themonthly.com.au/issue/2009/february/1319602475/kevin-rudd/global-financial-crisis#mtr

Sarkees, M. R., & Zunes, S. (1994). Disenchantment with the 'New World Order': Syria's Relations with the United States. *International Journal of Law, Crime and Justice, 49*(2), 355–377.

SIlver, L., Devlin, K., & Huang, C. (2021). *Large Majorities Say China Does Not Respect the Personal Freedoms of Its People.* https://www.pewresearch.org/global/2021/06/30/large-majorities-say-china-does-not-respect-the-personal-freedoms-of-its-people/.

Small, M., & Singer, J. D. (1976). The War-Proneness of Democratic Regimes, 1816–1965. *The Jerusalem Journal of International Relations, 1*, 57–69.

Smith, E. J. (2021). *Pacific puzzle: How China and Australia fit in to Solomon Islands protests.* SBS News: Dateline. Retrieved 5 December from https://www.sbs.com.au/news/dateline/pacific-puzzle-how-china-and-australia-fit-in-to-solomon-islands-protests.

Solomon, L. (2014, 25 April). UN is de facto dead; The UN no longer counts in the world. Like the League of Nations, it will thankfully disappear. *National Post.* https://journal.probeinternational.org/2014/04/25/the-un-is-de-facto-dead/

Stuenkel, O. (2016). *Post-Western world: How emerging powers are remaking global order.* Cambridge, UK: Polity Press.

Walker, C., & Ludwig, J. (2017, 16 November). The Meaning of Sharp Power: How Authoritarian States Project Influence. *Foreign Affairs.* https://www.foreignaffairs.com/articles/china/2017-11-16/meaning-sharp-power

Weiss, J. C. (2020, 16 July). China's Self-Defeating Nationalism: Brazen Diplomacy and Rhetorical Bluster Undercut Beijing's Influence. *Foreign Affairs.* https://www.foreignaffairs.com/articles/china/2020-07-16/chinas-self-defeating-nationalism

World Bank. (2021). *World Bank Data: GDP (Current US$).* Retrieved 4 December from https://data.worldbank.org/indicator/NY.GDP.MKTP.CD?end=2020&most_recent_value_desc=true&start=1960&view=chart.

Yergin, D., & Stanislaw, J. (2002). *The Commanding Heights: The Battle for the World Economy.* New York: Simon & Schuster.

10

THE COVID-19 PANDEMIC AND ITS IMPACT IN SUB-SAHARAN AFRICA

Geostrategic dynamics and challenges for development

Matthias Rompel

Introduction

Scrutinizing the impact of the global COVID-19 in sub-Saharan Africa, it can be argued that while epidemiological and health impacts of COVID-19 in sub-Saharan Africa are (so far) less severe than anticipated, economic and social impacts are dramatic. Specifically, the rise in extreme poverty and inequality due to the pandemic and the increase in food insecurity and hunger are great concerns. The COVID-19 pandemic accelerates existing crises, puts development gains at stake, and might shape the continent for years to come.

And on top of this state of play, the global access to COVID-19 vaccines reveals further structural inequalities and advances new geostrategic challenges and opportunities. While the rapid development of vaccines for COVID-19 has been a huge scientific success, the politics of providing equal access on a global scale have been a failure. On one hand, multilateral solutions for a fair and equal global vaccine distribution were promoted but were slow and worked far from being perfect. On the other hand, a race to secure vaccine doses by countries of the Global North emerged and gave room for a vaccine diplomacy of different players to increase their respective spheres of influence. However, the African Union (AU) has responded to the call and developed an ambitious political agenda to build local production capacity for vaccines (COVID-19 and beyond) and other pharmaceutical supplies, to overcome the structural dependency in the long run.

Corona as a 'polypandemic'

Some two years into the global corona pandemic, the state of play in Africa still bears a paradox: The least infected are the most affected. The health impacts of

DOI: 10.4324/9781003273844-10

the pandemic in sub-Saharan Africa remain relatively low compared to other regions as Europe, Asia, and the Americas. The World Health Organization (WHO) estimates that by the end of December 2021, approximately 281.8 million COVID-19 cases have been confirmed with more than 5.4 million deaths globally, while in the Americas, 102.2 million confirmed COVID-19 cases with 2.4 million deaths have been reported, 99.1 million confirmed cases with more than 1.6 million deaths in Europe, and 44.9 million confirmed cases with 720,545 deaths in Southeast Asia. In Africa, about 7.1 million confirmed cases and 155,675 deaths were reported (WHO, 2021). If we assume these figures as a reasonable reflection of reality, only 2.9% of the global COVID-19 deaths occurred on the African continent, while the total population in Africa is equivalent to about 17% of the global population.

A range of factors have been discussed as being responsible for the relatively low burden of COVID-19 disease in Africa. These factors include demographics, effective public health interventions, potential cross-protection from previous exposure to other coronaviruses, and, of course, data availability and reporting issues, meaning limitations of COVID-19 testing, which may have resulted in an undercounting of infections and deaths. The demographic factor seems to be of high relevance since age has been observed as a significant individual risk factor for COVID-19-related mortality (most deaths occur in persons above the age of 65). The percentage in this risk group of people above 65 years of age and hence vulnerable to severe COVID-19 in Germany – taken as a proxy for demographic structures in countries of the Global North – amounts to 21% of the population, while the same group in southern Africa consists of only 3% of the population; the median age in many countries in Africa ranges around 18 years of age, while e.g. the median age in Germany is about 43 years. These distinctions in the demographic structure of societies in Europe vis-à-vis African societies (with a much younger population, both in terms of median age and share of older citizens) might be the leading factor to explain lower morbidity and mortality rates of COVID-19 in Africa (Adams *et al.*, 2021).

Other factors mentioned above include effective public health interventions by African governments. This encompasses the fact that many African regions have a strong track record with handling diseases and coming up with timely and appropriate public policies and public health interventions. Such experiences include – inter alia – the different Ebola epidemics in West Africa over the past decades. And indeed, governments in Africa were quick to respond to the initial global COVID-19 wave in early 2020 and reacted timely in introducing outbreak mitigation (including lockdowns), physical distancing, and quarantine measures. Ivory Coast, for instance, implemented enhanced screening measures for passengers arriving from China as early as 2 January 2020 (Loembé *et al.*, 2020). It has also been highlighted that a lower disease burden in African countries might be attributed to cross-protection to infection due to previous exposure of reasonable parts of the population with other locally circulating coronaviruses. Another relevant factor might be an underreporting of COVID-19 cases, including

COVID-19-related deaths, due to insufficient data collection and limited testing capacities. Current data may not reflect the true dimensions of the disease in Africa. According to WHO, testing levels vary significantly across countries in Africa, while testing levels remain relatively low as compared to other regions in the world (Adams *et al.*, 2021).

However, beyond a possibly lower caseload in health systems, the impact of the COVID-19 pandemic on livelihoods on the African continent has been dramatic. While governments responded swiftly to the pandemic with policies that reduce human interaction and slow the spread of the virus, respective measures had negative effects on informal and formal economic activities, labour participation, and productivity. Household consumption decreased, and food and nutrition insecurity increased, as well as poverty – both in absolute and relative terms (UNDP, 2021). The pandemic caused a sharp decline in living standards and rising food insecurity. A drop in employment, income, and access to markets and services has been observed in the mainly informal economies in Africa, translating into high levels of food insecurity. Many households reported being unable to meet basic nutritional needs. According to one study conducted in Burkina Faso, Ghana, Kenya, Rwanda, Sierra Leone, and other countries of the Global South, the median of reported income losses at household level was 70%, while the reported loss of employment was at median of 29%. In all countries, schools were closed, and respondents also reported reduced access to health services, including prenatal and preventive care, and vaccinations (Egger *et al.*, 2021). The reduced utilization of health services provides for a grim outlook on long-term effects in the management of diseases like HIV, malaria, and tuberculosis. According to a survey of the Global Fund to Fight AIDS, Tuberculosis and Malaria (GFATM), prenatal care visits dropped by two-thirds between April and September 2020, and consultations for children under 5 dropped by three-quarters. As a consequence, it is estimated that twice as many people around the world could be at risk of dying from malaria. And there could be 400,000 additional deaths from tuberculosis in the next few years and 500,000 extra deaths from HIV/AIDS (GFATM, 2021). Appiah points out: "The coronavirus's real death toll, then, has to be calculated not just in deaths from Covid, but also in deaths that would otherwise have been prevented, from malaria, TB, HIV, diabetes and more" (Appiah, 2021).

Globally, it is estimated that between 119 and 124 million additional people were pushed into extreme poverty in 2020 due to COVID-19, while the estimated COVID-19-induced poor is set to rise to between 143 and 163 million in 2021 (Lakner *et al.*, 2021). Due to this dynamic, a first increase in global poverty rates since the 1990s can be recorded (UNOCHA, 2020).

The International Monetary Fund (IMF) estimated an overall economic contraction of 3.2% for Africa in 2020 (IMF, 2020), while reductions in gross domestic product (GDP) growth in 2021 range from minus 2.6% to minus 10.6% across different African countries (UNDP, 2021). The COVID-19 pandemic has significantly reduced economic growth and altered patterns of international economic interaction. While we are still in the midst of the crisis, there is real concern that the majority of macroeconomic effects will not be temporary but will disproportionately shift long-term development pathways in low- and middle-income countries, offsetting some of the gains made towards achieving the Sustainable Development Goals (SDGs) in recent decades (UNDP, 2021). While longer-term macroeconomic effects will vary from country to country, some common patterns can be described. It has been recorded since early 2020 and is further forecast that COVID-19 reduces international flows of trade, remittances, and foreign direct investments (FDI); drives up poverty most likely up to 2050; increases mortality over the next decade (mostly from communicable diseases); and increases child mortality. On trade flows at country level, COVID-19 has caused simultaneous reductions in imports and exports for most African economies. Since most African countries had negative trade balances (higher imports than exports) before COVID-19, there are nearly no net changes in the trade balances; however, the trade volume has substantially decreased. Besides trade, COVID-19 has significantly reduced FDIs and remittances flows to African countries. These factors will reduce tax earnings and hence strongly reduce fiscal space for governments (and in the case of remittances as well for individual households), leading also to rising debt-to-GDP ratios. In South Africa, e.g. average annual growth rates as high as 4.5% will be required to stabilize the debt-to-GDP ratio without severe cutbacks on government spending (UNDP, 2021). Suffice to say that such GDP growth rates are clearly out of reach for South Africa in the years to come. GDP is forecast to grow between 1% and 1.9% in 2022 and between 0.6% and 1.6% in 2023 in South Africa (OECD, 2021).

In fragile settings, there are fears that tensions might escalate following reductions in government spending for health, education, and security, due to stressed public households (UNDP, 2021). Some authors suggest that such pressure along with already-existing political tensions might push the political and social order to a tipping point in fragile states (Moyer, sub-Saharan Africa, Kaplan, 2020).

Beyond the health dimensions of COVID-19, the impacts of the pandemic will be long-term and far-reaching regarding economic structures, patterns of international trade, and negative implications for government investment and human development (health, education, poverty alleviation, and child mortality) (UNDP, 2021).

These dynamics illustrate the earlier mentioned statement: On a continental scale, the least infected (in terms of caseload of COVID-19 cases in health systems) are the most affected (in terms of economic and social impact of the pandemic). The effects on households in the economic and social domains have been mainly triggered not by the pandemic itself but by containment measures and international dynamics (e.g. reduction in international trade and travel). So, in a way, in much of Africa, the main engine of destruction around the COVID-19 pandemic hasn't been the disease itself (with its first-order health effects) but the second-order economic effects of the pandemic.

Against this background, the COVID-19 pandemic must be understood to be much more than a health crisis. It can be described as a global and multifaceted crisis, with serious short-term and long-term implications. Due to the multidimensional character of the impact, it has been argued by a report of the Munich Security Conference (MSC) that the impacts of COVID-19 translate into multiple pandemics rather than just one. The MSC report describes COVID-19 as a "polypandemic that is undermining development progress, exacerbating state fragility, and potentially further eroding international cooperation". And further: "If left unmitigated, the coronavirus pandemic and the pandemics that accompany it, including those of hunger, inequality, and authoritarian rule, will disproportionately hit those populations that were most vulnerable to begin with" (MSC, 2020: 6).

However, to contain the consequences of the pandemic, both for first- and second-order effects, there is one effective tool to limit the further dynamic of COVID-19. This is vaccination. The availability of vaccines will be discussed in the following section.

Access to vaccines

"No one is safe before everyone are safe". That is how Dr Tedros Ghebreyesus, the Director General of WHO, has put it to the point: Access to COVID-19 vaccination is the pathway to get out of the global pandemic. And while the dynamic of the pandemic is different in each part of the world, the pandemic highlighted vast inequalities within and between countries and regions. Access to vaccines might be the most striking example of these inequalities. In most countries of Europe, more than 60% of the population have been vaccinated against COVID-19 by November 2021, while only some 5% of citizens in Africa were fully vaccinated by that time. The limiting factor in this first phase of vaccination rollout has clearly been the supply side, the availability of vaccines. Rolling forward at current pace, a widespread vaccination coverage in Africa might only be achieved from 2023 on. This is a long time for the pandemic to take further footholds in African countries and for new strains of the virus to develop.

Heads of States and Governments of G20 countries met at the end of October 2021 in Rome and acknowledged that vaccines are amongst the most important tools against the pandemic. They also underscored (again) that extensive COVID-19 immunization is a global public good. At the same time, they reaffirmed the quantitative targets of WHO and committed to accelerate efforts to reach it:

> To help advance toward the global goals of vaccinating at least 40 percent of the population in all countries by the end of 2021 and 70 percent by mid-2022, as recommended by the World Health Organization (WHO)'s global vaccination strategy, we will take steps to help boost the supply of vaccines and essential medical products and inputs in developing countries

> and remove relevant supply and financing constraints. We ask our Health Ministers to monitor progress toward this end and to explore ways to accelerate global vaccination as necessary.
>
> *(Rome G20 Declaration: 2)*

This declaration of intent has largely been missed by the end of 2021: The target for achieving full vaccination of 40% of the people in every country by the end of 2021 has been missed across Africa. Only 9% of the population on the continent have been fully vaccinated by the end of December 2021. Only seven African countries have reached the 40% target (three of them small island countries), namely Seychelles, Mauritius, Morocco, Tunisia, Cabo Verde, Botswana, and Rwanda (Mwai, 2021). So let's scrutinize why we have seen so limited progress in vaccine supply and vaccination rates in sub-Saharan Africa. WHO, together with partners, as the US, the European Union (EU), and Germany amongst others, was early to create a multilateral approach to COVID-19 medication and vaccination. In February 2020, they launched the 'Access to COVID-19 Tools Accelerator' (ACT-A). Part of this mechanisms is the COVAX facility (spelled out as 'COVID-19 Vaccines Global Access'), serving as the vaccine pillar of ACT-A. COVAX dwells on established trends in global health, such as a disease-specific or 'vertical' approach (vis-à-vis a 'horizontal' or systems approach), and a focus on health technologies, as well as a preference for market solutions to address public health issues. COVAX was set up for pooled procurement and equitable distribution of COVID-19 vaccines, particularly created to increase access for medium- and low-income-countries. It is co-led by existing multilateral agents, namely the Coalition for Epidemic Preparedness Innovations, the Global Alliance for Vaccines and Immunization (GAVI), and the WHO, alongside key delivery partners. The US, the EU, and its member states invested substantial amounts of money into COVAX. Initially, it was envisioned to supply 20% of the demand of participating countries by the end of 2021, accumulating to 2.3 billion vaccine doses, out of which 1.8 billion were meant to cater for medium- and low-income countries. But the challenges are huge. And progress has been limited. Only 910 million doses were delivered by COVAX by the end of 2021. Beyond a general critique on COVAX on its limited success for bringing about global vaccine equity, it has been outlined that also the governance structures of COVAX, the downsides of its design as a public–private-partnership model, and its role in the ongoing financialization of global health might be problematic. It has been pointed out that COVAX conflates public health risk and corporate financial risk, leading it to privilege concerns of pharmaceutical companies over those of most participating countries (especially low- and lower-middle-income countries) (Stein, 2021).

After the first inoculants became available at the end of 2020, a scramble for the relatively few available quantities of the vaccines evolved. A dynamic for which the term 'vaccine nationalism' was coined: While the US, the EU, and other governments of the Global North were instrumental in pushing for multilateral mechanisms for fair and equitable distribution of vaccines through COVAX, they faced the political pressure to deliver access to vaccinations for their own populations. This led to trade-offs in their political management of vaccine procurement and to an ambivalent international approach to procuring and distributing COVID-19 vaccines at times when vaccine doses were not yet available in broader volumes. The US and the EU managed to secure the lion's share of the available production of vaccines from producers in their region (Moderna, Astra-Zeneca, BioNTech/Pfizer) in order to secure access to vaccines for their own populations. The US even put up an export ban for COVID-19 vaccines. WHO and many health experts pointed out early on that from a vantage point of a global disease management, health care workers around the globe should be the first ones to become vaccinated, then people at higher risk of severe disease, then those in areas where the disease is spreading rapidly, and only then, the rest of the population. Yet, national interest, domestic political pressure, and purchasing power of richer countries made them buy available vaccine supplies at the expense of the very same multilateral platform COVAX, for which creation was based on the recognition that a free-market system is unlikely to ensure equitable vaccine access on a global scale and was developed to avoid the international scramble for vaccines.

On the production side, the Serum Institute of India (SIU), providing more than 60% of global vaccine supply, was an early mover and managed to establish a licence production for Astra-Zeneca. A respective agreement was signed in June 2020, and shipment of vaccines to developing countries started mid-January 2021. And hopes for sufficient supplies for COVAX were built on the capacities of SIU. However, also SIU was placed with an export ban by the Indian government when a massive wave of COVID-19 infections surged in India in April 2021. COVID-19 vaccine export only resumed at the end of October 2021 after the export ban was lifted.

The vaccine nationalism was put into metaphorical language in early 2020 by Serbia's president Aleksandar Vucic, when he compared the situation around COVID-19 vaccine availability to the sinking of the Titanic, where everyone wanted a lifeboat only for themselves (Economist, 2021). In a way, the speedy availability of vaccines as a tool to fight the pandemic might be described as huge success of science; at the same time, the inability to deliver an equitable distribution of these vaccines on a global scale can be seen as a political failure. The latter also providing room to further international dynamics, which are discussed in the next section.

The rise of vaccine diplomacy

The realities of vaccine nationalism and global vaccine inequity gave rise to a new geopolitical dynamic, to vaccine diplomacy. Early 2021, China and Russia started major vaccine diplomacy operations. Ever since they have sent millions of COVID-19 vaccines developed in their countries (mainly Sputnik

V, Sinopharm, and Sinovac) to countries in sub-Saharan Africa. The strategic objectives of these operations were not difficult to read: Through vaccine diplomacy, China and Russia have been trying to extend their long-term presence in the developing world. Both countries seized the opportunity to improve on their reputation as reliable partners committed to global health. Accordingly, the provision of masks, ventilators, other medical equipment, and eventually vaccines against COVID-19 has – despite being the most effective tool against the global pandemic – also become a geopolitical instrument. As Lina Benabdallah documented for the Washington Post:

> Sierra Leone television channels broadcast live footage of China's Sinopharm vaccine doses landing in Freetown's Lungi Airport on Feb. 26, adding to an expanding list of African countries receiving vaccine doses from China. Just a day earlier, Senegal President Macky Sall took his Sinopharm jab live on television, then tweeted an appeal for all Senegalese to get vaccinated. In Zimbabwe, President Emmerson Mnangagwa hailed China for its donation of 200,000 Sinopharm vaccine doses, describing them as "a light at the end of a dark tunnel".
>
> *(Washington Post, 2021)*

It has been pointed out that the success of the vaccine diplomacy by China and Russia has been clouded by questions over the efficacy of the vaccines and under-delivery in promised volumes (Kier, sub-Saharan Africa, Stronski, 2021).

A more detailed scrutiny reveals, however, that China's humanitarian and medical assistance to Africa is not new: China has been rendering medical support to African countries for a long time, e.g. through the deployment of Chinese medical teams: "The Chinese government estimates that since 1963 more than 22,000 Chinese medics have been sent to Africa, where they have treated approximately 220 million patients" (Bayes, 2021: 25). The COVID-19 pandemic has become an opportunity for China to share its medical expertise and medical knowledge more widely in the continent, and, of course, to shape a narrative of strengthened China–Africa ties and, more generally, to showcase the success of the Chinese development (and societal) model. In this sense, the overseas medical assistance during the pandemic has been described as being part of a 'Health Silk Road', a health-focused extension of the Belt and Road Initiative (Bayes, 2021: 18).

Structural inequalities in vaccine production capacity

Before the COVID-19 pandemic hit, the EU was the world's largest producer of vaccines. The pre-pandemic market for vaccines was divided into two spheres: Rich countries in the Global North have been supplied mainly by EU and US vaccine production capacity, while India has been the main producer for the Global South (Jeanrenaud *et al.*, 2021). With COVID-19, China and Russia entered the stage as main producers for COVID-19 vaccines, mainly targeting their own populations and the population of developing countries. COVID-19 has shown that this market structure provides clear limitations to a fair and equitable access to vaccines and to successfully handling a global public health security crisis.

More so, the realities in global vaccine production also revealed a structural dependency of African countries: 99% of vaccines utilized in African countries and about 80% of its medicines are currently imported to the continent, meaning only 1% of the demand of inoculants are produced locally (about 12 million doses per year, mainly yellow fever jabs produced at the Institute Pasteur in Senegal). Africa, hence, remains in a critical dependency regarding vaccine supply, and this reaches far beyond the current discussions on COVID-19 vaccines.

The AU has prioritized the pharmaceutical industry over the past decades: A Pharmaceutical Manufacturing Plan for Africa, which identified the importance of strengthening the industry, was already endorsed by the AU Heads of State and Government Summit in 2007. The African Medicines Regulatory Harmonization Initiative was launched in 2009 and has fostered significant developments on regulatory harmonization at the level of regional organizations. The initiative has actually been the predecessor to the African Medicines Agency, which has been established by treaty in 2019 as the regulatory body for pharmaceuticals and has entered force in November 2021 when 15 member states had ratified the treaty. But for the time being, Africa still stays behind in the global effort of vaccine production, also due to the limitations of its pharmaceutical industry, challenging the very fight against the COVID-19 pandemic and other diseases, and the establishment of resilient health supply chains on the continent.

These structural issues come at a cost. The Economist Intelligence Unit (EIU) developed an economic model to calculate the cost of vaccine inequality between countries and regions. The calculations from August 2021 paint a sobering picture: They forecast that countries with less than 60% of the population vaccinated against COVID-19 by mid-2022 will register GDP losses totalling around 2 trillion USD in 2022–2025 (which is roughly equivalent to the annual GDP of France). "Emerging countries will shoulder around two-thirds of these losses, fuelling poverty and further delaying their economic convergence with more developed countries" (EIU, 2021: 4).

However, African governments have reacted to the challenge, have identified the problem, and raised their ambitions: The first ever African Vaccine Manufacturing Conference was convened by the AU and the Africa Centre for Disease Control and Prevention in April 2021 and launched the Partnership for African Vaccine Manufacturing (PAVM), with the ambition to locally produce 60% of Africa's total vaccine requirements by 2040, including those to fight the COVID-19 pandemic and other vaccines required for routine immunization (vaccines against measles, polio, yellow fever, and, in future, possibly against malaria and HIV/AIDS). The ambition was formulated against the backdrop of AU's Agenda 2063. Agenda 2063 was initially adopted by the Heads of State and

Governments of the AU in 2015 as the development plan for the next 50 years (the call for such agenda was first made in 2013, 50 years after the predecessor of AU, the Organisation of African Unity, was founded). It is intended to serve as a master plan for transforming Africa into a global powerhouse of the future. The blueprint of such global powerhouse includes a strong competitive pharmaceutical industry. Also, the launch of the African Continental Free Trade Area (AfCFTA) earlier in 2021 offers a window of opportunity to accelerate progress towards the outlined goals. The PAVM has reviewed initial progress in a stakeholder meeting in early December 2021 in Kigali, Rwanda, and endorsed a continental strategy, a framework for action. The framework for action prioritizes eight key programmes, including an ambitious pooled-procurement mechanism, strengthening national regulatory agencies, a vaccine-manufacturing fund, and programmes to increase coordination of technology transfers, regulation, research, sub-Saharan Africa development, and infrastructure.

On G20 level and at the World Trade Organization (WTO), a discussion around a waiver for intellectual property rights and patents has been looming over the first two years of the pandemic, also as a reaction to the unequal global access to vaccines. India and South Africa made the initial call in October 2020 and suggested a waiver for all WTO member states on the implementation of certain provisions of the TRIPS Agreement regarding prevention, containment, and treatment of COVID-19 (TRIPS is a multilateral agreement on intellectual property rights such as copyright, patents, and protection of undisclosed information or trade secrets, which came into effect in 1995). The opponents of such waiver argue that a patent waiver would be of symbolic nature only, since patents are not the important bottleneck for vaccine manufacturing in African countries but technology transfer, availability of trained staff, quality infrastructure, the regulatory environment, a research and development ecosystem, and trade barriers between countries. These challenges are the reason why pharmaceutical companies see the first step in the production of vaccines in African countries in the 'fill and finish', with a backward integration of further production steps in future. In South Africa, the local company Aspen Pharmacare started mid of 2021 with fill and finish of COVID-19 vaccines on behalf of Johnson and Johnson, sub-Saharan Africa; a further fill and finish production line for COVID-19 vaccines shall be established still in 2021 by the South African BioVac Institute, with support of the German vaccine producer BioNTech. Both initiatives are expected to lead to a combined capacity of 500 million doses of additional COVID-19 vaccines per annum by the end of 2022. This would be a substantial milestone in broadening the vaccine-manufacturing capacity on the continent.

However, more efforts are needed to deliver on the ambitious goals of AU to produce 60% of Africa's total vaccine demands on the continent by 2040. And some players came forward to support AU and member states in their efforts through major new initiatives in their development policy: The EU and its member states came up with an initiative to support PAVM and the AU in reaching the set targets. The rationale for EU is the political imperative of supporting progress on vaccine manufacturing and access to (COVID-19 and other) vaccines in Africa. But from a political economy point of view, the initiative can also be read as an attempt to counterbalance the EU's political decision to block a WTO waiver for intellectual property rights on COVID-19 vaccines. While protecting its own vaccine industry in their intellectual property rights, the EU had to deliver other means to render political support to AU and African countries to support them in overcoming the structural inequalities in vaccine production. To this end, the EU initiated a 'Team Europe Initiative (TEI)' on 'Manufacturing and Access to Vaccines, Medicines and Health Technologies (MAV+) in Africa'. Entities from different European member states and from different domains are brought together under the umbrella of the TEI: In partnership with the private sector, European financing institutions, the European Commission, and member states' agencies aim at creating leverage on establishment or expansion of companies in the pharma and health care technology sectors in Africa. The president of the European Commission has pledged 1 billion Euro for this initiative, and EU member states joined in, e.g. Germany has already committed an additional amount of 500 million Euro in financing guarantees, loans, and grants (mainly channelled through development cooperation) for the support of vaccine-manufacturing capacities in South Africa, Senegal, Ghana, Rwanda, and at AU level. Private-sector players are stepping in as well, e.g. the German vaccine producer BioNTech, who signed memoranda of understanding with the governments of Senegal and Rwanda to establish vaccine production capacities beyond COVID-19 in the respective countries. The COVAX Vaccine Manufacturing Task Force and the ACT-A Vaccine Manufacturing Working Group chaired by South Africa and Germany have been dealing with vaccine-manufacturing capacity constraints in low- and middle-income countries and with an initial focus on COVID-19 vaccines. They have established a technology transfer hub model, and WHO has announced in June 2021 that the first hub focusing on mRNA vaccines will be established in South Africa. The respective mRNA hub is built on the idea of a reverse engineering of an existing mRNA vaccine (the Moderna COVID-19 vaccine, for which Moderna has already declared not to enforce intellectual property rights), in order to build capacity for production, regulation, associated research, sub-Saharan Africa development, and basically the development of an entire ecosystem for vaccine production. South Africa has been vocal in establishing itself as a hub for vaccine production in the region, making it clear that it would use its position for delivering to other countries on the African continent.

These initiatives – if delivered successfully – have indeed the potential to fundamentally change the current structural inequalities in global vaccine production and supply chains. However, further political initiatives on addressing market failures and on shaping global demand for vaccines will be needed to sustain the efforts and to structure supply and demand, since supply only will not guarantee that new industries will survive competition on the global vaccine market in the long run (Sampath, 2021). The biggest long-term challenge for an economically viable vaccine production on the African continent might lie on the demand side since these vaccines will likely be more expensive than imports.

The shaping of a global supply in anti-retroviral drugs for HIV/AIDS treatment since the early 2000s might offer interesting lessons. On HIV/AIDS drugs, national and international agencies have worked together to shape global markets towards public health objectives, particularly to promote the supply of drugs to low-income countries. These efforts have focused mainly on market failures around pricing and access in reducing supplies and buyer risks and promoting security of supply by bringing together public, private, and non-profit actors. GAVI, the Vaccine Alliance (previously the Global Alliance for Vaccines and Immunization), is another example for such public–private global health partnership, which was set up in 2000 to address the low vaccine rollout in low- and middle-income countries. GAVI has been instrumental in pooling demand from low- and middle-income countries and offering financing for vaccines. It has put forward the concept of Advanced Market Commitment (AMC), following the idea that public funds should be committed in advance to buying vaccines that are needed in developing countries. However, Stein argues, that AMCs were explicitly promoted as a bulwark against changing intellectual property regimes. Stein moreover underlines that whether corporate subsidies (as being built into AMCs) can be justified might depend largely on the contractual details of AMCs, since they are highly complicated contracts and might quickly turn from reasonable subsidy of the private sector to a perfect waste of aid (Stein, 2021).

On the final objective to vaccinate broader populations against a disease, it must be noted that beyond sufficient supply of vaccines, there are more issues to consider for a successful rollout of vaccination campaigns: Factors include people's willingness to get vaccinated and countries' capacity to distribute the doses and to manage vaccination campaigns. Vaccination campaigns for a whole population are rather complex endeavours. Trust of the population in the inoculants and willingness to get vaccinated are paramount. Beyond this, trained health workers, a functioning public health system, supply chains, and cool-chain logistics way into rural areas are needed. Many African countries have plenty of experience in vaccination campaigns for children, yet insufficient experience in vaccination programmes for the whole population. Malawi, for instance, had to incinerate about 20,000 doses of Astra-Zeneca coronavirus vaccines in May 2020 out of a first shipment of 100,000 doses, since initial uptake of the vaccination campaign has been low and trust of citizens in the jabs has been low (BBC, 2021).

Conclusion

The geopolitical implications of the global COVID-19 pandemic continue playing out. For Africa, the paradox remains, that the least infected are the most affected: COVID-19 has (so far) in global comparison impacted with the least burden of disease in Africa (in numbers of infections and deaths). At the same time, African countries suffer tremendously by the 'polypandemic' corona has brought about. Early lockdowns and other measures to contain the disease have acted as an accelerant of other crises looming. Food and nutrition insecurity, stunting, economic inequalities, and extreme poverty are on the rise again in sub-Saharan Africa. Developmental gains of the past decades and progress towards the SDGs are at stake. The pandemic has also created strategic risks and opportunities for countries in Europe, the US, China, Russia, and India. While Europe and the US were fast to secure vaccine supply for their own populations (only), they had to face the allegation to impede equity in global vaccine distribution. The criticism was emphasized by the fact that while pushing successfully for multilateral solutions in vaccine distribution (mainly through ACT-A/COVAX), the EU, its member states, and the US showed resistance against waiving patents for COVID-19 vaccines. China and Russia (and for a certain time India) forged on this situation and established a strong vaccine diplomacy in offering their own vaccines to countries of the Global South. Over time, particularly the EU and its member states have come out clearly with the objective to support the AU and its member states in their ambition to develop their own manufacturing capacity for vaccines, pharmaceuticals, and other medical supplies. The emerging AfCFTA seems to provide further opportunities for this trajectory.

Such course might strengthen the AU and African countries striving for independence in pharmaceutical production in the long run. However, with a global market on vaccines, the question whether such production in African countries will prove to be economically viable remains open for now. The dynamics in a global pharmaceutical market and the development of mechanisms to shape the worldwide demand for vaccines have not yet received sufficient attention.

References

ACT Accelerator Facilitation Council sub-Saharan Africa Vaccine Manufacturing Task Force (2020): Report to the G20. 20th October, 2021, https://www.who.int/publications/m/item/act-accelerator-facilitation-council-vaccine-manufacturing-working-group---report-to-the-g20

Adams, Janica; Mary J. MacKenzie; Adeladza Kofi Amegah (2021): The Conundrum of Low COVID-19 Mortality Burden in sub-Saharan Africa: Myth or Reality? *Global Health: Science and Practice*. 2021 Sep 30; 9(3), 433–443.

Appiah, Kwame Anthony (2021): A Tale of Two Pandemics: The True Cost of COVID in the Global South. *The Guardian*, 23.11.2021.

Bayes, Tom (2021): Wielding Influence in the Age of Coronavirus. *How the Chinese Communist Party Shapes Narratives and Builds Influence in Africa*. Berlin: Konrad Adenauer Foundation.

BBC (2021): Malawi Burns Thousands of Expired AstraZeneca Covid-19 Vaccine Doses. *BBC News*, 19.5.2021.

Economist (2021): Vaccine Diplomacy Boosts Russia's and China's Global Standing. 29.4.2021.

Egger, Dennis; Eduard Miguel; Shana S. Warren; Ashis Shenoy; Elliott Collins; *et al.* (2021): Falling Living Standards during the COVID-19 Crisis: Qualitative Evidence from Nine Developing Countries. *Science Advances*, 7 February 2021.

EIU (2021): *Pandemic: Will the World Suffer from "Long Covid"? Clarity in an Uncertain World*. London: Economist Intelligence Unit.

G20 Declaration (2021): G20 Rome Leaders' Declaration. 30/31 October 2021.

GFATM (2021): *The Impact of COVID-19 on HIV, TB and Malaria Services and Systems for Health*. Geneva: The Global Fund to Fight AIDS, Tuberculosis and Malaria. April 2021.

Guetta-Jeanrenaud, Lionel; Niclas Potiers; Reinhilde Veugelers (2021): A World Divided: Global Vaccine Trade and Production. *Bruegel Blog Post*. https://www.bruegel.org/2021/07/a-world-divided-global-vaccine-trade-and-production/

IMF (2020): *World Economic Outlook Update, June 2020*. Washington, DC: International Monetary Fund.

Kier, Grace; Paul Stronski (2021): Russia's Vaccine Diplomacy is Mostly Smoke and Mirrors. *Carnegie Endowment for International Peace*. August 2021.

Lakner, Christoph; Nishant Yonzan; Daniel G. Mahler; *et al.* (2021): *Updated Estimates of the Impact of COVID-19 on Global Poverty: Looking Back at 2020 and the Outlook for 2021*. Washington: World Bank. January 2021.

Loembé, Marguerite Massinga; Akhonda Tshangela; Stephanie J. Salyer; Jay K. Varma; Ahmed E. Ogwell Ouma; John N. Nkengasong (2021): COVID-19 in Africa: The Spread and Response. In: *Nature Medicine*, 26, 999–1003 (2020).

Moyer, Jonathan D; Oliver Kaplan (2020). Will the Coronavirus Fuel Conflict? In: *Foreign Policy*. Availableathttps://foreignpolicy.com/2020/07/06/coronavirus-pandemic-fuel-conflict-fragile-states-economy-food-prices/

MSC (2020): Polypandemic. Munich Security Report Special Edition on Development, Fragility, and Conflict in the Era of Covid-19. Munich: Munich Security Conference. November 2020.

Mwai, Peter (2021): COVID-19 Vaccinations: African Nations Miss WHO Target. In: *BBC*, 31.12.2021. Available at https://www.bbc.com/news/56100076

OECD (2021): *South Africa Economic Snapshot. Economic Forecast Summary*. Organisation for Economic Co-operation and Development. Paris, December 2021.

Sampath, Padmashree Gehl (2021): Market Shaping and Market Access in the Global Vaccines Market - Approaches for the Future. Paper prepared for the Deutsche Gesellschaft für Internationale Zusammenarbeit (GIZ) GmbH. Eschborn.

Stein, Felix (2021): Risky Business: COVAX and the Financialization of Global Vaccine Equity. *Globalization and Health*, 17/2021, 112.

UNDP (2021): *Analysing Long-Term Socio-Economic Impacts of COVID-19 across Diverse African Contexts*. New York: United Nations Development Programme.

UNECA (2021): *Macroeconomic Impact of COVID-19 on Africa: Evidence from an Africa-wide Aggregate Macro-econometric Model*. Addis Ababa: United Nations Economic Commission for Africa.

UNOCHA (2020): *Under-Secretary-General for Humanitarian Affairs and Emergency Relief Coordinator Mark Lowcock – Remarks in Conversation with the Center for Strategic and International Studies on Covid-19's Next Cascade of Crises sub-Saharan Africa Choices Before the World's Leaders*. New York: United Nations Office for the Coordination of Humanitarian Affairs, July 22, 2020.

Washington Post (2021): Don't Believe the Hype about China's 'Vaccine Diplomacy' in Africa, 5.3.2021

WHO (2021): *WHO Coronavirus Disease (COVID-19) Dashboard*. December 28, 2021. Geneva: World Health Organization.

11

ECONOMIC AND SOCIAL PROSPERITY IN TIME OF COVID-19 CRISIS IN THE EUROPEAN UNION

Angeles Sánchez

Introduction

In the setting of the European Union (EU), the main pillars of the welfare state are to alleviate income inequality and reduce poverty, protect the population from insecurity that may arise from adverse situations such as unemployment or illness, and facilitate the population's access to preferred or merit goods (i.e. education, health, and housing). In the specific case of the EU, since its constitution in 1957, the European values of freedom, democracy, equality, and the rule of law have made possible European integration as well as improving peoples' prosperity and well-being (European Commission, 2020; Stiglitz, 2020). In this sense, it is noteworthy that following the accession to the EU from 2004 of the 11 Baltic, Eastern, and Central European countries plus Cyprus and Croatia, both poverty and income inequality levels in the EU as a whole increased, due to the worse situation of the newcomers. Especially in the case of poverty levels in the 15 former Member States in 2004, the percentage of the population *at risk of poverty or social exclusion*, which is the official measure of poverty in the EU, ranged from 16.1% in the Netherlands to 30.9% in Greece. All the new countries, except Slovenia and Cyprus, had higher rates in 2005 (for instance, 61.3% Bulgaria, 47% Romania, 46.3% Latvia, and 45.3% Poland). However, the process of convergence with the rest of the Member States was fast so that in 2008, the maximum value of the poverty rate in the EU dropped to 44.8% in Bulgaria (EUROSTAT, Income and Living Conditions [ilc_peps01]). All in all, the Member States studied in this chapter[1] fall into a group of countries in the world with very high human development. Furthermore, following their accession to the EU from 2004, the new Member States registered higher increases in their Human Development Index (HDI) than the rest of the Member States (United Nations, 2020a).

DOI: 10.4324/9781003273844-11

Regarding the budgetary effort in public policies (based on information from the International Monetary Fund [IMF], Government Finance Statistics), it is worth noting that over the period 2000–2019, the average public expenditure in the EU28 is 47% of gross domestic product (GDP) versus 33.71% in Australia and 35.56% in the United States. For 2020, the forecast is increments between 7 and 10 percentage points in all of these territories. Government social expenditure is obtained by adding spending on preferred goods and social protection, and it represents the public programmes that are most effective in reducing economic and social inequalities (Coady *et al.*, 2021; Furceri *et al.*, 2021). Government social expenditure has also registered in this period a greater weight in the EU28 (33.8%) than in other territories, such as 23.11% in Australia and 23.61% in the United States (IMF, Government Finance Statistics).

Within the government expenditure of the Member States, foreign aid finances the promotion of the economic development and welfare of developing countries. With the Lisbon Treaty (2009), development policy was incorporated to the external action of the EU being poverty eradication one of the main focuses. The Official Development Assistance (ODA) of each Member State is complemented by the ODA of the EU as an institution, and the European Commission is the coordinator (Muñoz-Gálvez, 2012). Taking as a reference the target of 0.7% of gross national income (GNI) dedicated to ODA, the average EU Collective ODA over the period 2010–2020 is 0.46%. In other words, the objective is not achieved as a whole. Contributions by Sweden, Luxembourg, Germany, and Denmark to foreign aid are higher than 0.7%, whereas the rest do not reach the target. Notwithstanding the foregoing, the EU and its 27 Member States together spent 0.50% of the EU's GNI in 2020, representing 46% of global ODA. This figure is above the 0.26% average of non-EU countries (e.g. 0.19% Australia and 0.17% United States) spent in 2020 by the members of the OECD-Development Assistance Committee (European Commission, 2021a).

Despite these figures, the global financial crisis that began in 2008 (hereafter GFC of 2008) exposed some weaknesses of the EU countries. As discussed more deeply in a next section, income inequality and poverty rates have reached very high levels. The main explanations would be greater income reductions for the population with lower incomes. This is due to the augmented loss of relative weight of wages in the national income that had already been recorded since the 1980s and also as a consequence of the policies of sustainability of public finances carried out in the EU since 2011 (Agnello and Sousa, 2014; Piketty and Sáez, 2013; Sánchez and Pérez-Corral, 2018). Subsequently, the COVID-19 pandemic has put the achievement of the Sustainable Development Goals (SDGs) of the United Nations at risk; among them, SDG 1 focused on eradicating poverty in all its forms everywhere. Loss of income is expected to affect the vulnerable strata of society more than other socio-economic strata. Thus, income inequality and poverty will increase around the world and also in the EU (European Commission, 2020; Fetting, 2020; United Nations, 2020b). Specifically, the *indicator people at risk of poverty or social exclusion* has increased from 21.4% of the population in 2019 to 22% in 2020 (EUROSTAT, Income and Living Conditions [ilc_peps01]). The information available for some Member States in EUROSTAT on indicators of income inequality would also confirm the forecast of an increase. For example, in Germany, the Gini index would increase from 29.7 in 2019 to 34.4 in 2020 (EUROSTAT, Income and Living Conditions [ilc_di12]).

The increase in income inequalities has aroused great interest in the study of its consequences in different areas of well-being. Studies show that societies with less inequality in the income distribution enjoy longer life expectancy, as well as fewer rates of mortality, school dropout, mental illness, and drug abuse (Lewer *et al.*, 2020; Wilkinson and Pickett, 2009). More importantly, the persistence of income inequality represents a threat to the sustainability of social welfare because it prevents the social mobility of minors from families with lower incomes (Esping-Andersen, 2016). Furthermore, empirical works for European nations and Organisation for Economic Co-operation and Development (OECD) countries state a negative relationship between income inequality and economic growth (Cingano, 2014; Dabla-Norris *et al.*, 2015; Sánchez and Pérez-Corral, 2018). In any case, inequality in the distribution of income could foster political instability and undermine the social consensus required to adjust to large shocks and, therefore, reduce the pace and stability of economic growth (Berg *et al.*, 2012; OECD, 2015).

In this setting, the reduction of income inequalities is one of the priorities of the political agendas in many countries. The aim is to curb social resentment and the rise of populist and protectionist sentiments that could lead to political instability (OECD, 2015). It could be said that the EU has learned from its past mistakes. In order to confront the negative effects of COVID-19 shock, the EU has chosen 'expansive economic policies', such as the rise of government expenditure and the approval of the Next Generation EU funds to foster the recovery after the pandemic (European Commission, 2021b).

This chapter has two objectives. The first is to analyse the connection between poverty, income inequality, and human development with the economic cycle and the public policies carried out over the past two decades in the EU. The second objective is to study in what position the 27 Member States were in 2019 to cope with the social and economic effects of the COVID-19 pandemic or any other potential shock.

To this end, the 'An Overview of the EU in the Past Two Decades' section presents an overview of the EU in the past two decades, focusing on the two major crises: GFC of 2008 and the COVID-19 crisis. In the 'Human Development in the EU at the Pre-COVID Stage' section, and following the United Nations' methodology, a composite HDI is constructed according to the socio-economic context of the EU. More specifically, indicators of enhanced capabilities are selected instead of indicators of basic capabilities. In addition, in the 'Human Development in the EU and European Values' section, a composite index of governance is built on the basis of the self-reported assessment of the socio- economic agents (citizens, experts, and enterprises) regarding the degree of compliance with the European values of freedom, political stability, and rule of law. The combination of information on human development and perception of compliance with European values that determine the prosperity of citizens allows the 27 Member States in 2019 to be classified into four typologies, as well as discussing which Member States are better prepared for the next challenges. Finally, the 'Conclusions' section summarises the main conclusions.

An overview of the EU in the past two decades

In economics, it is of interest to study changes or temporal variation variables because they reflect the behavioural patterns of the agents analysed and enrich the analysis. Figure 11.1 shows the evolution over the past two decades of economic growth (annual variation rate of GDP) in the EU, as well as the annual variation rate of government expenditure. The main socio-economic changes in the EU are also addressed. These facts are reviewed in the sections below.

Stability and growth pact and enlargement of the EU

In 1990, the steps towards the Economic and Monetary Union were initiated. In January 2002, the Euro was introduced as the single currency. In an area where there is a single currency, a single monetary policy and an exchange rate policy controlled by the European Central Bank are required. However, the fact that fiscal policy is designed in a discretionary manner by national governments can make it easier for countries to run deficits, as their cost is distributed among all

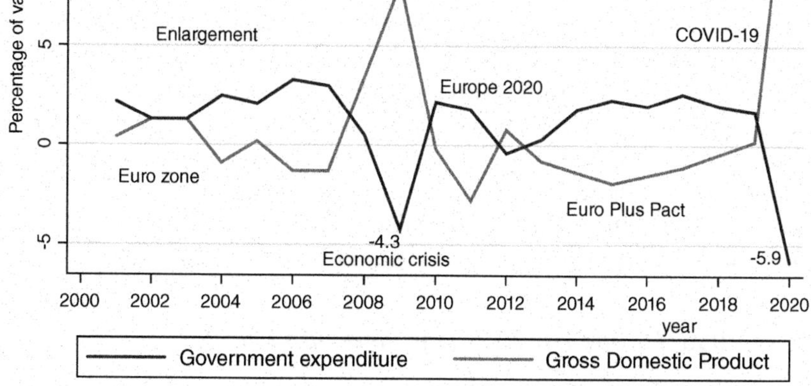

FIGURE 11.1 Annual variation rate of GDP and government expenditure in the EU of 28 Member States, 2001–2020 (%).

members of the euro area creating a number of spillover effects. The Member States therefore decided that coordination of their fiscal policies was necessary and signed the Stability and Growth Pact (SGP) in 1997. The SGP established as rules to be adhered to by the Member States, among others, a limit of 3% of GDP for the government deficit and 60% of GDP for government debt. In accordance with the European Semester framework by which public finances are approved and monitored (government spending, taxes, deficits, and public debts), every Member State presents their budgetary commitments. The European Commission is responsible for reviewing the programmes. If the criteria are not met, the European Council launches an excessive deficit procedure based on the Commission's recommendations, which may lead to the payment of sanctions (European Commission, 2012).

In parallel, in May 2004, ten countries joined the EU: Czechia, Cyprus, Estonia, Hungary, Latvia, Lithuania, Malta, Poland, Slovakia, and Slovenia. In 2007, Bulgaria and Romania joined and, finally, Croatia in 2013. Thus, from 2013, we speak about the EU of 28 Member States (EU28) until 2020, when the United Kingdom ceased to be a member of the EU. From that moment, there are 27 Member States (EU27).

In short, the euro area or Eurozone is currently constituted by 19 Member States. Denmark chose to keep its national currency. The remaining seven countries have not yet adopted the single currency but will join the euro area when they meet the necessary conditions: Bulgaria, Croatia, the Czechia, Hungary, Poland, Romania, and Sweden. Most of these are the Member States that joined the Union from 2004 onwards.

The 11 countries of the former Soviet Union are denominated as emerging economies as in the years prior to the transition process they shared the same kind of social and economic policies (Bastagli *et al.*, 2012; Roaf *et al.*, 2014). Focusing on the weight of the public sector in the economy in emerging countries, several aspects are noteworthy. Firstly, this group of countries makes a smaller budgetary effort than the EU as a whole. Government expenditure is lower, and they have maintained their gap of around six percentage points since joining the EU until the last year studied (Figure 11.2).

Secondly, the comparison between the 11 emerging countries and the remaining 17 countries reveals statistically significant differences in terms of tax structure or relationship between direct and indirect taxes – and the social government expenditure. In emerging Member States, the tax structure is less progressive than in the rest of Member States, and they show a smaller budgetary effort in social government expenditure (see Sánchez and López-Corral, 2018).

GFC of 2008, Europe 2020 Strategy, and Euro Plus Pact

The negative effects of the collapse of the housing bubble in the United States that were transmitted to the rest of the world reached the EU from 2008 onwards. As Figure 11.1 shows, in the GFC, the annual economic growth rate of the

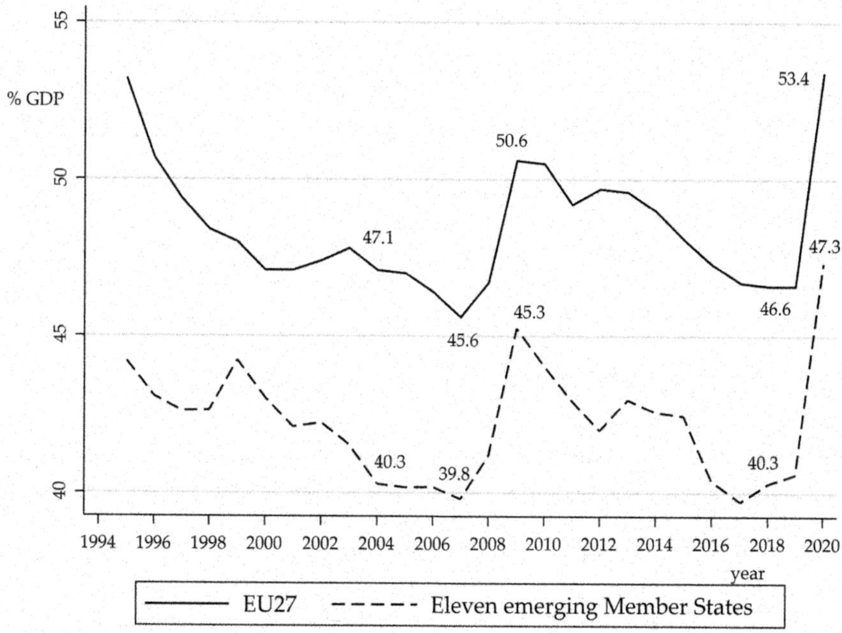

FIGURE 11.2 Government expenditure in the EU of 27 Member States and the emerging Member States, 1995–2020 (% GDP).

EU28 slowed sharply from 2008 onwards, registering negative values in 2009 (−4.3%) and 2012 (−0.4%). In fact, the EU28, as a whole, technically entered economic recession in the second quarter of 2008 and could be considered to have emerged from recession in the second quarter of 2013 (see EUROSTAT, Quarterly National Accounts [namq_10_gdp]). To respond to the adverse effects of the crisis, expansionary counter-cyclical fiscal policies were initially chosen, as reflected by the increase in government expenditure in 2009 (from 46.4% of GDP in 2008 to 50.2% in 2009) (Figure 11.2).

In June 2010, the European Council approved the Europe 2020 Strategy to coordinate all Member States' efforts to collectively exit stronger from the GFC of 2008 and turn the EU into a smart, sustainable, and inclusive economy that delivers high levels of employment, productivity, and social cohesion (European Commission, 2010, preface). Probably one of the most remarkable aspects of Europe 2020 Strategy is that it constituted a new vision of Europe's social market economy for the 21st century. The construction of a Social Europe, which has been a primary objective since the creation of the European Economic Commission in 1957, is reinforced by the definition of the social market economy (in the Europe 2020 Strategy) as an integrated social, economic, and political order, characterised by an economic market policy and at the same time a social policy that regulates the former (European Commission, 2010, p. 3). The latter is its main difference from economic neoliberalism.

To accomplish these priorities of a smart, sustainable, and inclusive economy, the Member States had undertaken to achieve eight targets by 2020 in the areas of employment, research and development, education, environmental protection, and poverty. The introduction of targets to promote a more environmentally sound economy and social targets for education and the fight against poverty represented a step forward. Nevertheless, the major drawbacks of the Europe 2020 Strategy are likely to be, firstly, the assumption that social cohesion would follow from economic growth (see Sánchez and Ruiz-Martos, 2018) and, secondly, its coincidence in timing with the GFC of 2008. The Europe 2020 Strategy was approved before the true extent of the GFC of 2008 was known. The reforms that were intended to be carried out in the Europe 2020 Strategy went in the opposite direction to the budgetary adjustment and austerity measures that were implemented by the Member States to deal with the GFC of 2008. Indeed, the worsening of macroeconomic indicators, especially public deficit above 3% of GDP in most Member States, as well as the risk of bankruptcy in some of them, led all Member States to prioritise the sustainability of public finances, signing the 2011 Euro Plus Pact (European Council, 2011).

The measures approved in the Euro Plus Pact, inspired by the proposals of Reinhart and Rogoff (2009), focused especially on controlling public spending to contain the public deficit and, subsequently, reducing debt to boost economic growth. The main conclusion of Reinhart and Rogoff (2009) for the Eurozone was that if government debt rose above 90% of GDP, it would negatively affect economic growth. The effectiveness in containing government spending is shown in Figure 11.1, which, since 2010, has recorded negative changes until 2019. Government deficits were reduced in virtually all Member States to below 3% of GDP and economic growth rates recovered. However, the fiscal consolidation measures exerted great pressure on EU economic, social, and territorial cohesion, which have been core EU objectives since its foundation.

The ratio of total disposable income received by 20% of the population with the highest income to that received by 20% of the families with the lowest income (S80/S20) indicates that in 2019 in the EU28, the richest families earned 5.1 times more than the poorest ones (Figure 11.3). More importantly, the evolution shows that in the 15 years for which information is available, income inequality has not been reduced and even increased in 2014 and 2015 as a consequence of the policy of government expenditure containment.

Regarding poverty, the Europe 2020 Strategy aimed, among its objectives, to reduce the number of people at risk of poverty or social exclusion by 20 million. For that, a new multidimensional poverty index was developed for being used by all the Member States: *people at risk of poverty or social exclusion* (AROPE). The AROPE index incorporates three dimensions: monetary poverty, severely materially deprived people, and households with low work intensity. For its construction, the head-counting methodology is followed with the union criterion. More specifically, it calculates the percentage of the population that in one or more of the three dimensions registers values below the established thresholds (60% of

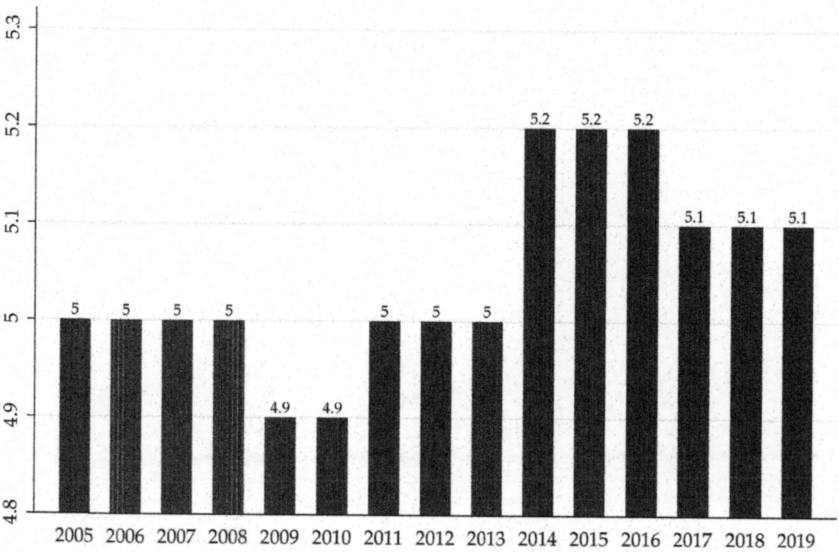

FIGURE 11.3 Income inequality in the EU of 28 Member States, 2005–2019.

the country's median income, inability to enjoy four or more items out of nine from a list of deprivations items,[2] and households where members worked less than 20% of their potential). AROPE is also calculated for the population under 18 years of age and provides an approximation of multidimensional child poverty.

Table 11.1 shows the pace of poverty in the EU by breaking down by gender, child poverty, and severely materially deprived people. This last indicator is a measure of extreme poverty in the context of the EU (see Bradshaw and Movshuk, 2019).

All the concepts of poverty worsened from 2009 onwards as a result of the GFC of 2008 and the fiscal measures taken; likewise, all the rates have worsened again in 2020. Starting with the AROPE for all the population, Sánchez and Ruiz-Martos (2018) estimated that in order to meet the poverty target of Europe 2020 Strategy, the AROPE should reach the value of 18.7% in 2020. As shown in Table 11.1, the rate for 2020 (22%) is far from that target. Inequalities in the EU are also reflected in the fact that in all the years analysed, women have higher poverty rates than men and poverty also affects households with children more. That is, children are the most vulnerable group in the EU. This fact is especially serious since child poverty represents a threat for sustainability of societal well-being in terms of both economic development and social stability (Esping-Andersen, 2016; Sánchez and Navarro, 2021). The extreme poverty rates are lower than the at-risk-of-poverty rates in all the years shown in Table 11.1, but the reality is that there are extremely poor households in all the years and also in all the EU countries.

All in all, the economic crisis and the policy measures to combat its effects pushed the EU away from the scope of an inclusive growth strategy able to foster improvement of living standards and shared prosperity across all social groups.

TABLE 11.1 Percentage of people at risk of poverty or social exclusion in the European Union

Year	*AROPE total*	*AROPE males*	*AROPE females*	*AROPE less than 18 years*	*Extreme poverty*[a]
2008	23.7	22.3	25.1	26.5	8.5
2009	23.3	22.0	24.5	26.5	8.2
2010	23.8	22.7	24.8	27.6	8.4
2011	24.3	23.2	25.4	27.3	8.8
2012	24.8	23.8	25.8	28.1	9.9
2013	24.6	23.7	25.5	27.9	9.6
2014	24.4	23.6	25.3	27.8	8.9
2015	23.8	23.1	24.5	27.1	8.1
2016	23.5	22.6	24.4	26.4	7.5
2017	22.4	21.5	23.3	24.9	6.6
2018	21.8	20.8	22.8	24.2	5.9
2019	21.4	20.4	22.3	23.4	5.5
2020[b]	22.0	21.1	22.8	23.7	6.3

[a]Measured by severely materially deprived people.
[b]The United Kingdom is not included.
Adapted from EUROSTAT, Statistics on Income and Living Conditions [ilc_peps01].

The shock of COVID-19

Despite the fact that it is too early to assess the full effects of the COVID-19 crisis, the European Commission's forecasts indicate that the EU27 as a whole will reach the 2019 level of real GDP by mid-2022. Compared to other economies, this rate of recovery is slower. For example, Australia and the United States are expected to return to pre-crisis levels of GDP by 2021 (European Commission, Directorate General for Economic and Financial Affairs, AMECO dataset). Likewise, there are remarkable differences in performance across as well as within sectors in the EU. Overall digital and healthcare industries have performed well, whereas sectors that are dependent on human contact and interaction have experienced substantial hits by the COVID-19 crisis (see de Vet *et al.*, 2021).

In the field of income distribution and people's living conditions, the severity and depth of the social and economic crisis caused by the COVID-19 pandemic are expected to lead to an increase in income inequalities and poverty in the EU, representing a serious threat to the achievement of the UN's SDGs (European Commission, 2020; Fetting, 2020). Women, young people, migrants, people with temporary employment, and people with a lower level of education are suffering more than other groups from increased income inequality and poverty levels (Fasani and Mazza, 2020; Furceri *et al.*, 2021). In this sense, the information available in 2020 shows that in the countries with the largest population size of the EU27, poverty has increased in 2020 compared to 2019. The Member States most negatively affected by the COVID-19 crisis in terms of poverty are Germany and Spain. The case of Germany is especially serious because the AROPE for all the population increased 6.6 percentage points in 2020, the AROPE for less than 18 years increased 10.6 points (from 15% to 25.6%), and the AROPE for people aged 65 years increased 4.3 percentage points (EUROSTAT, Statistics on Income and Living Conditions [ilc_peps01]).

The EU's response to this situation has been different from the GFC of 2008. The EU has approved the Next Generation EU (Euro 750 billion) to build a more resilient, sustainable, and fair Europe through large-scale financial support for investments and reforms. In 2020, the Member States have increased their government expenditure by 7–10% over the previous year, and the financial stability budget targets have been temporarily put on hold. As Figure 11.1 illustrates, in 2020, EU GDP fell by 5.9 percentage points from the previous year and government expenditure grew by 16.6 percentage points from 45.8% of GDP in 2019 in the EU28 to 53.4% of GDP in 2020.

More importantly, in March 2021, the European Commission put forward the European Pillar of Social Rights Action Plan to enhance social rights and to strengthen the European social dimension across all policies of the Union. The main lines of action that should guide policy decisions in Member States are equal opportunities, fair working conditions, and social protection and inclusion (European Commission, 2021c). Consistent with the UN SDGs, three targets to be reached by 2030 have been proposed: at least 78% of the population aged 20 to 64 should be in employment, at least 60% of all adults should be participating in training every year, and there should be a reduction in the number of people at risk of poverty or social exclusion by 15 million, including at least 5 million children.

Human development in the EU at the pre-COVID stage

Having reviewed the contextual framework of the EU as a whole and the main economic changes that have occurred over the past two decades, in this section, the study focuses on the level of the Member State. More specifically, and following the UN methodology, a composite HDI is constructed according to the socio-economic context of the EU (referred to here as the EU-HDI). The 27 Member States' 2019 data are compared on the basis of the EU-HDI so that conclusions can be drawn regarding the position of the Member States to face the social and economic effects of the COVID-19 shock.

Materials and methods for building the EU-HDI

As is well known, the HDI of the United Nations is a composite index constructed from four indicators: *life expectancy at birth, expected years of schooling, mean years of schooling*, and *GNI*. The composite index EU-HDI proposed in this study is a summary measure of achievements in four key dimensions of human development: a long and healthy life, equal opportunities in life, inclusion, and a decent standard of living (see Table 11.2).

TABLE 11.2 Single indicators of EU-HDI in 2019

Dimension	*Single indicator*	*Minimum*	*Maximum*
Health	Healthy life years at birth (no. years)	51.4	73.3
Equal opportunities	Young people in employment or in education and training (% of 15–29 years)	71.5	94.3
Inclusion	Population unaffected by severe material and social deprivation (%)	63.2	98.6
Standard of living	GNI per capita (2017 PPP$)	15,424	72,712

In comparison with the HDI of the United Nations, the main difference in the selection of single indicators is that, on the ground of the different socio-economic contexts of the EU, basic capabilities have been replaced with enhanced capabilities. More specifically, instead of *life expectancy at birth*, *healthy life years at birth* is considered because people are living longer, and what matters is the number of years that a person at birth is expected to live without any severe or moderate health problems. This indicator also monitors health as a productive or an economic factor, since increases in *healthy life years at birth* not only improve the situation of individuals but also result in lower levels of public health care expenditure.

As education indicators, the United Nations considers *expected years of schooling* and *mean years of schooling*. In the EU, two opposite phenomena coexist in terms of human capital. On the one hand, schooling is compulsory and funded by the public sector at least until the age of 16 or having completed upper secondary education (level 3 in the International Standard Classification of Education, UNESCO). But on the other hand, some Member States have very high school dropout rates. In other words, there is a certain polarity in human capital so that in the same country, there are high rates of population with tertiary education and high rates of school dropout (e.g. Spain). Thus, the two indicators of the United Nations would not reflect reality on the ground. The chosen indicator is the percentage of the young population between 15 and 29 who have a job or are involved in education or training. Indeed, this indicator is obtained by subtracting the value of the indicator *young people neither in employment nor in education and training* from 100, which is considered a headline indicator in the Social Scoreboard for the European Pillar of Social Rights Action Plan to foster equal opportunities (European Commission, 2021c).

Poverty and social exclusion harm individual lives and limit opportunities for people to achieve their full potential by affecting their health and well-being and lowering educational outcomes (Esping-Andersen and Cimentada, 2018; Richardson *et al.*, 2020). Within the EU setting, consisting of developed countries, there are vulnerable households that suffer both material and social deprivation in a severe way. In such cases, the risk of trans-generational poverty reduces the opportunities to lead a successful life. This causes poverty to persist and hence creates more inequality, which can lead to long-term loss of economic productivity from whole groups of society, thus hindering inclusive and sustainable economic growth. All these ideas justify consideration of the dimension of inclusion into the EU-HDI. Specifically, to account for the capability of economic and social inclusion, the percentage of people not affected by severe material and social deprivation is calculated by subtracting the *severe material and social deprivation rate*[3] from 100. This is a headline indicator in the Social Scoreboard for the European Pillar of Social Rights Action Plan to foster social protection and inclusion (European Commission, 2021c).

Finally, as an indicator of standard of living, the same indicator as per HDI of the United Nations (United Nations Statistics Division) was adopted: GNI per capita converted to international dollars in purchasing power parity (PPP) of 2017. GNI is the aggregate income of an economy generated by its production and its ownership of factors of production, less the incomes paid for the use of factors of production owned by the rest of the world, converted to international dollars using PPP rates, divided by midyear population. More specifically, the natural logarithm of GNI per capita is used to account for the fact that each additional dollar of income has a smaller effect on expanding capabilities (Anand and Sen, 2000).

The idea is that those EU Member States that have a higher level of human development because their inhabitants have a greater expectation of healthy life, and with a vulnerable young population (without employment or training) as a lower proportion of their young people, are less affected by severe material and social deprivation and enjoy higher incomes. Thus, these Member States will be in a better position to cope with the negative socio-economic effects of the COVID-19 shock.

Table 11.3 presents the descriptive statistics of the four indicators selected as a proxy of the human development dimensions for the 27 Member States in 2019. The values of Pearson's coefficient of variation indicate that the largest territorial differences arose in GNI per capita. The Member States that joined the EU in 2004 and afterwards registered the lowest values. The cases of Luxembourg and Ireland stand out with the highest values, equivalent to three times the GNI per capita of Bulgaria. The second indicator with big disparities is healthy life years at birth. People enjoy a healthy and large life in Sweden (73.3 years) and Malta (73.2 years) and the shortest in Latvia (53.1 years). There is a difference of more than 20 years. Overall, it might be deduced that southern countries, in addition to Sweden and Ireland, enjoy more years of healthy life at birth. In the equal opportunities dimension, Italy and Greece reached the worst performances with around 20% of its young people without work and without being involved in education or training. By far, Romania and Bulgaria registered the worst figures in severe poverty: 25% of the population experienced severe material and social deprivation.

TABLE 11.3 Descriptive statistics of single indicators for building the EU_HDI in 2019 (n = 27)

Country	*Healthy life years at birth (no. years)*	*Young people in employment or in education and training (% of 15–29 years)*	*Population not affected by severe material and social deprivation (%)*	*GNI per capita (2017 PPP$)*
Austria	57.3	91.7	97.3	56,197
Belgium	62.4	88.2	93.7	52,085
Bulgaria	66.3	83.3	77.5	23,325
Croatia	57.4	85.8	95.4	28,070
Cyprus	62.5	85.9	96.8	38,207
Czechia	62.0	90.2	97.9	38,109
Denmark	58.9	90.4	96.2	58,662
Estonia	55.8	90.2	97.3	36,019
Finland	56.4	90.5	98.1	48,511
France	64.1	87.0	92.7	47,173
Germany	66.3	92.4	97.0	55,314
Greece	66.0	82.3	84.2	30,155
Hungary	61.7	86.8	89.1	31,329
Ireland	69.6	88.6	92.8	68,371
Italy	68.3	77.8	93.6	42,776
Latvia	53.1	89.7	92.4	30,282
Lithuania	57.5	89.1	90.3	35,799
Luxembourg	62.6	93.5	98.6	72,712
Malta	73.2	92.1	95.0	39,555
Netherlands	61.0	94.3	97.2	57,707
Poland	62.5	88.0	96.5	31,623
Portugal	59.2	90.8	94.4	33,967
Romania	60.2	83.2	75.2	29,497
Slovakia	56.2	85.5	94.1	32,113
Slovenia	60.9	91.2	97.8	38,080
Spain	69.9	85.1	92.3	40,975
Sweden	73.3	93.7	98.5	54,508
Mean	62.4	88.4	93.4	42,634.1
Maximum	73.3	94.3	98.6	72,712.0
Minimum	53.1	77.8	75.2	23,325.0
CV	8.53	4.44	6.33	30.32

Note. CV is Pearson's coefficient of variation.
Adapted from EUROSTAT, Healthy Life Years by Sex [hlth_hlye]; EUROSTAT, Educational Attainment Level and Transition from Education to Work [EDAT_LFSE_35__custom_1020966]; EUROSTAT, Income and Living Conditions [ILC_MDSD11]; United Nations Statistics Division [http://hdr.undp.org/en/indicators/195706#].

According to the HDI of the United Nations, the EU-HDI is the geometric mean of normalised indicators for each of the four dimensions. In order to transform the single indicators (*x*) expressed in different units into a range between 0 and 1, the re-scaling method is applied. The normalisation formula is:

$$I_{ij} = \frac{x_{ij} - \text{minimum}(x_j)}{\text{maximum}(x_j) - \text{minimum}(x_j)}$$

where I_{ij} is the normalised indicator *j* on the Member State *i*.

As maximum values we take the maximum value of the indicator across Member States in 2019. In order to prevent that the numerator becomes zero, as minimum value we take the minimum value of the indicator across Member States over the period in which the information is available: 2010–2019 for *Healthy life years at birth*, 2010–2019 for *Young people in employment or in education and training*, 2015–2019 for *Population not affected by severe material and social deprivation*, and 2000–2019 for *GNI per capita*.

The EU-HDI in a Member State is the geometric mean of the four normalised indicators:

$$\text{EU-HDI}_i = \left(I_{i1} * I_{i2} * I_{i3} * I_{i4}\right)^{\frac{1}{4}}$$

This method is partially compensatory, and the four single indicators have the same weight.

Results of the EU-HDI

Table 11.4 displays the results of EU-HDI and HDI of 27 Member States in 2019, as well as the ranking of countries according to these measures and the variation in the ranking of countries from EU-HDI to HDI. At a first glance, the association between both indices is quite high (Pearson's coefficient of correlation is 0.81, $p < 0.01$; and the Spearman's rank correlation is 0.85, $p < 0.01$). Nevertheless, there are some remarkable findings. The countries that exhibit major changes in the rankings are Malta, Portugal, Poland, and Hungary, which rise five or more positions, and Finland, Latvia, Denmark, and Estonia, down from five to ten places. Focusing on the top, the six best positions in HDI (first quartile) are achieved by Ireland, Germany, Sweden, the Netherlands, Denmark, and Finland. However, the six best positions in the EU-HDI, which considers enhanced capabilities, are achieved by Sweden, Ireland, Luxembourg, Malta, Germany, and the Netherlands. Malta improves ten positions because, after Sweden, it has the highest number of healthy life years at birth and because only 8% of its young people are unemployed or do not participate in an education or training programme. On the contrary, Finland and Denmark are penalised in the

TABLE 11.4 Comparisons of the EU-HDI and the HDI of the United Nations in 2019 (27 Member States)

Country	*EU-HDI*	*Rank EU-HDI (1)*	*HDI*	*Rank HDI (2)*	*Variation (2)–(1)*
Austria	0.662	13	0.922	9	−4
Belgium	0.706	8	0.931	7	−1
Bulgaria	0.441	25	0.816	27	2
Croatia	0.496	23	0.851	25	2
Cyprus	0.649	14	0.887	18	4
Czechia	0.690	11	0.900	13	2
Denmark	0.691	10	0.940	5	−5
Estonia	0.543	21	0.892	16	−5
Finland	0.610	16	0.938	6	−10
France	0.698	9	0.901	12	3
Germany	0.837	5	0.947	2	−3
Greece	0.533	22	0.888	17	−5
Hungary	0.570	19	0.854	24	5
Ireland	0.841	2	0.955	1	−1
Italy	0.589	18	0.892	15	−3
Latvia	0.386	27	0.866	21	−6
Lithuania	0.547	20	0.882	19	−1
Luxembourg	0.838	3	0.926	8	5
Malta	0.837	4	0.895	14	10
Netherlands	0.774	6	0.944	4	−2
Poland	0.632	15	0.880	20	5
Portugal	0.606	17	0.864	22	5
Romania	0.413	26	0.828	26	0
Slovakia	0.485	24	0.860	23	−1
Slovenia	0.680	12	0.917	10	−2
Spain	0.715	7	0.904	11	4
Sweden	0.943	1	0.945	3	2
CV	22.05		4.17		

Note. CV is Pearson's coefficient of variation ($n = 27$).
HDI values are adapted from United Nations (2020a). Human development report 2020. The next frontier: Human development and the Anthropocene.

EU-HDI since their numbers of healthy life years at birth (56.4 and 58.9, respectively) are very low in comparison with the rest of the Member States. At the bottom, it is worth noting the best position that Portugal and Hungary occupy in the EU-HDI. The main strength of Portugal is that only 9% of its young people are unemployed or do not participate in an education or training programme. Hungary has in its favour a higher number of healthy life years at birth in comparison to the other countries placed at the bottom.

Another remarkable aspect is that inequalities, measured by Pearson's coefficient of variation, are much higher in the EU-HDI than in the United Nations' HDI. This finding is explained because inequality is typically higher across enhanced capabilities (see United Nations, 2019). In other words, it is easier to achieve convergence in basic capabilities, but when a minimum level of well-being or development is reached and improvement is sought, disparities increase.

Human development in the EU and European values

The EU-HDI provides a picture of where Member States are ranked in dealing with the negative socio-economic effects of the COVID-19 shock. The diagnosis or ranking of the Member States on the basis of the objective indicators synthesised in the EU-HDI shows the relative position of each Member State in the EU27 group. However, especially in times of crisis, it is worth remembering the European values of freedom, democracy, equality, and the rule of law that have inspired the EU since its constitution, and which should be respected by all Member States that want to enjoy the economic benefits of the EU. These values determine the future and prosperity of citizens as they directly affect social welfare and the evolution of the economy.

To this end, in the study, the assessment of citizens, experts, and enterprises regarding the degree of compliance with these values is incorporated. Specifically, the subjective or self-reported information on five indicators of quality of governance provided by the project the Worldwide Governance Indicators of the World Bank (www.govindicators.org) is considered. The five indicators of governance studied are defined as follows.

1 *Voice and Accountability* reflects the perceptions of the extent to which a country's citizens are able to participate in selecting their government, as well as freedom of expression, freedom of association, and a free media.
2 *Political Stability and Absence of Violence* measures the perceptions of the likelihood of political instability and/or politically motivated violence, including terrorism.
3 *Government Effectiveness* reflects the perceptions of the quality of public services, the quality of the civil service and the degree of its independence from political pressures, the quality of policy formulation and implementation, and the credibility of the government's commitment to such policies.
4 *Regulatory Quality* reflects the perceptions of the ability of the government to formulate and implement sound policies and regulations that permit and promote private-sector development.
5 *Rule of Law* reflects the perceptions of the extent to which agents have confidence in and abide by the rules of society, and in particular the quality of contract enforcement, property rights, the police, and the courts, as well as the likelihood of crime and violence.

All five indicators are measured on the same scale and are transformed in such a way that higher values indicate a better situation. Specifically, in our sample of 27 Member States, the indicators range from 0 (weak) to 2.5 (strong) governance performance. From these five indicators, a Governance Index has been constructed by calculating the arithmetic mean, thus assuming the possibility of compensating.

Figure 11.4 displays the results of comparing the values of the EU-HDI and the Governance Index in 2019. It has differentiated between the group of 11 emerging Member States and the rest. Overall, there is a positive relationship between both indices so that higher levels of human development are linked to a better perception of the quality of governance or compliance with the European values of freedom, democracy, rule of law, political stability, quality of public services, etc. The incorporation of the median lines of both indices allows establishing a classification of the Member States into four groups.

The countries located in the upper-right quadrant are in the best position in 2019 in both human development and governance to face the negative effects of the COVID-9 shock. In this group of ten countries, Czechia is the only country in the emerging group because it reaches just the median in the Governance Index. In human development, its strengths are the human capital of its young population and the low incidence of severe material and social deprivation. In addition to Czechia, the group is made up of five of the six founding countries of the EU (Belgium, France, Germany, Luxembourg, and the Netherlands), two Scandinavian countries (Sweden and Denmark), and Austria, all of them with a developed welfare state. Finally, the case of Ireland is the opposite of the case of Czechia. Ireland's greatest weaknesses are in the human capital of its young population and in the incidence of severe material and social deprivation. Despite

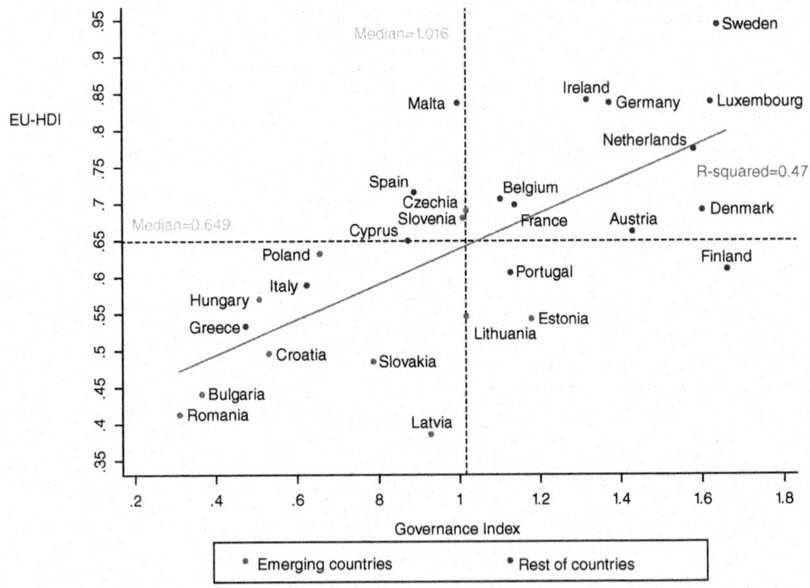

FIGURE 11.4 Association between the EU-HDI and the Governance Index in the EU of 27 Member States in 2019.

these weaknesses, Ireland scores high on the EU-HDI due to its income. Ireland is the EU country that has recorded the highest economic growth rates since 2014 with an average GDP growth rate of 9.2% in the 2014–2020 period. In fact, in 2020, all Member States registered negative growth except Ireland, which registered an increase of 5.9% compared to 2019. From a social welfare point of view, the key question is whether all groups or parts of Irish society benefit from the high levels of income generated.

On the contrary, nine countries make up the group with the lowest performance in both indices (lower-left quadrant). All of them are emerging countries except Italy and Greece. Italy registers the lowest value in the indicator young people who are unemployed or do not participate in an education or training programme and receives a very low rating in compliance with the rule of law and political stability. Greece, despite having been in the EU since 1981, registers very similar values to the rest of the emerging countries of this group in the indicators of human development (low GNI per capita, high rate of youth people unemployed and youth not involved in education or training programmes, and high levels of severe deprivation). Greece also shares with the emerging countries in this quadrant a very low assessment in all the indicators of governance.

Finally, with regard to the remaining two quadrants where a smaller number of Member States are located, all of them are very close to the Member States that have a better situation, although improvements in governance would be necessary in Spain and Cyprus. The exceptions are likely to be Lithuania and Estonia with a lower human development explained by their low income levels and low numbers of healthy life years at birth.

Conclusions

Since its constitution in 1957, the European values of freedom, democracy, equality, and the rule of law, in addition to the economic integration, are considered key drivers of improving peoples' prosperity and well-being in the EU. Over time, the EU has become increasingly integrated while facing major economic changes and shocks. From the analysis conducted in this chapter, three key findings emerge.

Firstly, the creation of the Economic and Monetary Union, with the implementation of the single monetary policy, has meant that countries lost part of their autonomy. Additionally, the pact to advance in the coordination of fiscal policy, signed by the 27 Member States, implies that the objectives established in terms of public finances have to be respected by all of them. At the same time, the incorporation of 11 new countries from Eastern Europe, with different economic and social principles, represented a major challenge for the EU.

Secondly, the Europe 2020 Strategy, which was intended to be a new boost to the social market economy, was largely counteracted by the context of the GFC of 2008. Precisely to try to get out of the public debt crisis, the EU opted for fiscal consolidation measures, approved in the Euro Plus Pact 2011, which managed to reduce public deficits but, arguably, at the cost of the prosperity and well-being of Europeans. This context of reduction in government spending was also noted in the foreign aid so that the EU28 Collective ODA, which represented 0.46% of GNI in 2010, was reduced until 0.43% in the following four years.

Finally, faced with the threat that the COVID-19 pandemic poses to economic and social welfare in terms of poverty and inequality, which would distance it from the SDGs, the EU's response has been very different from the response given to the GFC of 2008. On the budgetary front, there has been a strong push for expansionary policies with the Next Generation EU, which is an additional fund equivalent to the 66.6% of the total EU budget for the period 2021–2027 in order to foster the recovery after the pandemic. This approach to increasing budgetary effort has also been applied to development policy. The EU27 Collective ODA in 2020 has increased by Euro 8.8 billion compared to 2019, representing 0.50% of GNI. Complementary to the ODA, in 2021, the EU has approved a specific package of over Euro 40 billion to support partner countries' efforts in tackling the coronavirus pandemic. More importantly, EU is collectively committed to providing 0.7% of GNI as ODA within the time frame of the 2030 Agenda (European Commission, 2021a). In the sphere of values or institutions, the European Pillar of Social Rights Action Plan, approved in March 2021, aims at enhancing social rights and strengthening the European social dimension across all policies of the Union. Most importantly, the access to Next Generation funds will be conditional on compliance with the European Pillar of Social Rights.

On the basis of the results of the EU-HDI and the Governance Index, the position of the 27 Member States in 2019 in terms of prosperity, as well as to deal with the negative effects of the COVID-19, could be summarised as follows.

The three Scandinavian countries together with Luxembourg are the highest ranked in terms of quality of their institutions and European values, whereas the lowest ranked countries are Romania, Bulgaria, Greece, and Hungary. However, Denmark and Finland do not rank in the first position in human development because they are penalised in human development for their low values in healthy years of life.

Despite having been in the EU for more than 15 years, emerging countries and Greece register the lowest values, both in human development and in governance. Traditionally, these countries register GNI per capita below the EU27 average, but they have not known or have not wanted to take advantage of the opportunity of integrating and participating in the economic and social benefits that the EU represents.

Within the emerging countries, it is worth noting four cases that show a different behaviour to the group of emerging countries. Czechia and Slovenia are supported by the human capital of their young populations and with a very low incidence of severe deprivation, as well as compliance with the European values of freedom, democracy, equality, stability, and the rule of law, are very close to the group with more developed welfare states and, therefore, have a greater capacity to recover from shocks such as the COVID-19 pandemic. Estonia and Lithuania are highly valued for respecting and promoting European values that, in turn, determine the quality of their governance. However, in addition to low income, the low healthy life years at birth slow down their human development. That is, they have converged with the EU in terms of governance, but they still maintain the gap in human development.

Notes

1 Taking into account that the United Kingdom left the EU in 2020 after the Brexit process, this study analyses both a EU of 27 Member States (EU27) and a EU of 28 Member States (EU28) that includes the United Kingdom. In retrospective analyses and whenever the information is available, EU28 is chosen. For 2020, EUROSTAT does not provide information on poverty and income inequality for the United Kingdom.

2 Severely materially deprived people experience at least four out of nine of the following deprivation items: cannot afford (i) to pay rent or utility bills; (ii) keep home adequately warm; (iii) face unexpected expenses; (iv) eat meat, fish, or a protein equivalent every second day; (v) a week holiday away from home; (vi) a car; (vii) a washing machine; (viii) a colour TV; or (ix) a telephone.

3 The *severe material and social deprivation rate* is defined as the proportion of the population experiencing an enforced lack of at least 7 out of 13 deprivation items (1–6 related to the individual and 7–13 related to the household): (1) having internet connection, (2) replacing worn-out clothes by some new ones, (3) having two pairs of properly fitting shoes, (4) spending a small amount of money each week on him/herself, (5) having regular leisure activities, (6) getting together with friends/family for a drink/meal at least once a month, (7) capacity to face unexpected expenses, (8) capacity to afford paying for one-week annual holiday away from home, (9) capacity to being confronted with payment arrears, (10) capacity to afford a meal with meat, chicken, fish, or vegetarian equivalent every second day, (11) ability to keep home adequately, (12) have access to a car/van for personal use, and (13) replacing worn-out furniture.

References

Agnello, L. and Sousa, R. M. (2014). How does fiscal consolidation impact on income inequality? *Review of Income and Wealth, 60*(4), 702–726.

Anand, S. and Sen, A. (2000). The income component of the human development index. *Journal of Human Development and Capabilities, 1*(1), 83–106.

Bastagli, F., Coady, D., and Gupta, S. (2012). Income inequality and fiscal policy. *IMF Staff Discussion Note, SDN/12/08.*

Berg, A., Ostry, J. D., and Zettelmeyer, J. (2012). What makes growth sustained? *Journal of Development Economics, 98*(2), 149–166.

Bradshaw, J., and Movshuk, O. (2019). Measures of extreme poverty applied in the European Union. In H. P. Gaisbauer, G. Schweiger, and C. Sedmak (Eds.), *Absolute poverty in Europe: Interdisciplinary perspectives on a hidden phenomenon* (1st ed., pp. 39–72). Bristol University Press. https://doi.org/10.2307/j.ctvf3w3zg.7

Cingano, F. (2014). Trends in income inequality and its impact on economic growth. *OECD Social, Employment and Migration Working Papers, 163.* OECD Publishing. https://doi.org/10.1787/5jxrjncwxv6j-en

Coady, D., D'Angelo, D., and Evans, B. (2021). Fiscal redistribution, social welfare and income inequality: 'doing more' or 'more to do'? *Applied Economics*. https://doi.org/10.1080/00036846.2021.1990840

Dabla-Norris, E., Kochhar, K., Suphaphiphat, N., Ricka, F., and Tsounta, E. (2015). Causes and consequences of income inequality: A global perspective. *IMF Staff Discussion Note, 15/13*. International Monetary Fund. https://www.imf.org/external/pubs/ft/sdn/2015/sdn1513.pdf

de Vet, J.M. *et al.* (2021). *Impacts of the COVID-19 pandemic on EU industries*. Publication for the Committee on Industry, Research and Energy, Policy Department for Economic, Scientific and Quality of Life Policies, European Parliament. https://www.europarl.europa.eu/RegData/etudes/STUD/2021/662903/IPOL_STU(2021)662903_EN.pdf

Esping-Andersen, G. (2016). *Families in the 21st century*. Stockholm: SNS Förlag. https://www.sns.se/en/articles/families-in-the-21st-century/

Esping-Andersen, G., and Cimentada, J. (2018). Ability and mobility: The relative influence of skills and social origin on social mobility. *Social Science Research, 75*, 13–31. https://doi.org/10.1016/j.ssresearch.2018.06.003

European Commission. (2010). *EUROPE 2020 a Strategy for Smart, Sustainable and Inclusive Growth*. COM(2010) 2020.

European Commission. (2012). *Excessive Deficit Procedure (EDP): Five Member States Assessed*. MEMO/12/7. https://ec.europa.eu/commission/presscorner/detail/en/MEMO_12_7

European Commission. (2020). *2020 Strategic Foresight Report. Charting the Course towards a More Resilient Europe*. COM(2020) 493 final.

European Commission. (2021a). *Questions and Answers: Preliminary Figures on 2020 Official Development Assistance*. QANDA/21/1704. https://ec.europa.eu/commission/presscorner/detail/ro/qanda_21_1704

European Commission. (2021b). *The EU's 2021–2027 Long-Term Budget and NextGeneration EU. Facts and Figures*. Publications Office of the European Union. https://op.europa.eu/en/publication-detail/-/publication/d3e77637-a963-11eb-9585-01aa75ed71a1/language-en

European Commission. (2021c). *The European Pillar of Social Rights Action Plan*. Publication Office of the European Union. https://op.europa.eu/webpub/empl/european-pillar-of-social-rights/en/

European Council 24/25. (March 2011). *Annex I: The Euro Plus Pact*. Stronger Economic Policy Coordination for Competitiveness and Convergence. https://www.consilium.europa.eu/uedocs/cms_data/docs/pressdata/en/ec/120296.pdf

Fasani, F., and Mazza, J.A. (2020). *Vulnerable Workforce: Migrant Workers in the COVID-19 Pandemic*. Join Research Center, Publications Office of the European Union. https://doi.org/10.2760/914810, JRC120730

Fetting, C. (2020). *Impacts of the COVID-19 Pandemic on Sustainable Development and the SDGs in Europe*. ESDN Report, July 2020.

Furceri, D., Loungani, P., Ostry, J., and Pizzuto, P. (2021). The Rise in Inequality after Pandemics: Can Fiscal Support Play a Mitigating Role? *IMF Working paper, WP/21/120*.

Lewer, D., Jayatunga, W., Aldridge, R. W., Edge, C., Marmot, M., Story, A., and Hayward, A. (2020). Premature mortality attributable to socioeconomic inequality in England between 2003 and 2018: An observational study. *The Lancet Public Health, 5*(1), e33–e41. https://doi.org/10.1016/S2468-2667(19)30219-1

Muñoz-Gálvez, E. (2012). European Development Aid: How to be more effective without spending more? *Notre Europe-Policy paper, 57.* Institut Jacques Delors. https://institutdelors.eu/wp-content/uploads/2018/01/developmentaid_e.munozgalvez_ne_july12.pdf

OECD. (2015). Inequality and fiscal redistribution in emerging economies. In OECD (Ed.), *In It Together: Why Less Inequality Benefits All* (pp. 291–332). Paris, OECD Publishing.

Piketty, T., and Sáez, E. (2013). Top Incomes and the Great Recession: Recent Evolutions and Policy Implications. *IMF Economic Review, 61*, 456–78.

Reinhart, C. M., and Rogoff, K. S. (2009). *This time is different. Eight Centuries of Financial Folly.* Princeton, NJ: Princeton University Press.

Richardson, D., Carraro, A., Cebotari, V., Gromada, A., and Rees, G. (2020). *Supporting Families and Children Beyond COVID-19: Social Protection in High-Income Countries.* Florencia (Italia): UNICEF Office of Research – Innocenti.

Roaf, J., Atoyamn, R., Joshi, B., and Krogulski, K. (2014). *25 Years of Transition: Post-Communist Europe and the IMF*, Regional Economic Issues Special Report, Washington D.C., International Monetary Fund.

Sánchez, A., and Navarro, M. (2021). Public policies of welfare state and child poverty in the European Union. *Sustainability, 13*(5), 2725. https://doi.org/10.3390/su13052725

Sánchez, A., and Pérez-Corral, A.L. (2018). Government social expenditure and income inequalities in the European Union. *Hacienda Pública Española/Review of Public Economic, 27*(4), 133–156. https://www.ief.es/docs/destacados/publicaciones/revistas/hpe/227_Art5.pdf

Sánchez, A., and Ruiz-Martos, M. (2018). Europe 2020 Strategy and citizens' life satisfaction. *Journal of Happiness Studies, 19*, 2315–2338. https://doi.org/10.1007/s10902-017-9928-0

Stiglitz, J. (2020). *Rewriting the Rules of the European Economy: An Agenda for Growth and Shared Prosperity.* New York, WW Norton and Company, Inc.

United Nations. (2019). *Human Development Report 2020. Beyond Income, Beyond Averages, Beyond Today: Inequalities in Human Development in the 21st Century.* http://hdr.undp.org/en/content/human-development-report-2019

United Nations. (2020a). *Human Development Report 2020. The Next Frontier: Human Development and the Anthropocene.* http://hdr.undp.org/en/content/human-development-report-2020

United Nations. (2020b). *Shared Responsibility, Global Solidarity: Responding to the Socio-Economic Impacts of COVID-19.* https://unsdg.un.org/sites/default/files/2020-03/SG-Report-Socio-Economic-Impact-of-Covid19.pdf

Wilkinson, R., and Pickett, K. (2009). *The Spirit Level. Why More Equal Societies Almost Always Do Better.* London: Allen Lane.

12

COVID-19 IMPACTS ON PACIFIC ISLAND COUNTRIES

Making an already bad situation worse

Mark McGillivray

Introduction

Pacific Island Countries (PICs) have in recent decades been vulnerable to changes in international commodity prices, natural environment events such as cyclone and floods, political instability and spread of infectious diseases, causing low and highly volatile economic growth rates. This is despite PICs being among the world's largest recipients of foreign development aid relative to population and size of economies. COVID-19 adds to and endogenously interacts with this vulnerability.

This chapter analyses the various impacts of COVID-19 on PICs. Its focus is not on all PICs but on the Pacific small island states group, which consists of Fiji, Kiribati, Marshall Islands, The Federated States of Micronesia, Nauru, Palau, Samoa, Solomon Islands, Tonga, Tuvalu and Vanuatu.[1] The chapter develops an impacts analytical framework for COVID-19. This framework is important given its predictive orientation, given that the pandemic's impacts are yet to be fully observed, with the overall COVID-19 situation still highly fluid. This framework is relevant to all countries, but in particular the Pacific small island states group. It distinguishes between direct health impacts and those arising from endogenous behavioural responses owing to public and private aversion behaviour due to the fear of infection. The second category of impacts includes those on income poverty and other development achievement indicators.

The chapter commences by outlining the above-mentioned analytical framework. It then examines the vulnerability of Pacific small island states to external exogenous shocks. This is followed by looking at available, albeit limited, evidence of the impacts of COVID-19 on these states. The chapter argues that almost all these impacts have been transmitted through, and have exacerbated by,

DOI: 10.4324/9781003273844-12

existing and well-known vulnerabilities to exogenous shocks. The chapter then briefly examines the response overseas development aid response of Australia to COVID-19 in the Pacific small island states group in this context, arguing that this approach needs not just to build health systems capability but also to address the broader vulnerabilities through which exogenous shocks such as COVID-19 are endogenously transmitted.

Analytical framework

COVID-19 is a classic exogenous shock. The standard definition of such a shock is a sudden event beyond the control of the authorities that has a significant negative impact on the economy and society. This does not imply that the impact of the shock cannot be mitigated by governments and other agents; just the onset of the shock cannot readily be prevented. The COVID-19 situation is highly fluid, and its full impacts are yet to be observed. All that can be done at this stage is to observe and respond to the unfolding crisis with the evidence and resources at hand. Figure 12.1 helps in this regard. It identifies categories of anticipated impacts of COVID-19 and the channels through which they are expected to emerge. The context is generic, applying both within and among countries. It has been adapted from a number of other exogenous shock impact analyses, with modification and augmentation.[2]

As Figure 12.1 suggests, the predicted impacts of COVID-19 obviously commence with its direct and indirect impacts on sickness and death. COVID-19 will place pressure on health care resources, with resources being allocated to people with the virus and away from other sick people, which can further contribute to the number of sick and dead people, particularly in developing countries with weak health systems. There will also be associated mental health impacts owing to the stress the virus causes, including among those who do not have it. These impacts can be observed over both the short and long run, even if the number of infections and deaths owing to COVID-19 does not escalate. The longer-run, lingering effects include a reduction in human capital, defined as the physical abilities, knowledge and social and personality attributes that produce economic and other values.

These health impacts have a number of flow-on effects that can lead to further adverse impacts. These include the endogenous public- and private-sector behavioural impacts resulting from the fear of contagion. This behaviour can include the closing or restricting of places of employment, governments closing land borders and restricting entry of citizens from other countries and restricting entry of returning citizens from abroad. This also motivates private decision makers to disrupt trade, travel and commerce by cancelling commercial flights and reducing cargo and shipping services. The central point about the behavioural impacts is that the initiating exogenous shock (be it COVID-19 or others) can have profoundly adverse impacts even if there is no contagion. All that is required is a fear of contagion leading to aversion behaviour. And, of

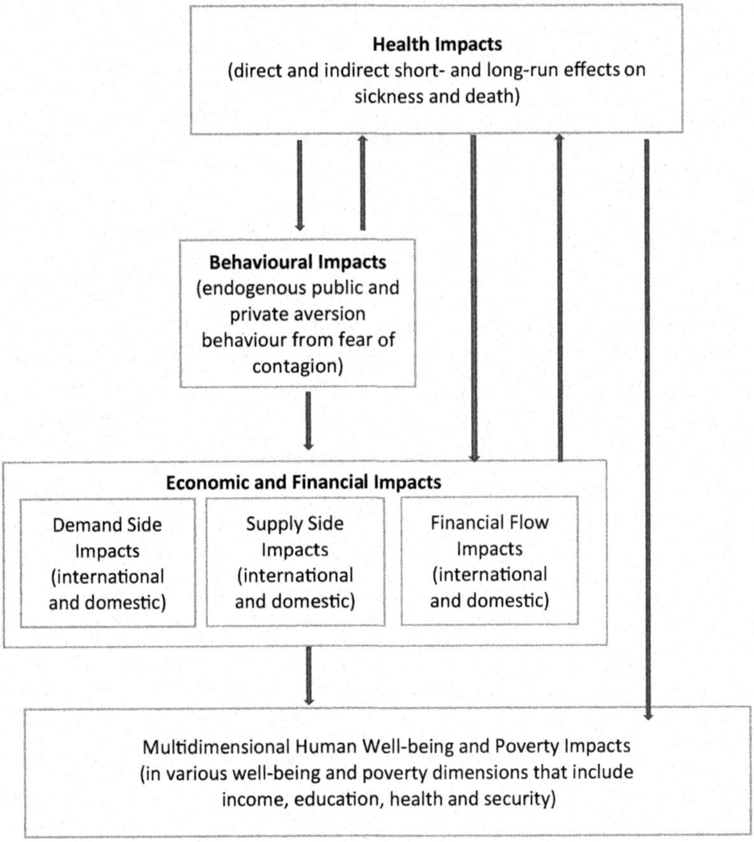

FIGURE 12.1 COVID-19 anatomy of predicted impacts.

course, this behaviour will limit further spread of the infection in question, as the upward-pointing arrow in Figure 12.1 indicates.

These behavioural impacts, which are essentially on decision making, then lead to a range of economic and financial impacts, such as the restricted labour mobility, tourism, export and import of goods and services and flows of capital (including remittances). Research on the behavioural impacts of infectious disease outbreaks such as the severe acute respiratory syndrome epidemic of the early 2000s, and the swine flu epidemic of 2009, suggests that flow-ons from these impacts (on economic and financial variables) contribute up to 90% of the total economic impact of these types of outbreaks (Lee and McKibben, 2003). It will be argued below that endogenous aversion behaviour due to the fear of COVID-19 contagion has had major impacts on the Pacific small island states.

The adverse consequences do not stop with the impacts on economic and financial variables, due to both the aversion behaviour and the direct impacts of increased sickness and death. They include negative impacts on multidimensional well-being and poverty, transmitted through both the economic and financial variables directly from the increased sickness and death (noting that health is a well-being and poverty dimension). The impacts on poverty (and social inclusivity more generally) will be particularly pronounced in poorer nations, with relatively large shares of people living just above income poverty lines and with relatively low levels of multidimensional well-being. These people are particularly vulnerable to the flow-on effects of exogenous shocks. This, in turn, means that the broader impacts of exogenous shocks will fall primarily on the poor and near poor.

Pacific small island states' vulnerability

The vulnerability of small island states to exogenous shocks is well recognised in research and policy circles (see, for example, McGillivray *et al.*, 2010; Scandurra *et al.*, 2018). There have been many attempts to construct composite indices that highlight the vulnerability of these states (see, for example, Briguglio, 1995; Briguglio *et al.*, 2009; Center for Environment and Development, 2002; Guillaumont, 2008, 2009; Turvey, 2007; United Nations Committee for Development Policy (UNCDP), 2008). Asso and Meddeb (2021) extend and update this research with arguably a more comprehensive multidimensional vulnerability index (MVI). The MVI augments the Economic Vulnerability Index (UNCDP, 2008), with measures of financial vulnerability.[3]

The MVI was calculated for 126 mainly low- and middle-income countries using the latest available data available in late 2020. The results for Pacific small island states are extremely revealing, emphasising just how vulnerable they are to exogenous shocks. MVI scores for these and selected other countries are shown in Figure 12.2 and Table 12.1. The other countries that are selected are the three nations with the lowest MVI scores calculated by Asso and Meddeb (2021). Using MVI scores, Asso and Meddeb (2021) divide countries into four groups: very high vulnerability (those with MVI scores above 43), high vulnerability (with an MVI score in the range of 32 to less than 43), medium vulnerability (MVI score in the range of 21 to less than 32) and low vulnerability (score of less than 20).

MVI scores for the Pacific small island states group range from 52.7 to 31.4, for Kiribati and Nauru, respectively. Strikingly, each of the countries, Kiribati, Marshall Islands, Palau, Tonga, Tuvalu and the Federated States of Micronesia, is ranked among the top ten most vulnerable countries of those assessed by Asso and Meddeb (2021). Each of the other Pacific small island states falls into the high vulnerability group, with the exception of Nauru. Nauru has the lowest MVI score of these countries and is classified as medium multidimensional vulnerability. What has driven the high and very high vulnerability assessments of the Pacific small island states countries is a reliance on tourism and/or remittances, together with remoteness and proportion of people living in lowly elevated coastal areas (Asso and Meddeb, 2021).

A consequence of the vulnerability of the Pacific small island states group is very low economic performance. As shown in Table 12.2, this group has lower per

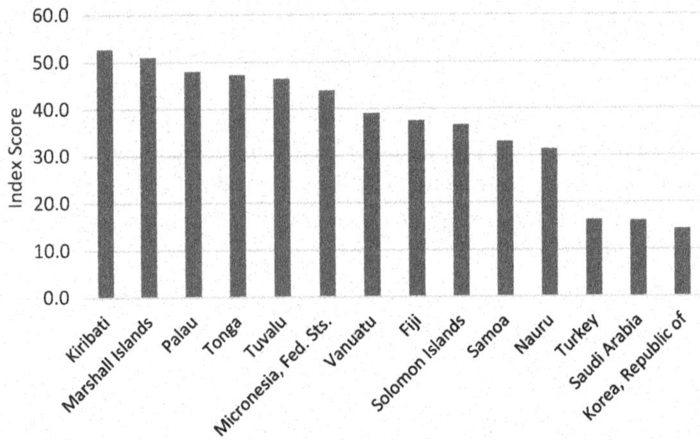

FIGURE 12.2 Multidimensional vulnerability of Pacific small island states and selected other countries.

TABLE 12.1 Multidimensional vulnerability of Pacific small island states and selected other countries, 2021

	MVI score	*MVI rank*	*Vulnerability classification*
Kiribati	52.7	1	Very high
Marshall Islands	51.0	2	Very high
Palau	48.0	4	Very high
Tonga	47.3	5	Very high
Tuvalu	46.5	6	Very high
Micronesia, Federated States of	43.9	8	Very high
Vanuatu	39.1	13	High
Fiji	37.5	26	High
Solomon Islands	36.6	33	High
Samoa	33.0	49	High
Nauru	31.4	55	Medium
Turkey	16.3	124	Low
Saudi Arabia	16.1	125	Low
Korea, Republic of	14.3	126	Low

Source of data: Asso and Meddeb (2021).

capita gross domestic product (GDP) growth rates than all other geographic regions of predominantly developing (low- and middle-income) countries. Adding the other sovereign countries of the PICs group (Papua New Guinea, Niue and Cook Islands) does not change this conclusion. These statistics are interesting in their own right, but adding to this interest is that the Pacific small island states group is by a large margin the most heavily aided, relative to GDP, in the developing country world. We note this in passing but will return to aid later in this chapter.

TABLE 12.2 Pacific small island states and selected other country group growth rates and aid receipts, 1980–2020

	GDP per capita growth		
	Growth rate (%) 1980–2020	*Growth rate variation*[a] *1980–2020*	*Aid to GDP ratio*[b] *(%) 1980–2020*
Pacific Island Small States	1.84	1.83	10.43
South Asia	5.54	0.46	1.01
Sub-Saharan Africa	2.91	0.82	3.83
Middle East and North Africa	2.80	1.13	1.00
Latin America and Caribbean	2.17	1.16	0.27

[a] Growth rate variation is measured by the coefficient of variation of annual growth rates over the period in question.

[b] The measure of aid shown is net disbursements of official development assistance (see World Bank, 2021, for further details).

Sources of data: World Bank (2021) for growth and aid and author calculations for growth variation.

COVID-19 infection: direct impacts on health

Limited data availability with respect to a wide range of statistics is a well-known problem in PICs. Some COVID-19 data are published, however, including those relating to reported cases and on the extent of vaccination. The most recent data at the time of writing this chapter are shown in Table 12.3. Also shown in this table are data for other regions of predominantly non-high-income countries (that is, low- and mainly middle-income countries) and for the world as a whole. The data shown on total cases are cumulative, in that included are the number of people currently with and who have previously had COVID-19. These data allow us some insight into the direct impacts of COVID-19, identified in the first box in Figure 12.1.

Arguably, the key message of Table 12.3 is that the story of COVID-19 infection in the Pacific small island states group, and the deaths arising from this, is primarily one about Fiji. What is meant by this statement is that 99.9% of cases and all resulting deaths except one in this group have been in Fiji. All other countries in this group have had less than 10 cases, with the exception of Solomon Islands, which has had 20 cases. The only other death in this group has been recorded in Vanuatu. This of course may well change in the future. The incidence of cases measured the number of cases relative to population size. The incidence of cases defined in this way in Fiji is 5.74%, which in October 2021 was higher than that for the world as a whole and for Africa and Asia. The incidence in Africa will clearly increase much further as time progresses, which should be noted. One might think that with the exception of Fiji, any adverse impacts

TABLE 12.3 Reported COVID-19 cases and vaccinations as of October 19, 2021

	Reported cases			*Reported deaths due to COVID-19*			
	Number	*% of population*	*Vaccinated people (% of population)*	*Number*	*% of population*	*Vaccinated people (% of population)*	*Fully vaccinated people (% of population)*
Fiji	51,846	5.74	69	663	0.073	69	57
Kiribati	2	0.00	35	0	0	35	7
Marshall Islands	4	0.01	*	0	0	*	*
Micronesia, Federated States of	1	0.00	*	0	0	*	*
Nauru	0	0.00	70	0	0	70	67
Palau	8	0.04	42	0	0	42	40
Samoa	3	0.00	58	0	0	58	37
Solomon Islands	20	0.00	16	0	0	16	4
Tonga	0	0.00	47	0	0	47	28
Tuvalu	0	0.00	52	0	0	52	39
Vanuatu	4	0.00	19	1	0.000	19	9
Pacific Small Island States	51,888	2.02	43	664	0.026	43	29
Africa	8,444,411	0.61	8	215,909	0.358	8	5
Asia	78,141,449	1.67	55	1,156,573	0.025	55	40
South America	38,137,617	8.78	65	1,164,829	0.266	65	47
World	241,573,517	3.07	48	4,913,600	0.003	48	36

*Data not reported.

Source of data: Richie *et al*. (2021).

on Pacific small island states will be nil or extremely negligible given the tiny or non-existent COVID-19 cases in the remainder of these countries. This of course is a naive expectation, focusing on direct impacts and ignoring a central message of Figure 12.1, which is that there can be significant adverse impacts of endogenous aversion behaviour. This point is taken up in what follows.

Also clearly evident from Table 12.3 are the low rates of vaccination of people in Kiribati, Solomon Islands and Vanuatu. No more than 9% of the populations of these countries are fully vaccinated in these three countries. While not as low as the double vaccination rate for Africa (which is a particularly disturbing 5%), the rates in these three countries are well below the rate for the world as a whole (which is 36%). The double vaccination rate for the Pacific small island states group is 28%, which lags behind that for Asia, South America and the world as a whole.

COVID-19 flow-on impacts

Direct impacts on health of the pandemic in the Pacific small island states are at least in part identified above. Let us now consider the second and subsequent round of impacts predicted by the analytical framework outlined in Figure 12.1 that can be observed from current data.

Endogenous behavioural responses quickly emerged from the onset of the pandemic in early 2020. As Edwards (2020) notes, PICs reacted very quickly to the pandemic by closing international borders. Edwards further notes that this is primarily why the direct health impacts of the pandemic have been low or non-existent but that the economic impacts of these policy responses have been severe. We return to the second of these points below. Vanuatu in March 2020 commenced turning away international tourist cruise ships in fear of COVID-19 infection. Fiji, Cook Islands, Samoa and Tonga quickly followed by placing bans on selected international air arrivals. The Vanuatu prime minister has announced that, in response to concerns over the spread of COVID-19, there will be a temporary restriction on all seasonal work schemes in which Vanuatu workers participate in New Zealand and Australia (The Spinoff, 2020). Australia and New Zealand subsequently temporarily suspended its labour mobility schemes, in which PICs are principal suppliers of workers. A particular consequence of the restriction on international arrivals in the Pacific small island states is that labourers on Chinese construction sites around the Pacific have also been unable to return to work, slowing the pace of Chinese-led construction, which has become a major feature of infrastructure construction throughout the PICs (Dayant and Pryke, 2020).

The flow-on implications, observed and potential, of these endogenous aversion behavioural responses are enormous, as Figure 12.2 suggests. Consideration of these impacts takes us back to the vulnerability of Pacific small island states discussed above, to reliance on tourist revenue, remittance inflows and foreign direct investment (FDI). Pacific small island states' data on these inflows, together with data on official development assistance (aid) inflows, are shown in Figure 12.3. The data on remittances cover the period up to 2020, which is the latest year for which data are available. The latest year for which data are available on the other inflows shown in Figure 12.3 are for 2019, which obviously predate the COVID-19 pandemic.

What Figure 12.3 emphasises is the enormous reliance of Pacific small island states on external revenues.[4] Since 2008, tourism revenue has been at least 20% of GDP. Remittances have been approximately 6.2% and 7.9% of GDP since 2001. Aid inflows were just under 10% of GDP in 2019, having trended downwards from 17% in 1994 to 13.65% in 2011. Intuition tells us that given the enormous levels of these inflows relative to GDP, any reduction in these inflows will have significant adverse impacts on the Pacific small island states, tourism in particular. This is consistent with research on aid, remittances and FDI impacts on economic growth on PICs, which concludes that growth would be lower in these countries in the absence of their inflows, especially remittances (see, for example, Feeny and McGillivray, 2010; Feeny *et al.*, 2013, 2014; Hansen and Headey, 2010).[5] While the impacts of COVID-19 on FDI and aid and remittances remain an open question, its impacts on tourism and remittances will almost certainly be significantly negative given the above restrictions on international travel.[6] Given that tourism revenue flows for the Pacific small island states group as a whole have been more than 20% of GDP in each year since 2008, and are as high as 43% and 35% in Vanuatu and Palau, any decline in these flows will almost certainly have a major advanced impact on this group of countries.

What are the flow-on impacts of the COVID-19 exogenous shock on multidimensional well-being and poverty? It is very difficult to answer this question given the paucity of data on these conditions in the PICs and that we are still in the midst of the pandemic and cannot therefore realistically observe its full impacts. Moreover, we do not have rigorous evidence of impact and its extent; just likely associations rather than causal linkages between COVID-19 and the variables of interest.

An indicator of the economic or income dimension of well-being is GDP per capita. Annual growth data on this indicator (measured in constant prices) for the years from 1980 to 2020 are shown in Figure 12.4, for the Pacific small island states group and for developing countries as a whole. GDP per capita growth rate data for the individual Pacific small island states show a sobering, concerning picture. GDP per capita growth was low in these countries in 2019, being 0.78%. It plummeted to –13.03% in the first COVID-19 pandemic year of 2020. GDP per capita growth also fell, but by a much smaller margin, to –1.89%. Growth rates for individual Pacific small island states were as low as –-19.36% and –-11.38% in Fiji and Vanuatu, respectively. That the decline in the Pacific small island states is much larger is consistent with its very high vulnerability to exogenous shocks, with the impact of COVID-19 both adding to and interacting with (being transmitted via) this vulnerability.

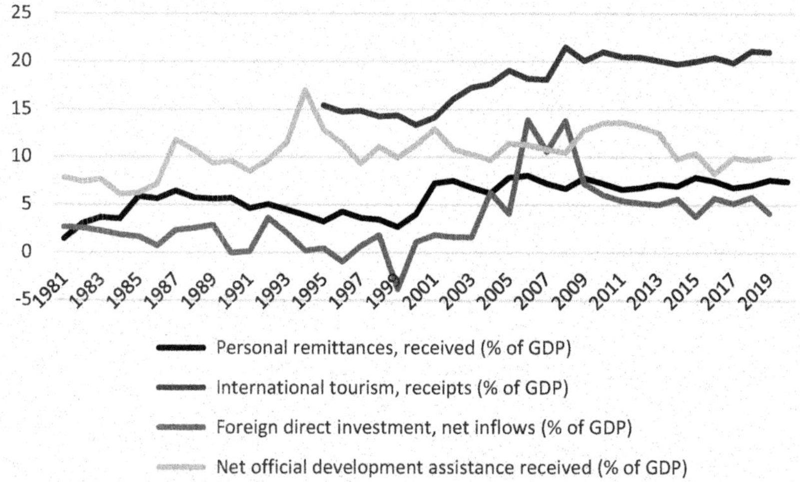

FIGURE 12.3 External inflows of Pacific small island states, 1980–2020.

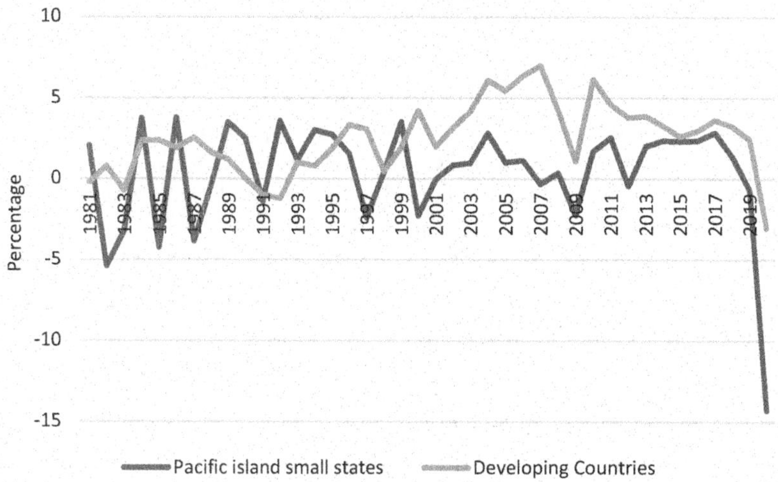

FIGURE 12.4 Annual GDP per capita growth rates, 1980–2020.

As speculated above, the poor and near poor will be particularly vulnerable to COVID-19. Among other factors, they cannot as easily self-isolate as other groups and have lower pre-existing levels of health and less access to health services. The most comprehensive source of reasonably reliable poverty data is the World Bank's Poverty and Equity Database, which is included in World Bank (2021). It does not report poverty data for the Pacific small island states group as a whole owing to the lack of information. Income poverty data are available in World Bank (2021) for some countries but only up to 2013. The exception to this is Fiji, for which income poverty data for the year 2019 are reported. The percentage of the Fijian population living below the national income poverty line in 2019 was 29.9%. This will almost certainly increase substantially given the Fijian data presented above, particularly that on the direct impacts of COVID-19. What will almost certainly happen is that COVID-19 will increase the depth of poverty (how far below the poverty line) of the poor in Fiji owing to the direct impacts of the pandemic.

Official development assistance

Pacific small island states are among the world's largest recipient of official development assistance. As shown above, as a group these countries received more than 10% of its combined GDP in such assistance, and it only surpassed by tourism revenue as its principal source of foreign revenue. Official development assistance, or aid as it is more popularly known, has a dubious reputation in PICs. There is much controversy surrounding it. There are some who argue that it has failed the Pacific. This argument in essence is that despite very large levels of aid relative to GDP, economic growth in the Pacific is among the lowest and most variable and lowest of country groups in the world. A more sophisticated and less reactionary critique asks what economic growth rates among PICs would have been in the absence of aid. As was noted earlier, there is empirical evidence that growth rates would have been marginally lower in its absence.

Australia provides more development aid to the PICs, including the small island states group that has been the focus of this chapter, than any other donor nation. Owing to this and the level of aid to Pacific small island states, Australia's response to COVID-19 to them is especially important.

The Australian Department of Foreign Affairs and Trade (DFAT) launched a new development policy *Partnerships for Recovery: Australia's COVID-19 Development Response* in May 2020 (DFAT, 2020). It incorporates a regional COVID-19 response with a focus on Asia and the Pacific. Health security, the maintenance of social stability (with respect to education, governance and decreasing violence against women) and stimulating economic recovery are the three pillars of the next policy. The overall focus of the health security pillar is on improving health systems through funding regional programmes. It is self-evidently appropriate that health systems be supported in a COVID-19 context as it has long been recognised that they struggle in most if not all Pacific small island states. This will help deal with the direct impacts of COVID-19, as defined in this chapter. But we must keep in mind that these impacts have, to date, been zero or negligible in all these states except Fiji. But the indirect impacts stemming from endogenous pandemic aversion behaviour, which have been transmitted though pre-existing and very well-known vulnerabilities, have and will be immense. A more enlightened and developmentally effective response is to also address the broader vulnerabilities through which exogenous shocks such as COVID-19 are endogenously transmitted, increasing general resilience to exogenous shocks in Pacific small island states.

Conclusion

This chapter looked at actual and potential impacts of COVID-19 on Pacific small island states. For the purposes of this chapter, this group is delineated as Fiji, Kiribati, Marshall Islands, The Federated States of Micronesia, Nauru, Palau, Samoa, Solomon Islands, Tonga, Tuvalu and Vanuatu. This group is the most multidimensionally vulnerable to exogenous shocks like COVID-19 in the world. Low and highly volatile per capita economic growth rates, among the lowest and most volatile in the world, and difficulties in promoting and sustaining achievements in well-being are consequences of this vulnerability. These countries are among the world's largest recipients of foreign development aid relative to GDP. The chapter presented evidence and conceptual reasoning that COVID-19 adds to and interacts with this vulnerability. In short, the chapter made the case that COVID-19 makes an already bad situation worse.

Official development assistance (aid as it is more commonly known) is a vital external flow to Pacific small island states. Aid to PICs is a controversial topic. While there is some evidence that economic growth would be lower in these countries in the absence of aid, critics of it are correct to note that aid should have had a much larger impact on them given the amounts of aid they have been allocated over time. Australia, the largest donor of official development assistance to the Pacific, has responded to the COVID-19 pandemic with an increased focus on health security in the region. This is appropriate, as it will reduce the direct impacts of the pandemic on Pacific small island states and could well improve their capacity to respond to it should infection rates increase. Yet, as this chapter has argued, what is fundamentally needed from donors are broader attempts to reduce the very high extents of vulnerability to exogenous shocks of these states: reducing the various dimensions of this vulnerability will limit the propensity through which exogenous shocks such as COVID-19 are endogenously transmitted.

Notes

1 This group is recognised and used for analytical and policymaking purposes, by such groups as the World Bank (see World Bank, 2021). PICs not included in the group include PNG, owing to its relatively large size but PIC standards; Niue and Cook Islands, as a constitutional birth right of its citizens is New Zealand citizenship; New Caledonia, Wallis and Futuna and French Polynesia, which are French external territories; and Guam and the Northern Mariana Islands, which are external territories of the United States; and, Tokelau, which is an external territory of New Zealand.

2 See, in particular, World Bank (2014), *The Economic Impact of the 2014 Ebola Epidemic: Short- and Medium-Term Estimates for West Africa*, World Bank, Washington DC, 2014. Figure 12.1 is adapted from an earlier version presented in Carpenter and McGillivray (2020).

3 Despite being labelled an economic vulnerability index (EVI), the EVI also includes measures of what are interpreted as financial, geographic and environmental vulnerabilities. These measures are export concentration, share of agriculture in GDP, instability of agricultural production, instability of exports of goods and services,

share of total population living in drylands, share of total population living in lowly elevated coastal zones, remoteness and number of victims of disasters. The financial instability measures added to the EVI to form the MVI are tourism revenues as share of exports, remittances as percentage of GDP and FDI as a percentage of GDP (Asso and Meddeb, 2021).

4 On remittances, Feeny *et al.* (2013) find that economic growth during the years from 1971 to 2010 in PICs would have been negative in the absence of remittance inflows.

5 A major component of remittances sent to PICs comes from their workers in Australia and New Zealand who participate in seasonal work programs in these countries. These workers send money back to their home countries while in Australia and New Zealand and also bring money back on completion of their work programs.

References

Asso, J. and R. Meddeb (2021), *Towards a Multidimensional Vulnerability Index*, Discussion Paper, United Nations Development Programme Human Development Report Office, New York.

Briguglio, L. (1995), "Small Island Developing States and their Economic Vulnerabilities", *World Development* 23: 1615–1632.

Briguglio, L., G. Cordina, N. Farrugia and S. Vella (2009), "Economic Vulnerability and Resilience: Concepts and Measurements", *Oxford Development Studies* 37: 229–247.

Center for Environment and Development (2002), "Vulnerability and Small Island States", *UNDP Policy Journal* 1: 49–81.

Dayant, A. and J. Pryke (2020), "Anticipating Covid-19 in the Pacific", Lowey Institute, Sydney, March 16.

DFAT (2020), *Partnerships for Recovery: Australia's COVID-19 Development Response*, Department of Foreign Affairs and Trade (DFAT), Canberra.

Edwards, R. (2020), "Bubble In, Bubble Out: Lessons for the COVID-19 Recovery and Future Crises from the Pacific", World Development 135: 105072.

Feeny, S. and M. McGillivray (2010), "Aid and Growth in Small Island Developing States", *Journal of Development Studies* 46(5): 828–854.

Feeny, S., M. McGillivray and S. Iamsiraroj (2013), "Remittances and Economic Growth: Larger Impacts in Smaller Countries?", *Journal of Development Studies* 50(8): 1055–1066.

Feeny, S., S. Iamsiraroj and M. McGillivray (2014), "Growth and Foreign Direct Investment in the Pacific Island Countries", *Economic Modelling* 37(C): 332–339.

Guillaumont, P. (2009), "An Economic Vulnerability Index: Its design and Use for International Development Policy", *Oxford Development Studies* 37:193–228.

Guillaumont, P. (2010), "Assessing the Economic Vulnerability of Small Island Developing States", *Journal of Development Studies* 46(5): 828–854.

Hansen, H. and D. Headey (2010), "The Short-run Macroeconomic Impact of Foreign Aid to Small States: An Agnostic Time Series Analysis", *Journal of Development Studies* 46(5): 877–896.

Lee, J.-W. and W.J. McKibben (2003), *Globalization and Disease: The Case of SARS*, Working Paper 2003/16, Australian National University, Canberra, 2003.

McGillivray, M., W. Naudé and. A.U. Santos-Paulino (2010), "Vulnerability, Financial Flows and State Failure in Small Island Developing States", *Journal of Development Studies* 46(5): 815–827.

Ritchie, H., E. Mathieu, L. Rodés-Guirao, C. Appel, C. Giattino, E. Ortiz-Ospina, J. Hasell, B. Macdonald, D. Beltekian and M. Roser (2021), *Coronavirus Pandemic*

(COVID-19), Our World In Data, Oxford. Retrieved from https://ourworldindata.org/coronavirus on October 29, 2021

Scandurra, G., A.A. Romano, M. Ronghi and A. Carfora (2018), "On the Vulnerability of Small Island Developing States: A Dynamic Analysis", *Ecological Indicators* 84: 382–392.

The Spinoff (2020), "Covid-19 and the Pacific: How the Islands Nations Hope to Fend off the Pandemic", Auckland, March 19.

Turvey, R. (2007), "Vulnerability Assessment of Developing Countries: The case of Small-Island Developing States", *Development Policy Review* 25: 243–264.

UNCTAD (2020), *Investment Trends Monitor. Impact of the COVID-19 Pandemic on Global FDI and GVCs. Updated Analysis March 2020.* UNCTAD, Geneva.

United Nations Committee for Development Policy (2008), *Handbook on the Least Developed Country Category: Inclusion, Graduation and Special Support Measures*, United Nations Committee for Development Policy and Department of Economic and Social Affairs, New York.

World Bank (2014), *The Economic Impact of the 2014 Ebola Epidemic: Short- and Medium-Term Estimates for West Africa*, World Bank, Washington DC.

World Bank (2021), *World Development Indicators*, World Bank, Washington DC.

13

COVID-19 VACCINES AND GLOBAL HEALTH DIPLOMACY

Canada and France compared

Stephen Brown and Morgane Rosier

Introduction

The COVID-19 pandemic has disrupted the delivery of foreign aid while increasing the need for international assistance. However, the extent to which the crisis is truly transforming the foreign aid *regime* remains an open question. Other than a renewed emphasis on social services and well-being, most trends associated with the pandemic are actually accelerations of processes that were already in place, such as a growing proportion of aid being directed to humanitarian assistance and the increased reliance on local partners in the Global South (Brown, 2021b). Despite the universal recognition of the need for a concerted global effort to fight the novel coronavirus, one of the most significant reinforced trends has been the growth of self-interest in foreign aid, not only in the rationale for aid but also in how short-term national interests have eclipsed medium- and long-term national and common interests. This contradiction is especially apparent in donor countries' acquisition and distribution of COVID-19 vaccines.

This chapter compares Canada's and France's policies and practices regarding COVID vaccines. It asks to what extent they advance domestic interests versus international ones and what the impact is on their influence in the world. The two countries are especially interesting case studies among "traditional" aid donors as they both have a history of global health diplomacy, and their respective leaders during the first years of the pandemic, Prime Minister Justin Trudeau and President Emmanuel Macron, shared a dynamic leadership style and a desire to play an increasingly important role on the world stage. As such, the pandemic provided them with an opportunity to exercise that commitment, predisposing Canada and France to be potential champions of multilateral cooperation to fight COVID-19. Indeed, both countries quickly embraced, at the rhetorical level, the

DOI: 10.4324/9781003273844-13

need to address the global crisis via multilateral channels, including to ensure an equitable distribution of vaccines.

How they acted, however, differed considerably. The Canadian government took a strong "Canada First" position, in spite of verbal and financial support for multilateral responses, and impeded patent waivers that would increase global vaccine production. By taking actions that would prolong the pandemic at the global level, Canada also behaved to the detriment of its global "soft power". France, on the contrary, acted more multilaterally and strategically and reversed its initial self-interested position on intellectual property rights. We argue that Canada's and, to a lesser extent, France's domestic policy objectives undermined their global health diplomacy efforts and ultimately acted against their own interests, both in terms of health outcomes and being able to exercise influence in global affairs, especially in the Global South. By emphasizing approaches characterized by selfishness and charity, rather than equity and justice, they also, along with their counterparts in the Global North, undermined the credibility of Northern aid donors more generally and the legitimacy of the aid regime.

To make this argument, we begin by presenting an overview of the concepts of soft power and public health diplomacy. We then analyse, in turn, the cases of Canada and France, based on publicly available documentation, including government statements, media reports and analyses by scholars and practitioners. When examining the governments' actions, we draw on Harman *et al.*'s (2021) normative hierarchy of the three means of fighting vaccine inequity: Most ethical is the "pooling, temporary waivers, or suspension of IP [intellectual property]" (Harman *et al.*, 2021, p. 2). Second is multilateral charity, epitomized by the flawed COVAX initiative. The most problematic is bilateral (country-to-country) charity, because

> it is unclear if this will be done for free, at a lower cost, tied to diplomacy or conditionality, or crucially, when these vaccines will be made available, where they will go, or how many will be delivered. The bilateral charity approach has little to do with equity and more to do with geopolitics, wealth and aid dependency.
>
> *(Harman et al., 2021, p. 1)*

Taking into account that analytical framework, we structure our comparison of Canada and France via five related questions. First, mainly as background, what was each country's experience in support to the health sector in the Global South and in global health diplomacy? Second, what was its discourse on global COVID vaccination? Third, how did it conduct its domestic vaccine procurement? Fourth, how did it proceed in international vaccine donations, and how did it support multilateral initiatives? Fifth, what was its position on vaccine-related intellectual property rights? The coherence and inconsistencies in Canada's and France's rhetoric and actions, as well as the similarities and differences between the two countries, help us trace a nuanced picture and tease out its implications.

Soft power, global health diplomacy and multilateral responses

Soft power is generally understood as "the ability to get what you want through attraction rather than coercion or payments" (Nye, 2004, p. x), as opposed to hard power, which refers to the use by states of material resources as a means of pressure, in particular military force. Soft power rests on more intangible attributes, particularly cultural and political, on which a country's reputation and thus its influence on the global stage depend (Chung, 2011). It allows for more peaceful solutions, as well as considerable savings in terms of human, material and financial resources when compared to coercive initiatives. The notion of soft power thus makes it possible to conceive of state discourses and initiatives through a reputational lens and the construction and maintenance of a positive image on the world stage.

COVID-19 constituted an opportunity for states to boost their image by demonstrating leadership in responding to this global health and economic crisis in an equitable way. At the global level, while some countries had long been strongly involved in what is known as global health diplomacy, others jumped on the bandwagon and "emerging" countries became more active. Global health diplomacy refers to "multi-level and multi-actor negotiation processes that shape and manage the global policy environment for health" (Kickbusch *et al.*, 2007, p. 230). According to Kickbusch (2011), "foreign policy can be used to promote health goals", but it can also "endanger health" (p. 1). For instance, international trade and patent laws restrict the possibility of producing affordable medicines, prioritizing the profits of pharmaceutical companies and national interests over the health of millions (Brunet-Jailly, 2016; Gopakumar, 2016; Sharun and Dhama, 2021).

Increasing the supply of vaccines is urgently required to save lives and prevent further spread of the coronavirus. Reducing the global caseload would also decrease the odds of dangerous new variants emerging, which is in all countries' best interest. Many companies have been expanding their manufacturing capacity, but it is nowhere near sufficient – and they have proven extremely reluctant to voluntarily licence other companies to manufacture them on their behalf. Despite characterizations of COVID vaccines as a "global public good", something with the potential to benefit everyone, everywhere, most remain very much *private* goods, under the control of powerful profit-seeking companies whose interests do not necessarily align with principles of equity, solidarity, justice or, in fact, global public health. As a result, the only remaining option to increase manufacturing is "to move towards involuntary production upscaling" (Meijer *et al.*, 2021, p. 1).

In the interest of global well-being, international agreements and domestic laws already allowed states to individually and collectively authorize the manufacturing of generic vaccines without the patent holders' permission, for which they would nonetheless be compensated, known as compulsory licencing. Under certain circumstances, including during a public health emergency such as a pandemic, the World Trade Organization's (WTO) Trade-Related Aspects of Intellectual Property Rights (TRIPS) Agreement permits such a process to take place without first attempting to obtain the patent-holder's permission, i.e., without seeking voluntary licencing. The majority of the world's countries, including China, Russia and the United States, expressed support for a temporary TRIPS waiver that would further weaken intellectual property rights to facilitate the expansion of manufacturing of generic COVID vaccines. Initially proposed by India and South Africa in October 2020, such a waiver can only be granted under WTO rules if there is a consensus among member states.

The manufacturing and distribution of prophylactic medical products are subject to a subcategory of global health diplomacy, namely vaccine diplomacy, which "refers to almost any aspect of global health diplomacy that relies on the use or delivery of vaccines" (Hotez, 2014, p. 2). Vaccines are a precious instrument of soft power, even "national security assets", used to pursue political and diplomatic objectives in an uneven playing field in which poorer countries generally have access to vaccines last (Pannu and Barry, 2021, p. 744).

The COVID-19 pandemic quickly led to the creation of an international solidarity mechanism: the Access to COVID-19 Tools Accelerator (ACT-A), co-coordinated by Gavi, the Vaccine Alliance (Gavi), the Coalition for Epidemic Preparedness Innovations and the World Health Organization (WHO). Invoking principles of equity and justice, wealthier countries committed to funding this mechanism designed to ensure "equitable access to COVID-19 tests, treatments, and vaccines" for all countries regardless of their purchasing power, because "no-one is safe until everyone is safe" (WHO, n.d., para. 1 and 4). In particular, access to vaccines is a major challenge for low-income countries as "[t]he endgame is no longer simply how to make the best vaccine in the laboratory, but rather how vaccines will be purchased and used appropriately" (Hotez, 2001, p. 863).

ACT-A includes the COVAX initiative for COVID-19 vaccines. In particular, the COVAX Advanced Market Mechanism (AMC), financed mainly through wealthy countries' official development assistance, was created to ensure low- and middle-income countries could have equitable access to vaccines. To do so, COVAX was meant to pool vaccine resources, either bought by COVAX or donated by countries, and distribute them according to need, determined according to a country's population size, target vaccination rate and possible acute outbreaks (Berkley, 2021). COVAX aimed to vaccinate only 20% of poor countries' inhabitants, far below wealthier countries' own targets, a disparity that Zimbabwean philanthropist Strive Masiyiwa called "a deliberate global architecture of unfairness" (quoted in Merelli, 2021).

COVAX, however, did not live up to those initial goals. Although it allows all countries regardless of their revenue to request vaccine doses, in practice, while self-financing countries are guaranteed an access to vaccines in proportion to the amount they contribute, vaccine supplies for poorer countries depend on funding availability, as the head of Gavi has recognised (Berkley, 2021). The mechanism's fatal flaw is that it relies on charitable donations and market mechanisms. It has been unable to purchase the planned number of doses because wealthy countries displayed a tremendous degree of "vaccine nationalism" and locked in supplies via direct contracts with pharmaceutical companies, especially of the premium mRNA vaccines, buying enough to inoculate their population multiple times over. They resisted the loosening of intellectual property rights (Sharun and Dhama, 2021), which would have helped increase vaccine production and availability. COVAX's ability to purchase supplies on the global market was further limited by India's five-month moratorium in April 2021 on exports of its version of the AstraZeneca vaccine, enacted to deal with an escalating case rate at home, revealing the problem with COVAX's overreliance on a single country as its main supplier. With a limited ability to buy doses on its own, for most of 2021, COVAX had to rely on in-kind donations of mainly surplus vaccines. However, wealthy countries also failed to meet their pledges of vaccine donations and funding to permit COVAX to cover the needs of poorer countries while authorizing booster shots for their populations before even health workers and vulnerable populations could be vaccinated in the Global South (Ghebreyesus, 2021a, 2021b).

So-called emerging countries and rivals, China, India and Russia, undertook their own COVID vaccine diplomacy, which had the potential to disrupt Western countries' selfish dynamics. Prior to the pandemic, India produced more than half of the world's vaccines and had a long track record of providing affordable medicines across the world (Brunet-Jailly, 2016; Sharun and Dhama, 2021). However, after initially being a major source of COVAX's vaccines and donating millions of doses to neighbouring countries even before vaccinating a significant proportion of its own population, India temporarily banned COVID vaccine exports. Despite China's early use of vaccines as a diplomatic tool to the benefit of poorer countries, the country encountered supply problems, there were suspicions that China would withhold the provision of vaccines to countries criticizing its human rights records and doubts persisted on the efficacy of Chinese vaccines against variants (Keaten, 2021; Mashal and Yee, 2021; Wee, 2021). In August 2020, Russia was the first country to approve a vaccine against COVID-19. However, concerns rapidly spread regarding Sputnik V's quality, including the conduct of its trials and transparency on results (Mahase, 2020). Moreover, stepping up production proved very challenging, and Russia faced delivery delays due to a lack of technical capacity and experienced personnel, as well as shortages in supplies (Ivanova and Nikolskaya, 2021). Moreover, not all of those countries' vaccines received WHO approval.

The hope of a widely available and highly effective vaccine coming from China, India or Russia proved disappointing, stymying their efforts to conduct global public health diplomacy. We now turn to the cases of Canada and France to analyse to what extent these "traditional" Western donors acted from the perspective of soft power and used vaccine diplomacy to further their own interests or, instead, to promote solidarity and justice through fair and equitable access to COVID vaccines.

Canada: not walking the talk

For this first case study, we examine, in turn, the five issue areas identified in our analytical framework as applied to Canada.

Global health diplomacy

Health had been an explicit area of focus of Canadian foreign aid since at least 2000 (Canada, 2002). Most prominently, the Conservative government of Stephen Harper strongly promoted its Muskoka Initiative for Maternal, Newborn and Child Health, launched in 2010. By 2014, it had committed Cdn$8.5 billion (US$6.8 billion) to the initiative, a sizeable investment. Despite this generosity, it was criticized for a number of shortcomings, notably its exclusion of abortion services even where legal in order to please the Conservative Party's base, which tarnished the Initiative's reputation internationally (Brown, 2018). Under the Justin Trudeau Liberal government, Canada expanded the focus to "sexual and reproductive health and rights".

While many analysts praise Canada's development assistance and global influence in the area of health since the late 1990s, especially when delivered via multilateral channels (Ruckert, Labonté and Lencucha, 2019; Weldon and Hoffman, 2021), most are also quite critical of the distance between rhetoric and reality. A common refrain is that Canada could do much more, not only or even primarily by increasing its budget allocations but also rather by spending its funds better. Authors have variously found assistance to the health sector to have been too stingy, too narrow, too short term and ad hoc, too self-interested and/or overemphasizing services, while paying insufficient attention to the social determinants of health and health care infrastructure (Huish, 2021; Huish and Spiegel, 2012; Spiegel and Huish, 2009). Several sources highlight contradictions between global health objectives and other dimensions of Canadian foreign policy, as well as the lack of greater global leadership (Nixon *et al.*, 2018; Percival, 2018; Weldon and Hoffman, 2021). COVID presented Canada with a new leadership opportunity, but the government failed to seize it and, moreover, took other steps that were detrimental to its global reputation, even as it espoused valiant rhetoric.

Vaccine distribution rhetoric

From the outbreak of the pandemic, the Canadian government emphasized the importance of multilateral vaccination efforts and of the fundamental principles of solidarity, equity and justice with regard to access to vaccines – at least when addressing international audiences. For example, in July 2020, before any vaccines had been approved, Trudeau was the lead author of a statement signed by nine heads of state and heads of government that argued that:

> [we] must urgently ensure that vaccines will be distributed according to a set of transparent, equitable and scientifically sound principles. … A fair and effective vaccine allocation mechanism, guided by WHO advice and based on needs rather than means, should focus on saving lives and protecting health systems. We call on global leaders to commit to contributing to an equitable distribution of the covid-19 vaccine.
>
> *(Trudeau, 2020)*

In a similar vein, in September 2020, Minister of International Development Karina Gould declared that Canada was working to create a mechanism that would provide "a fair, equitable, accessible and affordable vaccine" at the global level (quoted in Blanchfield, 2020).

When addressing primarily domestic audiences, the Canadian government infused its rhetoric with more self-interest. For example, on different occasions, Gould made the case that "we will not be safe from COVID-19 in Canada until everyone, everywhere is" (quoted in Global Affairs Canada (GAC) 2020), "our health here depends on the health of the other 'over there'" (Gould, 2020) and "supporting other countries in their fight against COVID-19 is crucial to protect Canadians at home" (quoted in PMO, 2020). In May 2020, Trudeau (2020) invoked Canadian economic interests, arguing that "Canadian jobs and businesses depend on stable and productive economies in other countries – so it matters to us how everyone weathers this storm". These statements, despite the injection of self-interest, remained compatible with the principles of justice, equity and solidarity at the global level.

Vaccine procurement

Less compatible with the enlightened dimension of the self-interested rhetoric was Canada's actual domestic procurement. Widely criticized at home for an initially slow acquisition and rollout of vaccines when compared to the United States and the United Kingdom, the government overcompensated by aggressively signing contracts with a wide range of potential suppliers, sometimes paying a premium price to leapfrog over other purchasers in delivery timetables. Procurement Minister Anita Anand explained that the government wanted to make sure that "Canadians are at the front of the line" (quoted in Jones and Harris, 2020). Prioritizing its own citizens is to be expected of any government. However, in so doing, Canada became a record-breaking vaccine stockpiler. A *British Medical Journal* blog awarded Canada the "gold medal for top hoarder" for having purchased enough doses to fully vaccinate its entire population more than five times over (Benton *et al.*, 2021).

Given the finite global supply of doses, Canada's excessive deals with pharmaceutical companies – including purchases from the Serum Institute of India – meant that fewer doses were available on the market for other countries or COVAX to purchase. Moreover, Canada decided to access 1.9 million doses of the AstraZeneca vaccine from COVAX AMC. Although Canada was entitled to do so, exercising that option opened up Canada to additional criticism, as those doses would have otherwise gone to low- and middle-income countries that had not already secured sufficient or indeed any supplies for their populations (Usher, 2021). The government eventually decided to forego any further deliveries from COVAX, but only after it had more AstraZeneca doses that it could possibly need, given that its use had been almost entirely suspended in Canada over concerns regarding side effects and the newly widespread availability of the "more desirable" Pfizer and Moderna mRNA vaccines.

Canada's international reputation suffered from its patently selfish "Canada First" behaviour in its domestic vaccine acquisition and the indirect harm that such vaccine nationalism does to other countries (Brown, 2021a). Canada could, however, have redeemed itself through vaccine donations and measures to increase global vaccine manufacturing, but it failed to be sufficiently proactive in those areas as well.

Vaccine assistance

For a long time, the Canadian government refused to explain what it would do with its surplus doses once it had enough to vaccinate fully the Canadian population, even calling the scenario "hypothetical" (Lum, 2020). This reluctance was confusing, as the outcome was virtually certain, given the oversupply, and, moreover, governments must plan for multiple scenarios. In March 2021, the government stated that it would wait until vaccines had been made available to all Canadians before donating any doses to countries in need (Zimonjic and Cullen, 2021), unlike other donor countries such as France, New Zealand and Norway. The Liberal government was presumably worried about voters objecting to altruism, even though polls suggest that the public in Canada and other high-income countries was broadly supportive of donating a proportion of national vaccine supplies (Clarke *et al.*, 2021, p. 935).

In the meantime, Canada did make relatively generous financial contributions to the multilateral COVAX AMC initiative. In particular, Canada announced in September 2020 a donation of Cdn$220 million (about US$175 million) to buy vaccines for low- and middle-income countries and also contributed over Cdn$1 billion (US$800 million) for other forms of support to "equitable access to vaccines, tests and treatments" (Canada, 2021).

In August 2021, the month after receiving enough doses to vaccinate its entire adult population, Canada announced that it would donate "up to" 10 million doses of the Janssen/Johnson and Johnson vaccine (GAC, 2021a), which had been approved for use in Canada, but never actually distributed, presumably because of its inferior effectiveness compared to other options and the perceived risk of side effects, as well as the fact that the first shipment of doses from the United States to Canada had to be destroyed because they were contaminated. That commitment brought promised total to over 40 million doses to COVAX, but the government did not provide a timetable or deadline nor a breakdown of which vaccines it would be contributing. It has only rolled them out slowly and sometimes close to their expiry dates, which needlessly complicated logistics and ultimately risked them having to be destroyed (York, 2021). As of October 22, 2021, out of the 40 million committed to COVAX, it had donated only 3.7 million doses and actually delivered only 1.4 million doses (WHO, 2021a). At the end of October, Trudeau announced that Canada would donate "up to" 10 million doses of the Moderna vaccine (PMO, 2021).

In parallel, in August and September, the Canadian government donated 762,080 AstraZeneca doses bilaterally (government to government) in six countries in South America and the Caribbean (McGregor, 2021). The Canadian government presented only a vague rationale for distributing these vaccines bilaterally, as opposed to via the COVAX allocation and delivery mechanism. The choice can be presumed to be a desire to curry favour with the recipient government and the diaspora in Canada. If so, it was at best only partially successful, as observers noted the fact Canada only shipped the less desirable vaccine type. Trinidadian Canadian Pundit Vijay Persad Seetahal, who played a role in brokering the donation to his country of origin, stated that "After I make that solemn thanks to her [Canadian Minister of International Development Karina Gould], I am going to beg and ask her very nicely for Pfizer vaccines" (quoted in Ramdass, 2021).

Oddly for a multilateral mechanism, even doses that COVAX distributes are linked to the country that donated the vials. Canada's first AstraZeneca donations to COVAX, for instance, were announced as having been sent to Nigeria, Kenya and Niger (Gavi, 2021a), even though Canada actually played no role in selecting the recipients according to Global Affairs Canada (York, 2021). Even more confusingly, COVAX has identified shipments of the Chinese vaccine Sinopharm to Nicaragua and Zimbabwe as being Canadian-funded (McGregor, 2021).

Canada's vaccine donations were announced late, were delivered slowly and in an apparently ad hoc manner and consisted only of doses that Canada has no intention of ever using. They were not especially numerous (given the size of Canada's stockpile), and the total commitment compared poorly with the 1 billion vaccines that the United States had pledged to donate. As such, the credit that Canada's vaccine diplomacy could earn remained limited. The final possibility for a strong contribution to global public health would be leadership in expanding vaccine manufacturing, but Canadian immobilism rendered that scenario moot as well.

Intellectual property rights

Whereas some European countries such as Germany and the United Kingdom opposed a TRIPS waiver, Canada remained officially undecided more than a year after the proposal was made. In this context, sitting on the fence is not the same as abstaining from a vote; when a consensus is required, indecision is a form of blocking the adoption of the decision.

The Canadian government stonewalled by repeatedly asking for more evidence that intellectual property rights are the main barrier to expanded vaccine production and argued that a waiver was unnecessary because existing mechanisms permitted compulsory licencing without one. However, its reasoning was demonstrably false (Labonté *et al.*, 2021). For instance, Canada has its own compulsory licencing mechanism, known as Canada's Access to Medicines Regime (CAMR). In place since 2005, it has only been used once to date. The process is so cumbersome that the company in question, Apotex, decided never to engage with it again (Houston and Nickerson, 2021). Nonetheless, in March 2021, the Bolivian government signed a contract with Canadian company Biolyse to produce 15 million doses of the Janssen/Johnson and Johnson vaccine via compulsory licencing. The CAMR requires government approval before production can start. However, like for TRIPS, the Canadian government stalled. It neither approved nor rejected the request and refused to state when a decision would be made – to the dismay of the Bolivian government, which publicly criticised the gap between Canada's rhetoric and actions (Khan, 2021).

It is unclear why, given the global health emergency, the Canadian government was unwilling to support existing provisions for compulsory licencing, whether at home or internationally, based on apparently spurious and contradictory arguments. Such measures are of little or no threat to the profits of Canadian pharmaceutical companies and could in fact benefit Canadian generic drug manufacturers. It would also increase Canada's credibility as a supporter of global public health and thus contribute to Canada's soft power. Some sources speculate that the big COVID vaccine manufacturers pressured the Canadian government to block approval, using as leverage future access to vaccines and pharmaceutical company investment in manufacturing in Canada (Abbas, 2021, pp. 14, 17; Khan, 2021; Moss, 2021, p. 13). Whatever the reason, Canada was unwilling to act in that area as well, let alone play a leadership role, to the detriment of its international reputation.

France: strategic posturing

We now turn to the case of France, once again examining the five issue areas outlined in the introduction.

Global health diplomacy

The French government defined health as one of the five sectoral priorities of its foreign assistance in 2018. In particular, it reaffirmed its commitment to fighting pandemics through contributions to multilateral organizations (Ministry of Economy, Finance and Recovery [MEFR], 2018). In 2021, it reiterated this focus on health in its law on inclusive development and the fight against global inequalities, which frames health as a global public good (Légifrance, 2021).

France has been a major actor in global health diplomacy for decades, albeit not always consistently. An enduring feature is France's focus on African countries with which it has long-lasting colonial ties, in line with its overall foreign assistance strategy (Ministry for Europe and Foreign Affairs [MEFA], 2021a). In the early 2000s, France shifted from mostly bilateral initiatives to allocating most of the aid dedicated to health to multilateral initiatives (Donor Tracker, n.d.; Goblé, 2011). Indeed, France in the past 20 years has led and participated in major multilateral endeavours dedicated to fight epidemics and pandemics: it is the second-largest public donor to the Global Fund to Fight AIDS, Tuberculosis and Malaria (Global Fund, n.d.; Canada is the seventh largest); it is a founding member of Unitaid, which is engaged in fighting epidemics in low- and middle-income countries; it had a role in the development of Gavi, and the International Finance Facility for Immunization, in particular. However, several analysts found this shift to be detrimental to the support of health systems in the long term, despite France's rhetoric (Atlani-Duault *et al.*, 2016; Kerouedan *et al.*, 2011). Moreover, using only multilateral channels for global health diplomacy risks minimizing France's efforts in terms of visibility and "exposes it to political volatility" (Atlani-Duault *et al.*, 2016, p. 2259).

In 2012, France adopted for the first time a strategy for international health cooperation, followed in 2017 by a more detailed strategy for global health. Both emphasize the fight against infectious diseases and the strengthening of health systems as priorities, and both place the geographical focus on Francophone Africa (MEFA, 2012, 2017). However, the latest strategy puts greater emphasis on international health security, including to "promote the fight against emerging diseases and guarantee access to essential public health products", notably vaccines for poorer countries (MEFA, 2017, p. 24).

Hence, France has significant experience in global health diplomacy and has made health a priority sector of its foreign policy over the past 20 years, preferring multilateral instances but making sure to maintain its influence in French-speaking Africa. The challenge for France is to continue (re)building its influence on the global stage by showing financial but above all political leadership for global health solidarity (Atlani-Duault *et al.*, 2016; Kerouedan *et al.*, 2011). France seized the opportunity presented by the COVID crisis to defend equitable access to vaccines through multilateralism both rhetorically and by leading key initiatives such as ACT-A and vaccine donations. However, it undermined its efforts by "bilateralizing" its multilateral support to serve its own interests.

Vaccine distribution rhetoric

Since the beginning of the COVID-19 pandemic, France has consistently appealed to values and principles of multilateralism, solidarity, justice and cooperation. As early as March 2020, France, as part of the G7 alongside Canada, co-published a statement asserting the crisis needs "a strongly coordinated international approach" (Élysée, 2020a, para. 2). In May 2020, leaders of France and three other European countries and top representatives of the European Union (EU) shared their "determination to work together, with all those who share our commitment to international cooperation. We are ready to lead and support the global response" and committed to "[make the vaccine] available, accessible and affordable to all" (Michel *et al.*, para. 8 and 11). In July 2020, France reiterated its commitment along with 18 representatives from European, Latin American and Caribbean countries. They declared their support for "the [ACT-A] initiative, which aims to speed up the development, production and fair and universal access to … vaccines against COVID-19 and strengthen health systems, especially in the most vulnerable countries and most disadvantaged sectors in our societies" (MEFA, 2020a, para. 6).

On its own, France has also advocated global solidarity and cooperation on multiple occasions, with the Minister for Europe and Foreign Affairs Jean-Yves le Drian calling for "international cooperation", "effective multilateralism" and "universal access to vaccines" (MEFA, 2020b, para. 1; MEFA, 2021b, para. 5). From the start, President Emmanuel Macron called for an international response to the multifaceted crisis and the involvement of all stakeholders and took part in the launch of ACT-A. He announced "France's commitments to this inclusive, comprehensive and cooperative vision of health" (Élysée, 2020b). In April 2021, after vaccines were approved and vaccination progressed rapidly in rich countries, he stated that "the time has come to share" because "our health also depends on what is happening in poorest countries" (Élysée, 2021). Albeit characterized by some self-interest, these stances are nonetheless in line with principles of solidarity and justice. France partly followed them for vaccine procurement, even though the EU's vaccine nationalism somewhat tarnished the idealistic rhetoric.

Vaccine procurement

France sources its COVID vaccines solely through multilateral channels, namely the EU. Contrary to Canada, it decided not to acquire any doses from COVAX, which can be considered in line with France's commitment to solidarity. As the EU secured almost three doses per person bilaterally even before any vaccine was approved (Overseas Development Institute [ODI], 2020), tapping into COVAX vaccine reserves would have further hindered poorer countries' access. Indeed, the EU negotiated opaque deals with pharmaceutical companies early on to ensure it would have enough vaccines for its own citizens, committing billions of dollars and indirectly excluding citizens in poorer countries from timely vaccination (European Commission, n.d.; Guéguen, 2021).

France thus showed solidarity, but only after it knew the EU had secured deals with vaccine manufacturers. In contrast, the French government demonstrated some leadership in providing vaccine assistance, looking to boost its reputation on the global stage and to affirm its position as a key actor in global health. Still, by instrumentalizing multilateral mechanisms, France appeared to resemble Harman *et al.*'s (2021) least desirable scenario of bilateral charity.

Vaccine assistance

When it became clear that COVAX could not secure enough doses directly from manufacturers, France was the first country to donate doses through this mechanism – even before its domestic vaccination was complete (Gavi, 2021b). As of October 2021, it has pledged to donate 120 million doses to COVAX (France 24, 2021a). France thus became second-most generous country regarding dose-sharing commitments through COVAX after the United States, albeit a distant second (WHO, 2021a). However, only 13.5 million doses had been delivered out of the 44.7 million that were officially considered donated as of October 22, 2021 (WHO, 2021a). Moreover, France provided mainly AstraZeneca vaccines shunned by the French population, as was primarily the case in Canada (France 24, 2021b; *Le Matin*, 2021).

If COVAX's initial purpose was to pool resources and then allocate them to low- and middle-income countries based on needs, the way Gavi, the media and sometimes governments framed vaccine donations and distribution casts doubts on the impartiality of the mechanism and France's intentions. Indeed, the multilateral initiative resembles a bilateral one in many instances, serving French interests and visibility in Africa in particular. For example, the media reported: "[Rwanda] received additional 247,000 doses of AstraZeneca through the COVAX mechanism, including 117,600 doses donated by the French government" (*East African*, 2021, para. 2); "France has donated 184,000 doses of AstraZeneca's (AZN.L) COVID-19 vaccine to Senegal through the COVAX vaccine-sharing facility" (Reuters, 2021, para. 1). A vaccine shipment received by Kampala reads, "Covid-19 Vaccine Donation from **FRENCH Government** to the Republic of Uganda" (*Independent*, 2021, emphasis in original).

In the case of Tunisia, the French government stated that "[t]his support will involve the imminent arrival of an initial French donation of 324,000 AstraZeneca vaccine doses through the COVAX initiative, following the Prime Minister's visit to Tunisia" (MEFA, 2021c, para. 3). Elsewhere, the French government referred to this donation without even mentioning COVAX (MEFR, 2021). However, the French government denied engaging in "'vaccine diplomacy or clientelism'" in favour of Francophone Africa: "It is Gavi's choice, that we fully support as Africa is the continent where vaccination campaigns are least advanced. But dose-sharing is also intended to serve other regions" (Liabot,

2021, paras. 9 and 10). Like in the Canadian case, it would be odd for France to decide where vaccines go, given that COVAX has an allocation mechanism based on need. The wording above suggests doses are not pooled and that donor countries can designate doses for certain recipient countries, as the initial US donation to COVAX, with detailed earmarks, seems to confirm (White House, 2021). France also donated vaccines bilaterally, for example, to Slovakia, following Harman *et al.*'s worst scenario of bilateral charity (Le Parisien, 2021a).

Moreover, France supported and even initiated multilateral endeavours dedicated to the fight against COVID-19, such as ACT-A. It did so with in-kind and financial contributions, even if some commitments have yet to be honoured. Indeed, French vaccine donations are in addition to a pledge of €200 million (US$250 million) to COVAX AMC (Gavi, n.d.) and €500 million (US$580 million) to support research and vaccine distribution through ACT-A (Reuters, 2020). However, those commitments appear to be relatively modest and sometimes arrived late compared to the significant bilateral initiative launched as early as April 2020 by France "COVID-19 – Health in Common" led by the French Development Agency. With a budget of €1.2 billion (US$1.4 billion), it aims to support mainly French-speaking African countries to respond to the COVID crisis in the short and longer term by reinforcing health systems (MEFA, 2020c).

France paved the way for vaccine sharing and pledged to provide more financial and in-kind support, to the benefit of its global reputation. However, if France were more committed to leadership and solidarity, it would have engaged in global health diplomacy to promote a more ethical approach to fighting vaccine inequity. A key measure would be fully supporting a loosening of intellectual property rights to step up vaccine production.

Intellectual property rights

France was initially opposed to weakening intellectual property protection to improve access to vaccines, including the proposed TRIPS waiver, aligning itself with the EU's stance. It argued that the priority should instead be vaccine-sharing, technology transfer, strengthening health systems and stepping up production (Élysée, 2021). However, in May 2021, the day after US President Joe Biden declared his support for a partial patent waiver (for vaccines only, not therapeutics or technology), Macron said he was "very favorable to a waiver of intellectual property … to make this vaccine a global public good" (Bertrand, 2021, para. 1). Later that month, he declared being in favour of "waiving any constraints in terms of intellectual property" (La Presse, 2021, para. 2). It was as if France suddenly remembered that it is committed to universal access to health as France views health as a global public good (Fabius, 2016). By supporting Biden's position, France acted from the perspective of soft power to promote global solidarity rather than charity and positioned itself as a leader alongside the United States.

France nonetheless tempered this *volte-face* by downplaying the potential of patent waivers, still pointing at the lack of technical and production capacities in the Global South, by exhorting producing countries like the United States to lift export bans on vaccines and components and by stating it was in favour of a "circumscribed waiver" of patents (Le Parisien, 2021b; Rovan, 2021, para. 3). Indeed, showing its support for intellectual property (IP) waivers seemed risk-free, as the EU has systematically opposed them (European Parliament, 2021; Hiault, 2021; Hiault and Turban, 2021), a consistent position hindering poor countries' access to medicines throughout the years and protecting patents held by European firms (Bassilekin, 2016; Gopakumar, 2016). Yet, in 2010, the European Commission recommended coherence between the EU's aid policy and its commercial interests, as well as to support the effective use of TRIPS provisions for poorer countries (European Commission, 2010).

In summary, France was rather opportunistic by positioning itself in favour of patent waivers only after the United States did and after more than enough vaccine doses were secured for its own citizens. It acted from the perspective of soft power to boost its image as a leader and an ally of the Global South but still did not promote a fully ethical approach, especially at the EU level.

Comparing national approaches

In many ways, Canada and France reacted rather differently to the COVID pandemic. The Canadian government took a strong "Canada First" position, in spite of verbal and financial support for multilateral responses, to the detriment of its global soft power. It stood out for its reluctance to share its vaccine stockpile, even after securing many times more doses than it could use, and also stonewalled efforts to facilitate the compulsory licencing of vaccines, which was essential – albeit not sufficient – to expand global vaccine production. The evident gap between rhetoric and actual practices laid bare a lack of strategic vision, leadership and commitment to equity.

The French government acted more multilaterally and strategically than Canada from the perspective of soft power. For instance, it procured its vaccines multilaterally (albeit regionally) and decided to support a TRIPS waiver. However, France acted only after the US government did and mainly from within the EU's strong "Europe First" position, remaining secure in the knowledge that the EU would protect the interests of French pharmaceutical companies. Thus, whereas Canada has erected obstacles to the lifting of vaccine patent protections, France fared slightly better in belatedly providing some rhetorical support for waivers but little leadership for what Harman *et al.* (2021, p. 1) describe as the superior approach to fighting vaccine inequity, which is to challenge "unethical intellectual property (IP) regimes".

Both countries contributed financially and in kind to the second-best approach, which is to say multilateral charity, via the COVAX initiative. However, their cash contributions were undermined by their purchase, alongside other wealthy countries, of vaccines directly from manufacturers, hampering COVAX's ability to buy the doses it needed to meet its distribution and vaccination targets. As a result, COVAX had to rely to a large extent on ad hoc donations of leftover doses, notably of vaccine types that Canada and France no longer wanted to use domestically.

Finally, France and Canada did partake in the most problematic approach to vaccine allocation, namely bilateral charity – although with a relatively small proportion of their in-kind donations. The quote above about the need to express gratitude and beg Canada for more vaccines, especially some of the more valued mRNA ones, starkly illustrates the neocolonial dimension of the bilateral charitable donation modality, as opposed to one based on equity or justice.

However, both countries' multilateral donations were "bilateralized", that is to say, COVAX allowed a specific number of physical doses to be identified as having been donated from them to specific recipient countries. This practice contradicted COVAX's foundational multilateral equity-based principles. Moreover, pairing donor and recipient countries reinforces the idea of national gratitude for bilateral charity in line with geostrategic self-interest and undermines universal and rights-based principles in global vaccine distribution and public health.

The controversial practice of earmarking multilateral donations raises questions regarding COVAX. If donor countries are using this multilateral mechanism to give bilaterally or at least seem to do so, COVAX becomes an instrument of rich countries' soft power and global health diplomacy – to the detriment of fair and equitable access to vaccines. Officially, donor countries should not be able to earmark their cash or in-kind donations to COVAX for specific recipient countries. But if they do not, why has COVAX's Independent Allocation of Vaccines Group drawn attention to "the need for countries which are sharing doses with COVAX to reduce/remove all earmarking" (WHO, 2021b)?

Notwithstanding expressions of gratitude, countries in the Global South have strongly criticized wealthy countries for their vaccine nationalism (Psaledakis, 2021). The increased emphasis on donor self-interest, even in the face of a global health emergency, is not new to the pandemic context. Rather, COVID has accelerated this pre-existing trend, observable since the 2008 global financial crisis (Mawdsley *et al.*, 2018). A *British Medical Journal* opinion piece described COVID vaccines' distribution as "crumbs from the rich person's table" and the broader charity model as "a catastrophic failure" (Benton *et al.*, 2021, para. 1). Multilateral charity thus appears to share some of the flaws of the bilateral charity model, beyond what Harman *et al.* (2021) had foreseen.

Conclusion and implications for the foreign aid regime

By acting in line with their short-term, mainly domestic, political objectives, France and especially Canada undermined their global health diplomacy, which they had been unevenly building up for decades. Ultimately, their choices are likely to prove detrimental to their medium- and long-term interests, not only in soft power terms but also because they slowed the global fight against COVID-19, which could have a boomerang effect by favouring the emergence of new variants and prolonging their own and global recovery. Although the two countries had some differences between them and other "traditional" donors will have their own particularities, the Canadian and French experiences do not appear to differ in any significant ways from those of their peers. Future research can confirm if that is indeed the case – or analyse any important differences.

Countries in the Global South are unlikely to forget how France and especially Canada shamelessly discarded their discourse of equity, justice and solidarity when it came to vaccine procurement, distribution and manufacturing. Inasmuch as these two countries' actions reflect a trend among "traditional" aid donors, they have further delegitimated the donors' altruistic and principled aid narrative and the broader foreign aid regime, already under strain. It remains to be seen the extent to which Canada's and France's global health diplomacy and soft power will be able to recover in a post-pandemic context – and to what extent countries of the Global South will be able to ensure more equitable multilateral responses to future crises. If they cannot count on international cooperation, they will have no choice but to focus on self-reliance.

Acknowledgements

The authors are grateful to Adam Rainis Houston for helpful comments. Stephen Brown thanks the University of Cambridge Centre for Gender Studies for hosting him during his work on this chapter, along with the Centre for Research on the Arts, Social Sciences and Humanities, and Clare Hall, as well as the Social Sciences and Humanities Research Council of Canada and the Leverhulme Trust for financial support. Morgane Rosier thanks the University of Ottawa for financial assistance through the Jacques Frémont Scholarship for International Graduate Students.

References

Abbas, M.Z. (2021). *Canada's political choices restrain vaccine equity: the Bolivia-Biolyse Case.* South Centre Research Paper. https://www.southcentre.int/research-paper-136-september-2021/

Amorim, C., Douste-Blazy, P., Wirayuda, H., Store, J.G., Gadio, C.T., Dlamini-Zuma, N. and Pibulsonggram, N. (2007). Oslo Ministerial Declaration—global health: a pressing foreign policy issue of our time. *The Lancet, 369*(9570), 1373–1378.

Atlani-Duault, L., Dozon, J.-P., Wilson, A., Delfraissy, J.-F. and Moatti, J.-P. (2016). State humanitarian verticalism versus universal health coverage: a century of French international health assistance revisited. *The Lancet, 387*(10034), 2250–2262.

Bassilekin, A. (2016). Chapitre 14 – La coopération ACP-UE et la santé publique: un partenariat pour le développement humain? In D. Kerouedan (Ed.), *Santé mondiale : Enjeu stratégique et jeux diplomatiques* (pp. 287–306). Presses de Sciences Po.

Benton, A., Majumder, M. and Yamey, G. (2021, August 20). The global health security agenda rewards rich nations for their selfish behaviour. *The BMJ Opinion.* https://

blogs.bmj.com/bmj/2021/08/20/the-global-health-security-agenda-rewards-rich-nations-for-their-selfish-behaviour/

Berkley, S. (2020, September 20). *COVAX explained.* Gavi, the Vaccine Alliance. https://www.gavi.org/vaccineswork/covax-explained

Bertrand, C. (2021, May 8). Vaccins contre le Covid-19: pourquoi Macron fait volte-face au sujet de la levée des brevets? *La Dépêche.* https://www.ladepeche.fr/2021/05/07/vaccins-contre-le-covid-19-pourquoi-macron-fait-volte-face-au-sujet-de-la-levee-des-brevets-9532440.php

Blanchfield, M. (2020, September 11). Health and policy experts criticize Canada's COVID-19 vaccine deals, call for international funding. *Globe and Mail.* https://www.theglobeandmail.com/canada/article-heath-and-policy-experts-criticize-canadas-covid-19-vaccine-deals/

Brown, S. (2018). All about that base? Branding and the domestic politics of Canadian foreign aid. *Canadian Foreign Policy Journal, 24*(2), 145–164.

Brown, S. (2021a). Canada's COVID-19 vaccine fix. *Canadian Foreign Policy Journal, 28*(1), 98–106.

Brown, S. (2021b). The impact of COVID-19 on development assistance. *International Journal, 76*(1), 42–54.

Brunet-Jailly, J. (2016). Chapitre 16 – Une introduction à la géopolitique du médicament. In D. Kerouedan (Ed.), *Santé mondiale: Enjeu stratégique et jeux diplomatiques* (pp. 335–364). Presses de Sciences Po.

Canada. (2002). *Canada making a difference in the world: a policy statement on strengthening aid effectiveness.* Canadian International Development Agency.

Canada. (2021, August 25). Canada's aid and development assistance in response to the COVID-19 pandemic. *Government of Canada.* https://www.international.gc.ca/world-monde/issues_development-enjeux_developpement/global_health-sante_mondiale/response_covid-19_reponse.aspx?lang=eng

Chung, R. (2011). Soft power. In D.K. Chatterjee (Ed.), *Encyclopedia of Global Justice* (1st ed., pp. 1019–1022). Springer.

Clarke, P.M., Roope, L.S.J., Loewen, P.J., Bonnefon, J.F., Melegaro, A., Friedman, J., Violato, M., Barnett, A. and Duch, R. (2021). Public opinion on global rollout of COVID-19 vaccines. *Nature Medicine, 27*(6), 935–936.

Donor Tracker. (n.d.). *France – global health.* https://donortracker.org/france/globalhealth

East African. (2021, May 28). Rwanda resumes nationwide vaccination against Covid-19. https://www.theeastafrican.co.ke/tea/news/east-africa/rwanda-nationwide-vaccination-covid-3417080

Élysée. (2020a, March 16). *Coronavirus: G7 Leaders' statement.* https://www.elysee.fr/en/emmanuel-macron/2020/03/16/coronavirus-g7-leaders-statement

Élysée. (2020b, April 24). *Conference to launch a global initiative on diagnostics, treatment and vaccines.* https://www.elysee.fr/emmanuel-macron/2020/04/24/conference-to-launch-a-global-initiative-on-diagnostics-treatment-and-vaccines.en

Élysée. (2021, April 25). *L'initiative Act-A a un an. Beaucoup a été accompli, tant reste à faire* [Video]. YouTube. https://www.youtube.com/watch?v=LYfMQ6Ic7kA

European Commission. (n.d.). *EU Vaccines Strategy.* https://ec.europa.eu/info/live-work-travel-eu/coronavirus-response/public-health/eu-vaccines-strategy_en

European Commission. (2010). *Communication from the Commission to the Council, the European Parliament, the European Economic and Social Committee and the Committee of the Regions – The EU Role in Global Health.* https://eur-lex.europa.eu/LexUriServ/LexUriServ.do?uri=COM:2010:0128:FIN:EN:PDF

European Parliament. (2021, September). *At a glance – World Trade Organization TRIPS waiver to tackle coronavirus.* https://www.europarl.europa.eu/RegData/etudes/ATAG/2021/690649/EPRS_ATA(2021)690649_EN.pdf

Fabius, L. (2016). Chapitre 7 – La santé au cœur de la politique étrangère française. In D. Kerouedan (Ed.), *Santé mondiale: Enjeu stratégique et jeux diplomatiques* (pp. 177–184). Presses de Sciences Po.

France 24. (2021a, September 26). France to double Covid vaccine doses for poorer countries. *France 24.* https://www.france24.com/en/live-news/20210925-france-to-double-covid-vaccine-doses-for-poorer-countries

France 24. (2021b, July 20). Vaccin Covid: toutes les doses d'AstraZeneca désormais destinées aux dons. *France 24.* https://www.france24.com/fr/info-en-continu/20210720-vaccin-covid-toutes-les-doses-d-astrazeneca-d%C3%A9sormais-destin%C3%A9es-aux-dons

GAC. (2020, June 27). Canada announces support for equitable access to new COVID-19 medical solutions. *Global Affairs Canada news release.* https://www.canada.ca/en/global-affairs/news/2020/06/canada-announces-support-for-equitable-access-to-new-covid-19-medical-solutions.html

GAC. (2021a, August 12). Canada announces new contribution to global vaccination efforts. *Government of Canada.* https://www.canada.ca/en/global-affairs/news/2021/08/canada-announces-new-contribution-to-global-vaccination-efforts.html

GAC. (2021b, August 4). Canada announces new vaccine contributions for regional partners. *Global Affairs Canada news release.* https://www.canada.ca/en/global-affairs/news/2021/08/canada-announces-new-vaccine-contributions-for-regional-partners.html

Gavi. (n.d.). *France.* https://www.gavi.org/investing-gavi/funding/donor-profiles/france

Gavi. (2021a, September 2). *Canada donates doses through COVAX – Nigeria, Kenya and Niger to receive first doses.* https://www.gavi.org/news/media-room/canada-donates-doses-through-covax-nigeria-kenya-and-niger-receive-first-doses

Gavi. (2021b, April 23). *France makes important vaccine dose donation to COVAX.* https://www.gavi.org/news/media-room/france-makes-important-vaccine-dose-donation-covax

Ghebreyesus, T. (2021a, August 4). *WHO Director General's opening remarks at the media briefing on COVID-19.* World Health Organization. https://www.who.int/director-general/speeches/detail/who-director-general-s-opening-remarks-at-the-media-briefing-on-covid-4-august-2021

Ghebreyesus, T. (2021b, September 23). *WHO Director-General's remarks at the Alliance for Multilateralism.* World Health Organization. https://www.who.int/director-general/speeches/detail/who-director-general-s-remarks-at-the-alliance-for-multilateralism_

Global Fund. (n.d.). *Government and public donors – France.* https://www.theglobalfund.org/en/government/profiles/france/

Goblé, M. (2011). 33. La coopération sanitaire française dans les pays en développement. In D. Kerouedan (Ed.), *Santé internationale: Les enjeux de santé au Sud* (pp. 423–430). Presses de Sciences Po.

Gopakumar, K. (2016). Chapitre 15 – L'accès aux médicaments et les droits de propriété intellectuelle, vus du sud. In D. Kerouedan (Ed.), *Santé mondiale: Enjeu stratégique et jeux diplomatiques* (pp. 307–334). Presses de Sciences Po.

Gould, K. (2020, May 1). Rebuilding a more resilient planet. *Thomson Reuters Foundation News.* http://news.trust.org/item/20200501102506-sxegy/

Guéguen, E. (2021, February 19). Achats européens des vaccins : un secret très bien gardé. *France Inter.* https://www.franceinter.fr/achats-europeens-des-vaccins-un-secret-tres-bien-garde

Harman, S., Erfani, P., Goronga, T., Hickel, J., Morse, M. and Richardson, E.T. (2021). Global vaccine equity demands reparative justice—not charity. *BMJ Global Health, 6*(6), 1–4.

Hiault, R. (2021, September 14). Vaccins anti-covid: la levée des brevets dans l'impasse. *Les Echos*. https://www.lesechos.fr/monde/enjeux-internationaux/vaccins-anti-covid-la-levee-des-brevets-dans-limpasse-1346099

Hiault, R. and Turban, P. (2021, June 1). Vaccins anti-Covid: toujours pas de consensus sur la levée des brevets à l'OMC. *Les Echos*. https://www.lesechos.fr/monde/enjeux-internationaux/vaccins-anti-covid-toujours-pas-de-consensus-sur-la-levee-des-brevets-a-lomc-1319622

Hotez, P.J. (2001). Vaccines as instruments of foreign policy. *EMBO Reports, 2*(10), 862–868.

Hotez, P.J. (2014). "Vaccine diplomacy": historical perspectives and future directions. *PLoS Neglected Tropical Diseases, 8*(6), e2808.

Hotez, P.J. (2019). Immunizations and vaccines: a decade of successes and reversals, and a call for "vaccine diplomacy". *International Health, 11*(5), 331–333.

Houston, A. and Nickerson, J. (2021, April 30). Why Canada should support the WTO waiver to expand access to COVID-19 medical technologies. *MSF Access Campaign—Medicines Are Not a Luxury*. https://msf-access.medium.com/why-canada-should-support-the-wto-waiver-to-expand-access-to-covid-19-medical-technologies-9ecdcc0f81ab

Huish, R. (2021). Beneath the skin: Canadian global health policy in the time of a pandemic. In Carment, D. and Nimijean, R. (Eds.), *Political Turmoil in a Tumultuous World* (pp. 105–123). Palgrave Macmillan.

Huish, R. and Spiegel, J. (2012). First as tragedy and then on to farce: Canadian foreign aid for global health. *Canadian Foreign Policy Journal, 18*(2), 244–246.

Independent. (2021, September 23). Uganda receives 655,000 doses of AstraZeneca Covid-19 vaccine. https://www.independent.co.ug/uganda-receives-655000-doses-of-astrazeneca-covid-19-vaccine/

Ivanova, P., and Nikolskaya, P. (2021, May 14). Big promises, few doses: why Russia's struggling to make Sputnik V doses. *Reuters*. https://www.reuters.com/business/healthcare-pharmaceuticals/big-promises-few-doses-why-russias-struggling-make-sputnik-v-doses-2021-05-14/

Jones, R.P. and Harris, K. (2020, August 5). Feds Sign Agreements with Pfizer, Moderna for millions of doses of COVID-19 vaccines. *CBC News*. https://www.cbc.ca/news/politics/vaccine-procurementanand-bains-1.5674820

Keaten, J. (2021, June 25). AP exclusive: diplomats say China puts squeeze on Ukraine. *Associated Press*. https://apnews.com/article/united-nations-china-europe-ukraine-health-a0a5ae8f735b92e39c623e453529cbb9

Kerouedan, D., Gonzalez-Canali, G., Balique, H. and Floury, B. (2011). Santé et développement: 50 ans de coopération française en Afrique. *Revue Mondes, Les Cahiers du Quai d'Orsay*, 7, 81–93. https://www.college-de-france.fr/media/dominique-kerouedan/UPL7969937300967349 75_Sant___et_d__veloppement___Cinquante_ans_de_coop__ration_fran__aise_en_Afrique.pdf

Khan, A. (2021, October 6). Canada lacks "political will" to waive COVID-19 vaccine patents, Bolivian minister says. *Global News*. https://globalnews.ca/news/8243635/bolivian-minister-canada-covid-vaccine-waiver/

Kickbusch, I. (2011). Global health diplomacy: how foreign policy can influence health. *British Medical Journal, 342*(7811), 1345–1346.

Kickbusch, I., Silberschmidt, G. and Buss, P. (2007). Global health diplomacy: the need for new perspectives, strategic approaches and skills in global health. *Bulletin of the World Health Organization, 85*(3), 230–232.

Labonté, R., Johri, M., Plamondon, K. and Murthy, S. (2021). Canada, global vaccine supply, and the TRIPS waiver. *Canadian Journal of Public Health, 112*(4), 543–547.

La Presse. (2021, May 18). Un sommet économique sur l'Afrique demande la levée des brevets sur les vaccins. https://www.lapresse.ca/international/afrique/2021-05-18/un-sommet-economique-sur-l-afrique-demande-la-levee-des-brevets-sur-les-vaccins.php

Légifrance. (2021). *LOI n° 2021-1031 du 4 août 2021 de programmation relative au développement solidaire et à la lutte contre les inégalités mondiales (1).* https://www.legifrance.gouv.fr/jorf/id/JORFTEXT000043898536

Le Matin. (2021, March 1). Français et Allemands boudent le vaccin AstraZeneca. https://www.lematin.ch/story/francais-et-allemands-boudent-contre-le-vaccin-astrazeneca-378921962918

Le Parisien. (2021a, March 7). Covid-19: la France donne 15000 doses du vaccin AstraZeneca à la Slovaquie. https://www.leparisien.fr/societe/sante/covid-19-la-france-donne-15000-doses-du-vaccin-astrazeneca-a-la-slovaquie-07-03-2021-W3YUCKV7KVAIVFP2IMGPSVXOMI.php

Le Parisien. (2021b, May 6). Vaccins anti-Covid: Emmanuel Macron se dit «tout à fait favorable» à la levée des brevets. https://www.leparisien.fr/economie/vaccins-anti-covid-emmanuel-macron-se-dit-tout-a-fait-favorable-a-la-levee-des-brevets-06-05-2021-KG244MTISRDVLLFXFX6QKTPX7M.php

Liabot, T. (2021, April 28). Covax: voici comment la France partage ses vaccins avec le reste du monde. *Le Journal du Dimanche.* https://www.lejdd.fr/Societe/covax-voici-comment-la-france-partage-ses-vaccins-avec-le-reste-du-monde-4041371

Lum, Z.-A. (2020, December 20). Too early for talk about Canada's "Hypothetical Surplus" of vaccines: Minister. *Huffington Post Canada.* https://www.huffingtonpost.ca/entry/canada-coronavirus-vaccine-surplus_ca_5fdfe4f0c5b60f8288576132

Mahase, E. (2020, August 13). Covid-19: Russia approves vaccine without large scale testing or published results. *British Medical Journal, 370*(3205). https://www.bmj.com/content/370/bmj.m3205

Mashal, M. and Yee, V. (2021, February 11). The Newest Diplomatic Currency: Covid-19 Vaccines. *The New York Times.* https://www.nytimes.com/2021/02/11/world/asia/vaccine-diplomacy-india-china.html

Mawdsley, E., Murray, W.E., Overton, J., Scheyvens, R. and Banks, G. (2018). Exporting stimulus and "shared prosperity": reinventing foreign aid for a retroliberal era. *Development Policy Review, 36*(S1), O25–O43.

McGregor, J. (2021, October 8). Canada has donated over 750,000 AstraZeneca vaccine doses internationally since late summer. *CBC News.* https://www.cbc.ca/news/politics/astra-zeneca-surplus-donations-1.6205150

MEFA. (2012). *France's strategy for international health cooperation.* https://www.diplomatie.gouv.fr/IMG/pdf/France_s_strategy_for_international_health_cooperation_cle85a144.pdf

MEFA. (2017). *France's strategy for global health.* https://www.diplomatie.gouv.fr/IMG/pdf/sante_mondiale_en_web_cle4c7677-1.pdf

MEFA. (2020a, July 10). *Statement by the Foreign Ministers from 18 countries in Europe, Latin America and the Caribbean, and the High Representative of the Union for Foreign Affairs and Security Policy – COVID-19.* https://www.diplomatie.gouv.fr/en/

country-files/americas/news/article/statement-by-the-foreign-ministers-from-18-countries-in-europe-latin-america

MEFA. (2020b, November 12). *Meeting of the alliance for multilateralism – statements by M. Jean-Yves Le Drian, Minister for Europe and Foreign Affairs, by video conference (Paris Peace Forum).* https://www.diplomatie.gouv.fr/en/french-foreign-policy/united-nations/multilateralism-a-principle-of-action-for-france/alliance-for-multilateralism/news-about-the-alliance-for-multilateralism/article/meeting-of-the-alliance-for-multilateralism-statements-by-m-jean-yves-le-drian

MEFA. (2020c, April 9). *La France lance, via l'AFD, l'initiative «Covid-19- Santé en commun» pour soutenir les pays d'Afrique.* https://www.diplomatie.gouv.fr/fr/politique-etrangere-de-la-france/developpement/evenements-et-actualites-sur-le-theme-du-developpement/evenements-et-actualites-sur-le-theme-du-developpement-2020/article/la-france-lance-via-l-afd-l-initiative-covid-19-sante-en-commun-pour-soutenir

MEFA. (2021a). *Development assistance – geographical priorities.* https://www.diplomatie.gouv.fr/en/french-foreign-policy/development-assistance/geographical-priorities/

MEFA. (2021b, February 24). *Multilateralism – Jean-Yves Le Drian's participation in the ministerial meeting of the Alliance for Multilateralism (video conference).* https://www.diplomatie.gouv.fr/en/french-foreign-policy/united-nations/multilateralism-a-principle-of-action-for-france/alliance-for-multilateralism/news-about-the-alliance-for-multilateralism/article/multilateralism-jean-yves-le-drian-s-participation-in-the-ministerial-meeting

MEFA. (2021c, July 11). *Tunisie – Entretien de Jean-Yves Le Drian avec son homologue.* https://www.diplomatie.gouv.fr/fr/dossiers-pays/tunisie/evenements/article/tunisie-entretien-de-jean-yves-le-drian-avec-son-homologue-11-07-21

MEFR. (2018, February 8). *Interministerial International Cooperation and Development Committee (CICID) – statement of conclusions.* https://www.tresor.economie.gouv.fr/Articles/6d8c888e-b5d2-4897-b7a3-aef7b6e606f1/files/1ec94c51-0e37-4054-a2a6-2cf5cd981ceb

MEFR. (2021, June). Brèves économiques de Tunisie et de Libye. https://www.tresor.economie.gouv.fr/Articles/5add6197-c29e-4d5d-8b1e-c30293fc4075/files/04850bbb-36c6-41c9-912d-e88c7e387185

Meijer, M., Verschuuren, M. and Weggen, E. (2021). COVID-19 vaccines a global public good? Moving past the rhetoric and making work of sharing intellectual property rights, know-how and technology. *European Journal of Public Health, 31*(5), 925–926.

Michel, C., von der Leyen, U., Conte, G., Macron, E., Merkel, A. and Solberg, E. (2020, May 3). *The global response: working together to help the world get better.* Élysée. https://www.elysee.fr/en/emmanuel-macron/2020/05/03/the-global-response-working-together-to-help-the-world-get-better

Moss, N. (2021, May 12). U.S.-backed vaccine waiver should force Canada to support initiative, say politicos. *Hill Times.* https://www.hilltimes.com/2021/05/12/u-s-backed-vaccines-ip-waiver-should-force-canada-to-support-initiative-say-politicos/297141

Nixon, S.A., Lee, K., Bhutta, Z.A., Blanchard, J., Haddad, S., Hoffman, S.J. and Tugwell, P. (2018). Canada's global health role: supporting equity and global citizenship as a middle power. *The Lancet, 391*(10131), 1736–1748.

Nye, J.S. (2004). *Soft power: the means to success in world politics* (1st ed.). Public Affairs.

ODI. (2020). *Infographics: principled aid index 2020.* https://odi.org/en/publications/multimedia/infographics-principled-aid-index-2020/

Pannu, J. and Barry, M. (2021). The state inoculates: vaccines as soft power. *The Lancet Global Health, 9*(6), 744–745.

Percival, V. (2018, February 21). On global health, Canada is not "back". *The Globe and Mail.* https://www.theglobeandmail.com/opinion/on-global-health-canada-is-not-back/article38032659/

PMO. (2020, September 25). New agreements to secure additional vaccine candidates for COVID-19. Prime Minister's Office. https://pm.gc.ca/en/news/news-releases/2020/09/25/new-agreements-secure-additional-vaccine-candidates-covid-19

PMO. (2021, October 30). Global Health and Economy: Prime Minister concludes productive first day of G20 Leaders' Summit in Italy. Prime Minister's Office. https://pm.gc.ca/en/news/news-releases/2021/10/30/global-health-and-economy-prime-minister-concludes-productive-first

Psaledakis, D. (2021, September 22). Developing nations' plea to world's wealthy at U.N.: stop vaccine hoarding. *Reuters.* https://www.reuters.com/world/developing-nations-plea-worlds-wealthy-un-stop-vaccine-hoarding-2021-09-22/

Ramdass, A. (2021, August 6). Browne requested vaccine donation from Canada... so did pundit. *Daily Express.* https://trinidadexpress.com/news/local/browne-requested-vaccine-donation-from-canada-so-did-pundit/article_7a54a75c-f716-11eb-af82-4b9f389c3f89.html

Reuters. (2020, May 4). Macron: France to pledge 500 million euros for global coronavirus vaccine hunt. https://www.reuters.com/article/us-health-coronavirus-eu-france-idUSKBN22G1NO

Reuters. (2021, June 3). France donates 184,000 AstraZeneca doses to Senegal via COVAX. https://www.reuters.com/world/africa/france-donates-184000-astrazeneca-doses-senegal-via-covax-2021-06-03/

Rovan, A. (2021, May 8). Covid-19: sceptique sur la levée des brevets, l'UE exhorte les États-Unis à exporter leurs vaccins. *Le Figaro.* https://www.lefigaro.fr/international/covid-19-sceptiques-sur-la-levee-des-brevets-les-vingt-sept-exhortent-les-etats-unis-a-exporter-leurs-vaccins-20210508

Ruckert, A., Labonté, R. and Lencucha, R. (2019). Health in Canadian foreign policy: the role of norms and security interests. *Canadian Foreign Policy Journal, 25*(3), 325–341.

Sharun, K. and Dhama, K. (2021). COVID-19 vaccine diplomacy and equitable access to vaccines amid ongoing pandemic. *Archives of Medical Research, 52*(7), 761–763.

Spiegel, J.M. and Huish, B. (2009). Canadian foreign aid for global health: Human security opportunity lost, *Canadian Foreign Policy Journal, 15*(3), 60–84.

Trudeau, J. (2020, May 26). Prime Minister's remarks on keeping Canadians safe and working with other countries to fight COVID-19. Prime Minister's Office. https://pm.gc.ca/en/news/speeches/2020/05/26/prime-ministers-remarks-keeping-canadians-safe-and-working-other-countries

UNICEF. (2021, July 18). https://www.unicef.org/tunisia/communiqu%C3%A9s-de-presse/la-france-fait-don-%C3%A0-la-tunisie-dun-lot-de-vaccins-linitiative-covax

Usher, A.D. (2021). A beautiful idea: how COVAX has fallen short. *The Lancet, 397*(10292), 2322–2325.

Wee, S.L. (2021, September 11). From Asia to Africa, China promotes its vaccines to win friends. *The New York Times.* https://www.nytimes.com/2020/09/11/business/china-vaccine-diplomacy.html

Weldon, I. and Hoffman, S.J. (2021). Harnessing Canada's potential for global health leadership: leveraging strengths and confronting demons. In R. W. Murray and P. Gecelovsky (Eds.), *The Palgrave Handbook of Canada in International Affairs* (pp. 483–510). Palgrave Macmillan.

White House. (2021, June 3). FACT SHEET: Biden-Harris administration unveils strategy for global vaccine sharing, announcing allocation plan for the First 25

Million doses to be shared globally. https://www.whitehouse.gov/briefing-room/statements-releases/2021/06/03/fact-sheet-biden-harris-administration-unveils-strategy-for-global-vaccine-sharing-announcing-allocation-plan-for-the-first-25-million-doses-to-be-shared-globally/

WHO. (n.d.). *What is the ACT-accelerator.* https://www.who.int/initiatives/act-accelerator/about

WHO. (2021a, October 29). Access to COVID-19 tools funding commitment tracker. *World Health Organization.* https://www.who.int/publications/m/item/access-to-covid-19-tools-tracker

WHO. (2021b, September 24). What needs to change to enhance Covid-19 vaccine access. Statement from the Independent Allocation of Vaccines Group of COVAX. *World Health Organization.* https://www.who.int/news/item/24-09-2021-what-needs-to-change-to-enhance-covid-19-vaccine-access

York, G. (2021, September 9). Canada donates soon-to-expire vaccines to Africa as global shortage worsens. *The Globe and Mail.* https://www.theglobeandmail.com/world/article-canada-donates-soon-to-expire-vaccines-to-africa-as-global-shortage/

Zimonjic, P. and Cullen, C. (2021, March 5). Canada to take COVAX vaccines, won't share doses until every Canadian is inoculated: Anand. *CBC News.* https://www.cbc.ca/news/politics/covax-anand-vaccine-timetable-1.5939270

14

STRONG CAPACITY AND HIGH TRUST

Perceptions of crisis management and increased nationalism among Chinese civil servants

Qun Cui, Lisheng Dong, and Tom Christensen

Introduction

The COVID-19 pandemic is not merely a severe public health crisis but also a far-reaching crisis that has long-term impacts on the landscape of world politics. One of the urgent issues that has emerged is the dynamic between the pandemic and growing nationalism. While it remains uncertain whether the world will be confronted with what some have called 'COVID-19 nationalism' (Bouckaert *et al.*, 2020) or global solidarity (Ozkirimli, 2020), or if the two tendencies can coexist (Bieber, 2020b; Wang, 2021), a general impression is that the global rise of nationalism will be a lasting consequence of the pandemic (Tisdall, 2020). But there is also a prediction that the post-pandemic world could herald a new era of global solidarity with increased interdependence, and enhanced authority, adaptability, resilience of the supranational union (Barbier-Gauchard *et al.*, 2021), with the increased role of administrators, specialists, and experts bringing professionalism back into fashion (Krastev, 2020).

Growing academic discussions focus on either government responses like expanding state authority domestically and searching for blame internationally or citizen sentiment linking minorities, racial groups, and specific communities as likely virus carriers. The COVID-19 crisis is not only about objective facts but also has important subjective or perceptional elements (Christensen and Ma, 2021). In particular, nation-states have engaged in a form of pandemic response competition, with, for example, Vladimir Putin telling Russian state TV in June 2020, 'So far we've done it better than nearly any other country in the world and I assess that by the end of this we will be the best in the world' (Givens and Mistur, 2021). Civil servants in public administration can also ask, 'Are we acting more appropriately and doing better than other countries?' Political and administrative elites are a group that is less abstract than the state and has access

DOI: 10.4324/9781003273844-14

to more symmetrical information about the pandemic than ordinary citizens. The perception of civil servants toward national crisis management strategies and performance, then, offers a core reflection and influencer of increasing or decreasing nationalism.

How a national crisis management response is perceived and how this perception shapes nationalism are characteristic of a wicked problem, in that the pandemic is transboundary, unique, and characterized by a high degree of uncertainty (Christensen *et al.*, 2007). At its core, the COVID-19 crisis affects humans as organisms rather than political systems, yet perceptions of the efficacy of responses to the crisis by democratic and authoritarian states challenge states' capacity and legitimacy differently in countries with different political systems and cultures. But comparing the rise of nationalism in democratic states during the pandemic is more obvious than the fluctuation of nationalism in authoritarian contexts, which has less empirical explanations. This is perhaps because the pendulum between nationalism and globalism is more noticeable and easier to observe in democracies like European Union states and the United States where political debates in two-party systems, electoral successes of far-right parties, and announcements of anti-migrant policies can be observed and measured. But the conflict between nationalists and liberalists is empirically difficult to capture in authoritarian systems, and firsthand data are not usually accessible.

This chapter examines Chinese nationalism through the lens of the Chinese political and administrative elites through an empirical study of how Chinese municipal civil servants perceive governance capacity and legitimacy of China's response to the pandemic. The chapter examines their perceptions and addresses the following questions:

- How do civil servants assess the pandemic crisis management capacity and legitimacy of China in comparison to other nation-states?
- What are plausible causal relations between such perceptions and changing nationalism?
- How can we interpret and explain the perception and relations from an organization theory perspective?

The chapter consists of five sections. The first section defines key concepts and possible relationships between crisis management and nationalism and briefly presents some theoretical frameworks. The second section outlines the Chinese context and its approach to combating the COVID-19 pandemic. The third section introduces the methodology and data sources. The fourth section explains how respondents perceived China's pandemic crisis management in comparative perspective and considers how perception and nationalism are intertwined (based on concepts of capacity and legitimacy). The fifth section analyzes the observed perceptions through demographic, structural, and cultural perspective lenses. The chapter concludes that Chinese civil servants perceived much higher capabilities and legitimacy of the pandemic crisis management by the Chinese government in comparison with Western governments or supranational agencies, and this perception is an ideological catalyst for the increasing nationalism among them.

Concepts and theoretical frameworks

Nationalism is 'a malleable and narrow ideology that values membership in a nation more highly than belonging to other groups' (Bieber, 2020a, 10). Another ideology is globalism, which associated with vaguely defined cosmopolitan elites, venues for cross-border collaboration, and technocratic expertise more generally (Helfer, 2019). The global rise of nationalism not only has its roots in the economic, political, and sociocultural new developments such as immigration, globalization, and regionalization (Gingrich and Banks, 2006) but also closely relates to global crises, like oil crisis, financial crisis, and refugee crisis. The mechanism causing nationalism during crisis is political or economic shocks pushing nationals to pin the blame on outsiders, taking self-protectionist actions and developing nativist sentiments (Wang, 2021). A notable example in the COVID-19 pandemic is criticism of the World Health Organization (WHO) and the United States' defunding of it (Bokat-Lindell, 2020). Further, crisis also constitutes a 'critical juncture' for state governance system, that is, how the state deals with a crisis before, during, and after its occurrence can also be a catalyst for nationalism. The processes by which government organizations mitigate, define, handle, and learn from crises are referred to as crisis management (Boin *et al.*, 2008).

There are two important dimensions in crisis management, namely governance capacity and legitimacy (Christensen and Ma, 2021). Governance capacity includes formal structural/procedural features and the use of resources and how these features work in practice (Christensen *et al.*, 2016). Lodge and Wegrich (2014) divide governance capacity into four types: analytical, coordination, regulation, and delivery capacity. Coordination capacity is about bringing together disparate organizations to engage in joint action; analytical capacity is about analyzing information and providing advice as well as risk and vulnerability assessments; regulation capacity is about control, surveillance, oversight, and auditing; and delivery capacity is about handling the crisis, exercising power, and providing public services in practice. A government's legitimacy, namely public perceptions of and attitudes toward policies and collective actions, strongly influences crisis management performance and may either enhance or undermine governance capacity (Christensen *et al.*, 2016). The concept of legitimacy can be distinguished as three main types: input, throughput, and output legitimacy (Schmidt, 2013). The distinction emphasizes that citizens' assessment and acceptance of governance actions in crises might be related to politics, participatory quality, and support for political parties (input); processes within the administrative apparatus (throughput); and policies, means, and measures (output) (Christensen *et al.*, 2016).

In authoritarian states, the relationship between crisis management and nationalism is a two-way process. First, nationalism could strengthen state capacity and consolidate the legitimacy of the existing political order, especially as a tool used by the elite to maintain political power in the face of internal or external pressure (Wang and Tao, 2021). Scholars have also long debated that authoritarian countries possess advantages over their democratic counterparts in dealing with crises (San *et al.*, 2021), not only through political institutions that have a strong coercive capacity, centralized decision-making and mandate-driven implementation capacity, and state-directed mobilization and cooperation capacity (Mao, 2021), but also, more importantly, citizens with nationalist norms, values, and beliefs are more compliant and supportive of these coercive and mobilized responses, which, in turn, strengthens these capacities. Second, the perceptions, attitudes, and trust toward the home country's performance of crisis management can help to fuel nationalism. Easton (1975, 449) argued that 'evaluation of outputs and performance may help to generate, and probably at all times will help to sustain, confidence in authorities'. High self-evaluation and downplaying others' performance could lead to a stronger division between the ingroup and outgroup ('othering'), as well as facilitating a feeling of national superiority. In accordance with the two dimensions of crisis management, the perception about performance includes two parts: first, whether states present themselves as being capable of coordinating, delivering, regulating, and analyzing the approach to the crisis, and second, whether the political systems, administrative apparatus, and policy measures are appropriate.

The perception toward crisis management performance can be shaped by individual factors such as demographic background, personality, and social interaction (Ma and Christensen, 2019). But since crisis management plays out in specific institutional, political, and organizational contexts that influence performance, the structural-instrumental perspective and the cultural-institutional perspective of organization theory help in understanding how governments deal with crises (Christensen *et al.*, 2016) and in explaining the variation in perceptions of crisis management efficacy among civil servants. From the structural-instrumental perspective, different governance capacities relate to specific organizational arrangements and instruments in crisis, such as realizing cooperation through hierarchy and networks, analyzing the crisis through expert-based decision-making, regulating the society through strong control measures, and delivering emergency supplies through top-down mobilization. From the cultural-institutional perspective, informal norms and values play key roles in shaping managerial attitudes and organizational behaviors (Christensen *et al.*, 2007). This can be interpreted by the perspective that is called 'the logic of appropriateness'. Action is seen as driven by rules of appropriate or exemplary behavior, organized into institutions. Rules are followed because they are seen as natural, rightful, expected, and legitimate (March and Olsen, 2004, 1). As governmental strategies and operating procedures are homogeneous and compatible with a state's historical traditions, administrative culture, polity features, and citizens' beliefs, civil servants are more likely to consider such approaches to be 'appropriate' and practices to be 'best'.

Context

Actions and behaviors toward a crisis can be situated around three primary stages: pre-crisis prevention, crisis management, and post-crisis outcomes (Bundy *et al.*, 2017, 1664). This process requires government agencies and various entities to work together to prepare for, handle, and recover from crises (Boin and Lodge, 2016). In the pre-crisis prevention stage, the 2002–2003 severe acute respiratory syndrome (SARS) outbreak has changed public health in many ways in China (Li and Gao, 2017). Since then, intensified actions have been taken to reduce the burden of infectious diseases (Wang *et al.*, 2008) and promote the 'reliability' of organizations (Bigley and Roberts, 2001). China established a systematic and integrated national crisis management system that consists of four pillars: response plans, institutional structures, response mechanisms, and legal framework (Lu and Xue, 2016, 415). China also invested substantially in building disease prevention and control systems and provided substantial funding to the Chinese Center for Disease Control and Prevention (CCDC) and its departmental counterparts at each local level (province, municipality, county). The National Health Commission is the central department that has administrative power to handle public health crises such as epidemics and pandemics, and the CCDC is the subordinate agency that possesses professional and technical capabilities. However, lessons learned from the SARS epidemic have been gradually forgotten, and the allocation of staff and resources of public health, in combination with continuous training, updating planning in preparation for unexpected and transboundary pandemic, is insufficient in most localities.

In the response phase of crisis management, local authorities in Wuhan city and Hubei province were initially unprepared for the severe consequences of the unknown virus. The bewildering pace, ambiguity, and complexity of COVID-19 overwhelmed normal modes of situation assessment (Boin, 2009, 372) and delayed efforts to administer, make sense of situation, and prompt treatment, contain, and fight the virus (Ang, 2020), until January 19, 2020. And when the third senior experts group dispatched by the National Health Commission confirmed that the virus was transmissible through human-to-human contact, nationwide intensive and draconian measures were triggered. All available resources were quickly mobilized to support the epicenter of the virus in Wuhan and Hubei, including 42,600 medical and 965 public health personnel. Quarantine measures, roadblocks, restrictions on daily movement, extensive measurement of individual body temperature, restrictions on overseas travels, and so on were imposed by government across regions and hierarchies (Tian *et al.*, 2020). Urban residential communities and villages became numerous grids, under which a city is divided into units according to geographical layout, convenient management, and integrity of management objects, and then used the prevention and control measures (Ling and Wen, 2020; Wei *et al.*, 2021) to screen, monitor, and trace public's health status and movements. By imposing such stringent measures, the spread was successfully contained, enabling the government to 'flatten the curve' to reduce the strain on the health system in less than three months.

The recovery phase began when the General Office of the State Council issued a notice focusing on further simplifying the process of production approval and optimizing governmental services to accurately and steadily promote the resumption of production on March 4 (Xu *et al.*, 2020). But enterprises, especially most small and medium-sized enterprises, were unable to resume work because of a shortage of epidemic mitigation materials, the inability of employees to return to work, disrupted supply chains, and reduced market demand (Lu *et al.*, 2020), so the formulation of supportive policies for enterprises was followed, such as cutting taxes and fees, providing government subsidies and financial services. In May 2020, the State Council issued the *Guidelines on Normalizing COVID-19 Prevention and Control.* The new instruments and strategies were introduced to prevent a rebound in the spread of the virus. First, the rapid development and wide use of 'big data' analytics and other emerging technologies provided the government with strong technological capabilities in monitoring, detecting, and responding to potential risks (Kummitha, 2020). For example, citizens were required to show a 'health code' on their phone before accessing public transport or entering indoor spaces. This restricted the movement of people who live or work in the medium- to high-risk areas. Second, public health measures such as mass vaccination and rapid antigen testing were undertaken; the deputy director of CCDC said at the press conference that by September 6, 2021, 77.6% of the Chinese population were vaccinated (Ying, 2021). Third, since most new infections came from abroad, China increased and enforced rules for identifying, tracking, quarantining, and restricting the movement of people who entered the country.

The above contextual situation illustrates a hybrid combination of successful performance and substantial funding toward pandemic crisis management in China. On the one hand, China managed to promptly bring the pandemic under effective control by quick coordination, resource mobilization, technology application, public cooperation, and wide citizen participation in a 'nationwide campaign'. On the other hand, the process of combating the virus has been prolonged (compared to most countries having already canceled restrictive policies), and civil servants have faced increased pressure on political accountability, and pandemic control needs continue to be prioritized over a return to the economic and social order, with citizens sacrificing more of their civic rights. Moreover, China has also adopted a complicated posture with both exclusionary nationalism, which imposes stringent measures toward outside threats, and cooperative globalism, which actively participates in global health governance. But this paradoxical relationship between globalism and nationalism has dominated the official discourses and policies in China (Hou, 2020) before COVID-19: on the one hand, the Chinese Communist Party (CCP) employed nationalism to legitimize the ruling party to counter the belief vacuum arising from the decline in the Maoist faith and the so-called intrusion of Western ideology (Yang and Chen, 2021); on the other hand, the CCP engages in multilateral institutions and world politics, and external reform ideas and influences are being diffused through public administration 'learnt from the West' processes (Christensen *et al.*, 2008). Therefore, with the intertwined crisis managing approach of globalism and nationalism, whether Chinese civil servants get more national identity, or be more outward-looking, and how the perception about crisis management capabilities and legitimacy interacts with their increased or decreased nationalism, needs more empirical exploration.

Data composition and analysis

The data are taken from several surveys of municipal civil servants who participated in the training programs of Qingdao School of Administration. In China, civil servants at all levels and departments are required to attend the official training provided by Party School and School of Administration. The program usually covers ideological education such as Marxism, Xi Jinping Thought, and history of Communist Party, and also specialized courses like public administration, finance, and law. During COVID-19, one of the authors conducted questionnaire surveys in her lecture 'Public Health Crisis Management'. The respondents total 210, who come from different institutions: party committee departments (48%), government departments (52.86%), and few from public security organs, state-owned enterprises, etc.; the respondents carry various ranks in administrative hierarchy: bureau-level cadres account for 8.57%, the next section-level cadres 73 (41.9%), the third-level officials 88 (34.76%), and the lowest-ranking office clerks 18 (13.33%). Among them, 96 (45.71%) respondents were directly involved in the prevention and control of COVID-19, while others did not; 7 (3.33%) and 82 (39.05%) respondents possess very well and well about the public health crisis management knowledge, while more than half (57.14%) only know a bit.

To test the perception about crisis management capabilities and legitimacy from a comparative perspective, respondents were asked a set of questions, and their perceptions were rated on a scale from 1 (very poor/not at all) to 5 (very good/extremely) on each of the five dimensions; 'not relevant' was also an option.

How do you assess the capabilities of following organizations' reaction to the COVID-19 pandemic?

How much do you trust the following organizations in their response to the COVID-19 pandemic?

a International organization (like the WHO)
b Overseas government (like the UK and the US)
c Chinese central government
d Chinese provincial government
e Chinese municipal government

f Chinese county government
g Chinese district/township government
h Chinese grassroots self-governing organization

To test the change of nationalism before and after the pandemic, respondents were given three statements and asked to describe their perceptions: 'decreased', 'remained the same', or 'increased'.

Comparing today with before the COVID-19 pandemic, please indicate how your attitude has changed:

State protects my rights and interests.
State has capacity to tackle the crisis.
State follows the appropriate rules, processes, and procedures when tackling the crisis.

Perception across comparative dimensions

As Tables 14.1 and 14.2 show, in terms of governance capacity during the COVID-19 pandemic, overseas governments such as the UK and the US were rated the lowest with 2.19 points, while the average score for the Chinese governments was more than 4.5 points. The similar result goes with trust. So, there are evident variations of perception across country and hierarchy dimensions: the Chinese municipal civil servants reported both stronger capabilities and higher level of trust toward domestic governments than foreign governments or supranational organizations; the supportive attitudes differ for governments at different levels of China's administrative system, as the central government ranked highest compared to lower levels of government.

Second, although the reported evaluation about domestic governance capacity and legitimacy is pretty high, there is a subtle difference. The respondents are more satisfied with the coordination capacity than delivery, regulation, and analytical capacity, based on the evaluation score on crisis management performance they gave in sequence from high to low is multiple organization mobilization (4.6), emergence resource allocation (4.39), public livelihood guarantee (4.39), public opinion control (4.36), technology application (4.36), economic regulation and development (4.31), risk monitoring and early warning (4.07), scientific innovation (4.08), and investigation and learning (4.32). In addition, the civil servants in our sample strongly agree with the statements that 'state follows appropriate rules, processes and procedures when tackling the crisis' (4.73), agree with 'government do well on information publicity' (4.08), but less agree with 'I have influence on the government's crisis management policy formulation and implementation' (3.25), showing higher agreement with output legitimacy like appropriateness of policies, means, and measures than throughout legitimacy like government transparency and input legitimacy like participatory quality.

TABLE 14.1 The Chinese civil servants' assessment of different organizations' COVID-19 crisis management capabilities

Organization	*Average (E)*	*Standard deviation*
International organization (like the WHO)	3.28	1.089
Overseas government (like the UK and the US)	2.19	1.090
Chinese central government	4.83	0.610
Chinese provincial government	4.74	0.658
Chinese municipal government	4.73	0.717
Chinese county government	4.69	0.695
Chinese district/township government	4.65	0.751
Chinese grassroots self-governing organization	4.60	0.790

N = 210.

TABLE 14.2 The Chinese civil servants' trust toward different organizations' COVID-19 crisis management

Organization	*Average (E)*	*Standard deviation*
International organization (like the WHO)	3.39	1.067
Overseas government (like the UK and the US)	2.53	1.059
Chinese central government	4.81	0.605
Chinese provincial government	4.68	0.732
Chinese municipal government	4.66	0.78
Chinese county government	4.59	0.815
Chinese district/township government	4.5	0.876
Chinese grassroots self-governing organization	4.41	0.904

N = 210.

Third, when it comes to comparing the national pride sentiment prior to and after COVID-19, the survey showed a tendency of increasing nationalism among the civil servants. The most respondents think after pandemic, they put more faith in state having capacity to tackle the crisis (193, 91.9%), and the state acts appropriately and rationally when tackling the crisis (189, 90%). But fewer respondents (154, 73.33%) choose attitude increase in 'the state protects my rights and interests'. The survey also finds that the perception of governance capacity and legitimacy of home country does interlink with increasing nationalism among the civil servants. As Table 14.3 shows, Pearson's coefficient is greater than 0, and the significance is less than 0.05, indicating the higher evaluation respondents have about the supranational organization like the WHO and domestic government that are more inclined to improve the cognition about the state protecting the individuals' well-being, having required capacity, acting appropriately after pandemic, and vice versa. The similar result goes with trust. Therefore, the civil servants' perception of the domestic crisis management capacities and legitimacy does have significant influence on attitudes toward nation pride and belonging.

TABLE 14.3 Correlation analysis of the perception of different types and levels of organizations' COVID-19 crisis capacity affecting the changing attitude of national pride

	State protects my rights and interests	*State has capacity to tackle a crisis*	*State acts appropriately when tackling a crisis*
Supranational	0.303*	0.214*	0.219*
UK and US	0.04	−0.028	−0.037
Central	0.459*	0.660*	0.635*
Provincial	0.519*	0.551*	0.546*
Municipal	0.468*	0.522*	0.514*
County	0.534*	0.544*	0.532*
District/township	0.486*	0.468*	0.457*
Grassroots	0.415*	0.446*	0.432*

Note: * at a confidence level of 0.01, the correlation was significant.

On the contrary, the correlation between negative opinion of Western countries' crisis management and corresponding changes in attitudes is not significant.

Variation in perception: multivariate analyses

To explain the differences in civil servants' perceptions of capacity and trust during the pandemic, we choose following independent variables from demographic, structural, and cultural dimensions. The multivariate analysis is summed up in Table 14.4.

First, there are some relationships between gender and perceived capacity of international organizations; male respondents give higher rating to the WHO than females. But generally, the correlations related to demographic features like gender, age, and education are very weak.

Second, among administrative levels, department categories, whether participating in the COVID-19 crisis management process as independent variables, the correlations with the dependent variables are overall irrelevant. One of our hypotheses is that attitudes and behaviors of the civil servants can have impact in terms of structural characteristics: formal position in the hierarchy could have impact since the higher level comes with more decision-making power and the lower level faces more implementation pressure; the members of the party committee departments may be more likely to report pride in state capacity with political loyalty; experience of participating in the COVID-19 control directly could have more information symmetry and less influences from media reports, leading to the difference in perceptions. However, it turns out these structural features do not correlate with the civil servants' perception.

Third, professional knowledge appears to be associated with evaluation of and trust in supranational agencies and overseas governments, which means if the

TABLE 14.4 Summary of regression analysis by demographic, structural, and cultural features affecting perception of capacity and legitimacy

	Capacity evaluation			*Trust level*		
	Supranational	*Overseas*	*Central*	*Supranational*	*Overseas*	*Central*
Demographic features:						
Gender	0.011	0.283	0.233	0.159	0.868	0.301
Age	0.124	0.545	0.787	0.536	0.249	0.869
Education	0.606	0.215	0.894	0.937	0.103	0.656
Structural features:						
Administrative level	0.298	0.378	0.364	0.836	0.367	0.226
Department category	0.813	0.558	0.911	0.712	0.606	0.633
Participation in COVID-19 crisis managing	0.409	0.114	0.578	0.478	0.254	0.453
Cultural features:						
Professional knowledge	0	0.001	0.639	0.001	0.065	0.364
Centralization preference	0.210*	0.076	0.490*	0.179*	0.064	0.511*
Collectivism preference	0.226*	0.021	0.516*	0.214*	0.014	0.603*

Note: * indicates statistical significant finding.

respondent knows better about epidemiology and crisis management, he or she would look outside the performance and strategies across the world in a more rational way. But whether having the knowledge or not, all respondents give high score to domestic governments. The most important explanatory factors are centralization and collectivism preference in the culture dimension. The civil servants in our sample who agreed more with 'the COVID-19 crisis showed that the central government should furfure centralize the power from localities and society', 'I can sacrifice my individual rights if it is necessary for pandemic control', are also more likely to report both stronger capabilities and higher level of trust in governments of the home country.

Discussion

This chapter has demonstrated that the outputs and performances of China's COVID-19 crisis management were evaluated very highly by the Chinese municipal civil servants. This could help to increase the confidence in the authoritarian system. While civil servants have access to the messages from the media under state control, as political-administrative elites, they are also part of the 'system'. In the survey responses, when asked why crisis management strategies and performance in combating the COVID-19 pandemic differed between countries, the most common explanations are related to political institutions and structures: 70.95%, 45.24%, and 26.67% of the respondents chose the leadership of ruling party, the strategy of the national leader, and the policy design of central government as major differences, respectively. The remaining perceptions of differences were as follows: cultural orientation in society (20%), local government policy implementation (17.62%),[1] economic development level (10%), public health resources reserve (8.57%), and the message delivered by media (0.48%). In an authoritarian context like China, the civil servants' perceptions of the state capacities and legitimacy are mainly shaped by both institutional arrangements and culture preferences.

First, the 'all-of-Government' approach enhanced coordination capacity by bringing together disparate governmental organizations at different levels and of different types to work closely on decision-making and implementation under conditions of uncertainty and urgency. Strong coordination capacity means government agencies and various entities can work together to prepare for, handle, and recover from crises (Boin and Lodge, 2016). Vertically, China demonstrated strong leadership and central direction and clear-cut responsibilities and chains of command throughout the hierarchy (Rykkja and Lægreid, 2014). President Xi Jinping focused his attention on the pandemic in public speeches, and a nationwide, top-down action began: the Central Committee of the Communist Party (CCCP) set up the Leading Group for Pandemic Response, sent the Steering Group (the team leader is a vice premier) to Hubei, and organized the Chinese People's Liberation Army and other provinces and cities sending personnel and supplies. Each level of administration had its own Pandemic Prevention and Control Headquarters while accepting the steering and guidance from the superior and central government to keep a balance between centralization (strong leadership, hierarchical control, and command) and decentralization (flexibility, improvisation, diversity, and local autonomy) (Kettl, 2003). Horizontally, the State Council formulated the Joint Prevention and Control Mechanism spanning 32 ministries and set up functional groups based on medical treatment, scientific research, publicity, foreign affairs, logistics support, and so on. Similar cross-departmental coordination was also organized at each local level, and different departments worked together in teams and networks (Christensen and Lægreid, 2020). Since political centralization and intergovernmental coordination are conducive to effective information gathering and sharing, timely decision-making, and the implementation of crisis response strategies (Comfort, 2007), institutional quality of the COVID-19 crisis management has been improved (Persson and Povitkina, 2017).

Second, personnel control increased the regulatory capacity of state by providing the mechanism for supervising civil servants and public administrations to implement policies, same as top-down intensive and temporary regulations made a basis for mandatory directives that society and citizens need to comply.

Different from officials in democratic countries under electoral accountability, Chinese civil servants are accountable to their territorial Party Committees, their territorial leaders and their Party Committees' Organization Departments, and their departmental counterparts at superior levels. On January 28, 2020, the CCCP issued the *Notice on Strengthening the Party's Leadership, Providing Strong Political Guarantee to Win the Battle against COVID-19*, which introduced the evaluation and accountability mechanisms. The civil servants who have outstanding performance in control of the virus spread were to be praised, and those who were deemed irresponsible, implemented policy poorly, or behaved fraudulently were to be punished such as receiving admonishment talks, being transferred to other posts or removed from positions. The basis is mainly that the implementation of prevention and control measures is not strong enough, and the performance of duties is inadequate, which leads to the rebound and spread of the epidemic. For example, in Nanjing, the airport staff were infected during the disinfection of the aircraft, which led to the spread of the epidemic to the city. In this incident, many local leaders including the director of the Nanjing Municipal Health Commission were removed from their posts. This top-down personnel rewards and punishments mechanism provided local officials with incentives and mandates to implement policies effectively (Lam and Chan, 2015). China also differs from Western democratic countries in that instead of following laws passed in parliament, crisis management can be implemented quickly during times of uncertainty, instability, complexity, and ambiguity through top-down temporary regulations. Although China has laws such as the *Infectious Disease Prevention Act*, the law did not provide systematic and detailed guidance on how to address an unprecedented and unforeseeable crisis. By making and updating regulations quickly, the response can be both adaptive to the changing process of the pandemic and consistent to the new policy intent of the central government. However, because of risks from the level-by-level responsibility system and the pressure imposed by a strict administrative hierarchy, the civil servants in our sample showed less participation efficacy in responding to the pandemic ('I have influence on the government's crisis management policy formulation and implementation').

Third, powerful health care resource control and allocation reflected the delivery capacity that government is able to provide public services for citizens during crisis. Access to health care remains a critical pillar in dealing with the COVID-19 pandemic (Ho and Dascalu, 2020). Under the philosophy of 'leaving no one behind', the Chinese media delivered the messages that governments had done the utmost in facility construction and resource integration. For example, two hospitals were established in ten days to receive patients in Wuhan; shortages in personal protective equipment caused by rising demand resulted in the daily production capacity of masks in China exceeding 110 million units by the by the end of February 2020 (Zhang *et al.*, 2020). Further, China was at the forefront of global efforts to develop COVID-19 vaccines and has five fast-tracked candidates at the final stage, large-scale human clinical trials testing phase in 2020

(Yin *et al.*, 2021,), and by July, 2021, chief engineer of Chinese Ministry of Industry and Information Technology said at a press conference that China has already supplied 1.4 billion doses of free vaccines for domestic citizens, and estimates reveal that vaccine manufacturing capacity can reach 5 billion doses annually (Zhang, 2021). More importantly, the government presented itself as a 'wellbeing guardian' capable of quickly providing public goods including free and equitable access to COVID-19 treatments and vaccines.

Fourth, real-time risk communication and professional voices improved the analytical capacity by analyzing information, assessing risk, and adjusting strategies on the base of consensus among public administrations, professional expects, and public. Denied access to reliable information and online rumors aggravated public disorder and chaos in the early days of the pandemic. But soon after, the state became proactive in providing the necessary information to prevent widespread panic (Liu and Chan, 2018). Since January 21, 2020, the National Health Commission began publishing daily pandemic information on its website. Local governments also released timely information through press briefings and social media. Even the results of epidemiological investigations and new infected peoples' movements had been published. Combined with the official data, professional advice such as precautionary strategies based on health criteria were also provided. Further, public health experts and clinical specialists were invited to participate in and contribute to policy formulation and implementation processes. Experts played a vital role in risk communication, such as Zhong Nanshan, China's top respiratory expert, and Zhang Wenhong, a Shanghai-based infectious disease specialist. Such experts helped predict the pandemic's spread, interpret prevention and control policies, stabilize public sentiment, and eliminate hesitancy in receiving vaccine by addressing the media.

Fifth, 'all-of-society' mechanisms supported the picture of 'we're united as one' and 'circle the wagons'. Tackling crises depends not only on the government but also on public compliance and social mobilization and cooperation (Bynander and Nohrstedt, 2019). China's predominant crisis management approach has been characterized by campaign-style governance, which refers primarily to the temporary political mobilization of government and social resources to address urgent issues (Liu *et al.*, 2015). On the one hand, government uses the advantage of the authoritarian regime to regulate and coerce the society, such as control and oversight of the life and production activates in communities and workplaces. On the other hand, China tends be more supportive on state–society relationships in risk-managing processes. The assistance from non-state actors like civil society organizations (CSOs) encouraged to focus on specific themes of pandemic control, ranging from raising donations and purchasing emergency supplies to providing mental health initiatives. CSOs also took responsibility for isolating those residents who lived in 'high-risk' areas or have traveled back from there, helping solve practical life difficulties so they can stay at home (Zhang *et al.*, 2020). The integration of citizen-led volunteering and grassroots bureaucratic control helped to make government-led mobilization more rationalized, because structurally, this adds more elements of involvement in multilateral governance instead of only coercing by government, and culturally, it also makes sense of solidarity that individuals need to sacrifice some freedom to avoid threatening the overall safety and health.

Sixth, highlighting the West–China contrast enhanced the perceived output legitimacy of the Chinese crisis management. On the one hand, Chinese official media outlets portrayed China as a cooperative, responsible power in combating the global pandemic relative to some irresponsible and incapable Western powers (Yang and Chen, 2021). News like 'herd immunity strategy in the UK' and 'state governments criticize the failure of the US federal government' made the headlines; naturally the Chinese civil servants linked more infectious cases and higher death rates to the democratic countries' soft mitigation strategy, slow response, and confrontational policy. On the other hand, propagating the Chinese official discourse on the 'Community of Shared Destiny for Mankind' and 'Global Community of Health for All', the Chinese media showed that China proactively collaborated with multilateral institutions such as the United Nations, the WHO, and other G20 countries and provided funding and clinical support to developing countries affected by the global pandemic. Related news reporting and comments also included 'Trump Scapegoating of China' and 'Trump Referred to the "Chinese Virus"' (Boylan *et al.*, 2021). Such headlines furthered the view that international organizations like the WHO aligned with China, while the US-led external provocation was viewed as irrational and groundless, and the world should look up to and thank China (Christensen and Ma, 2021). Popular sentiment in China reflected this view, with a viral WeChat post asking the West, 'Why don't they just copy our homework?'

Seventh, the security-first, performance-paramount, and central authority worship culture strengthened the perception of capacity and legitimacy. Civil liberties—such as freedom of expression, religion, movement, assembly, and privacy, as well as due process and nondiscrimination—are crucial political values in a democratic society, but during times of national threat, these rights and liberties may be in conflict with the situational imperatives of security (Etzioni, 2005). The pandemic broke out first in China, and the Chinese civil servants perceived high risks in their environment, so they were motivated to relinquish some civil rights and tolerated unprecedented intervention in exchange for societal security. Another key factor was the lack of appreciation for procedural justice in China's legal and political traditions. China, since Deng Xiaoping, has taken a pragmatic strategy of 'performance legitimacy', which means that the government relied on accomplishing concrete goals such as economic growth, social stability, and national unity, to retain its legitimacy (Zhu, 2011). So, lower quality of participation efficacy, accountability, transparency, representation, and inclusiveness in input and throughput legitimacy can be traded off with better output legitimacy that matches the civil servants' expectations: specifically, fewer cases of infections and a stable political order. In addition, the nationalist ideology had already been created to sustain the legitimacy of the ruling party and promoted through a top-down approach in an instrumentalist fashion in China (Zhao, 2000). The Chinese state and party are integrated and inseparable (Zhu, 2011)—strong leadership, a noncompetitive regime and a unitary state, and capable central government are required. Accordingly, the results of our survey proved culture preference for strengthening centralization, that most respondents agreed 'corona crisis showed that the central government should furfure centralize the power from localities and society', and this result related to the perception of both stronger capabilities and higher level of trust in governments of the home country.

Conclusion

The main finding from our survey was that the Chinese civil servants perceived much higher capabilities and legitimacy of the pandemic crisis management by the Chinese government in comparison with Western governments or supranational agencies. When it comes to explaining variations in perception, China has individual cultural preferences for centralization and collectivism, but this is also related to the specific institutional, political, and culture contexts in which the Chinese civil servants we surveyed are embedded. First is the adaptive and campaign-style crisis management through institutional modification, including a series of policy adjustments in government structures, administrative regulations, and accountability mechanisms, which temporarily solved institutional frictions between different levels and types of actors. Second is the reputation management strategies that designed and maintained multiple positive images of China as a transparent government, a world leader in response to the pandemic, a public welfare guardian, and national solidarity, which influenced civil servants' beliefs, attitudes and expectations.

While the existing literature suggests that the COVID-19 crisis itself caused the increasing nationalism, this chapter proved that the perception of crisis management strategies and performance could be a core reflection and influencer too. A benefit of this perception of high-performance evaluation and trust was that the Chinese civil servants' national pride and sense of belonging increased significantly from an already high level during the pandemic crisis. The Chinese case could be reflection of other authoritarian countries, that they may reap the benefits of strong coordination capability and output legitimacy in crisis management and then exacerbate pursuit of quick results and bias against democratic institutions, but neglecting procedural justice, normalized accountability, institutionalized coordination, and learning from others in the post-COVID-19 era. However, another lesson that authoritarian countries can learn from China is nationalism in crisis times is not necessarily extreme or exclusionary but takes elements of globalism in respecting public health professionals, coordinating international assistance, and cooperation. Therefore, the challenge ahead for China is using both nationalism and globalism to enhance the governance capacity and legitimacy in the long term and reach a better balance between emphasizing the national identity of 'Chinese characteristics' and seeking statecraft when look outward.

Note

1 According to the 1982 Constitution, China has three levels of local government: province (autonomous regions or centrally administered municipalities), county (autonomous county or county-level city), and township (ethnic township, town). In reality, however, four levels of local government exist for most of the country. Between the province and county, there is a level of prefectural government as the provincial government's dispatched office without its own People's Congress. But many cities carrying this rank are full-fledged level of government with their People's Congresses (Zhong, 2015). In practice, the civil servants regard all other levels except for the central government as the local government. Here, the local government refers to all four levels of province, municipality, county, and township.

References

Ang, Y. Y. (2020). When COVID-19 meets centralized, personalized power. *Nature Human Behaviour, 4*, 445–447.

Barbier-Gauchard, A., Dai, M., Mainguy, C., Saadaoui, J., Sidiropoulos, M., Terraz, I., and Trabelsi, J. (2021). Towards a more resilient European Union after the COVID-19 crisis. *Eurasian Economic Review, 11* (2021) 321–348.

Bieber, F. (2020a). Global nationalism in times of the COVID-19 pandemic. *Nationalities Papers, 50*(1), 13–25.

Bieber, F. (2020b). *Debating nationalism: The global spread of nations.* London, Bloomsbury Academic.

Bigley, G. A., & Roberts, K. H. (2001). The Incident Command System: High-Reliability Organizing for Complex and Volatile Task Environments. *The Academy of Management Journal, 44*(6), 1281–1299.

Boin, A. (2009). The new world of crises and crisis management: Implications for policymaking and research. *Review of Policy Research, 26*(4), 367–377.

Boin, A., and Lodge, M. (2016). Designing resilient institutions for transboundary crisis management: A time for public administration. *Public Administration, 94*(2), 289–298.

Boin, A., McConnell, A., and Hart, P. T. (Eds.). (2008). *Governing after crisis: The politics of investigation, accountability and learning.* Cambridge: Cambridge University Press.

Bokat-Lindell, S. (2020). Is the Coronavirus killing the World Health Organization. *The New York Times.* Accessed September 20, 2021. https://www.nytimes.com/2020/07/07/opinion/Coronavirus-world-health-organization.html.

Bouckaert, G., Galli, D., Kuhlmann, S., Reiter, R., and Van Hecke, S. (2020). European coronationalism? A Hot Spot Governing a Pandemic Crisis. *Public Administration Review*, 10.1111/puar.13242. Advance online publication.

Boylan, B. M., McBeath, J., and Wang, B. (2021). US–China relations: Nationalism, the trade war, and COVID-19. *Fudan Journal of the Humanities and Social Sciences, 14*(1), 23–40.

Bundy, J., Pfarrer, M. D., Short, C. E., and Coombs, W. T. (2017). Crises and crisis management: Integration, interpretation, and research development. *Journal of Management, 43*(6), 1661–1692.

Bynander, F., and Nohrstedt, D. (2019). *Collaborative crisis management: Inter-organizational approaches to extreme events* (pp. 1–12). Routledge.

Christensen, T., and Lægreid, P. (2020). Balancing governance capacity and legitimacy: How the Norwegian government handled the COVID-19 crisis as a high performer. *Public Administration Review, 80*(5), 774–779.

Christensen, T., Lægreid, P., and Røvik, K. A. (2007). *Organization theory and the public sector: Instrument, culture and myth*. Aldershot, UK: Ashgate.

Christensen, T., Lægreid, P., and Rykkja, L. H. (2016). Organizing for crisis management: Building governance capacity and legitimacy. *Public Administration Review, 76*(6), 887–897.

Christensen, T., Lisheng, D., and Painter, M. (2008). Administrative reform in China's central government—how much learning from the West? *International Review of Administrative Sciences, 74*(3), 351–371.

Christensen, T., and Ma, L. (2021). Comparing SARS and COVID-19: Challenges of governance capacity and legitimacy. *Public Organization Review, 21* (2021), 629–645.

Comfort, L. K. (2007) Crisis management in hindsight: Cognition, communication, coordination, and control. *Public Administration Review, 67*(S1), 189–197.

Easton, D. (1975). A re-assessment of the concept of political support. *British Journal of Political Science, 5*(4), 435–457.

Etzioni, A. (2005). *How patriotic is the Patriot Act?: Freedom versus security in the age of terrorism*. Abingdon, Routledge.

Gingrich, A., and Banks, M. (Eds.). (2006). *Neo-nationalism in Europe and beyond: Perspectives from social anthropology*. New York: Berghahn Books.

Givens, J. W., and Mistur, E. (2021). The sincerest form of flattery: Nationalist emulation during the COVID-19 pandemic. *Journal of Chinese Political Science, 26*(1), 213–234.

Helfer, L. R. (2019). The ILO at 100: Institutional innovation in an era of populism. *AJIL Unbound, 113*, 396–401.

Ho, A., and Dascalu, I. (2020). Global Disparity and solidarity in a pandemic. Global Disparity and solidarity in a pandemic. *Hastings Center Report, 50*(3), 65–67.

Hou, X. (2020). The paradox of nationalism and globalism: China's participation in global capitalism. *The Wiley Blackwell Companion to Race, Ethnicity, and Nationalism*, 119–128.

Kettl, D. F. (2003). Contingent coordination: Practical and theoretical puzzles for homeland security. *The American Review of Public Administration, 33*(3), 253–277.

Krastev, I. (2020). Seven early lessons from the Coronavirus. *European Council on Foreign Relations*.

Kummitha, R. K. R. (2020). Smart technologies for fighting pandemics: The techno- and human-driven approaches in controlling the virus transmission. *Government Information Quarterly, 37*(3), 101481.

Lam, W. F., and Chan, K. N. (2015). How authoritarianism intensifies punctuated equilibrium: The dynamics of policy attention in Hong Kong. *Governance, 28*(4), 549–570.

Li, Z., and Gao, G. F. (2017). Infectious disease trends in China since the SARS outbreak. *The Lancet Infectious Diseases, 17*(11), 1113–1115.

Ling, C., and Wen, X. (2020). Community grid management is an important measure to contain the spread of novel Coronavirus pneumonia (COVID-19). *Epidemiology and Infection*, 148, e167.

Liu, N. N., Lo, C. W.-H., Zhan, X., and Wang, W. (2015). Campaign-style enforcement and regulatory compliance. *Public Administration Review, 75*(1), 85–95.

Liu, Y., and Chan, R. H. Y. (2018). The framework of crisis-induced agenda setting in China. *Asia and the Pacific Policy Studies, 5*(1), 18–33.
Lodge, M., and Wegrich, K. (2014). Administrative capacities. In *The Governance Report* 2014 (pp. 27–48). Oxford: Oxford University Press.
Lu, X., and Xue, L. (2016). Managing the unexpected: Sense-making in the Chinese emergency management system. *Public Administration, 94*(2), 414–429.
Lu, Y., Wu, J., Peng, J., and Lu, L. (2020). The perceived impact of the COVID-19 epidemic: Evidence from a sample of 4807 SMEs in Sichuan Province, China. *Environmental Hazards, 19*(4), 323–340.
Ma, L., and Christensen, T. (2019). Government trust, social trust, and citizens' risk concerns: Evidence from crisis management in China. *Public Performance and Management Review, 42*(2), 383–404.
Mao, Y. (2021). Political institutions, state capacity, and crisis management: A comparison of China and South Korea. *International Political Science Review, 42*(3), 316–332.
March, J. G., and Olsen, J. P. (2004). The logic of appropriateness. *In The Oxford handbook of political science.* Accessed November 11, 2021. https://www.oxfordhandbooks.com/view/10.1093/oxfordhb/9780199604456.001.0001/oxfordhb-9780199604456-e-024.
Ozkirimli, U. (2020). Coronationalism? *Open Democracy*, April 14, 2020. Accessed October 8, 2021. https://www.opendemocracy.net/en/can-europe-make-it/coronationalism/
Persson, T. A., and Povitkina, M. (2017) 'Gimme Shelter': The role of democracy and institutional quality in disaster preparedness. *Political Research Quarterly, 70*(4), 833–847.
Rykkja, L. H., and Lægreid, P. (2014). Coordinating for crisis management in Norway after the terrorist attack in 2011. In *Organizing for coordination in the public sector* (pp. 66–77). London: Palgrave Macmillan.
San, S., Bastug, M. F., and Basli, H. (2021). Crisis management in authoritarian regimes: A comparative study of COVID-19 responses in Turkey and Iran. *Global Public Health, 16*(4), 485–501.
Schmidt, V. A. (2013). Democracy and legitimacy in the European Union revisited: Input, output and 'throughput'. *Political Studies, 61*(1), 2–22.
Tian, H., Liu, Y., Li, Y., Wu, C.-H., Chen, B., Kraemer, M. U. G., Li, B., Cai, J., Xu, B., Yang, Q., Wang, B., Yang, P., Cui, Y., Song, Y., Zheng, P., Wang, Q., Bjornstad, O. N., Yang, R., Grenfell, B. T., Pybus, O. G., and Dye, C. (2020). An investigation of transmission control measures during the first 50 days of the COVID-19 epidemic in China. *Science, 368*(6491), 638–642.
Tisdall, S. (2020). Power, equality, nationalism: How the pandemic will reshape the world. *The Guardian, 28*, 717.
Wang, Z. (2021). From Crisis to Nationalism? *Chinese Political Science Review, 6*(1), 20–39.
Wang, Z., and Tao, Y. (2021). Many nationalisms, one disaster: Categories, attitudes and evolution of Chinese nationalism on social media during the COVID-19 pandemic. *Journal of Chinese Political Science, 26*, 525–548 (2021)
Wang, L., Wang, Y., Jin, S., Wu, Z., Chin, D. P., Koplan, J. P., and Wilson, M. E. (2008). Emergence and control of infectious diseases in China. *The Lancet, 372*(9649), 1598–1605.
Wei, Y., Ye, Z., Cui, M., and Wei, X. (2021). COVID-19 prevention and control in China: Grid governance. *Journal of Public Health, 43*(1), 76–81.
Xu, X., Wang, S., Dong, J., Shen, Z., and Xu, S. (2020). An analysis of the domestic resumption of social production and life under the COVID-19 epidemic. *PLoS One, 15*(7), e0236387.

Yang, Y., and Chen, X. (2021). Globalism or nationalism? The paradox of Chinese official discourse in the context of the COVID-19 outbreak. *Journal of Chinese Political Science, 26*(1), 89–113.

Ying, N. (2021). 77.6% of the Chinese population were vaccinated. Chinanews, September 7, 2021. Accessed October 2, 2021. https://baijiahao.baidu.com/s?id=1710248690827758349andwfr=spiderandfor=pc

Yin, F., Wu, Z., Xia, X., Ji, M., Wang, Y., and Hu, Z. (2021). Unfolding the determinants of COVID-19 vaccine acceptance in China. *Journal of Medical Internet Research,* 23(1), e26089.

Zhang, S., Wang, Z., Chang, R., Wang, H., Xu, C., Yu, X.,4 Cai, Y. (2020). COVID-19 containment: China provides important lessons for global response. *Frontiers of Medicine, 14*(2), 215–219.

Zhang, X. X. (2021). 5 billion vaccines can be produced annually. Xinhuanews, July 16, 2021. Accessed October 1, 2021. http://www.gov.cn/xinwen/2021-07/16/content_5625452.htm

Zhu, Y. (2011). 'Performance legitimacy' and China's political adaptation strategy. *Journal of Chinese Political Science, 16*(2), 123–140.

Zhao, S. (2000). Chinese nationalism and its international orientations. *Political Science Quarterly, 115*(1), 1–33.

15

CHINA'S INWARD- AND OUTWARD-FACING IDENTITIES

Post-COVID challenges for China and the international rules-based order

Yan Bennett

Introduction

Since its opening up in the late 1970s, China has been considered a rising power because of its international aspirations and economic growth, which has been 'the fastest sustained expansion by a major economy in history' (Morrison, 2019, p. 1). Chinese leaders are determined to see China reach high-income status, which they hope will be sometime during its 14th Five-Year Plan (2021–2025) period (Chu, 2021). For this ambitious goal to be achieved, China must aggressively engage in economic development, overcome the middle-income trap, accelerate the growth of its domestic markets and technological capabilities, and engage in deepening reforms, all within the next four years.

In the past decade, China's intense economic growth has been marked by the establishment of state-led plans that include development projects around the world. The Belt and Road Initiative (BRI), launched in 2013 by Chinese Communist Party (CCP) General Secretary Xi Jinping, is intended to be an extensive assemblage of development and investment initiatives stretching from East Asia to Europe, significantly expanding China's economic and political influence. The BRI allows China to cultivate new investment opportunities and markets and will catapult China into high-income status by helping to raise Chinese personal incomes and domestic consumption.

While the BRI is not aid in the traditional Western sense, it has nonetheless been instituted as one of main planks in China's bold economic international development strategy (State Council Information Office, 2021). The BRI was written into the CCP charter at the 19th Party Congress in 2017. It was stated that the BRI will 'achieve policy, infrastructure, trade, financial, and people-to-people connectivity and thus build a new platform for international co-operation to create new drivers of shared development' (Xi, 2017b, para. 11). The particular

DOI: 10.4324/9781003273844-15

wording used by Xi indicates that China intends to follow a different international development strategy than that of other nations. As a core tenet of such a strategy, this chapter will show that the achievement of BRI objectives is an essential part of China's foreign policy. Enshrined within China's core principles, the BRI becomes 'impossible to abandon' and, moreover, is 'likely to impose on foreign states a corresponding obligation to engage with the Belt and Road if they want to engage with China' (Maçães, 2019, p. 41).

Many observers see China's contemporary state-to-state and multilateral interactions, including the BRI, as indicative of great power aspirations and advance the notion that China's growing strength will result in an adversarial contest with the United States and its allies (Mearsheimer, 2014). Beckley and Brands (2021), however, propose China has already peaked and, like one cornered, is engaging in desperate measures against what it sees as a closing window of opportunity; 'if there is a formula for aggression by a peaking power, China exhibits the key elements' (Beckley and Brands, 2021, para. 21).

Concurrent with BRI expansion and theories of China's global aspirations is the COVID-19 pandemic, which has allowed China to extend humanitarian assistance in the form of medical supplies and vaccine donations and sales. China has been using the pandemic to present itself as a responsible international leader through COVID-related aid while nurturing favourable public opinion at home. As this chapter observes, both the BRI and COVID-19 have placed Chinese humanitarian and development aid under scrutiny and criticism by developed nations, the 'Global North', while such measures are welcomed by the 'Global South' (Mahler, 2017, para. 1; Mulakala and Ji, 2020, p. 2). The mixed responses to China's COVID-19 assistance and BRI development aid provide discourse that help examine the effectiveness of China's soft power strategies. Some argue that China's extension of humanitarian assistance to countries with few resources, inadequate infrastructure, and weak public health systems provides an opportunity for China to improve its global image (Kuruwita, 2020, para. 9). Others, primarily in the Global North, see China taking advantage of a tragedy of its own making to extend the reach of its soft power over weak and vulnerable states. These commentaries have even interpreted China's humanitarian response as a 'whitewash' of its alleged initial domestic 'coverup' of the COVID-19 crisis and its initial draconian 'zero-covid' strategy, in which the central government 'locked people into their homes, forced patients to take untested medications, and imposed 40-day quarantines at gunpoint' (Bhattacharya and Boudreaux, 2021, para. 2). Yet another camp theorizes that China's humanitarian effort is just another factor in its wider geostrategic competition with the United States (Mulakala and Ji, 2020, para. 2).

In order to understand both internal and external narratives about China, critical discourse analysis utilizing social constructivism within international relations theory is employed, which places language and linguistic practices at the forefront of interpretation and helps us understand how 'discursive, linguistic, and textual boundaries justify certain claims to truth' (Debrix, 2003,

p. xii). Language has a constructivist function in that 'by doing what we do with each other and saying what we say to each other', 'we make the world what it is' (Onuf, 2012, p. 4). Underlying this interpretation is Foucault's notion of the relationships between discursive statements and how they lead to discursive formations and limitations (Foucault, 1972). This methodology heavily uses quoted text in order to examine these discursive interrelations, not to prove the truth of whatever they assert but to understand the current dialogue on and about China and how this has affected the development of China's inward and outward identities.

The first section is a summary of what China potentially envisions for a future world order in which it is a far more influential player, what norms and principles animate that world order, and what role the current great powers will play. The second section details the soft power outcomes of the BRI, focusing on its discursive effects. The third section offers an analysis of China's humanitarian aid initiatives through mask and vaccine diplomacy. The conclusion briefly evaluates China's soft power approach as implemented through development and humanitarian aid and how this may affect global norms and discourse.

China's rise in a liberal world order in transition

Within the context of geopolitical shifts in the 21st century, a more assertive Chinese statecraft has emerged under Xi, indicating that 'China now actively seeks to shape international norms and institutions and forcefully asserts its presence on the global stage' (Chatzky and McBride, 2020, para. 11). While China's foreign policy in the past has been characterized as 'hide your capacities and bide your time', Xi's more aggressive international activism deviates from this long-held aphorism (Doshi, 2019, para. 4). Lee's (2021) analysis of China's development model contends that 'China wants to benefit from the developments of the West without embracing its ideals and norms' and 'does not want to accept all the international rules and laws which it did not play a part in formulating' (p. 8). Discourse on China's international intentions tends to show that perceptions lean towards a belief that China is challenging American leadership on a number of fronts to realize a vision of China in which socialism with Chinese characteristics is upheld and a moderately prosperous society is built and the Chinese Dream of national rejuvenation is achieved (Xi, 2017b, para. 3).

As part of its international economic policy initiatives, the Global South looms large in China's narrative. In 1974, Mao Zedong proposed his 'Three Worlds' theory that the international system was divided into three worlds, with the 'third world' being where China and most of the world resided (Mao, 1994, p. 454). Other connections to the Global South have been articulated in the Five Principles of Peaceful Coexistence, namely, mutual respect for sovereignty and territorial integrity, mutual non-aggression, non-interference in each other's internal affairs, equality and mutual benefit, and peaceful coexistence, which Xi reiterated in 2014 at a joint meeting with India and Myanmar (Xi, 2014).

Courtney Fung (2016) argues that China's self-identification with the Global South remains highly salient despite its rising economic might. Overall, identification with the Global South is a central tenet of Beijing's worldview and its soft power approaches.

To predict how world order might be reshaped by China, scholars have applied a 'realist' or 'neorealist' paradigm on China's rise, in which competition between states is a zero-sum game and China's rise to great power status must inevitably undermine great powers in the liberal world order, particularly the United States (Friedberg, 2012; Mearsheimer, 2006, 2010, 2014; Roy, 2013; Tellis, 2013). By contrast, Larson posits China 'wants to restore its former status as a great power, but at the same time to preserve its culture and norms without assimilating Western liberal values' (Larson, 2015, p. 324). It seems that Larson's view is the more likely scenario in that China has shown it is developing a model of 'socialist political democracy showing distinctive Chinese characteristics', as stated in a 2005 white paper (State Council Information Office, 2005, p. 4). In a communique circulated in April 2013, the CCP leadership warned against universal values (*pushi jiazi*), civil society as a way to dismantle the Party's social foundation, neoliberalism, and questioning socialism with Chinese characteristics (Central Committee of the Communist Party of China's General Office, 2013). A synthesis of these directives implies that, implicit among the goals articulated in Xi's speech to the 19th CCP National Congress, China is to reassume its position as a great power not within the confines of the current world order but in a context that would better conform with the Chinese Dream of national rejuvenation and Chinese values. As viewed from the West, China has been seen as unwilling to accede to international norms on issues such as the promotion of human rights and civil liberties within its borders, reformation of its economy along the lines of the liberal economic model as required by the World Trade Organization (WTO), and observation of territorial boundaries in accordance with internationally established law, distinguishing China's rise from other nations that have flourished in the current liberal world order (Bader, 2016; de Graaff *et al.*, 2020; Fish, 2017; Larson, 2015; *Sources on Universal Values*, 2010; The debate over universal values, 2010). China's growing authoritarianism at home, increasingly nationalistic rhetoric, and progressively more assertive behaviour abroad appear to the West as corroborating evidence that Beijing is attempting to revise the status quo in ways that better suit its Chinese Dream.

Comprehending this complex interplay of discourse and action has been difficult for traditional scholars of international relations because when Xi speaks of China's 'peaceful rise' and states that it 'will never seek hegemony' (Wang, 2018, para. 6), Beijing is at the same time making threatening sorties near Taiwanese airspace (Buckley and Qin, 2021), building makeshift islands in the South China Sea to assert highly disputed territorial claims (Duong, 2015), and punishing its trade partners (Harrell *et al.*, 2018). At the same time, Xi has continued the official narrative of building a society based on harmonious relations between 'man and environment, between social classes, and between China and foreign countries' (Overholt, 2012, p. 135). Yet China's oppression of ethnic Uyghurs (Maizland, 2021), authoritarian extinguishment of human and civil rights in Hong Kong (Fan, 2021), and its increasingly threatening and belligerent foreign policy (Carter, 2019; Kelly, 2014; Pence, 2020) belie a 'harmonious' metanarrative. China's actions create cognitive dissonance with the effect of making interpretation of its actions more contested.

Many American observers now consider China to be the equivalent of the Cold War-era Soviet Union, that is, America's primary global competitor and ideological foe. Noted scholars John Mearsheimer and Graham Alison write about increased prospects for war when an emerging power challenges an existing hegemon (Allison, 2017; Mearsheimer, 2006, 2014, 2020). Even previously dovish American officials now consider China the 'most dynamic and formidable competitor in modern history' (Campbell and Ratner, 2018, p. 70). Cold War historian Melvyn Leffler notes, however, that analogizing this current competition as a new Cold War is misleading. Leffler argues that the context in which the 'China challenge' exists is much different than the environment that emerged following World War II (Leffler, 2019a, pp. 209–210). What others often fail to realize, Leffler asserts, is that China has many problems that will be difficult to overcome. Right in China's neighbourhood are challenges that include the economically strong countries of Japan and South Korea, a robust and nationalistic India, a revanchist Russia—which is now warring with Ukraine—and the continuing dilemma of Taiwan (Leffler, 2019b). China must balance against these regional powers in order to achieve geostrategic dominance, no easy feat, says Leffler (Leffler, 2019b).

Nonetheless, current thinking on China is not entirely wrong on the aggression and assertiveness of China's rise and now, perhaps, its apex. Michael Beckley and Hal Brands propose China's decades-long, supercharged advance is now encountering strong headwinds; China has peaked in terms of economic growth and is now encountering problems due to an ageing population and scarcity in natural resources. Additionally, China's increasingly steep slide to totalitarianism is causing it to lose 'access to the welcoming world that once enabled its advance'. Carl Minzner also notes China's rise has been significantly undermined by China's authoritarian revival exacerbated by social and political factors that are of its own making. Beckley and Brands observe that a likely and more frightening possibility is that China's leaders recognize they have arrived at 'peak China' and will act more belligerently because they are running out of time. They note that when a nation like China wants to reorder the world and sees that its time and ability to do so are waning, it will make a 'low-probability lunge for success rather than suffering a humiliating descent' (Beckley and Brands, 2021b, para. 3–4, 30). Xi's increasing risk tolerance may reflect Beijing's realization that its 'window of strategic opportunity is sliding shut', presaging a dangerous decade for the liberal world order (Erickson and Collins, 2021, para. 7).

Based on the preceding evidence and assuming China is not abiding by traditional international relations theories but one that is of its own making and oriented towards the goals of national rejuvenation, a degree of great power status, and the ability to defend its national interests from foreign interference, it appears that the contours of this international order do not include a China that intentionally seeks unipolar hegemony or a bipolar, Cold War–style world. What we know of China's intentions tends to show us that the framework is not addressing an international paradigm animated by traditional international relations theories, but one that is more limited to allowing Chinese national interests to prevail without question within its spheres of influence. This Chinese world order exhibits characteristics in which Chinese self-interest is the predominant guiding principle, it will advance the economic prosperity of other nations only if it helps to achieve Chinese interests, and freedom from foreign interference is fiercely defended. At the same time, China is not interested in assuming the traditional role of global leadership in the American-led post–World War II era. Rather, it will assume global leadership when it is beneficial to Chinese interests. Thus, this order is Sino-centric in scope with Chinese interests at the heart of its foreign policies and international initiatives, while, at the same time, it will usually only exhibit leadership when its interests are at stake.

Regarding its inward-facing identity, China is animated by fears of peak China, of internal forces competing with the Party for authority, and of an increasingly hostile world order. But simultaneously, it is attempting a reordering of global norms and necessitating the participation of other nations as economic partners and consumers. This reordering of global norms requires assertions of hard and soft power in ways that promote Chinese interests and national rejuvenation. As such, China's use of soft power involves shaping the preferences of others through appeal and attraction to achieve its objectives, including its continuing economic growth, the BRI, and requiring the concession and participation of other nations to achieve. As will be noted in the following sections, China's soft power strategies in development and humanitarian aid show that while it has some ability to influence, it may not be enough to shift the centre of gravity of this current international world order to itself, which seems especially true in an era of disruption.

The BRI's 'development' assistance

In a 2021 white paper, titled 'China's International Development Cooperation in the New Era', China detailed its plan of international development cooperation, defining development aid as the totality of its 'bilateral and multilateral efforts, within the framework of South-South cooperation, to promote economic and social development through foreign aid, humanitarian assistance, and other means' (State Council Information Office, 2021, p. 1). Included in this plan is support for the BRI, a significant infrastructure project that Beijing has explicitly stated is a major platform for its international development and cooperation strategy, which encompasses 'policy, infrastructure, trade, financial and people-to-people connectivity … a path towards peace, prosperity, opening up, innovation, green development, cultural exchanges, and clean government' (State Council Information Office, 2021, p. 3).

The current vision for the BRI includes creating a vast transportation network of railways, highways, border crossings, and both natural gas and oil pipelines that extend west to the former Soviet republics and south to the Indian subcontinent and Southeast Asia. The maritime prong includes extensive port development 'along the Indian Ocean, from Southeast Asia all the way to East Africa and parts of Europe' (Chatzky and McBride, 2020, para. 8). According to Xi, the BRI would 'break the bottleneck in Asian connectivity' and link Europe and East Asia 'while creating new geopolitical space for China in Eurasia' (Deng, 2021, p. 736; Xi, 2014b, para. 19). But Xi's grander strategic goal for the BRI is to build 'a global community of shared future' to address the 'deficit in peace, development, and governance' (Xi, 2017a, para. 10, 2019, p. 273).

The Chinese Ministry of Commerce has reported BRI-related investments exceeded US$110 billion in 2019, while in the same year, China's official development assistance (ODA) expenditures amounted to about US$5.9 billion (Kitano and Miyabayashi, 2020, p. 1; Liu, 2019, para. 12). However, much of BRI lending is off-the-books and unaccounted for in official records of government debt; even Chinese officials are unsure of China's total public and private lending portfolio (Hatton, 2021, para. 7). New evidence from AidData, a research lab at the University of William and Mary in the United States, shows that China hands out at least twice as much development money than the United States and other major powers, but 'with most of it coming in the form of risky high-interest loans from Chinese state banks' (Hatton, 2021, para. 1), differing significantly from traditional forms of ODA. AidData notes that from 2000 to 2017, China has granted or loaned money worth US$843 billion to 13,427 infrastructure projects in about 165 countries, with much of this linked to the BRI and saddling some Global South nations with risky debt (Wooley, 2021).

An example includes a Chinese loan for a winding railway in Laos, which, as one of the poorest countries in Southeast Asia, it struggles mightily to repay. Most of the railway line is owned by a Chinese entity, but Laos is responsible for repayment of the debt. Exacerbated by the pandemic, this deal has downgraded Laos's credit rating to junk status, in which sovereign default becomes a real possibility (Hatton, 2021, para. 13; Kawase, 2020, para. 1). On the brink of bankruptcy in late 2020, Laos sold a major national asset to China, 'handing over part of its energy grid for $600 m in order to seek debt relief from Chinese creditors … all before the railway has even begun operations' (Hatton, 2021, para. 14). Another example is Montenegro, a candidate to join the European Union (EU), which had to ask the EU for debt relief 'after it realized it could not repay China for the $1 billion highway funded through BRI' (Sacks, 2021, para. 8). Montenegro's Chinese debt is larger than its gross domestic product, and Montenegrin officials have said that the highway goes 'from nothing to nothing' (Schmitz, 2021, para. 2). In a 2018 study on 68 BRI-indebted countries, 23 were considered at risk of debt distress, and within that subset 8 nations were considered at risk of sovereign bankruptcy (Hurley *et al.*, 2018, pp. 1–2).

Two more stumbling blocks have complicated the BRI narrative for China. During the 2016 US presidential campaign, then candidate Donald Trump stumped on the issue of trade inequities and, after he became president, initiated a 'trade war' with China (Hass and Denmark, 2020, n.p.). Although he was defeated in the 2020 election, current president Joe Biden's China policy is much like Trump's but without the bluster. Trump-era trade tariffs towards China have remained in place, and American officials are in the process of crafting 'a strategy that deals with China as it is, rather than as they wish it were', indicating a harder line will be kept (Khalid, 2021, para. 14). In Europe, the EU and China negotiated the EU–China Comprehensive Agreement on Investment (CAI) with then German chancellor Angela Merkel, pushing through approval despite criticisms from EU diplomats and officials over the agreement's lack of labour rights protections, China's violations of human rights, and the transatlantic divisions it will cause with North America (von der Bruchard, 2020). Shortly after the CAI's approval, the EU sanctioned Chinese officials for human rights violations, and China retaliated quickly by sanctioning EU legislators and warned the EU to 'immediately stop interfering in China's internal affairs [and] abandon its confrontational approach' (*China Defiant after EU Warning over Trade Agreement*, 2021, n.p.). This has effectively halted the CAI's progress. What makes these two issues problematic for China's economic growth is that, as with the ancient Silk Road, the BRI is designed to reach Western markets and the rich consumers residing there.

The BRI is a particularly interesting soft power strategy to analyse. As Joseph Nye put it, '[T]his soft power—getting others to want the outcomes that you want—co-opts people rather than coerces them', by focusing on the agency of the recipient and concentrating on the ability to affect outcomes through attraction (Nye, 2008, p. 95). Leadership, then, is getting people to follow 'not only because you tell them to do so and enforce your orders but because they instinctively want to do it for you' (Nye, 2009, p. 161). However, as Janice Mattern points out, '[A]ttraction is a rather subjective experience', which raises issues about efficacy of soft power in the eyes of the intended target (Mattern, 2005, p. 584). Soft power, then, is about attraction but as determined through the agent, who is ultimately the arbiter of the success of such soft power assertions.

With regard to the BRI, a Sino-centric world order in which Chinese national interests reign uncontested and participation in such a world order comes with a price, is, unsurprisingly, not as appealing for the recipients as it is for China. When China launched the BRI in 2013, countries were initially eager to participate. Prior to the COVID-19 pandemic, a 2018 study examined sentiment towards the BRI by country and found that, generally, the BRI was considered most favourably by African nations and least favourably by South Asian nations. The highest-ranking regions in terms of positive perception were Central Asia and sub-Saharan Africa. Even at that time, however, several BRI loan recipients, primarily in Europe, held significantly negative attitudes (Garcia-Herrero and Xu, 2019).

Over time and with examples like Laos and Montenegro, it appears that nations have become wary of the long-term risks that the BRI poses. By 2020, African nations' opinions have begun to sour 'over the unilateral nature of the initiative, the lack of transparency and accountability to African countries, and the absence of direct benefit to those countries' economies', raising suspicions and fuelling local resentment (Venkateswaran, 2020, p. 1). In a growing number of African countries, such as Zambia, Nigeria, Kenya, Guinea, Sierra Leone, and the Democratic Republic of Congo, public opinion has turned against the BRI (Mishra, 2021). In the Association of Southeast Asian Nations region, including Malaysia, Indonesia, Thailand, and the Philippines, domestic public perceptions of China's so-called debt-trap diplomacy—the entrapment of states in persistent and sovereignty-constricting loan arrangements that primarily benefit China—and predatory lending have become an obstacle for the implementation of BRI projects within their borders (Jones and Hameiri, 2020, p. 3; Lam, 2020). Notably, a recent survey affirmed that a majority of Southeast Asians have little or no confidence in BRI project loans (Iwamoto, 2020). A Central European Institute of Asian Studies poll of Central European countries found that general perceptions of China have worsened during the pandemic, with the exception of Serbia and Russia (Turcsányi *et al.*, 2020).

Due to public sentiment and awareness of the dangers of Chinese debt, governments are quietly cancelling or pausing high-profile BRI projects, including those nations that once held favourable attitudes towards China (Wooley, 2021, n.p.). While it may be that foreign leaders publicly praise Beijing for addressing their unmet infrastructure needs—in a bid for China's continuing patronage—countries spanning Africa, Asia, Latin America, and Central and Eastern Europe are rejecting the BRI because of these concerns (Malik *et al.*, 2021). Altogether, the dialogical interactions have caused nations to reconsider their participation in the BRI when such benefits are set against what seems to be a growing amount of risk. Together with North American and European sentiment turning against China, this is to a degree squandering the BRI's momentum.

Mask diplomacy

On the issue of humanitarian assistance during the pandemic, China's contributions of medical supplies have helped it on a number of fronts and have been termed 'mask diplomacy' (Kowalski, 2021). China is the world's largest producer of low-tech medical supplies, such as testing swabs, surgical masks and gowns, hand sanitizers, and high-filtration masks, supplies known as personal protection equipment (PPE) (Bradsher, 2020). China has played a humanitarian role by offering countries access to these supplies as well as has used mask diplomacy as a soft power strategy (Gauttam *et al.*, 2020). China's People's Liberation Army (PLA), as well, engaged in mask diplomacy with military counterparts

(Legarda, 2020). While the amount of Chinese spending on its pandemic assistance is difficult to determine due to its methodology and opacity surrounding assistance, China has donated medical equipment to more than 150 countries, with a particular focus to Global South nations within its BRI network and those it is courting for the BRI (Kurtzer, 2020; Rudolf, 2021). What can be seen of Chinese donations include US$43 million to Nicholas Maduro's Venezuelan government, US$23 million to Brazil, and $9.5 million to Chile, for example (Urdinez, 2021). In Europe, Xi has pledged an undefined but substantial amount of medical supplies to the Czech Republic, Italy, Spain, Italy, Belgium, and France. Private individuals and corporations like Jack Ma, founder of Alibaba, and Huawei, have also engaged in mask diplomacy (Wong, 2020, para. 2).

For countries combatting the pandemic and in short supply of PPE, this assistance was invaluable. On a number of fronts, mask diplomacy has helped with China's soft power assertions in that it has helped to draw attention away from the CCP's initial coverup of the early response to the virus, allowed China the appearance of global leadership from a humanitarian perspective, and reinforced existing BRI investments in development spending. The PLA sent medical supplies to 56 countries around the world, of which 54 were within the BRI network (Nouwens, 2021). In Italy, for example, mask diplomacy has helped to decrease tensions and public criticisms of the BRI. Early in the pandemic, Italy faced large-scale health and socio-economic challenges that began to overwhelm its public health system. After Europe collectively failed to assist Italy, China provided much-needed support and was seen positively by many Italians traumatized by the pandemic (Chen, 2021).

Enabling China to engage in positive public diplomacy is one of the key drivers behind China's coronavirus assistance (Chen, 2021). In certain cases, mask diplomacy has helped to improve public opinion on China and counter criticisms about the BRI and allegations of debt-trap diplomacy through tactical delivery of instrumental support in a time of crisis. Nonetheless, China has found it more difficult to move Western elite opinion because they question the sincerity of Chinese offers of friendship and are critical of Chinese requirements for 'public displays of gratitude from other countries' as 'strange' and 'not in the tradition of the best humanitarian relief efforts' (Wong and Mozur, 2020, para. 20). What complicates matters even more is that it is unclear whether China is donating or selling PPE because of the opacity surrounding its humanitarian aid metrics (Kurtzer, 2020). China exported more than US$1.4 billion of pandemic supplies in early 2020 with 'scores of countries signing contracts' according to the Chinese Foreign Ministry (Wong and Mozur, 2020, para. 20), bringing into question whether such sales meet the definition of humanitarian aid.

In general, mask diplomacy met China's goals of influencing opinion in the specific countries where Chinese PPE was received, but the Global North has nevertheless perceived China's growing influence more negatively after COVID and 'as a threat to be reckoned with more firmly' (Transatlantic Trends, 2020, p. 6). In the context of Western elite discourse on China, mask diplomacy as a tool for winning hearts and minds has proven largely ineffective with Western journalists and scholars claiming 'the image of the country has worsened substantially in almost every European country' (Kowalski, 2021, p. 12). China's acts of generosity are heavily criticized by the Global North not only because they are contingent upon public demonstrations of gratitude but also in light of purported obfuscation of China's initial coverup of the COVID-19 outbreak and alleged obstruction of the World Health Organization's (WHO) investigation in the origins of COVID-19 (Westcott *et al.*, 2021), not to mention the 'lab leak' theory, in which it is suspected the CCP is covering up the virus's origin in the Wuhan Institute of Virology as part of gain-of-function research (Muller and Quay, 2021, para. 2). Such questions regarding China's responsibility for the global pandemic are fuelling the wider discourse on its authoritarian and subversive nature. Nevertheless, countries desperate for medical supplies are not terribly concerned about elite quarrels over COVID-19's origins or the WHO's investigation. Therefore, Chinese mask diplomacy falls on fertile ground in countries that already have favourable opinions of China, but mask diplomacy has not helped to change Western discourse on China's rise.

Vaccine diplomacy

While many wealthy countries have been able to vaccinate large portions of their populations and are currently in the process of rolling out COVID-19 vaccine boosters, most of the world is being left behind. Serbian president Aleksandar Vucic stated that 'today it's harder to get the vaccines than nuclear weapons' (*Vaccine Diplomacy Boosts Russia's and China's Global Standing*, 2021, para. 1). The World Bank warns that the vast majority of the world remains unvaccinated, especially the poorest nations, exacerbating inequality. Only 1.1% of the global population in low-income countries has received 'even one dose of a vaccine' (Banerjee and Blake, 2021, para. 10). It is estimated that 11 billion total doses will be produced by the end of 2021, but with almost all those doses promised to the Global North (Banerjee and Blake, 2021, para. 18).

This is further complicated by questions of the efficacy of the vaccines produced by different countries. The Pfizer-BioNTech and Moderna vaccines have been proven to be more effective than the Russian or Chinese ones but are not yet widely available to the Global South (Bremmer, 2021; MacKinnon and York, 2021). A Peruvian study of one of the Chinese vaccines, Sinopharm, found it only 50.4% effective against infection, and a Brazilian study has shown Sinovac, another Chinese vaccine, also to be 'barely 50% effective' (*Covid*, 2021, para. 14; Rochabrun and Liu, 2021, para. 1). Indonesia, Hong Kong, and Singapore have expressed alarm over the low efficacy of Chinese vaccines and mistrust of Chinese vaccines due to deaths and breakthrough cases (Aravindan and Lin, 2021; Dou and Mahtani, 2021; Widianto and Lamb, 2021). Adding fuel to this controversy is China's refusal to release data to national health agencies, which increases worries of the Chinese vaccines' low efficacy and raises questions about what else China is hiding (Dou and Mahtani, 2021). Scientists have additionally warned that 'developing nations that choose to use them could end up lagging behind countries that select Pfizer or Moderna' (Ives, 2021, para. 9).

As with mask diplomacy, China is using vaccine diplomacy as a way to sway public opinion and to also undergird its development efforts by focusing on BRI countries (Huang, 2021). A harder edge to this soft power initiative is that China is also pressuring countries to drop diplomatic recognition of the Republic of China in Taiwan and as coercion to manipulate diplomatic outcomes (Rogin, 2021; Strangio, 2020; *Taiwan Says China Exploiting Vaccines*, 2021). However, China's vaccine diplomacy has encountered several obstructions, including contentions that the so-called vaccine donations have actually been sales for profit to countries in crisis. In a recent study based on open-source data, China's vaccine diplomacy appears to consist largely of a small 'free sample' that then 'results in the purchase of the vaccine, this time in millions of doses' (Karásková and Blablová, 2021, para. 4).

With vaccine diplomacy, China has been accused of being more heavy-handed than in its other attempts to shape international public opinion. Questions of the vaccine's efficacy and China's refusal to release relevant data have created an even more hazardous landscape than did mask diplomacy. Nonetheless, many nations in the Global South have had no access to vaccines and care little about efficacy or lab leak theories and simply desire to protect their citizens from the virus with any means available to them. A narrative that Global South countries readily accept is that Western world powers are stockpiling doses, while China is seen as 'manufacturing its vaccines with the goal of distributing them throughout the Global South and amassing influence in developing countries neglected by its Western rivals' (Bodetti, 2021, para. 9).

In general, vaccine diplomacy has met China's goals of influencing opinion in the specific countries where it was received, such as Serbia and Global South nations; however, increasingly negative perceptions of China in advanced economies soared during the pandemic (Silver *et al.*, 2020; Transatlantic Trends, 2020; Turcsányi *et al.*, 2020). This shows that the pandemic only accelerated already-existing negative sentiment towards China and that its mask and vaccine diplomacy gained limited success in only a couple countries where negative public opinion previously existed, like Italy and the Czech Republic (Kowalski, 2021).

Conclusion

Disrupted by the pandemic, the world continues to face a worldwide global crisis. For a well-resourced country like China, the pandemic could have been a prime opportunity to recontour the international world order to better suit its aims and objectives. This opportunity, however, has been difficult for China to fully utilize. Prior to the pandemic, dominant narratives of China's rise were progressively laden with predictions of the demise of the liberal world order and an end to American leadership. Despite its vast investment in development and humanitarian aid, China has not been able to substantively shift sentiment in its favour, and the pandemic accelerated some already negative sentiment towards China. An emergent narrative now proposes that China is in decline and may act in increasingly rash and dangerous ways to lunge for success.

This admittedly Western narrative is further complicated by attempting to understand Chinese long-term objectives through a realist or neorealist theoretical lens. This chapter proffers a view to understanding China through discursive analysis, examining what it says about itself and its intentions, on the one hand, and then comparing this with its actions in development and humanitarian aid, on the other. From this perspective, it is possible to see that China is likely not seeking American-style hegemony but rather great power status in a Sino-centric world order using a soft power strategy. In this world order, Chinese economic prosperity and close connections to the Global South are apparent, as is a determination to defend its interests using unorthodox means. China's self-interests shine through as the ultimate objective in all its endeavours, including its international development and humanitarian aid programmes.

Although the pandemic offered an exceptional opportunity to disrupt the current global governance system, China was unable to fully realize this opportunity, partially because of its own missteps in allowing debt diplomacy to negatively impact its reputation, but more importantly, because China's self-interest in these loans were and are too evident to BRI loan recipients. Sentiment in BRI loan-recipient countries is beginning to turn against China because the short-term benefits seemingly did not justify the long-term costs, in which economic sovereignty becomes threatened, helping to fuel the Global North's discourse of the insidious nature of the BRI.

China's humanitarian aid during the pandemic was another opportunity not fully realized. Damaging allegations, whether or not true, have centred on the possibility of the virus originating in a Wuhan lab leak, the lack of efficacy of Chinese vaccines, and Chinese sales of what others view as humanitarian aid. This went hand in hand with the narrative created by deliberately withholding Chinese vaccine data and intentionally tying humanitarian aid to its economic interests in the BRI, all of which have combined to 'unmask' China's broader strategic intentions. Both mask and vaccine diplomacy were significant opportunities for China to show generosity and leadership, but these efforts foundered upon China's determination to press its self-interest so overtly.

Nevertheless, China does provide millions of dollars in humanitarian aid to nations in need, and it does have influence in regions that hold strategic importance to the United States, Europe, and their allies. Greater sensitivity is needed to the geopolitical implications of this influence. China's connection to the Global South is still an important instrument in PRC statecraft as it pursues its own version of great power status. The Global North can use the pandemic to rethink the ways in which it interacts with and aids the Global South. As to China's global aspirations and prospects of a Sino-centric world order, it must counter with deeds and actions the evolving narrative that it is a growing threat to the liberal world order.

References

Allison, G. (2017). *Destined for war: Can America and China escape Thucydides's trap?* (Reprint ed.). Boston, MA: Mariner Books.

Aravindan, A., and Lin, C. (2021, June 19). *Singapore sees early rush for Sinovac vaccine.* Reuters. https://www.reuters.com/world/asia-pacific/singapore-sees-first-day-rush-sinovac-vaccine-2021-06-18/

Bader, J. A. (2016). *How Xi Jinping sees the world...and why* (Order From Chaos Project, Report No. 2). Washington D.C.: The Brookings Institution.

Banerjee, R., and Blake, P. (2021). *'Absolutely unacceptable' vaccination rates in developing countries* (No. 17) [Transcript]. The Development Podcast, World Bank. Retrieved 20 October 2021. https://www.worldbank.org/en/news/podcast/2021/07/30/-absolutely-unacceptable-vaccination-rates-in-developing-countries-the-development-podcast

Beckley, M., and Brands, H. (2021a, October 1). China is a declining power—And that's the problem. *Foreign Policy.* https://foreignpolicy.com/2021/09/24/china-great-power-united-states/

Beckley, M., and Brands, H. (2021b, October 7). The end of China's rise. *Foreign Affairs.* https://www.foreignaffairs.com/articles/china/2021-10-01/end-chinas-rise

Bhattacharya, J., and Boudreaux, D. J. (2021, August 4). Eradication of COVID is a dangerous and expensive fantasy. *Wall Street Journal.* https://www.wsj.com/articles/zero-covid-coronavirus-pandemic-lockdowns-china-australia-new-zealand-11628101945

Bodetti, A. (2021, January 15). *China's vaccine diplomacy in the Middle East.* The Diplomat. https://thediplomat.com/2021/01/chinas-vaccine-diplomacy-in-the-middle-east/

Bradsher, K. (2020, July 5). China dominates medical supplies, in this outbreak and the next. *The New York Times.* https://www.nytimes.com/2020/07/05/business/china-medical-supplies.html

Bremmer, I. (2021, August 2). Why the Chinese and Russian vaccines haven't been the geopolitical wins they were hoping for. *Time.* https://time.com/6086028/chinese-russian-covid-19-vaccines-geopolitics/

Buckley, C., and Qin, A. (2021, October 3). In a surge of military flights, China tests and warns Taiwan. *The New York Times.* https://www.nytimes.com/2021/10/03/world/asia/china-taiwan-flights-airspace.html

Campbell, K. M., and Ratner, E. (2018, April). The China reckoning: How Beijing defied American expectations. *Foreign Affairs, 97*(2). https://www.foreignaffairs.com/articles/china/2018-02-13/china-reckoning

Carter, E. B. (2019, January 22). Diversionary aggression in Chinese foreign policy. *Brookings Institution.* https://www.brookings.edu/articles/diversionary-aggression-in-chinese-foreign-policy/

CentralCommitteeoftheCommunistPartyofChina'sGeneralOffice. (2013). *Communiquéon thecurrentstateoftheideologicalsphere(DocumentNo. 9).* https://digichina.stanford.edu/work/communique-on-the-current-state-of-the-ideological-sphere-document-no-9/

Chatzky, A., and McBride, J. (2020). *China's massive belt and road initiative.* Council on Foreign Relations. https://www.cfr.org/backgrounder/chinas-massive-belt-and-road-initiative

Chen, W. A. (2021, July 3). COVID-19 and China's Changing Soft Power in Italy. *Chinese Political Science Review* (2021), 1–21. https://doi.org/10.1007/s41111-021-00184-3

China Defiant after EU Warning Over Trade Agreement. (2021, May 21). Associated Press. https://apnews.com/article/china-europe-trade-agreements-global-trade-business-cf73bb19ff7a13ddfa87a45d8441aef1

Chu, D. (2021, March 10). Projection on China's high-income country status draws attention to quality of development, deepening reforms. *Global Times*. https://www.globaltimes.cn/page/202103/1218011.shtml

COVID: What Do We Know about China's Coronavirus Vaccines? (2021, January 14). BBC News. https://www.bbc.com/news/world-asia-china-55212787

Debrix, F. (2003). *Language, agency, and politics in a constructed world.* Abingdon: Routledge.

de Graaff, N., ten Brink, T., and Parmar, I. (2020). China's rise in a liberal world order in transition. *Review of International Political Economy, 27*(2), 191–207.

Deng, Y. (2021). How China builds the credibility of the Belt and Road Initiative. *Journal of Contemporary China, 30*(131), 734–750.

Doshi, R. (2019, January 22). Hu's to blame for China's foreign assertiveness? *Brookings Institution.* https://www.brookings.edu/articles/hus-to-blame-for-chinas-foreign-assertiveness/

Dou, E., and Mahtani, S. (2021, March 23). China's vaccine diplomacy stumbles as clinical trial data remains absent. *Washington Post*. https://www.washingtonpost.com/world/asia_pacific/china-coronavirus-singapore-data/2021/03/23/7a0582ca-8afc-11eb-a33e-da28941cb9ac_story.html

Duong, H. (2015, June 15). Massive island-building and international law. *Asia Maritime Transparency Initiative*. https://amti.csis.org/massive-island-building-and-international-law/

Erickson, A. S., and Collins, G. B. (2021, October 18). A dangerous decade of Chinese power is here. *Foreign Policy*. https://foreignpolicy.com/2021/10/18/china-danger-military-missile-taiwan/

Fan, W. (2021, February 25). China's campaign to crush democracy in Hong Kong is working. *Wall Street Journal*. https://www.wsj.com/articles/chinas-campaign-to-crush-democracy-in-hong-kong-is-working-11614268174

Fish, E. (2017, February 4). Why's Beijing so worried about western values infecting China's youth? *ChinaFile*. https://www.chinafile.com/features/whys-beijing-so-worried-about-western-values-infecting-chinas-youth

Foucault, M. (1972). *The archaeology of knowledge* (1st American ed.). New York: Pantheon Books.

Friedberg, A. L. (2012). *A contest for supremacy: China, America, and the struggle for mastery in Asia* (1st ed.). New York: W. W. Norton and Company.

Fung, C. J. (2016). Global South solidarity? China, regional organisations and intervention in the Libyan and Syrian civil wars. *Third World Quarterly, 37*(1), 33–50.

Garcia-Herrero, A., and Xu, J. (2019). *Countries' perceptions of China's Belt and Road Initiative: A big data analysis* (Working Paper No. 1). Bruegel. https://www.ssrn.com/abstract=3430318

Gauttam, P., Singh, B., and Kaur, J. (2020). COVID-19 and Chinese global health diplomacy: geopolitical opportunity for China's hegemony? *Millennial Asia, 11*(3), 318–340.

Harrell, P., Rosenberg, E., and Saravalle, E. (2018). *China's Use of Coercive Economic Measures*. Center for New American Security. https://www.cnas.org/publications/reports/chinas-use-of-coercive-economic-measures

Hass, R., and Denmark, A. (2020, August 7). More pain than gain: How the US-China trade war hurt America. *The Brookings Institution*. https://www.brookings.edu/blog/order-from-chaos/2020/08/07/more-pain-than-gain-how-the-us-china-trade-war-hurt-america/

Hatton, C. (2021, September 29). China: Big spender or loan shark? *BBC News*. https://www.bbc.com/news/world-asia-china-58679039

Huang, Y. (2021, July 26). Vaccine diplomacy is paying off for China. *Foreign Affairs*. https://www.foreignaffairs.com/articles/china/2021-03-11/vaccine-diplomacy-paying-china

Hurley, J., Morris, S., and Portelance, G. (2018). *Examining the debt implications of the Belt and Road Initiative from a policy perspective* (Policy Paper No. 121). https://www.cgdev.org/sites/default/files/examining-debt-implications-belt-and-road-initiative-policy-perspective.pdf

Ives, M. (2021, June 19). Singapore allows Sinovac shots, but casts doubt on their effectiveness. *The New York Times*. https://www.nytimes.com/2021/06/19/world/singapore-sinovac.html

Iwamoto, K. (2020, January 16). 7 of 10 ASEAN members favor China over US: Survey. *Nikkei Asia*. https://asia.nikkei.com/Politics/International-relations/7-of-10-ASEAN-members-favor-China-over-US-survey

Jones, L., and Hameiri, S. (2020). *Debunking the myth of 'debt-trap diplomacy' how recipient countries shape China's Belt and Road Initiative*. Chatham House, The Royal Institute of International Affairs. https://www.chathamhouse.org/sites/default/files/2020-08-25-debunking-myth-debt-trap-diplomacy-jones-hameiri.pdf

Karásková, I., and Blablová, V. (2021, March 24). *The logic of China's vaccine diplomacy*. The Diplomat. https://thediplomat.com/2021/03/the-logic-of-chinas-vaccine-diplomacy/

Kawase, K. (2020, September 24). Laos credit downgrade signals 'real' default risk as China looms. *Nikkei Asia*. https://asia.nikkei.com/Economy/Laos-credit-downgrade-signals-real-default-risk-as-China-looms

Kelly, R. (2014, May 28). Chinese foreign policy: Belligerence is internally motivated. *The Interpreter*. https://www.lowyinstitute.org/the-interpreter/chinese-foreign-policy-belligerence-internally-motivated

Khalid, A. (2021, October 4). Biden is keeping key parts of Trump's China trade policy. Here's why. *NPR*. https://www.npr.org/2021/10/04/1043027789/biden-is-keeping-key-parts-of-trumps-china-trade-policy-heres-why

Kitano, N., and Miyabayashi, Y. (2020). *Estimating China's foreign aid: 2019–2020 preliminary figures*. JICA Ogata Sadako Research Institute for Peace and Development. https://www.jica.go.jp/jica-ri/publication/other/l75nbg000019o0pq-att/Estimating_Chinas_Foreign_Aid_2019-2020.pdf

Kowalski, B. (2021). China's mask diplomacy in Europe: Seeking foreign gratitude and domestic stability. *Journal of Current Chinese Affairs*, 50(2), 209–226.

Kurtzer, J. (2020, November 17). China's humanitarian aid: Cooperation amidst competition. *Center for Strategic and International Studies*. https://www.csis.org/analysis/chinas-humanitarian-aid-cooperation-amidst-competition

Kuruwita, R. (2020, April 15). *China to the rescue in Sri Lanka*. The Diplomat. https://thediplomat.com/2020/04/china-to-the-rescue-in-sri-lanka/

Lam, A. (2020, October 15). Domestic politics in Southeast Asia and local backlash against the Belt and Road Initiative. *Foreign Policy Research Institute*. https://www.fpri.org/article/2020/10/domestic-politics-in-southeast-asia-and-local-backlash-against-the-belt-and-road-initiative/

Larson, D. W. (2015). Will China be a new type of great power? *The Chinese Journal of International Politics*, *8*(4), 323–348.

Lee, L. T. (Ed.). (2021). *Chinese people's diplomacy and developmental relations with East Asia: Trends in the Xi Jinping era*. Routledge. https://www.taylorfrancis.com/books/9781003027560

Leffler, M. P. (2019a). Avoiding another Cold War. *China International Strategy Review, 1*(2), 205–212.

Leffler, M. P. (2019b, December 2). China Isn't the Soviet Union. Confusing the two is dangerous. *The Atlantic.* https://www.theatlantic.com/ideas/archive/2019/12/cold-war-china-purely-optional/601969/

Leffler, M. P. (2021, January 26). Defeating today's top threats requires rethinking our idea of national security. *Washington Post.* https://www.washingtonpost.com/outlook/2021/01/26/defeating-todays-top-threats-requires-rethinking-our-idea-national-security/

Legarda, H. (2020). The PLA's mask diplomacy (China Global Security Tracker No. 7; China Security and Risk Tracker). *Merics.* https://merics.org/en/tracker/plas-mask-diplomacy

Liu, Z. (2019, December 12). BRI helps build lasting economic and trade relations. *Chinadailyhk.com* https://www.chinadailyhk.com/articles/215/40/66/1576124709841.html

Maçães, B. (2019). *Belt and Road: A Chinese world order.* Hurst.

MacKinnon, M., and York, G. (2021, February 19). G7 falls behind Russia, China and India in 'vaccine diplomacy'. *The Globe and Mail,* A1.

Mahler, A. G. (2017). Global South. In *Oxford Bibliographies Online.* Oxford University Press.

Maizland, L. (2021). *China's repression of Uyghurs in Xinjiang.* Council on Foreign Relations. https://www.cfr.org/backgrounder/chinas-repression-uyghurs-xinjiang

Malik, A. A., Parks, B., Russell, B., Lin, J. J., Walsh, K., Solomon, K., Zhang, S., Elston, T.-B., and Goodman, S. (2021). *Banking on the Belt and Road* (p. 166). AidData at the William and Mary University. https://www.aiddata.org/publications/banking-on-the-belt-and-road

Mao, Z. (1994). *Mao Zedong on diplomacy.* Foreign Languages Press.

Mattern, J. B. (2005). Why 'Soft power' isn't so soft: Representational force and the sociolinguistic construction of attraction in world politics. *Millennium, 33*(3), 583–612.

Mearsheimer, J. J. (2006, April). China's unpeaceful rise. *Current History, 105*(690), 160–162.

Mearsheimer, J. J. (2010). The Gathering Storm: China's challenge to US power in Asia. *The Chinese Journal of International Politics, 3*(4), 381–396.

Mearsheimer, J. J. (2014). *The tragedy of great power politics* (Updated ed.). W. W. Norton and Company.

Mearsheimer, J. J. *The Great Delusion.* (2020, February 13). Department of Political Science, Carleton College. https://www.youtube.com/watch?v=nZVIaXFN2lU

Minzner, C. (2018). *End of an era: How China's authoritarian revival is undermining its rise* (Illustrated ed.). Oxford University Press.

Mishra, A. (2021, October 9). China's BRI continues to remain popular amongst Africans despite intense backlash. *Observer Research Foundation.* https://www.orfonline.org/expert-speak/chinas-bri-continues-to-remain-popular-amongst-africans-despite-intense-backlash/

Morrison, W. M. (2019). China's economic rise: History, trends, challenges, and implications for the United States (No. RL33534). *Congressional Research Service.* https://crsreports.congress.gov/product/pdf/RL/RL33534

Mulakala, A., and Ji, H. (2020, April 29). COVID-19 and China's soft-power ambitions. *The Asia Foundation.* https://asiafoundation.org/2020/04/29/covid-19-and-chinas-soft-power-ambitions/

Muller, R., and Quay, S. (2021, June 6). The science suggests a Wuhan lab leak. *Wall Street Journal.* https://www.wsj.com/articles/the-science-suggests-a-wuhan-lab-leak-11622995184

Nouwens, M. (2021). The evolving nature of China's military diplomacy: From visits to vaccines. *The International Institute for Strategic Studies*. https://www.iiss.org/blogs/research-paper/2021/05/china-military-diplomacy

Nye, J. S. (2008). Public diplomacy and soft power. *The ANNALS of the American Academy of Political and Social Science, 616*(1), 94–109.

Nye, J. S. (2009). Get smart: Combining hard and soft power. *Foreign Affairs, 88*(4), 160–163.

OECD. (2018). The Belt and Road Initiative in the global trade, investment and finance landscape. In *OECD Business and Finance Outlook 2018*. OECD Publishing.

Onuf, N. (2012). *Making sense, making worlds: Constructivism in social theory and international relations*. Taylor and Francis Group.

Overholt, W. H. (2012). Reassessing China: Awaiting Xi Jinping. *The Washington Quarterly, 35*(2), 121–137.

Pence, E. (2020, October 8). To understand China's aggressive foreign policy, look at its domestic politics. *Council on Foreign Relations*. https://www.cfr.org/blog/understand-chinas-aggressive-foreign-policy-look-its-domestic-politics

Ren, D. (2020, March 16). China boosts face mask production by five-fold, stoking glut concerns. *South China Morning Post*. https://www.scmp.com/business/companies/article/3075289/china-boosts-face-mask-production-capacity-450-cent-month

Rochabrun, M., and Liu, R. (2021, August 13). *Peru study finds Sinopharm COVID vaccine 50.4% effective against infections*. Reuters. https://www.reuters.com/world/americas/peru-study-finds-sinopharm-covid-vaccine-504-effective-against-infections-2021-08-13/

Rogin, J. (2021, April 22). The United States can't ignore China's vaccine diplomacy in Latin America: The Chinese are deploying vaccines for political leverage. *The Washington Post*.

Roy, D. (2013). *Return of the dragon: Rising China and regional security* (1st ed.). Columbia University Press.

Rudolf, M. (2021). *China's health diplomacy during COVID-19* (SWP Comment 2021/C 09; p. 8). Stiftung Wissenschaft und Politik.

Sacks, D. (2021, September 21). Europe's global gateway plans to counter China, but questions remain. *Council on Foreign Relations*. https://www.cfr.org/blog/europes-global-gateway-plans-counter-china-questions-remain

SAIS-CARI. (n.d.). Data: Chinese global foreign aid. *China Africa Research Initiative*. http://www.sais-cari.org/data-chinese-global-foreign-aid

Sanger, D. E. (2021, October 22). Biden said the U.S. would protect Taiwan. But it's not that clear-cut. *The New York Times*. https://www.nytimes.com/2021/10/22/us/politics/biden-taiwan-defense-china.html

Schmitz, R. (2021, June 29). How a Chinese-built highway drove Montenegro deep into debt. *NPR*. https://www.npr.org/2021/06/28/1010832606/road-deal-with-china-is-blamed-for-catapulting-montenegro-into-historic-debt

Silver, L., Devlin, K., and Huang, C. (2020). *Unfavorable views of China reach historic highs in many countries*. Pew Research Center. https://www.pewresearch.org/global/2020/10/06/unfavorable-views-of-china-reach-historic-highs-in-many-countries/

Sources on universal values: Background to the debate. (2010, September 29). *The Economist*. https://www.economist.com/blogs/asiaview/2010/09/sources_universal_values

State Council Information Office. (2005). *Building of Political Democracy in China* (White Paper). State Council Information Office. http://www.chinadaily.com.cn/english/doc/2005-10/19/content_486206.htm

State Council Information Office. (2021). *China's international development cooperation in the new era*. State Council Information Office. http://english.scio.gov.cn/whitepapers/2021-01/10/content_77099782.htm

Strangio, S. (2020, November 5). *China's Southeast Asian 'Vaccine Diplomacy' comes into relief.* The Diplomat. http://www.proquest.com/docview/2457446768/abstract/59EA3E9A6FC049B7PQ/1

Taiwan says China exploiting vaccines for political gain. (2021, June 3). Associated Press. https://apnews.com/article/health-taiwan-china-coronavirus-pandemic-80e3020948fc85e0e1d5a89b1a5b2255

Tellis, A. J. (2013). U.S.-China relations in a realist world. In D. Shambaugh (Ed.), *Tangled titans: The United States and China* (1st ed., pp. 75–102). Rowman and Littlefield.

The debate over universal values. (2010, September 30). *The Economist*. http://www.economist.com/asia/2010/09/30/the-debate-over-universal-values

Transatlantic Trends. (2020). *Transatlantic opinion on global challenges before and after COVID-19* (Transatlantic Perspectives on Global Challenges). Bertelsmann Foundation; The German Marshall Fund of the United States; Institut Montaigne. https://bfna.org/politics-society/transatlantic-trends-2020/

Turcsányi, R. Q., Šimalčík, M., Kironská, K., and Sedláková, R. (2020). *European public opinion on China in the age of COVID-19: Differences and common ground across the continent* (Sinophone Borderlands Project). Central European Institute of Asian Studies. https://ceias.eu/wp-content/uploads/2020/11/COMP-poll-report_3.pdf

Urdinez, F. (2021). *China's improvised mask diplomacy in Chile*. Carnegie Endowment for International Peace. https://carnegieendowment.org/2021/04/06/china-s-improvised-mask-diplomacy-in-chile-pub-84251

Vaccine diplomacy boosts Russia's and China's global standing. (2021, April 29). *The Economist*. http://www.economist.com/graphic-detail/2021/04/29/vaccine-diplomacy-boosts-russias-and-chinas-global-standing

Venkateswaran, L. (2020). *China's Belt and Road Initiative: Implications in Africa* (ORF Issue Brief No. 395). Observer Research Foundation. https://www.orfonline.org/research/chinas-belt-and-road-initiative-implications-in-africa/

von der Bruchard, H. (2020, December 29). *Merkel pushes EU-China investment deal over the finish line despite criticism*. Politico. https://www.politico.eu/article/eu-china-investment-deal-angela-merkel-pushes-finish-line-despite-criticism/

Wang, Y. (2018, December 18). *China will 'never seek hegemony,' Xi says in reform speech*. Associated Press. https://apnews.com/article/financial-markets-ap-top-news-international-news-asia-china-4c9476378e184f238845337ba442715c

Westcott, B., Yee, I., and Xiong, Y. (2021, July 22). *COVID-19 origins: Chinese government rejects WHO plan for second phase of origins study*. CNN. https://www.cnn.com/2021/07/22/china/china-who-second-origin-study-intl-hnk/index.html

What's behind the China-Taiwan divide? (2021, May 26). BBC News. https://www.bbc.com/news/world-asia-34729538

Widianto, S., and Lamb, K. (2021, June 17). *Hundreds of vaccinated Indonesian health workers get COVID-19, dozens in hospital*. Reuters. https://www.reuters.com/world/asia-pacific/hundreds-indonesian-doctors-contract-covid-19-despite-vaccination-dozens-2021-06-17/

Wong, B. (2020, March 25). *China's mask diplomacy*. The Diplomat. https://thediplomat.com/2020/03/chinas-mask-diplomacy/

Wong, E., and Mozur, P. (2020, April 14). China's 'donation diplomacy' raises tensions with U.S. *The New York Times*. https://www.nytimes.com/2020/04/14/us/politics/coronavirus-china-trump-donation.html

Wooley, A. (2021, September 29). AidData's new dataset of 13,427 Chinese development projects worth $843 billion reveals major increase in 'hidden debt' and Belt and Road Initiative implementation problems. *The First Tranche: AidData's Blog*. https://www.aiddata.org/blog/aiddatas-new-dataset-of-13-427-chinese-development-projects-worth-843-billion-reveals-major-increase-in-hidden-debt-and-belt-and-road-initiative-implementation-problems

Xi, J. (2014a, June 28). *Five principles of peaceful coexistence anniversary*. China.org.cn. http://www.china.org.cn/world/2014-07/07/content_32876905.htm

Xi, J. (2014b, August 11). *Connectivity Spearheads Development and Partnership Enables Cooperation*. Embassy of the People's Republic of China in the Republic of Indonesia. https://www.fmprc.gov.cn/ce/ceindo/eng/jrzg/t1211795.htm

Xi, J. (2017a, May 14). *Full text of President Xi's speech at opening of Belt and Road forum*. Xinhua. http://www.xinhuanet.com/english/2017-05/14/c_136282982.htm

Xi, J. (2017b, October 18). *Secure a decisive victory in building a moderately prosperous society in all respects and strive for the great success of socialism with Chinese characteristics for a new era*. Xinhua. http://www.xinhuanet.com/english/download/Xi_Jinping's_report_at_19th_CPC_National_Congress.pdf

Xi, J. (2019). *The Belt and Road Initiative* (1st ed.). Foreign Languages Press.

16

SOFT POWER AND THE POLITICS OF FOREIGN AID

The case of Venezuela

Anthea McCarthy-Jones

Introduction

During the Cold War, Venezuela was presented as one of the leading examples of a Latin American democracy that simultaneously resisted authoritarianism and communism in favour of the US-led rules-based world order (Tsvetkova *et al.*, 2019). A key reason for Venezuela's unwavering support of US initiatives and interests, both regionally and internationally, rested on its own reliance on US aid to support and protect its fledgling democracy. As a result, Venezuela's support for the United States remained the status quo until the late 1990s. By this time, however, Venezuela's political environment has shifted markedly, providing the fertile conditions for the election of Hugo Chávez and the beginning of radical transformation, which would become known the Bolivarian Revolution. The Bolivarian Revolution became the centre piece of President Chávez's efforts to re-invoke nationalistic sentiments amongst the population as a tool to support Venezuela's move away from US influence in the region and internationally.

In the early 2000s, President Chávez developed a foreign policy framework that vigorously pursued Venezuelan independence through his vision of a multipolar world. These efforts led to a serious deterioration of relations with the United States while simultaneously providing openings for the rapid development of new partnerships that facilitated the exercise of soft power by China and Russia in the region. However, almost 20 years on the establishment of these arrangements have not led to the promised greater political and economic independence for Venezuela, nor for the redistribution of wealth to alleviate poverty (Rodríguez, 2008). Instead, they have created a new and deeply problematic type of dependence on China and Russia that has become more acute under the leadership of Nicolás Maduro. Despite President Maduro facing significant challenges

DOI: 10.4324/9781003273844-16

to his legitimacy and leadership, Russian and Chinese economic assistance has been instrumental in his ability to hold on to power in Venezuela. This support has allowed Maduro and his government to resist significant US pressure in the form of economic sanctions against the Venezuelan regime and largely ignore persistent accusations from the international community that under Maduro's watch, Venezuela has morphed into a 'mafia state', defined as a state that 'is run as a criminal organization in which the country's political leader presides over a network of family and friends who make private gains from state action' (McCarthy-Jones and Turner, 2021).

The complex situation that has been unravelling in Venezuela over the past several years has included ongoing shortages of food, water, medication, and electricity, and rising crime, homicide, poverty, and inequality rates have created the largest mass exodus of the population in Venezuelan history. Venezuela has the largest amount of oil reserves in the world (BP, 2021) and, like other resource dependent 'petrostates', has been afflicted by weak institutions, poor governance, corruption, and reluctant foreign investment (Cheatham *et al.*, 2021). While such political and economic issues culminated in the emergence of an unprecedented humanitarian crisis, the unfortunate timing of these events placed the government and population in an extremely fragile position prior to the COVID-19 pandemic.

This chapter adopts an international relations perspective to analyse shifting political and economic environments in Venezuela to explain how Venezuela transformed itself from being a key proponent of the US-led rules-based order during the 20th century to a key protagonist of a Latin American movement to pursue an alternative rules-based world order at the beginning of the 21st century. By drawing on concepts such as radical pan-Americanism, multipolarity, and examples of Latin American regional integration, this chapter will demonstrate how Venezuela's radical approach to policy-making at the beginning of the 21st century provided a new stage for global political rivalries and enabled the extraordinary use of soft power in the region by China and Russia. However, as this chapter will demonstrate, despite Venezuela's ability to quickly develop important economic relationships with emerging powers outside of the Western Hemisphere, these ties have not been enough to insulate Venezuela from successive internal political and economic crises. In the absence of foreign investment over the past 20 years, Chinese and Russian use of soft power in Venezuela has remained purely transactional rather than transformational in nature and therefore has been incapable of affecting real change in the country and its fortunes. The analysis will demonstrate that the culmination of these factors over time explains why Venezuela found itself in such a vulnerable and problematic position before the onset of the COVID-19 global pandemic. The chapter develops a case study of how the pandemic has exacerbated the pre-existing crises in Venezuela and accelerated the consolidation of the mafia state in Venezuela, which has led to unprecedented levels of crime and corruption that have hampered the state's ability to deliver health services during the pandemic.

Venezuela and rules-based order in the 20th century

Unlike many Central and South American nations that only began to shift away from authoritarianism towards democracy during the third wave of democratisation, Venezuela's successful transition to what became known as the *Punto Fijo* model of democracy, based on a corporatist pact between leading political figures, was complete by 1958 (García-Guadilla and Mallen, p. 64). This democratic transition occurred on the back of almost 150 years of continuous authoritarian rule that dated back to Venezuela's declaration of independence from the Spanish in the early 19th century. Consequently, Venezuela's model of democracy was founded on a power-sharing agreement between three leading political parties at the time, namely, Acción Democrática, Comité de Organización Política Electoral Independiente: Partido Social Cristiano, and Unión Republicana Democrática. Central to the agreement that established democracy in Venezuela was a clear consensus between all three political parties that the viability of *Punto Fijo* democracy could only be sustained with the tacit support of the United States (McCoy and Meyers, 2004).

Venezuelan foreign and domestic policy in this period was influenced by close diplomatic and military ties with the United States, which effectively privileged Venezuelan military officers and tied their interests to the interests of the government (Trinkunas, 2002). Beginning with Venezuela's President Betancourt and carried on by subsequent leaders, Venezuela became a leading proponent of many US-led initiatives in the region during the Cold War. For example, Venezuela was an early supporter of US President Kennedy's Alliance for Progress, which sought to combine US efforts in Latin America to support economic, social, and democratic initiatives in the region. Venezuela bolstered the international prestige of its fledgling democracy through proactive diplomacy in a range of regional and international forums such as the Organization of American States (OAS), the Organization of Petroleum Exporting Countries (OPEC), and the United Nations (UN).

During the Cold War, Venezuela was one of the strongest champions of democracy and one of the loudest critics of communist influence in the region. This uncompromising approach, termed the Betancourt Doctrine (Rabe, 1996), took aim at communist and authoritarian Latin American governments by directly challenging their continuing participation in regional institutions and involved proposals to expel regional outliers such as Cuba from the OAS (Ellner, 2008, 62). Beyond these partisan actions, Venezuela also provided the impetus for an important organisational addition to the rules-based order for resource-rich developing nations. Venezuelan envoys strongly advocated for an international consensus on oil production and distribution to which they found a very receptive audience amongst oil-exporting countries in the Middle East. These diplomatic efforts in the early 1960s eventually paved the way for the establishment of OPEC, which continues to be a vital institution for oil-exporting countries in the 21st century (Yergin, 1992). These developments allowed Venezuela to create more favourable market conditions for its greatest natural asset, oil.

Since the beginning of the 20th century, oil has remained the most important variable in Venezuelan decision-making because it has often determined the stability of Venezuela's economic and political environments. This has been described by authors such as Tinker Salas (2009, 237) as an 'enduring legacy' and has led to important developments such as the decision to nationalise the oil industry and the creation of the state-owned oil company Petróleos de Venezuela (PDVSA) in the early 1970s. However, this legacy has provided as many problems as it has opportunities for the country. The abundance of oil has produced an almost mono-economy highly dependent on the state-run industry to generate almost all the government's revenue. Over time, and despite innovative efforts to establish organisations and operational framework to manage its greatest asset, Venezuela has been unable to escape the grips of the resource curse or 'Dutch disease' where governments are subjected to the boom and bust cycle of single resource economies and the political instability reliance on one sector of the economy entails (Ianchovichina and Onder, 2017). Further, the 1980s and early 1990s were characterised by distinct oil-related economic and political crises which culminated in an attempted coup d'état in 1992 in response to neoliberal reforms required by loans from the International Monetary Fund (IMF). Following this event, the remainder of the 1990s saw the collapse of 'elite democracy' (a form of 'trickle down democracy' beginning with citizens voting for the president but with no local elections in Venezuela and the beginnings of a regime in the 'grey zone', not fully democratic but demonstrating few authoritarian tendencies while the institutions of the state worked in the interests of the political and military elite (Diamond, 2002, 22–23).

Hugo Chávez and the pursuit of a multipolar world

Hugo Chávez's entrance into Venezuelan politics in the late 1990s challenged the predominance of the traditional party system in Venezuela and offered voters a new but largely untested social justice alternative to the elite politics that had come to define the *Punto Fijo* era (1958–1998). In the penultimate month before the 1998 presidential election, Chávez made significant gains in broadcasting his message to voters, which saw him move clear of other candidates and win the election by a comfortable margin. However, President Chávez had inherited a dysfunctional system that was plagued with inefficiencies and irregularities. Moreover, international events such as OPEC's decision to raise production quotas in November 1997, coupled with the UN Special Commission's decision to permit increased Iraqi oil exports, caused the price of oil to slump making it difficult for the new president to effect rapid change in the economy (Lichtblau, 1999, 3). Instead, President Chávez chose to introduce the Venezuelan population to his vision of a Bolivarian Revolution, named in honour of South America's liberator, Simón Bolívar, to overcome the elite politics of the preceding decades (Shifter, 2006). According to President Chávez, the Bolivarian Revolution was to be the vehicle for advancing and significantly improving the standard of living in

Venezuela through community organisation from the ground up (Aló Presidente No. 245, 2006). The Bolivarian Revolution became the label to describe President Chavez's decision to enact widespread restructuring of Venezuela's governance architecture, which included the drafting of a new constitutional and a redesign of the Venezuelan parliamentary system, which included the creation of a unicameral parliament to replace the existing bicameral structure and corresponding electoral reforms to support these new arrangements (McCarthy-Jones, 2014). While the revolution was embraced by an array of different communities especially in low socio-economic areas of the country, other sectors of the Venezuelan population began to organise and display strong opposition and open hostility to the government's attempts to revolutionise the country. At the time, President's Chávez's radical Bolivarian Revolution, which melded the ideas of Simón Bolívar with more general socialist principles and values, appeared to be at odds with most other Latin American governments (McCarthy-Jones, 2014). However, the outlier status that Chávez had quickly cultivated would soon be met with considerable support from a new political tide that was about to sweep the continent.

Beginning with the election of Hugo Chávez, the Pink Tide refers to the electoral phenomenon that brought a range of left-leaning governments to power in Chile, Brazil, Argentina, Uruguay, Bolivia, Nicaragua, Ecuador, and Guatemala during the early 2000s (Blofield *et al.*, 2017). The Pink Tide was essential to the establishment of a campaign that identified the space and demand for new regional projects and institutions that could provide an alternative to the US-led agenda (Chodor, 2015). These projects focused on augmenting economic and political integration through the establishment of regional institutions. In particular, President Chávez took a leading role in prioritising the urgent need to establish an institutionalised body that's mandate in the region, which went well beyond simply dealing with matters of trade.

The Union of South American Nations was formally established in 2006, followed by the introduction of its Constitutive Treaty in May 2008. The importance of the Treaty is that it unequivocally clarifies that the 'focus of the organisation is on cooperation and common policies in non-trade areas' (Chodor and McCarthy-Jones, 2013, 216). This regional institution has since proven to be an effective forum for dealing with regional political issues and has enabled South American states to effect change outside of traditional US-dominated forums such as the Organisation of American States. Another important institutional development during this time was the establishment of Bank of the South (*Banco del Sur*). This project is based on the principles of self-determination and regional cooperation and was created to act as an alternative source of Third World financing to the IMF (McCarthy-Jones and Greig, 2011).

It is important to note that in pursuing these novel alternative institutions that challenged US influence in the region, Chávez heavily drew on the original vision of regional integration as described by Venezuela's historical hero Simón Bolívar almost 200 years before. Bolívar himself noted the importance of institutional independence as the key to ensuring the permanent expulsion of oppressors and tyrannical laws from the region (Bolívar in Bushnell, 2003). These Bolivarian ideas also provided the basis for Chávez's desire to achieve a greater level of regional integration in the 21st century, and the Pink Tide countries provided the necessary support to move these ideas forward so that they could include other countries from the broader Latin America region. They combined to act as the glue for the endogenous concept of radical pan-Americanism to manifest as a guiding principle for future regional integration. Radical pan-Americanism at its core is a concept inspired by 'local popular struggles against imperialist power and through the recognition of a shared history' (McCarthy-Jones and Greig, 2011, 231). It unapologetically provided a framework for Latin American nations to imagine regional possibilities and governance beyond the existing orthodoxy. The establishment of the Community of Latin American and Caribbean States in 2010 represented the potency of these radical ideas and their ability to transform into vibrant examples of regional institutionalism independent of the United Sates (Chodor, 2015; McCarthy-Jones and Greig, 2011).

The significant regional adjustments that occurred because of the combined efforts of Pink Tide nations were not just limited to the reduction of US influence in hemispheric politics through the institutional changes outlined above. For the first time since the Cold War ended, Central and South American nations were well positioned to seize on new strategic and economic opportunities offered by great powers beyond the historical arrangements established with the United States. Under the leadership of President Chávez, and in direct conflict with US interests at the time, Venezuela was one of the first Latin American nations to vigorously pursue new partnerships with nations such as China and Russia.

Engaging China

China's deeper engagement with Venezuela began in the early 2000s. According to Briceño-Ruiz and Molina-Medina (2020, 148), [B]ilateral relations were modest in 1999: China and Venezuela had signed just 19 agreements up to that year, but from 1999 onward, more than 400 agreements have been signed, of which about 200 are fully operational. Initially, President Chávez's overtures to China formed part of Venezuela's new foreign policy agenda that promoted the idea of a multipolar world through engagement with a range of partners in the Global South (Sabatini, 2014). However, the internal instability in Venezuela between 2002 and 2004, which included an attempted coup d'état, a national oil strike, and a referendum that sought to recall Chávez from his role as president, temporarily halted the development of external relations with China. Following these events President Chávez took it upon himself to reinvigorate relations by travelling to China on diplomatic missions on a variety of occasions. As a result, the importance of the emerging bilateral relationship between China and Venezuela was consolidated through a series of bilateral agreements, including the 'oil-for-loans scheme' negotiated by President Hugo Chávez in 2007. These agreements mostly supported exchanges in the areas of energy, science and technology, infrastructure, agriculture, food production, social housing, and healthcare (Briceño-Ruiz and Molina-Medina, 2020; Ríos, 2013). Cooperation with China has enabled Venezuela to be the recipient of more than $60 billion in financial loans with many of these funds being provided by the China Development Bank and the Bank of China (Navone, 2021). The foundations established during Chávez's time in power have continued to chart the course of Chinese–Venezuelan relations in a post-Chávez era.

Following the death of President Chávez in 2013, his successor President Nicolás Maduro has gone to great lengths to maintain close relations between the two nations. For example, President Xi Jinping's visit to Venezuela in July 2014 was heralded by Maduro an example of the close cooperation between both nations, with Maduro concluding at the time that 'China's development model is a worthy lesson for our country to learn from' (China Daily, 2014). Similar to Chávez, Maduro has prioritised the Chinese government by making two official presidential visits to China, attending high-level talks in Beijing on at least one occasion, to discuss new financing projects for more than US$20 billion ((Briceño-Ruiz and Molina-Medina, 2020; El Universal, 2015). The Joint Development Plan between Venezuela and China (2015–2025) was also reached because of Maduro's continued advocacy of China's integral role in the development of Venezuela's economic future (Soler, 2021).

However, it is important to note that despite the plethora of high-level forums held, the many tranches of loans that have been secured and the frequent injection of Chinese money into Venezuela's economy, the exact nature of many of these deals remains largely unknown. This is because China and Venezuela have mutually maintained an opaque cover over the finer details of each deal they negotiate. The intended lack of transparency, especially in relation to the oil-for-loans model of financing, is a key reason for the ongoing scrutiny and criticism of the programme by the international community (Rendon, 2018).

While President Chávez may have intended and perhaps hoped this long-standing agreement could cut Venezuela's dependence on the United States, the stark reality is that Venezuela simply replaced one asymmetrical relationship with another (Ferchen, 2020). In 2021, the oil-for-loans agreements are appearing more like a 'debt trap' rather than a benign use of soft power by China (Balding, 2017). This point becomes clearer when the new oil import tax recently imposed by China is taken into consideration (Primer Informe, 2021).

These types of recent decisions by the Chinese government significantly hurt vulnerable countries, especially mono-economies like Venezuela that have spent the past two decades naively building an unhealthy reliance on China. This is why, after 20 years and billions of dollars later, China's assistance has not prevented Venezuela, be it economically or politically, lurching from one crisis to the next. Ultimately, China has used its soft power in the region to entice vulnerable nations with generous short-term benefits that mask exploitative agreements that are designed to produce long-term dependency on China (Rendon,

2018). However, China is not the only emerging power that has found lucrative opportunities in Venezuela over the past two decades. Since 2000, Russia has also created a significant foothold in Latin America, which at the time was strongly encouraged by President Chávez and continues today under the leadership of President Maduro.

Russian connections

Similar to China's experience, the Russian government was also an early recipient of targeted diplomatic overtures by President Chavez as early as 2000. Chávez saw Russia as an integral part of his vision of a truly multipolar world. Over the following years, Presidents Chávez and Putin met in person three times to sow the seeds of a new era of Russian–Venezuelan relations in the 21st century, and it is no coincidence that Russian–Venezuela relations expanded when both nations were experiencing deteriorating relations with the United States.

Over the years Venezuela has been able to use Russia, and vice versa, as a tool to counterbalance US influence both at home and further abroad. For example, from 2005, President Chávez began using his Russian connections to source a reliable supply of weaponry and equipment for the Venezuelan Armed Forces and other state-sanctioned armed actors. As Rouvinski (2021, 26) points out, 'Venezuela also became the largest buyer of Russian arms in the Western Hemisphere, after purchasing 100,000 Kalashnikov automatic rifles, 24 Su-30MK2 fighter jets, and about 50 helicopters, at a total cost estimated at $4 billion'. At the time these acquisitions assisted Chávez to adopt a more assertive stance against its US-backed neighbour Colombia and more generally against US influence in the region. Herbst and Marczak (2019) highlight the importance of 2008 Russian decision to send strategic bombers to Venezuela to participate in joint naval exercises in the Caribbean as a direct response to US backing of pro-Western influences in Ukraine and Georgia.

Beyond these types of events that create 'tit-for-tat' point scoring opportunities for Russia's geo-strategic competition with the United States, early on cooperation with Venezuela also afforded significant economic advantages. Russian oil companies began to explore investment opportunities in Venezuela, most notably advanced through Russia's main state-owned oil company Rosneft (Lowe and Sagdiev, 2019). At different times, other Russian companies attempted to enter the Venezuelan market; however, the chaotic and unchecked business environment in Venezuela that had already eroded the ease of doing business made it almost impossible for smaller ventures to remain viable. This has meant that Rosneft has effectively been the only Russian company to have a continuous presence in Venezuela since Presidents Chávez and Putin first established contact over two decades ago (Rouvinski, 2021). Until its final departure in 2020, Rosneft had played a vital role in developing and managing strategies that enabled Venezuela to bypass a series of US sanctions that had been placed on Venezuela's oil industry.

The fruits of Russian–Venezuela relations over the past 20 years are not always clear to see, and what remains is a complex and compromising arrangement for both nations. Critics have claimed that Russian money has allowed the Maduro government to remain viable in spite of extreme economic and political challenges over the past five years (Herbst and Marczak, 2019). Indeed, some reports have gone so far as to state that Venezuela has relied on Russian money to pay the salaries of the Venezuelan Armed Forces (Berg and Martínez Fernández, 2019; Berwick, 2019). It is estimated that Venezuela still owes just over $15 billion to Russian companies and the Russian government for a range of items. These include Russian-made fighter jets, development of Venezuelan oilfields, and other foreign direct investment projects funded by the Russian government (Herbst and Marczak, 2019, 7). However, despite the continuing climate of crisis in Venezuela, President Putin appears resolute in his support for the Maduro regime.

The impact of President Chávez's pursuit of a multipolar world in the early 2000s is still evident today. These actions provided openings for new emerging powers such as China and Russia to use soft power strategies to increase their imprint in the Latin American region. These new arrangements have supported Venezuela's reticence to abide by a US-led order in hemispheric and world affairs, at times even allowing Venezuela to sidestep the full brunt of economic sanctions placed on the Maduro regime by the United States. Despite this, these relationships have been unable to steady the course in Venezuelan economic and political spheres. To demonstrate this point, this chapter will now move to a detailed discussion of the political and economic crises that have engulfed Venezuela since 2014 and in the lead-up to the COVID-19 pandemic.

Venezuela's internal crises (2014–2019)

The death of Chávez in 2013 and subsequent leadership transition from Chávez to Maduro marked the beginning of a significant change in fortunes for Venezuela and its new president. Despite being promoted as Chávez's hand-picked successor, Nicolás Maduro proved to be a much less popular candidate, winning the election by only 1.49% of the vote (CNE, 2015). Despite initial attempts to emulate the unique style of his predecessor, President Nicolás Maduro's poor leadership and inability to manage the increasingly complex economic and social problems engulfing Venezuela boiled over in early 2014. What began as sporadic and unconnected protests by disgruntled citizens in January 2014 rapidly evolved into a nationwide movement that swept the country (Sequera, 2014). Important leaders in the opposition such as Leopoldo Lopez began coordinating nationwide demonstrations, and the protests evolved into the phenomenon known as 'guarim basin', in which protestors practised acts of civil disobedience and in some cases violence against the state (Ellner, 2017). The response from the Maduro government was swift and heavy-handed and ultimately resulted in 43 people killed in 2014 (PROVEA 2014). Amid the 2014 protests, the Maduro government was confronted with another predicament when the price of oil plummeted on the international market (Rosales, 2019). The twin impacts of prolonged social unrest and the collapsing price of oil were significant, and ever since, Maduro and his government have gone to great lengths to retain control over the country and its population. This has included a preference to deploy armed community groups (*colectivos*), the military, intelligence, and policing agencies to quell rather than appease disobedient segments of the population.

Moreover, when political rivals experienced electoral success in parliament, Maduro and his government simply circumvented them by creating comparable parallel institutions to replace existing ones. For example, in 2015, when a coalition of the opposition groups won a super-majority in the National Assembly, Maduro's response was to invent a National Constituent Assembly (NCA) and proclaim that it held superior institutional power over all pre-existing institutions and processes (Hellinger, 2019). The opposition boycotted the election of delegates to the NCA leading to the inevitable outcome of a NCA comprising Maduro supporters. According to Hellinger (2019, 1) in 2017, '[T]he NCA took legislative powers for itself, away from the National Assembly, under Article 349 of the existing constitution, which is intended to avoid obstruction of a constitutional assembly's work'. These events demonstrate that parliamentary institutions that previously provided checks and balances in Venezuela's political system have either been stymied or made redundant by the Maduro government when they no longer serve the interests of the regime. The next step for Maduro government to consolidate power and fabricate the appearance of legitimacy was to hold an upcoming presidential election. Controversially, Maduro called the election six months early, which drastically reduced the opposition's capacity to select a candidate and develop a strong campaign to run against the incumbent president. As a result, a sizeable section of the opposition once again chose to boycott the election. In the end, the 2018 presidential election resulted in a very small voter turnout, under 50%, when compared with previous elections (Hellinger, 2019). Despite Maduro's assertions that his electoral win provided a mandate for his position as the legitimate president of Venezuela, the legitimacy and fairness of the 2018 elections remain heavily disputed.

In January 2019, a radical challenge to the Maduro government presented itself in the form of Juan Guaidó, a relatively unknown political figure who had recently been elected as president of the National Assembly. Guaidó, on behalf of members of the National Assembly, cited Article 233 from the Venezuelan Constitution (1999) to declare the position of president of Venezuela vacant and therefore support his claim to act as interim president of Venezuela. To be clear, this specific article from the Venezuelan Constitution enables an interim president to replace a sitting president 'upon abandonment of his position, duly declared by the National Assembly' (BVG, 1999, Article 233). Thus, Venezuela found itself in a paradoxical situation whereby two people for very different reasons were simultaneously claiming to be the true and legitimate president of the country.

Despite members of the international community, including the United States and the United Kingdom, clambering to show unequivocal support for Maduro's new challenger, these actions did not affect the desired outcome. Rather than creating the necessary conditions that could force Maduro from power, Guaidó's challenge only served to provide clarity as to which members of the international community categorically supported Maduro and which did not. The United States doubled down on its efforts to counter Russia's support of the Maduro regime by introducing a range of sanctions specifically targeting the oil industry and key members of Maduro's support base (US Dept. Treasury, 2021). Russia initially used these sanctions to manoeuvre its state-owned oil company Rosneft into a position where it could act as a temporary economic lifeline for Maduro's regime by keeping PDVSA afloat (Kurmanaev, 2019a). The chaotic events of 2019 also provided opportunities for Russia to reaffirm their commitment to President Maduro's leadership in Venezuela through very public but mostly symbolic displays of support (Kurmanaev, 2019a). For example, David Smilde (2019, 1) points out that in early April, 'two Russian military planes carrying 35 tons of unspecified equipment and 100 soldiers landed at the international airport in Caracas'. However, as will be explained in the next section, while the seemingly resolute Russian support of Maduro was maintained throughout 2019, a very different picture of Russian–Venezuelan relations emerged in 2020.

Venezuela's decline, regardless of whether one focuses on economic, political, or social factors, is so extreme and unprecedented that it is difficult to grasp. Between 2014 and 2019, Venezuela's gross domestic product (GDP) shrank by just over 60% (Kurmanaev, 2019b). Hyperinflation, which was forecast to exceed 10 million percent by the end of 2019, has ravaged the value of the *Bolívar* (Hernandez and Monaldi, 2016; IMF, 2021). Oil production has dwindled to half its capacity when compared with levels over a decade ago, and almost 5 million Venezuelans have fled the country since 2015 (IMF, 2021; Kurmanaev, 2019b). During 2019, the country experienced severe electricity shortages, which resulted in nationwide blackouts that at times plunged up to 90% of the population into darkness (Smilde, 2019).

The majority of the population that remained in Venezuela have been left to scrounge out an existence from irregular activities such as buying and selling basic goods through illicit markets or operating through rudimentary barter systems to source everyday items. However, this reliance on illicit or irregular activities is not limited to just the Venezuelan citizenry. Since 2014, the Venezuelan state under the leadership of Maduro has itself been implicated in a range of illicit activities, ranging from money laundering to international drug trafficking, and in 2018, Venezuela was accused of fostering a state-crime nexus whereby the government has begun to function as a 'mafia state' (InSight Crime, 2018). This nexus has continued to grow unabated and is a key reason as to why Venezuela was in an even weaker position than most countries to manage the impending effects of the COVID-19 crisis.

COVID-19 and beyond

By the end of 2019, it seemed that President Maduro had managed to fend off Juan Guaidó's multiple attempts to affect a swift transfer of presidential power and had comfortably settled into a quasi-war of attrition with his political rival. Even more surprising was his regime's ability to overcome the US sanctions that discouraged foreign investment from long-standing partners in the oil industry. Maduro had retained the support of the Venezuelan military as well as important allies such as China and Russia, and so it seemed like Maduro had miraculously snatched victory from the jaws of defeat. This is precisely why at the beginning of the pandemic Rosneft's sudden withdrawal from Venezuela in April 2020 was a significant loss to the security blanket that Maduro has spent much of 2019 carefully crafting.

The combination of flawed risk assessments in conjunction with problematic political agendas that were driven by geo-strategic aspirations created a Russian myopia towards the reality of doing business in Venezuela. Rouvinksi (2021, 29) succinctly points out that previously 'Rosneft's motivations for doing business with Venezuela, despite mounting problems, involved politics first and economics a far distant second'. The impact of US sanctions on Rosneft Trading and TNK Trading, part of the US approach to targeting the Maduro regime through PDVSA, finally became too much even for Russia's state-owned juggernaut Rosneft to bear (Rondeaux, 2020; Rouvinski, 2021). This sudden shift by Russia foreshadowed growing problems for the Maduro regime as the seriousness of the COVID-19 pandemic became clearer and Venezuela's need for external assistance to deal with the crisis became even more acute.

Health crises and the harm they cause are to a large degree determined by pre-existing political, social, and economic environments within a country. As Van Praag and Arnson (2020, 1) argue, '[V]iruses thrive in the context of poverty and inequality, where dire living conditions make large segments of the population vulnerable to disease and healthcare and social services are inadequate or practically non-existent'. Since 2014, the short- and long-term impacts of Venezuela's decline meant that the country was already in a severely compromised position to adequately respond to an extraordinary and unprecedented event such as a global pandemic. For example, in 2019, Human Rights Watch described the country's ailing health system as being in a state of 'utter collapse with increased levels of maternal and infant mortality; the spread of vaccine-preventable diseases, such as measles and diphtheria; and increases in numbers of infectious diseases such as malaria and tuberculosis' (HRW, 2019, 1).

When the first cases of COVID-19 in Venezuela were confirmed in March 2020, the government appeared to be developing a sufficient response to the evolving health emergency (Berwick *et al.*, 2020). Venezuela's borders were closed, while government and health officials attempted to establish quarantine protocols and the strict enforcement of these new measures. In theory, these measures should have gone some way to preventing the spread of the disease; however, a particularity of pre-existing circumstances in Venezuela have proven to be the main obstacles that have stymied the government's approach to the threat of COVID-19. For example, the deteriorating infrastructure in Venezuela that has been neglected by the Maduro government since 2014 could not support large sections of the population to be house-bound for extended periods of time due to unstable electricity supplies, problematic access to running water, and functioning sewage (Van Praag and Arnson, 2020).

Unlike many developed countries that were able to smoothly transition many jobs in the formal economy to an online work environment, Venezuela's workforce could not. This is because an outcome of the protracted economic crisis in Venezuela has been the systematic shrinking of the public and private sectors, which have forced a significant section of the population to draw their livelihoods from the informal or black-market economy (Dalby, 2020). This unique set of labour and market conditions has meant that the Venezuelan population has remained much more mobile since the beginning of the pandemic to ensure continued income into many households across the country (Van Praag and Arnson, 2020). Unfortunately, this unusual phenomenon has caused the Maduro government to deploy oppressive measures against the civilian population in an attempt to contain the spread of the virus. Early in the pandemic, the Venezuelan military and security agencies were given primary responsibility for enforcing state border restrictions and curfews across the country.

Venezuela's reliance on the armed forces and other security and intelligence agencies to act as the key problem solvers for complex situations is not unique with many Latin American nations opting for a militarised response to the threat of COVID-19 (Mani, 2020). However, this has provided the military with an even stronger and more salient role in Venezuelan society. This is particularly problematic due to the extremely chequered recent history of the armed forces and security agencies, which have been accused of fostering the emergence a of state-crime nexus in Venezuela. For example, members of the Venezuelan Armed Forces are considered to be key leaders in the Venezuelan criminal organisation that traffics large quantities of cocaine internationally, known as the Cartel de los Soles (Cartel of the Suns) (InSight Crime, 2018). This has occurred alongside increasing attacks by the Maduro government on the last vestiges of democratic processes in the country. In 2020, Freedom House reported that during the early stages of the global pandemic, the Maduro regime made specific moves to diminish the prospect of future free and fair elections in Venezuela (Watson and Moley, 2020). For instance, Maduro once again turned to the Venezuelan Supreme Court (comprising only government supporters) to sidestep the National Assembly's powers to create a new National Electoral Council (Watson and Moley, 2020). Further, the impact of the COVID-19 pandemic has been the cause for blatant attempts to consolidate his authoritarian rule over Venezuela, to the point of not recognising the humanitarian crisis (thus preventing aid agencies from providing assistance) and using food to obtain loyalty (Otis, 2019; *The Economist*, 2021).

In February 2021, Venezuela commenced vaccinations for COVID-19 by offering the Russian-developed Sputnik V and the Chinese-produced Sinopharm. The Venezuelan government announced that its vaccination timeline would enable approximately 70% of the population to be vaccinated by the end of 2021 (Reuters, 2021c). However, it has been reported that despite requests from Venezuela for greater access to vaccines, the Venezuelan government has received only a total 3.5 million does from Russia and China (Reuters, 2021a). Furthermore, according to López Loyo, González and Espara (2021), Maduro's proclamation in late December 2020 that his government had successfully negotiated the supply of a further 10 million doses of the Sputnik V vaccine never 'materialised'. The continued inability of the Venezuelan government to secure a stable supply of vaccines for its population is one of the most acute problems confronting the government, arguably through poor governance, including the lack of a documented vaccination plan (López Loyo *et al.*, 2021). Again, the Venezuelan government's lack of transparency and reticence to release health data, especially in relation to COVID-19, makes it difficult to paint a clear picture of Venezuela's current situation. However, López Loyo, González and Esparza (2021) estimate that the most likely figure of total vaccinations is less than 200,000, and the number of doses earmarked for frontline healthcare workers is negligible.

The health crisis and vaccination problems endure in the greater context of the economic quagmire currently engulfing Venezuela. For example, a national survey of living conditions known as the Encovi Report (2021) approximates that Venezuela's GDP shrank 74% between 2014 and 2020. Moreover, researchers working at Andrés Bello Catholic University in Caracas have determined that in 2021, three in four Venezuelans live in extreme poverty, which they attribute as an outcome of both the COVID-19 pandemic and fuel crisis that have been plaguing Venezuela's economy since early 2020 (BBC, 2021). Reuters (2021) has reported that according to the Venezuelan Finance Observatory, year-on-year inflation is approximately 1,743%, and the minimum wage has been reduced to only US$2.50 per month. Finally, in early October 2021, Venezuela was forced to implement a second monetary overhaul in just under three years. The Maduro government's solution to the ills of hyperinflation is to simply remove six zeros from the national currency the *Bolívar* (Reuters, 2021b). While this approach will not resolve any of the extreme economic problems in the country, it will in the short term allow government, business, and ordinary citizens to streamline their accounting processes.

Despite many attempts by the Maduro government to source solutions internally and externally to the ongoing economic, social, political, and health problems, Venezuela finds itself in the unenviable position of being one of the most incapable countries in the world to deal with the impacts of the global pandemic. In early October 2021, the World Health Organization documented cumulative cases of COVID-19 to be 367,672 and 4,454 deaths, but these rather modest figures do not tell the real story of Venezuela's experience of dealing with

COVID-19 (WHO, 2021). In the past, figures provided to international organisations by the Venezuelan government have been heavily criticised as being unreliable due to the lack of transparency concerning data collection methods and analyses (Van Praag and Arnson, 2020). The low levels of transparency and opaque nature of governance and politics in Venezuela make it difficult to accurately reflect the true position that Venezuela finds itself, and this is most likely the desired outcome of the Maduro government (*The Economist*, 2021).

Conclusion

Venezuela's political trajectory has experienced steep twists and turns over the 20th and 21st centuries. During the Cold War, Venezuela was an exemplary model of a thriving Latin American democracy that unapologetically denounced authoritarianism and communism influence in the region and regarded the United States as its natural ally in the region. However, after years of mismanagement, by the late 1990s, the shortcomings of Venezuela's elite democracy were laid bare. New political candidates took centre stage, and the old style of *Punto Fijo* democracy was discarded in favour of the promises a newcomer offering radical change. Hugo Chávez rapidly set about revolutionising all aspects of Venezuelan politics and society, and prime amongst his objectives was to cut Venezuela's historical dependence on the United States. Drawing on endogenous concepts such as radical pan-Americanism and multipolarity as interpreted by President Chávez, Venezuela's radical foreign policy choices in the early 2000s sought to establish new connections with emerging powers outside of the Western Hemisphere. These actions opened the gates for China and Russia to rapidly establish footholds in the Latin American region that enabled the projection of their soft power. As this chapter has demonstrated, while this soft power has taken the form of significant economic assistance to Venezuela, it has only ever been motivated by transactional rather than transformational exchanges. This is why the pursuit of a multipolar world and independence from the United States through close ties with China and Russia has not delivered a more stable and prosperous environment for Venezuela. Instead, over the past 20 years, Venezuela has lurched from economic crisis to political crisis and back again. Propped up by Chinese and Russian money, President Maduro has maintained power in Venezuela despite his government's inability and at times unwillingness to manage the serious economic and social problems in Venezuela. However, this has come at a significant cost. Almost two decades ago, Venezuela was riding high on a wave of radical pan-Americanism that created significant regional movements for change such as the Pink Tide. Today Venezuela finds itself as a pariah in its own region and further abroad. This placed Venezuela in a particularly precarious position right before the onset of the COVID-19 pandemic. Venezuela's experience is as unique as it is extreme; however, its current situation should serve as a cautionary tale for other countries considering the short- and long-term effects of engaging with China's and Russia's transactional soft power approaches.

References

Aló Presidente. (2006). *Program No. 245, 29 January 2006 – Transcript*. Venezuelan Ministry for Communication and Education.

Balding, C. (2017). Venezuela's Road to Disaster Is Littered with Chinese Cash. *Foreign Policy*. https://foreignpolicy.com/2017/06/06/venezuelas-road-to-disaster-is-littered-with-chinese-cash/ (Accessed 26 January 2022).

Berg, R. C. and Martínez Fernández, A. (2019, 2 May). Venezuela Is Armed to the Hilt. *Foreign Policy*. https://foreignpolicy.com/2019/05/02/venezuela-is-armed-to-the-hilt/

Berwick, A. (2019, 22 August). Special report: How Cuba Taught Venezuela to Quash Military Dissent. *Reuters*. https://www.reuters.com/article/us-venezuela-cuba-military-specialreport-idUSKCN1VC1BX.

Berwick, A., Nara, M. and Kinosian, S. (2020, 14 March). Venezuela Confirms Coronavirus Cases Amid Public Health Concerns. *Reuters*. https://www.reuters.com/article/us-health-coronavirus-venezuela/venezuela-confirms-coronavirus-cases-amid-public-health-concerns-idUSKBN2102DR.

Blofield, M., Ewig, C. and Piscopo, J.M. (2017). The Reactive Left: Gender Equality and the Latin American Pink Tide. *Social Politics: International Studies in Gender, State and Society*, *24*(4), 345–369.

Bolívarian Government of Venezuela [BGV]. (1999). *Constitution of the Bolívarian Republic of Venezuela*. Caracas: Venezuelan Ministry of Communication and Information.

BP. (2021). Statistical Review of World Energy 2021. https://www.bp.com/content/dam/bp/business-sites/en/global/corporate/pdfs/energy-economics/statistical-review/bp-stats-review-2021-full-report.pdf (Accessed 24 January 2022).

Briceño-Ruiz, J. and Molina Medina, N. (2020). China–Venezuela Relations in a Context of Change. In R. Bernal-Meza and L. Xing (Eds.), *China–Latin America Relations in the 21st Century*. International Political Economy Series (pp. 147–168). Palgrave MacMillan.

British Broadcasting [BBC]. (2021 October 2). Venezuela Crisis: Three in Four in Extreme Poverty, Study Says. https://www.bbc.com/news/world-latin-america-58743253

Bushnell, J. (2003). *El Libertador: Writings of Simon Bolivar*. Oxford: Oxford University Press.

Cheatham, A., Roy, D. and Labrador, R.C. (2021). *Venezuela: The Rise and Fall of a Petrostate*. Council on Foreign Relations. https://www.cfr.org/backgrounder/venezuela-crisis (Accessed 22 January 2022).

Chodor T. (2015) The Pink Tide: Counter-Hegemonic Potentials. In Chodor, T. (Ed.), *Neoliberal Hegemony and the Pink Tide in Latin America*. International Political Economy Series (pp. 147–161). London: Palgrave Macmillan.

Chodor, T., and McCarthy-Jones, A. (2013). Post-Liberal Regionalism in Latin America and the Influence of Hugo Chávez. *Journal of Iberian and Latin American Research*, *19*(2), 211–223.

CNE (Consejo Nacional Electoral). (2015). Statistics. *Consejo Nacional Electoral*. http://www.cne.gov.ve/web/documentos/estadisticas/e15_01.pdf.

Dalby, C. (2020). Game Changers 2020: How Black Markets Became the New Normal. *InSight Crime*, December 23. https://insightcrime.org/news/analysis/gamechanger-black-markets-new-normal/

Diamond, L. (2002). Thinking About Hybrid Regimes. *Journal of Democracy*, *13*(2), 21–35.

Ellner, S. (2008). *Rethinking Venezuelan Politics: Class, Conflict, and the Chávez Phenomenon*. Boulder, CO: Lynne Rienner Publishers.

Ellner, S. (2017). Venezuela's Fragile Revolution: From Chávez to Maduro. *Monthly Review*, 69(5), 1–14.

El Universal. (2015 January 4). Maduro Travels to China to Seek Support in the Face of Falling Oil Prices [*Maduro viaja a China para buscar apoyo ante caída de precios del petróleo*]. El Universal. https://www.eluniversal.com.co/mundo/maduro-viaja-china-para-buscar-apoyo-ante-caida-de-precios-del-petroleo-181161-NVEU278432.

Encovi. (2021). *Encuesta Nacional de Condiciones de Vida* [National Survey of Living Conditions]. Instituto de Investigaciones Económicas y Sociales, Universidad Católica Andrés Bello. https://assets.websitefiles.com/5d14c6a5c4ad42a4e794d0f7/6153ad6fb92e4428cada4fb7_Presentacion%20ENCOVI%202021%20V1.pdf

Ferchen, M. (2020). China-Venezuela Relations in the Twenty-First Century: From Overconfidence to Uncertainty. United States Institute for Peace Special Report No. 484. https://www.usip.org/publications/2020/09/china-venezuela-relations-twenty-first-century-overconfidence-uncertainty (Accessed 26 January 2022).

García-Guadilla, M.P. and Mallen, A. (2019). Polarization, Participatory Democracy, and Democratic Erosion in Venezuela's Twenty-First Century Socialism. *The Annals of the American Academy of Political and Social Science, 681*(1), 62–77.

Hellinger, D. (2019, 7 February). *Venezuela crisis explained: a tale of two presidents.* The Conversation. https://theconversation.com/venezuela-crisis-explained-a-tale-of-two-presidents-111198.

Herbst, J.E. and Marczak, J. (2019, 12 September). Russia's Intervention in Venezuela: What's At Stake? *Atlantic Council.* https://www.atlanticcouncil.org/in-depth-research-reports/report/russias-intervention-in-venezuela-whats-at-stake/

Hernández, I. and Monaldi, F. (2016). Weathering Collapse: An Assessment of the Financial and Operational Situation of the Venezuelan Oil Industry. CID Working Paper Series 2016.327, Harvard University. https://dash.harvard.edu/bitstream/handle/1/37366358/327.pdf?sequence=1andisAllowed=y

HRW [Human Rights Watch]. (2019, 4 April). Venezuela's Humanitarian Emergency Large-Scale UN Response Needed to Address Health and Food Crises. *Human Rights Watch.* https://www.hrw.org/report/2019/04/04/venezuelas-humanitarian-emergency/large-scale-un-response-needed-address-health

Ianchovichina, E. and Onder, H. (2017). Dutch Disease: An Economic Illness Easy to Catch, Difficult to Cure. *Brookings Institution.* https://www.brookings.edu/blog/future-development/2017/10/31/dutch-disease-an-economic-illness-easy-to-catch-difficult-to-cure/ (Accessed 22 January 2022).

IMF [International Monetary Fund]. (2021). Venezuela: Country Data. *International Monetary Fund.* https://www.imf.org/en/Countries/VEN#countrydata.

InSight Crime. (2018). Venezuela: a Mafia State? *InSight Crime.* https://insightcrime.org/investigations/venezuela-mafia-state/

Kurmanaev, A. (2019a). Why Is Russia Helping Venezuela? *New York Times*, March 8. https://www.nytimes.com/2019/03/08/world/americas/russia-venezuela-maduro-putin.html.

Kurmanaev, A. (2019b). Venezuela's Collapse Is the Worst Outside of War in Decades, Economists Say. *New York Times*, May 17. https://www.nytimes.com/2019/05/17/world/americas/venezuela-economy.html.

Lichtblau, J. (1999). The Oil Price Collapse and Its Consequences. In *State of the Petroleum Industry.* Washington, DC: US Senate Committee. https://eprinc.org/download/Oil_Price_Collapse.PDF.

López Loyo, E. S., González, M. J. and Esparza, J. (2021). Venezuela Is Collapsing without COVID-19 Vaccines. *The Lancet, 397*(0287), 1806.

Lowe, C. and Sagdiev, R. (2019, 14 March). How Russia Sank Billions of Dollars into Venezuelan Quicksand. *Reuters*. https://www.reuters.com/investigates/special-report/venezuela-russia-rosneft/.

Mani, K. (2020, 21 April). The Soldier Is Here to Defend You. Latin America's Militarized Response to COVID-19. *World Politics Review*. https://www.worldpoliticsreview.com/articles/28700/from-peru-to-venezuela-military-forces-take-the-lead-in-coronavirus-responses

McCarthy-Jones, A. (2014). Ploughing the Sea. In a World of Regions Venezuela's Role in Reviving Latin American Regionalism for the Twenty-First Century. In L. Angosto-Ferrández (Ed.), *Venezuela and the International Politics of Discontent Democracy, Revolution and Geopolitics in Latin America*. New York: Routledge, pp. 67–86.

McCarthy-Jones, A. and Greig, A. (2011). Somos hijos de Sandino y Bolivar: Radical Pan-American Traditions in Historical and Cultural Context. *Journal of Iberian and Latin American Research*, *17*(2), 231–248.

McCarthy-Jones, A. and Turner, M. (2021). What Is a "Mafia State" and how is one created? *Policy Studies*.

McCoy, J. L. and Myers, D. J. (Eds.). (2004). *The Unravelling of Representative Democracy in Venezuela*. Baltimore, MD: The Johns Hopkins University Press.

Navone, A. (2021). *Could China Play a Role in Venezuela's Crisis?* United States Institute of Peace. https://www.usip.org/publications/2021/07/could-china-play-role-venezuelas-crisis (Accessed 26 January 2021).

Otis, J. (2019). *Lives Are At Risk: Venezuelan Charities Struggle under Shortages and Intimidation*. NPR. https://www.npr.org/2019/06/11/731648645/lives-are-at-risk-venezuelan-charities-struggle-under-shortages-and-intimidation (Accessed 26 January 2022).

Penfold-Beccera, M. (2007). Clientelism and Social Funds: Evidence from Chávez's Missions. *Latin American Politics and Society, 49*(4), 63–84.

Primer Informe (2021). La historia de cómo Chávez hizo caer a Venezuela en la trampa de deuda china [The Story of How Chavez Brought Venezuela into the Chinese Debt Trap]. *Primer Informe*. https://primerinforme.com/2021/02/17/la-historia-de-como-chavez-llevo-a-venezuela-a-la-trampa-de-deuda-china/

Provea. (2014 June 24). Venezuela 2014: Protestas y Derechos Humanos [Venezuela 2014: Protests and Human Rights]. *PROVEA*. https://issuu.com/proveaong/docs/informe-final-protestas2.

Rabe, S. G. (1996). The Caribbean Triangle: Betancourt, Castro, and Trujillo and U.S. Foreign Policy, 1958–1963. *Diplomatic History, 20*(1), 55–78.

Rendon, M. (2018, 3 April). When Investment Hurts: Chinese Influence in Venezuela. *Centre for Strategic and International Studies*. https://www.csis.org/analysis/when-investment-hurts-chinese-influence-venezuela

Reuters. (2021a). COVAX Aims to Resolve Venezuela COVID-19 Vaccine Roadblocks after Maduro Ultimatum. *Reuters*, July 7. https://www.reuters.com/world/americas/covax-aims-resolve-venezuela-covid-19-vaccine-roadblocks-after-maduro-ultimatum-2021-07-06/

Reuters. (2021b). Venezuela Subtracts Six Zeros from Currency, Second Overhaul in Three Years. *Reuters*, October 2. https://www.reuters.com/world/americas/venezuela-subtract-six-zeros-currency-second-overhaul-three-years-2021-10-01/

Reuters .(2021c). Venezuela Begins Vaccinating 2-Year-Old Children with Cuban Doses–Vice President. https://www.reuters.com/business/healthcare-pharmaceuticals/venezuela-begins-vaccinating-2-year-old-children-with-cuban-doses-vice-president-2021-11-08/ (Accessed 26 January 2022).

Ríos, X. (2013). China and Venezuela: Ambitions and Complexities of an Improving Relationship. *East Asia, 30*, 53–65.

Rodríguez, F. (2008). An Empty Revolution: The Unfulfilled Promises of Hugo Chávez. *Foreign Affairs*, *87*(2), 49–58, 60–62.

Rondeaux, C. (2020 April 3). Why Russia's Oil Giant, Rosneft, Abruptly Cut Its Ties with Venezuela. *World Political Review*. https://www.worldpoliticsreview.com/articles/28655/what-does-rosneft-cutting-ties-with-venezuela-mean-for-russia-venezuela-relations

Rosales, A. (2019) Radical Rentierism: Gold Mining, Cryptocurrency and Commodity Collateralization in Venezuela. *Review of International Political Economy, 26*(6) 1311-1332.

Rouvinski, V. (2019) Russian-Venezuelan Relations at a Crossroads. Woodrow Wilson International Center for Scholars. https://www.wilsoncenter.org/sites/default/files/russiavenezuela_report_rouvinski_final.pdf.

Rouvinksi, V. (2021) Venezuela: Russia's Gordian Knot in Latin America. In C. J. Arnson (Ed.), *The Ties that Bind*. Woodrow Wilson International Center for Scholars, pp. 20–53. https://www.wilsoncenter.org/sites/default/files/media/uploads/documents/LAP_210510-Venezuelas%20Authoritarian%20Allies-V5.pdf.

Sabatini, C. (2014). Meaningless Multilateralism: In International Diplomacy, South America Chooses Quantity over Quality. *Foreign Affairs*. https://www.foreignaffairs.com/articles/south-america/2014-08-08/meaningless-multilateralism (Accessed 26 January 2022).

Sequera, V. (2014 February 22). Student Protest over Campus Rape Attempt Lit Fuse behind Venezuelan Unrest. *The Star*. https://www.thestar.com/news/world/2014/02/22/student_protest_over_campus_rape_attempt_lit_fuse_behind_venezuelan_unrest.html.

Shifter, M. (2006). In Search of Hugo Chávez. *Foreign Affairs*. https://www.foreignaffairs.com/articles/venezuela/2006-05-01/search-hugo-ch-vez (Accessed 26 January 2022).

Smilde, D. (2019 April 4). Venezuela's Power Struggle Reaches a Tense Stalemate, as Human Suffering Deepens. *The Conversation*. https://theconversation.com/venezuelas-power-struggle-reaches-a-tense-stalemate-as-human-suffering-deepens-114545

Soler, A. (2021 August 23). Venezuela and China: Strong Bond or Empty Words? Debt, Sanctions and Taxes Put This South-South Relation to the Test. *Global Voices*, August 23. https://globalvoices.org/2021/08/23/venezuela-and-china-strong-bond-or-empty-words/.

The Economist. (2021, 13 November). Six Ways Nicolás Maduro Stays in Power in Venezuela. https://www.economist.com/the-americas/six-ways-nicolas-maduro-stays-in-power-in-venezuela/21806197 (Accessed 26 January 2022).

Tinker Salas, M. (2009). *The Enduring Legacy: Oil, Culture, and Society in Venezuela*. Durham, NC: Duke University Press.

Trinkunas, H. A. (2002). The Crisis in Venezuelan Civil-Military Relations. *Latin American Research Review*, *37*(1), 41–76.

Tsvetkova, N., Kheifets, V., Sytnik, A. and Tsvetkov, I. (2019). Venezuela in U.S. Public Diplomacy, 1950s–2000s: The Cold War, Democratization, and the Digitalization of Politics. *Cogent Social Sciences*, 5, 1.

United States Department of Treasury. (2021). Financial Sanctions – Venezuela. https://home.treasury.gov/policy-issues/financial-sanctions/faqs/topic/1581

Van Praag, O. and Arnson, C. (2020). A Crisis within a Crisis. *Wilson Centre.* https://www.wilsoncenter.org/sites/default/files/media/uploads/documents/A%20Crisis%20Within%20a%20Crisis_Venezuela%20and%20COVID-19%20%281%29.pdf

Watson, C. and Moley, J. (2020 August 31). Pandemic and Persecution in Venezuela. *Freedom House.* https://freedomhouse.org/article/pandemic-and-persecution-venezuela

WHO [World Health Organisation] (2021 October 4). COVID-19 Bolivarian Republic of Venezuela. https://covid19.who.int/region/amro/country/ve

Yergin, D. (1992). *The Prize: The Epic Quest for Oil, Money and Power.* New York: Free Press.

17

NATIONALIST POLITICS, ANTI-VACCINATION AND THE LIMITS OF THE RULES-BASED WORLD ORDER IN AN ERA OF PANDEMICS

The case of Tanzania

Japhace Poncian

Introduction

The world has, since December 2019, been engulfed in panic following the manifestation of the coronavirus disease (COVID-19). This panic stems from the real danger and threat posed by COVID-19 to public health and global socio-economic and political systems for three major reasons. First, COVID-19 is a new virus that spreads rapidly and to which the world knows little about it (Nicomedes and Avila, 2020). Second, although there are variations in fatality rates for COVID-19 across countries, comorbidities and age groups (Koh, Geller, and VanderWeele, 2021; Rosa *et al.*, 2021; Surendra *et al.*, 2021), and later, variants of the virus reportedly spread faster than the original variant. Since its beginnings in late 2019, COVID-19 infected a total of 363 million people worldwide by 28 January 2022, with a total of 5.63 million reported deaths (WHO, 2022). Third, the disease has been shown to have adverse effects not only on public health and the general health systems but also on several other socio-economic systems including tourism and international travel, gender-based violence, amplifying existing socio-economic inequalities, and taking a toll on social services delivery, among others (CCSA, 2020; Dlamini, 2021; Kideghesho *et al.*, 2021; Leburu-Masigo and Kgadima, 2020). Finally, since its eruption in 2019, several variants of the virus have been reported, some of which are said to be more contagious and cause more severe conditions such as the Delta variant (Janik *et al.*, 2021). This suggests that COVID-19 mutates continually making efforts to curb it harder (Vasireddy *et al.*, 2021). The World Health Organization (WHO), a key international organ at the helm of COVID-19 pandemic management, has issued a protocol for managing and controlling the pandemic spread and infection. The key measures purported to be useful in managing and limiting the spread of the virus include washing and sanitising hands, observing social

DOI: 10.4324/9781003273844-17

distance, vaccination, avoiding gatherings, and wearing a face mask. Whereas these measures are internationally accepted for addressing the pandemic, there have, in practice, been variations in the uptake of the COVID-19 protocol across countries. The manifestation of the variation in COVID-19 protocol uptake has taken a form of vaccine nationalism, anti-vaccine movements, COVID-19 denialism, and modification in some measures such as, for instance, emphasising the use of locally made face masks instead of the medically approved ones. This variation can, among other factors, be attributed to populist politics in individual countries and the growing mistrust between the governed and the governors (Devine *et al.*, 2021; Khemani, 2020).

All across the world, political response to COVID-19 has followed populist sentiments with some governments resorting to anti-science and the attack on critical thinking (Lee and Johnstone, 2021). Political leaders in both developed and developing countries such as the United States, Brazil, the Philippines, and Tanzania, among others, have been on record for disregarding existing scientific and expert understanding of COVID-19 (Burni and Tamaki, 2021; Hedges and Lasco, 2021; Kiptinness and Okoye, 2021; Lee and Johnstone, 2021). Underpinning this populist response to COVID-19 is the waning faith and trust in internationalism as well as historical perceptions held mostly by Third World Countries that international institutions have imperialistic tendencies to exploit human and natural resources of poor countries (Pevehouse, 2020; Ross, 2020).

This chapter draws on Tanzania's response to the COVID-19 pandemic to highlight the limitations of the international rules-based order in addressing social and public health emergencies in the face of increasing populism and nationalism. The chapter restricts itself to an examination of Tanzania's response to COVID-19 under the late President John Magufuli. In examining how President Magufuli's administration responded to COVID-19, the chapter advances an argument that COVID-19 has helped show that the 'rules-based' world order remains elusive in an age of reinvigorated nationalism. In presenting this argument, the chapter begins with a review of the rules-based world order within the context of rising nationalist and populist politics and how these feature in the global response to the pandemic. This helps provide context within which to understand Tanzania's broader nationalist politics under President Magufuli and how these shaped the country's response to COVID-19. Finally, the chapter draws some implications for internationalism.

The rise in nationalist politics and the plight of internationalism

Over the recent past, nationalist and populist politics have become the norm in numerous countries, including the Philippines, Brazil, the United Kingdom, the Netherlands, Venezuela, the United States, Spain, and Tanzania. Nationalist and populist politics have become prominent so much that some analysists are worried about the future of regional integration and international cooperation as can be attested by Brexit (Elias, 2009; Frieden, 2021; Pevehouse, 2020). Whereas this is becoming common, nationalist and populist politics are by no means new in international politics. Nationalist politics have been around throughout history and were, for instance, a major political force in interwar Europe with the rise of fascist regimes. They have been around so much that some researchers think their recent manifestation should not be a call for concern (Bieber, 2018).

As an ideology, nationalism has been a common feature of international politics for a long time. It generally connotes prioritising one's nation over all other nations and other social groups, or in other words, the right to national self-determination especially when this has to do with how nations respond and/or object to internationalism (Elias, 2009). Nationalism is, according to Bieber (2018, p. 520), an ideology 'which values membership in a nation greater than other groups … seeks distinction from other nations, and strives to preserve the nation and give preference to political representation by the nation for the nation'. Whereas internationalism and global cooperation, remarkable features of global economics particularly during the 1990s, emphasise nations coming together in collaboration for the common good of all nations (Obstfeld, 2021), nationalism emphasises an inward-looking strategy with individual nations prioritising their own self-interest and affiliation (Bollyky and Bown, 2020). Most recently, however, a major emphasis with nationalism has been an anti-globalisation and anti-internationalism rhetoric, which seeks to prioritise domestic considerations and needs at the expense of international cooperation (Frieden, 2021).

Whereas nationalism in its Westphalian sense has been an enduring feature of international relations since the 17th century (Jensen, 2016), there has been an increase in incidences of nationalist politics in recent years that go beyond the generally accepted ideas of national sovereignty and self-determination. This raises a fundamental question on why nationalist politics have gained some currency in the world today and what this means for internationalism. Arguably, it has been shown that neoliberal globalisation has affected nations and people severely as to produce citizens who are angry and suspicious of immigration and globalisation as well as the political establishment (Besley and Persson, 2021; Bonikowski *et al.*, 2019). Confidence in globalisation has been shown to have been undermined even in regions such as Europe where globalisation was embraced (Woods *et al.*, 2020). Further, it has been argued that globalisation started losing its appeal after the terrorist attacks on the United States in September 2001 (Frieden, 2018; Sluga, 2013). More recently, increased globalisation reflected in neoliberal economic reforms since the 1980s has been shown to have accelerated income inequality across countries and increasing insensitivity of international economic forces over growing domestic political pressure (Frieden, 2021). Interestingly, nationalistic politics occurring in the United States under President Trump and in the United Kingdom under Prime Minister Johnson have partly 'undone' the concept of globalisation as an inevitable force and encouraged a sovereign approach to governing national interactions or 'globalism' (see de Percy, Chapter 9). Apart from the economic consequences of globalisation, a backslide in democratic governance in countries such as Hungary, Turkey, and Venezuela has been encouraged where less democratic regimes are increasingly using nationalism to gain legitimacy (Frieden, 2021).

Further sources of an increase in lack of trust in the liberal international order include global shifts in economic power manifested in the military and economic rise of China and other emerging economies, an increase in illiberal non-state actors, deep-seated problems with the legitimacy of political elites, and social and racial problems in various countries (Hameiri and Jones, 2018; Ikenberry, Parmar, and Stokes, 2018). China's rise as an economic power on the back of anti-US nationalism can be traced back to the neglect of China in the international fora following the end of the Cold War (Bin, 1996; Jian, 2003). Although China has since found acceptance and recognition in the international liberal order, its foreign policy has in many ways undermined the globalisation project especially with respect to liberal ideals held dear by Western powers. For instance, whereas the Western powers have emphasised observance of liberal ideals in their foreign policy to Africa and the rest of the developing world, China has advanced a policy of non-interference in domestic affairs, which appears to undermine the liberal international order (Gonzalez-Vicente, 2015; Po and Sims, 2022; Sceats and Breslin, 2012). Chinese nationalism has also involved a growing distrust of the international order (see Cui, Dong, and Christensen, this volume, Chapter 14). This especially is the case, as we shall see in the next section, with how China has consistently closed its doors to the international community when dealing with pandemics such as SARS in 2002–2003 and COVID-19 (Wright, 2021).

Nationalism, the rules-based world order, and response to COVID-19

The eruption of COVID-19 and its escalation into a global pandemic have exposed fragility of the rules-based world order in practice. The rules-based world order, a much debated concept, is used in the context of this chapter to refer to an international order comprising generally accepted legal and normative principles often modelled on liberal ideals of international law and order (Beeson and Chubb, 2021; Zala, 2016). While the rules-based world order has understandably been around throughout the post–World War II era, recent developments have shown that the theory and practice of the same are increasingly becoming fragile. For example, some developed nations supported multilateralism financially and rhetorically while at the same time behaved in ways that reduced their 'soft power', especially in the Global South (see Brown and Rosier, this volume, Chapter 13). Moreover, the COVID-19 pandemic and how different countries have adopted divergent responses to it point to the elusiveness of a rules-based world order especially as it relates to the WHO mandate. Hinting at the way COVID-19 is already affecting the rules-based world order, one analyst cautions that:

> [t]he novel coronavirus (COVID-19) pandemic, which has been rampaging across the globe, is catalysing profound changes unseen in a century.

> As this unprecedented transformation interacts and clashes with the current international order, an escalating contention between two ordering principles is on the horizon … Global governance calls for global wisdom and global responsibility, but the fierce rivalry between a multilateral order and a unilateral order is only getting more intense. Cooperation among major powers is difficult to achieve, particularly as China and the United States, the world's two largest economies, are increasingly going separate ways.
>
> *(Zongze, 2020, p. 34)*

Whereas it appears that the main driver of the challenge confronting the rules-based world order is the rivalry between the United States and China, it should be noted that nationalist politics around the world have made the challenge more serious. For example, national security concerns are increasingly used as an excuse to adopt medical protectionist policies in response to COVID-19. One analyst has captured this succinctly:

> In the United States, politicians from both major parties are demanding new 'Buy American' rules for government health spending. French President Emmanuel Macron is seeking 'full independence' in critical medical supplies by year's-end. Almost ninety countries are now blocking the export of medical goods. Twenty-nine are doing so with food.
>
> *(Steil, 2020, p. 191)*

The US–China rivalry manifesting in a trade war that predated COVID-19 had major ramifications on the existing world order. After coming to power in 2016, President Trump rode on a nationalist agenda dubbed 'Make America Great Again', which President Trump used to secure a presidential seat by exploiting public resentment amid wage inequality, rising debts, and job losses (Paszak, 2021). This agenda saw President Trump engage in a trade war with China around three key concerns: First, that China's chronically large trade surplus was depressing job creation in the United States; second, that China was using illegal and unfair methods to acquire US technology at a discounted price; and third, that China was seeking to weaken US national security and its international standing (Liu and Woo, 2018). This trade war and deteriorating US–China relations during President Trump's administration made matters worse for the international order during the COVID-19 pandemic. For instance, amid the COVID-19 pandemic, President Trump accused China of being responsible for the global spread of the virus and urged the United Nations to hold China accountable for its actions (Nichols and Holland, 2020). Further, President Trump accused WHO of being a 'puppet of China' by failing to hold China accountable and always being on China's side (BBC, 2020b). Following these accusations, President Trump announced his government's intention to withdraw US membership from WHO, a move that was described as 'unlawful' and a threat to global and US health and security (Gostin *et al.*, 2020). The US's accusations towards China and key global governance institutions such as the WHO underscored the threat that nationalist politics posed to the sanctity of the existing rules-based world order. It challenged the primacy of international coordination and cooperation in addressing global challenges and reduced trust in the global governance institutions (see Jakupec, Chapter 6).

Nationalist politics and their impact on the COVID-19 response did not only play out through the US–China rivalry but also through the COVID-19 'vaccine race' (Freymann and Stebbing, 2020). Vaccine nationalism has become a topical issue in the COVID-19 response. Vaccine nationalism refers, broadly, to a 'situation whereby governments take unilateral actions to provide their own populations with access to vaccines ahead of other countries' (Gruszczynski and Wu, 2021, p. 712). It rests on a controversial view that 'countries of the global north are ethically justified in prioritising their citizens over citizens of countries of the global south when it comes to the supply and rollout of COVID-19 vaccines' (Schuklenk, 2021, p. 99). Different countries have embraced the race to produce and secure vaccines as part of their national strategy to respond to and address the COVID-19 pandemic. This is underpinned by the reality that there has been limited global, coordinated access to vaccines during the pandemic (Vanderslott *et al.*, 2021). Vaccine nationalism has especially been more pronounced in advanced economies where governments have ordered millions of vaccine doses in order to inoculate their own people first, often with severe repercussions to developing economies that can hardly afford the vaccines (Gruszczynski and Wu, 2021; Zhou, 2021).

By January 2021, advanced economies had secured about 60% of the 7 billion vaccines that were sold even though these countries constitute only 14% of the global population (Gruszczynski and Wu, 2021). Even though the COVID-19 Vaccine Global Access Facility (COVAX) facility has been put in place at the global level to coordinate vaccine production, procurement, and supply mostly for the developing world, this has not been able to address the inequalities created by vaccine nationalism. For instance, whereas Haiti only received its first shipment of 500,000 vaccine doses in July 2021 for a population of 11 million, Canada had inoculated about 70% of the population with at least one dose, and 50% of the country's residents were fully vaccinated by July 2021 (Schuklenk, 2021). More importantly, although COVAX makes COVID vaccines accessible to developing countries, vaccine nationalism makes it harder for those vaccinated with some vaccine varieties such as the Indian-made version of AstraZeneca to travel to developed countries such as those in the European Union (Cheng, 2021). Indeed, while Trump administration officials had compared vaccine nationalism to putting on one's own oxygen mask in an airplane before helping others, the 'major difference, of course, is that airplane oxygen masks do not drop only in first class' (Bollyky and Bown, 2020). Vaccine nationalism has brought to the fore issues of global coordination and cooperation that privilege the developed world when it comes to pressing global challenges, thus questioning the efficacy of the existing rules-based world order.

Another important challenge to the rules-based world order during the COVID-19 pandemic is how nationalism has been deployed as an excuse not to adhere to the WHO COVID-19 protocol in some countries (Forman *et al.*, 2021; Whitehead and Perry, 2020). This is reflected in political resistance and opposition to vaccination, testing, and disclosure of COVID-19 information, and officially providing misinformation about COVID-19, among other forms of resistance. A typical example of this comes from Tanzania under the late President Magufuli's administration to which we now turn.

Nationalism and response to COVID-19 in Tanzania

Tanzania typifies countries where nationalist politics have impacted greatly on the efficacy of the COVID-19 response. Broader nationalist politics that have been around since 2005 exemplified in state developmentalism have taken a toll on Tanzania's response to COVID-19. From COVID-19 denialism to anti-vaccination and religion, nationalist politics have shaped how Tanzania under the late President Magufuli's administration responded to COVID-19, effectively undermining the rules-based world order.

Like other countries in Africa and worldwide, Tanzania was not spared from COVID-19. The first case of COVID-19 infection in Tanzania was announced on 16 March 2020, and it was reportedly an imported case (Tarimo and Wu, 2020). From that time, the country consistently took relevant measures as per the WHO COVID-19 response protocol, including screening and testing, daily disclosure of COVID-19 infections and deaths, and adhering to standard public control measures including face-masking, washing hands, and social distancing. By 29 April 2020, the total number of confirmed cases was 509 while that of deaths due to COVID-19 stood at 21 (BBC, 2020c; Buguzi, 2021). Between March and late April 2020, Tanzania took all necessary measures as prescribed by WHO in response to the pandemic, including fully testing and reporting on new infections and deaths and adopting partial lockdown by closing schools, colleges, and universities and banning public gatherings, social distancing, encouraging face-masking, washing hands, and sanitisation. However, whereas the government had banned all public gatherings from 17 March 2021 for a period of 30 days, a ban not lifted until June 2020, President Magufuli declared on 23 March 2020 that places of worship would not be closed as he claimed that COVID-19 could be overcome through prayer: 'We are not closing places of worship. That's where there is true healing. Corona is the devil and it cannot survive in the body of Jesus' (Edwards, 2020). This turn to a religious approach to address the pandemic subsequently became a key government strategy in response to the pandemic.

On 16 April 2020, President Magufuli declared three days of observing fasting and prayer to begin on Friday, 17 April, to Sunday, 19 April 2020, and involving all religions to pray for God's protection and healing from COVID-19 (VOA News, 2020). The president's urge to fast and pray and his statement that the virus could be overcome through prayer reportedly 'eased people's fears about the virus being an abnormal disease and created new hope across the country' (Mpota, 2020). Alongside a religious approach, the president and the Ministry of Health also encouraged Tanzanians to use traditional herbs (Mpota, 2020). This included such measures as steam inhalation, drinking herbs such as ginger and lemon, and procuring and encouraging the use of COVID Organics, a herbal drink received from Madagascar in May 2020 (Richey *et al.*, 2021).

As days went on, President Magufuli's administration changed its response strategy to a more non-scientific approach based on conspiracy theories. This began with a stoppage of disclosure of COVID-19 infection and mortality data, which meant that COVID-19 infections and deaths were for the last time disclosed on 29 April 2020. This then was followed, in early May 2020, by a government-commissioned investigation of the national laboratory that conducted COVID-19 tests and the test kits used for testing. Based on this investigation, President Magufuli reportedly said the imported test kits were faulty because they had returned positive results on a goat and a pawpaw (Paravicini, 2020; Richey *et al.*, 2021). This was followed by the suspension of the head of the national laboratory in charge of testing (Paravicini, 2020). On 7 June 2020, President Magufuli declared Tanzania free from COVID-19 while attending a Christian Sunday service in a church in Dodoma claiming that:

> [t]he corona disease has been eliminated thanks to God. I want to thank Tanzanians of all faiths. We have been praying and fasting for God to save us from the pandemic that has afflicted our country and the world. But God has answered us. I believe, and I'm certain that many Tanzanians believe, that the corona disease has been eliminated by God.
>
> *(BBC, 2020a)*

Alongside declaring Tanzania to be COVID-19 free, President Magufuli ordered schools and other institutions that were closed in March in response to COVID-19 to be opened (Makoni, 2021). He also rode on conspiracy theories and popular mistrust of the international community to drive an anti-masking agenda by cautioning Tanzanians to be careful with foreign donations to support fight against the pandemic. The president reportedly cautioned that:

> [w]e need to be careful because some of these donations to fight coronavirus could be used to transmit the virus. I want to urge you Tanzanians not to accept donations of masks, instead tell the donors to go and use them with their wives and children.
>
> *(BBC, 2020a)*

By cautioning Tanzanians over imported or donated masks, President Magufuli urged the nationals to use locally made face masks instead (Thomas, 2021). A similar caution was also issued by President Magufuli in January 2021, this time with additional caution regarding COVID vaccines:

> You should stand firm. Vaccinations are dangerous. If the White man was able to come up with vaccinations, he should have found a vaccination for AIDS by now; he would have found a vaccination [for] tuberculosis by now; he would have found a vaccination for malaria by now; he would have found a vaccination for cancer by now.
>
> *(Makoni, 2021, p. 566)*

By claiming the vaccines and imported face masks were not safe for Tanzanians, President Magufuli effectively drew on popular mistrust of the *mabeberu* (imperialists) and sought to drive a nationalist agenda encouraging locally relevant responses to the pandemic against those accepted by the international community (Richey *et al.*, 2021). All this said, how did Tanzania under President Magufuli get to this nationalist response to COVID-19 with disregard to WHO protocol and scientific knowledge?

It should be said outright here that President Magufuli's administration was known for its populist nationalist governance approach long before the COVID-19 pandemic. Between 2016 and 2019, for instance, Tanzania attracted much international media attention due to its resource nationalist strategy in the management of the country's extractive resources. President Magufuli's administration banned the export of raw mineral concentrates in favour of value addition; seized several containers of mineral concentrates at the port of Dar es Salaam; demanded that Acacia Mining Company Plc pay US$ 190 billion in taxes owed to the government; and enacted laws banning international arbitration, reasserting permanent sovereignty over natural resources, and providing for renegotiation of unconscionable contract terms as well as demanding for mandatory state participation in extractive projects (Jacob and Pedersen, 2018; Poncian, 2019, 2021). These developments created tension between President Magufuli's administration and multinational companies working in Tanzania, notably with Acacia Mining company whose mineral concentrate containers were seized by the government at the port (Jacob and Pedersen, 2018). At one time, President Magufuli reportedly threatened that multinational corporations would better pack and go to allow the government to allocate their mining sites to artisanal and small-scale miners (Poncian, 2019).

In shaking up the private sector, President Magufuli branded himself as an economic messiah taking Tanzania through an economic warfare against the robbery of its natural wealth perpetrated by multinational corporations and supported by the *vibaraka wa mabeberu* (accomplices of imperialists) (Poncian, 2019). Further, President Magufuli had adopted a development strategy akin to state developmentalism with a major focus on mega infrastructural projects in order to 'make Tanzania great again' (Nkobou and Ainslie, 2021; Paget, 2020). President Magufuli's nationalist strategies appear to have been grounded on a popular perception that foreign companies were exploiting Tanzania leaving behind no or little benefit; therefore, they need to be checked and monitored, a view President Magufuli rode on during his presidential election campaigns in 2015 (Poncian, 2019). His mistrust of the international capital informed much of his stance, a probable reason why he never visited any Western country during his presidential tenure.

Thus, when the COVID-19 pandemic commenced and the international community faltered in its agenda for countries to adopt and implement agreed measures against the pandemic, these were landing in Tanzania on a platform that was already fertile with nationalistic and anti-globalisation views. Further, the rules-based world order was impacted by the decisions of President Trump in the United States and President Xi Jinping in China, which had effectively weakened the WHO that struggled to respond effectively to the crisis, and multilateral institutions such as the G-7, the G-20, and the UN Security Council 'failed to rise to the occasion' (Patrick, 2020). President Magufuli's disregard of the COVID-19 response protocol should, therefore, be understood in this context. Nevertheless, religion and traditional herbs continued to be an important COVID-19 response strategy up until March 2021 when President Magufuli died from 'heart problems', sparking conspiracy theories amid alleged controversy about the circumstances of his death (Burke, 2021; Olewe, 2021).

What is more troubling, however, is how a rules-based world order failed to keep a poor country like Tanzania in check when it defaulted on WHO standards. WHO's response to Tanzania's approach to addressing the COVID-19 pandemic was limited to the WHO being able to do little more than urge the country to report the pandemic cases, share data, and implement public health measures to stop virus transmission (Makoye, 2021). In a statement issued in February 2021, the WHO referred to the pandemic response situation in Tanzania as 'concerning' and called on the country to 'implement the public health measures that we know work in breaking the chains of transmission, and to prepare for vaccination' (WHO, 2021). The fact that there was nothing more serious WHO could do to bring Tanzania to comply with accepted COVID-19 response strategy underscores how the geopolitical situation, the rivalry between the political leadership of the United States and China, and the rhetoric and financial support for multilateralism from developed nations while prioritising their own people exposed loopholes within the rules-based world order that effectively undermined the 'soft power' of the WHO and other multilateral institutions and hence their legitimacy. There was no mechanism in place to hold Tanzania accountable for shunning science in favour of religion, herbs, and conspiracy theories. Indeed, at the same time, President Trump was advocating unproven COVID-19 treatments (Niburski and Niburski, 2020) amid the US government's 'confusing, inconsistent, and counterproductive' pandemic response (Acemoglu, 2020). This raises the question: What can the international community do when a country defaults on rules set by global governance institutions such as the WHO? Since Tanzania could walk away with its anti-vaccination and COVID-19 denialism as much as the United States walked away with its threat to remove its membership from WHO suggests that, despite its institutions, technical expertise, and resilience (at least in the post-war era), the rules-based world order relies on cooperation to be effective, and, given recent events, it is clear that the existing rules-based world order is inherently fragile.

Conclusion

The spread of COVID-19 not only shocked the world in terms of its socio-economic and life impact but has also generated divergent response strategies across the world. While it would have been reasonable to expect a multilaterally based strategic response based on cooperation and coordination, COVID-19 has instead exposed the fragility of the existing rules-based world order. Instead, nationalism and populism have become key defining concepts of how countries have individually responded to the pandemic. Motivated by a growing distaste for globalisation in both developed and developing countries, the turn towards nationalist politics in addressing the pandemic suggests that COVID-19 has been a catalyst for change. This chapter has drawn on the case of Tanzania to examine how nationalism and anti-vaccination sentiments have exposed the fragility of the rules-based world order. It has shown that anti-globalisation sentiments have pushed several governments in both developed and developing countries to resort to nationalist politics in order to grapple with the consequences of the pandemic. Vaccine nationalism in the developed world has revitalised sentiments of exploitative and imperial North–South relations, rivalries between global economic powers such as China and the United States, increased mistrust in globalisation and global governance institutions, as well as bold national non-compliance with global COVID-19 pandemic response protocol. In effect, these have made countries prioritise their national interests at the expense of global coordination and cooperation. Evidence from Tanzania shows that the rules-based world order is increasingly under threat from a crisis of legitimacy. The WHO, while striving to keep countries focused on cooperative confrontation of the pandemic, has failed to wield its expert authority over countries such as Tanzania, while its very expertise has been under threat from the major global powers. Further, that countries such as Tanzania have decided to address the pandemic their own way by side-lining the established scientific expertise suggests that the rules-based world order is as strong as each individual country chooses to ascribe and comply with it. This is evident in how the rules-based world order became less relevant during President Magufuli's administration only to become relevant again under President Samia Hassan's administration, which has chosen to re-engage with the rules-based world order and multilateralism. Thus, this chapter has shown that nationalism, when given full expression in governance, reduces the impact of advances in science and international relations and exposes the fragility of the existing world order.

References

Acemoglu, D. (2020). The Coronavirus Exposed America's Authoritarian Turn: Independent Expertise Always Dies First When Democracy Recedes. *Foreign Affairs*, 23 March 2020. https://www.foreignaffairs.com/articles/2020-03-23/coronavirus-exposed-americas-authoritarian-turn (Accessed 28 January 2022).

BBC. (2020a). Coronavirus: John Magufuli Declares Tanzania Free of Covid-19. *BBC News*, Retrieved October 30, 2021, from https://www.bbc.com/news/world-africa-52966016?source=pepperjamandpublisherId=120349andclickId=3743820859

BBC. (2020b, May 19). Coronavirus: Trump Accuses WHO of being a "Puppet of China." *BBC News*. Retrieved from https://www.bbc.com/news/health-52679329

BBC. (2020c, June 8). Coronavirus: John Magufuli Declares Tanzania Free of Covid-19. *BBC News*. Retrieved from https://www.bbc.com/news/world-africa-52966016?source=pepperjamandpublisherId=120349andclickId=3743771322

Beeson, M., and Chubb, A. (2021). Australia, China and the Maritime 'Rules-Based International Order': Comparing the South China Sea and Timor Sea Disputes. *International Relations of the Asia-Pacific*, 21(2), 233–264.

Besley, T., & Persson, T. (2021). The Rise of Identity Politics: Policy, Political Organization, and Nationalist Dynamics. Working Paper, London School of Economics.

Bieber, F. (2018). Is Nationalism on the Rise? Assessing Global Trends. *Ethnopolitics*, *17*(5), 519–540.

Bin, Y. (1996). The China Syndrome: Rising Nationalism and Conflict with the West. *Asia Pacific Issues*, *27*, 1–7.

Bollyky, T. J., and Bown, C. P. (2020). The Tragedy of Vaccine Nationalism: Only Cooperation Can End the Pandemic. *Foreign Affairs*, September/October 2020. https://www.foreignaffairs.com/articles/united-states/2020-07-27/vaccine-nationalism-pandemic (Accessed 28 January 2022).

Bonikowski, B., Halikiopoulou, D., Kaufmann, E., and Rooduijn, M. (2019). Populism and Nationalism in a Comparative Perspective: A Scholarly Exchange. *Nations and Nationalism*, *25*(1), 58–81.

Buguzi, S. (2021). Covid-19: Counting the Cost of Denial in Tanzania. *BMJ*, *373*(n1052), 1–2.

Burke, J. (2021). Tanzania Leader Says Prayer Will Cure Covid, as Hospitals Overflow. *The Guardian*. Retrieved October 30, 2021, from https://www.theguardian.com/world/2021/feb/28/tanzania-leader-says-prayer-will-cure-covid-as-hospitals-overflow

Burni, A., and Tamaki, E. (2021). Populist Communication during the Covid-19 Pandemic: The Case of Brazil's President Bolsonaro. *Partecipazione e Conflitto*, *14*(1), 113–131.

Cheng, M. (2021, July 13). Immunized but Banned: EU Says Not All COVID Vaccines Equal. *Associated Press*. Retrieved from https://apnews.com/article/europe-business-lifestyle-health-travel-f678a53270470d9b35ce6259e48548bf

Devine, D., Gaskell, J., Jennings, W., and Stoker, G. (2021). Trust and the Coronavirus Pandemic: What Are the Consequences of and for Trust? An Early Review of the Literature. *Political Studies Review*, *19*(2), 274–285.

Dlamini, N. J. (2021). Gender-Based Violence, Twin Pandemic to COVID-19. *Critical Sociology*, *47*(4–5), 583–590.

Edwards, N. (2020). Tanzania's Mild Response to COVID-19 and Its Implications for the 2020 Elections. Retrieved October 30, 2021, from https://www.atlanticcouncil.org/blogs/africasource/tanzanias-mild-response-to-covid-19-and-its-implications-for-the-2020-elections/

Elias, A. (2009). *Minority Nationalist Parties and European Integration: A Comparative Study.* Oxford: Routledge.

Forman, R., Shah, S., Jeurissen, P., Jit, M., and Mossialos, E. (2021). COVID-19 Vaccine Challenges: What Have We Learned So Far and What Remains To Be Done? *Health Policy, 125*(5), 553–567.

Freymann, E. and Stebbing, J. (2020). China Is Winning the Vaccine Race: How Beijing Positioned Itself as the Savior of the Developing World. *Foreign Affairs*, 5 November 2020. https://www.foreignaffairs.com/articles/united-states/2020-11-05/china-winning-vaccine-race (Accessed 28 January 2020).

Frieden, J. (2018). The Backlash against Globalization and the Future of the International Economic Order. Paper prepared for a Policy Network volume, *The Next Phase of Globalisation: Capitalism and Inequality in the Industrialized World*, Harvard University, February 2018. URL: https://scholar.harvard.edu/files/jfrieden/files/frieden_future_feb2018.pdf (Accessed 28 January 2022).

Frieden, J. (2021). International Cooperation in the Age of Populism. In L. B. Pereira, M. E. Mata, and M. R. de Sousa (Eds.), *Economic Globalization and Governance* (pp. 303–314). Cham: Springer.

Gonzalez-Vicente, R. (2015). The Limits to China's Non-Interference Foreign Policy: Pro-State Interventionism and the Rescaling of Economic Governance. *Australian Journal of International Affairs, 69*(2), 205–223.

Gostin, L. O., Koh, H. H., Williams, M., Hamburg, M. A., Benjamin, G., Foege, W. H., … Kavanagh, M. M. (2020). US Withdrawal from WHO Is Unlawful and Threatens Global and US Health and Security. *The Lancet, 396*(10247), 293–295.

Gruszczynski, L., and Wu, C. (2021). Between the High Ideals and Reality: Managing COVID-19 Vaccine Nationalism. *European Journal of Risk Regulation, 12*(3), 711–719.

Hameiri, S., and Jones, L. (2018). China Challenges Global Governance? Chinese International Development Finance and the AIIB. *International Affairs, 94*, 573–593.

Hedges, K., and Lasco, G. (2021). Medical Populism and COVID-19 Testing. *Open Anthropological Research, 1*, 73–86.

Ikenberry, G. J., Parmar, I., and Stokes, D. (2018). Introduction: Ordering the World? Liberal Internationalism in Theory and Practice. *International Affairs, 94*(1), 1–5.

Jacob, T., and Pedersen, R. H. (2018). New Resource Nationalism? Continuity and Change in Tanzania's Extractive Industries. *Extractive Industries and Society, 5*(2), 287–292.

Janik, E., Niemcewicz, M., Podogrocki, M., Majsterek, I., and Bijak, M. (2021). The Emerging Concern and Interest SARS-CoV-2 Variants. *Pathogens, 10*(633), 1–13.

Jensen, L. (2016). The Roots of Nationalism: Introduction. In L. Jensen (Ed.), *The Roots of Nationalism: National Identity Formation in Early Modern Europe, 1600–1815* (pp. 9–27). Amsterdam: Amsterdam University Press.

Jian, Z. (2003). Chinese Nationalism and Its Foreign Policy Implications. In D.W. Lovell (Ed.), *Asia-Pacific Security: Policy Challenges* (pp. 108–125). Singapore: ISEAS Publishing.

Khemani, S. (2020). An Opportunity to Build Legitimacy and Trust in Public Institutions in the Time of COVID-19. *Research and Policy Briefs From the World Bank Malaysia Hub, 32*. https://papers.ssrn.com/sol3/papers.cfm?abstract_id=3602352

Kideghesho, J. R., Kimaro, H. S., Mayengo, G., and Kisingo, A. W. (2021). Will Tanzania's Wildlife Sector Survive the COVID-19 Pandemic? *Tropical Conservation Science, 14*, 1–18.

Kiptinness, E. M., and Okoye, J. (2021). Media Coverage of the Novel Coronavirus (Covid-19) in Kenya and Tanzania: Content Analysis of Newspaper Articles in East Africa. *Cogent Medicine, 8*(1), 1956034.

Koh, H. K., Geller, A. C., and VanderWeele, T. J. (2021). Editorial: Deaths from COVID-19. *JAMA*, *325*(2), 133–134.

Leburu-Masigo, G. E., and Kgadima, N. P. (2020). Gender-Based Violence during the Covid-19 Pandemic in South Africa: Guidelines for Social Work Practice. *Gender and Behaviour*, *18*(4), 16618–16628.

Lee, E., and Johnstone, M. (2021). Resisting politics of Authoritarian Populism during COVID-19, Reclaiming Democracy and Narrative Justice: Centering Critical Thinking in Social Work. *International Social Work*, *64*(5), 716–730.

Liu, T., and Woo, W. T. (2018). Understanding the U.S. -China Trade War. *China Economic Journal*, *11*(3), 319–340.

Makoni, M. (2021). World Report Tanzania Refuses COVID-19 Vaccines. *The Lancet*, *397*(10274), 566.

Makoye, K. (2021). WHO Urges Tanzania to Release Data on COVID-19. Retrieved October 30, 2021, from https://www.aa.com.tr/en/africa/who-urges-tanzania-to-release-data-on-covid-19/2151934#

Mpota, S. S. (2020). The Role of Religion and Traditional Medicines in Fighting COVID-19 in Tanzania. Retrieved October 30, 2021, from https://blogs.lse.ac.uk/africaatlse/2020/08/12/role-religion-traditional-medicines-covid19-tanzania-herbs-magufuli/

Nichols, M., and Holland, S. (2020, September 22). U.S.-China Tensions Take Center Stage at U.N. as Trump Accuses Beijing of Unleashing "Plague." *Reuters*. Retrieved from https://www.reuters.com/article/un-assembly-idUSKCN26D2KU

Niburski, K., and Niburski, O. (2020). Impact of Trump's Promotion of Unproven COVID-19 Treatments and Subsequent Internet Trends: Observational Study. *Journal of Medical Internet Research*, *22*(11).

Nicomedes, C. J. C., and Avila, R. M. A. (2020). An Analysis on the Panic during COVID-19 Pandemic through Online Form. *Journal of Affective Disorders*, *276*, 14–22.

Nkobou, A. T., and Ainslie, A. (2021). 'Developmental Nationalism?' Political Trust and the Politics of Large-Scale Land Investment in Magufuli's Tanzania. *Journal of Eastern African Studies*, *15*(3), 378–399.

Obstfeld, M. (2021). Globalization and Nationalism: Retrospect and Prospect. *Contemporary Economic Policy*, *39*, 675–690.

Olewe, D. (2021). John Magufuli: The Cautionary Tale of the President Who Denied Coronavirus. *BBC News*, 18 March 2021. https://www.bbc.com/news/world-africa-56412912 (Accessed 28 January 2021).

Paget, D. (2020). Again, Making Tanzania Great: Magufuli's Restorationist Developmental Nationalism. *Democratization*, *27.7* (2020), 1240–1260.

Paravicini, G. (2020). Africa Disease Centre Rejects Tanzania's Allegation That Its Coronavirus Tests Faulty. *Reuters* Retrieved October 30, 2021, from https://www.reuters.com/article/us-health-coronavirus-tanzania-tests/africa-disease-centre-rejects-tanzanias-allegation-that-its-coronavirus-tests-faulty-idUSKBN22J1FO

Paszak, P. (2021). *US-China Trade War: Origins, Timeline and Consequences*. Warsaw: Warsaw Institute.

Patrick, S. (2020). When the System Fails: COVID-19 and the Costs of Global Dysfunction. *Foreign Affairs*, July/August 2020. URL: https://www.foreignaffairs.com/articles/world/2020-06-09/when-system-fails (Accessed 28 January 2021).

Pevehouse, J. C. W. (2020). The COVID-19 Pandemic, International Cooperation, and Populism. *International Organization*, *74*(Supplement), E191–E212.

Po, S., and Sims, K. (2022). The Myth of Non-Interference: Chinese Foreign Policy in Cambodia. *Asian Studies Review, 46*, 36–54.

Poncian, J. (2019). Galvanising Political Support through Resource Nationalism : A Case of Tanzania's 2017 Extractive Sector Reforms. *Political Geography, 69*, 77–88.

Poncian, J. (2021). Resource Nationalism and Community Engagement in Extractive Resource Governance: Insights from Tanzania. *Review of African Political Economy, 48*, 529–551.

Richey, L. A., Gissel, L. E., Kweka, O. L., Bærendtsen, P., Kragelund, P., Hambati, H. Q., and Mwamfupe, A. (2021). South-South Humanitarianism: The Case of Covid-Organics in Tanzania. *World Development, 141*, 105375.

Rosa, F. G. De, Palazzo, A., Rosso, T., Shbaklo, N., Mussa, M., Boglione, L., … Corcione, S. (2021). Risk Factors for Mortality in COVID-19 Hospitalised Patients in Piedmont, Italy: Results from the Multicenter, Regional, CORACLE Registry. *Journal of Clinical Medicine, 10* (1951), 1–13.

Ross, K. R. (2020). Faith in Internationalism: Covid-19 and the International Order. *Transformation: An International Journal of Holistic Mission Studies, 37*(4), 276–285.

Sceats, S., and Breslin, S. (2012). *China and the International Human Rights System*. London: Chatham House.

Schuklenk, U. (2021). Editorial: Vaccine Nationalism – At This Point in the COVID-19 Pandemic: Unjustifiable. *Developing World Biotechnology, 21*, 99.

Sluga, G. (2013). *Internationalism in the Age of Nationalism*. Philadelphia: University of Pennsylvania Press.

Steil, B. (2020). Models for a Post-COVID US Foreign Economic Policy. In H. Brands and F. J. Gavin (Eds.), *COVID-19 and World Order: The Future of Conflict, Competition, and Cooperation* (pp. 191–203). Baltimore, MD: Johns Hopkins University Press.

Surendra, H., Elyazar, I. R. F., Djaafara, B. A., Ekawati, L. L., Saraswati, K., Adrian, V., … Hamers, R. L. (2021). Clinical Characteristics and Mortality Associated with COVID-19 in Jakarta, Indonesia: A Hospital-Based Retrospective Cohort Study. *The Lancet Regional Health-Western Pacific, 9*, 100108.

Tarimo, C. S., and Wu, J. (2020). The First Confirmed Case of COVID-19 in Tanzania: Recommendations Based on Lesson Learned from China. *Tropical Medicine and Health, 48*(25), 1–3.

The Committee for the Coordination of Statistical Activities (CCSA). (2020). *How COVID-19 Is Changing the World: A Statistical Perspective*. New York: CCSA.

Thomas, D. (2021). Is Magufuli's Covid-19 Response a Threat to the Region? Retrieved October 30, 2021, from https://african.business/2021/03/technology-information/magufulis-covid-19-negligence-threatens-region/

Vanderslott, S., Emary, K., Naude, W., Henry, J., English, M., Thomas, T., … Pollard, A. J. (2021). Vaccine Nationalism and Internationalism: Perspectives of 19 Vaccine Trial Participants in the United Kingdom. *BMJ Global Health, 6*, e006305.

Vasireddy, D., Vanaparthy, R., Mohan, G., Malayalad, S. V., and Atluri, P. (2021). Review of COVID-19 Variants and COVID-19 Vaccine Efficacy: What the Clinician Should Know? *Journal of Clinical Medicine Research, 13*(6), 317–325.

VOA News. (2020). Tanzanian President Declares 3 Days of National Prayer to Help Defeat Coronavirus. Retrieved October 30, 2020, from https://www.voanews.com/a/covid-19-pandemic_tanzanian-president-declares-3-days-national-prayer-help-defeat-coronavirus/6187740.html

Whitehead, A. L., and Perry, S. L. (2020). How Culture Wars Delay Herd Immunity: Christian Nationalism and Anti-vaccine Attitudes. *Socius: Sociological Research for a Dynamic World*, *6*, 1–12.

World Health Organisation [WHO]. (2021). WHO Director-General's Statement on Tanzania and COVID-19. Retrieved October 30, 2021, from https://www.who.int/news/item/20-02-2021-who-director-general-s-statement-on-tanzania-and-covid-19

World Health Organisation [WHO]. (2022). WHO Coronavirus (COVID-19) Dashboard. https://covid19.who.int/ (Accessed 28 January 2022).

Woods, E. T., Hughes, C., Schertzer, R., and Miller-idriss, C. (2020). COVID-19, Nationalism, and the Politics of Crisis: A BBC. (2020a). Coronavirus: John Magufuli declares Tanzania free of Covid-19. *BBC News*. Retrieved October 30, 2021, from https://www.bbc.com/news/world-africa-52966016?source=pepperjamandpublisherId=120349andclickId=3743820859

Zala, B. (2016). The Australian 2016 Defence White Paper, Great-Power Rivalry and a 'Rules-Based Order': An Imagined Correspondence between Carr, Bull and Bell. *Australian Journal of International Affairs*, *70*(5), 441–452.

18

COVID-19 CRISIS AND THE WORLD (RE-)ORDER

Max Kelly, Viktor Jakupec, and Michael de Percy

Introduction

The COVID-19 pandemic provides a rapidly evolving context dominating the public and media attention for close to two years at the time of writing this chapter. The impacts of the pandemic have shifted over time, from its initial position of a disease of the international travelling class, through a disease that disproportionately affected those already socially, economically, and otherwise marginalised. The fluidity of the situation makes it difficult to track a discourse in a clear fashion. Thus, even the most fundamental theoretical and practical analysis must remain flexible and can only be best presented as scenarios. Notwithstanding these challenges, pragmatically, historically, and theoretically, cognisant scholarly reflections may be beneficial for ascertaining the *Zeitgeist* of COVID-19 pandemic as a crisis almost two years in. The question, of course, is from which perspective should this discourse proceed.

The social determinants of health play out in the COVID space as much as they do with other diseases. However, it is increasingly apparent that the broader socio-economic and socio-political impacts of the COVID-19 pandemic are insidious and less discussed. There has been public discourse on the tensions between economic imperatives and public health imperatives, less explicitly framed by fiscal conditions and finally social conditions. These have played out in global health governance, in political discourses, and predominantly in public decision making about restrictions on publics unseen for decades. Lockdowns, movement restrictions, and stay-at-home orders have been framed around health/economy arguments and have proved politically complex. There are strong themes of uncertainty and disruption at international, national, and local levels, yet the structural causes of health remain as unaddressed as ever. The commitment of global leaders to addressing the pandemic remains embargoed within

DOI: 10.4324/9781003273844-18

political and economic concerns, rather than technical solutions, at a point of the pandemic where vaccines are available and reducing mortality and morbidity associated with the contracting of COVID-19.

The pandemic can be understood as a catalyst for change. Foreign aid and development have been side-lined by some Western nations struggling with the (geo-)political, social, and economic consequences of the pandemic, enabling China and Russia to exert 'soft power' in areas previously inaccessible. Global development is in a state of crisis with gains made under pre-COVID conditions in poverty, health, education, and many other areas now lost. Increasing challenges to the rules-based world order, founded at Bretton Woods, have already been seen in the rise of illiberal democracy, the swing away from globalisation, the rise of populism, and nationalism. Globally the shift from a unipolar world order, framed by the post–Cold War dominance of the US, has slowly given way to a more complex economic and power shift, from the North Atlantic to Asia, from the US as hegemon to a rising powers discourse, centred around US–China relations.

This chapter examines key themes emerging from the COVID-19 pandemic and its impact on the world order. Disruption has occurred at multiple levels, impacting many of the formal and informal institutions that order human life, ranging from 'social distancing' to challenging norms around working from home to outright defiance of the expertise of international institutions such as the World Health Organization (WHO). The concluding discussion focuses on how foreign aid is deeply challenged by pandemic-related drivers of political self-interest within the context of a rapidly changing global governance and world order.

Disruption and differentiated experiences of COVID-19, an evolving story

The National Intelligence Council (2021) notes that 'the ongoing COVID-19 pandemic marks the most significant, singular global disruption since World War II, with health, economic, political, and security implications that will ripple for years to come' (p. 2). Even as it stands today, the COVID-19 pandemic as a mega-crisis (discussed later) has exemplified the limitations, if not failures, of multilateral co-ordination of health crises and an incongruity between existing multilateral organisations such as the International Financial Institutions (IFIs), their funding levels, and upcoming health, political, economic, societal, and other challenges. At the nation state levels, there is a continuing and rising disparity between what people in low- and middle-income countries require and what aid agencies, national governments, and IFIs are able to provide. In other words, the COVID-19 pandemic as a mega-crisis is stretching the capacity of governments to maintain and increase services, thereby adding to the (by now) dwindling levels of trust into IFIs but with arguably limited capacity for aid agencies to address a growing shortfall between need and resources.

The COVID-19 pandemic has been experienced differently across regions. The Organisation for Economic Co-operation and Development (OECD) noted, in May 2021, the territorial dimensions of the COVID-19 pandemic, seen in infection and mortality rates, which differ regionally due to a variety of factors including differing access to health services, vulnerabilities to disease from demographics, and the underpinning social determinants of health. The WHO (2022) defines the social determinants of health as:

> the non-medical factors that influence health outcomes. They are the conditions in which people are born, grow, work, live, and age, and the wider set of forces and systems shaping the conditions of daily life. These forces and systems include economic policies and systems, development agendas, social norms, social policies and political systems.
>
> *https://www.who.int/health-topics/social-determinants-of-health#tab=tab_1*

The socio-economic impact of the pandemic will take considerably longer to empirically determine potential outcomes. Abidoye *et al.* (2021) assessed increases in poverty head counts. They modelled an increase of 626 million under a 'COVID Baseline' scenario and 753 million under a 'High Damage' scenario. Under a 'COVID Baseline' scenario, 86% of all people pushed into poverty by 2030 would live in countries with low and medium levels of human development and 79% under a 'High Damage' scenario. Of these, an estimated 41–169 million people will be directly pushed into poverty by the pandemic under the 'COVID Baseline' and 'High Damage' scenarios relative to the No-COVID scenario.

Prior to the pandemic, food and nutrition insecurity was on the rise, reversing improvements gained over the previous one and a half decades. Poverty, conflict, natural hazards, and climate change are all contributors to this reversal. There is increasing evidence of the disparities faced by those in lower income distributions.

The differentiated impact and response to the pandemic is perhaps well illustrated in the case of sub-Saharan Africa. Rompel (this volume, Chapter 10) outlines lower infection and mortality rates in many parts of the continent, highlighting potential underpinning factors as demography (lower age profiles), effective public health interventions, possible immune responses from previous exposure to other coronaviruses, and the potential of under-reporting contributing to some of the situation, due to data availability and reporting issues. However, he also draws on the concept of a reconceptualisation of the pandemic as a 'polypandemic'.

The notion of a 'PolyPandemic' was highlighted at the 2020 Munich Security Conference (MSC, 2020). It encompasses the very differentiated and diverse disruptions of the COVID-19 pandemic, including a hunger pandemic, a poverty pandemic, an authoritarianism pandemic, and further 'pandemics' in education, violence, and inequality, all of which are interpreted in complex ways.

In essence, the core argument around the notion of a polypandemic is of the mutually reinforcing nature of these 'pandemics'.

The impact of COVID-19 pandemic: an emerging picture

In order to gain a better understanding of the 'pandemics', it may be useful to provide a brief outline of impact from a selective geopolitical perspective.

McGillivray's assessment of the impact of COVID-19 in the Pacific (this volume, Chapter 12) highlights the nature of COVID as a classic exogenous shock. It can't be avoided, and it compounds existing vulnerabilities. Utilising a multidimensional lens, the Pacific is particularly vulnerable. McGillivray's argument is in line with Rompel, with regard to the mutually reinforcing nature of complex vulnerabilities. The former concludes that aid must focus on reducing existing vulnerabilities to limit the propensity of exogenous events to be transmitted to endogenous impacts. The fundamentals of this argument are straightforward, yet the context in which aid is committed and delivered by donors' countries is also impacted by the pandemic.

However, Grigoryev and Moriskina (this volume, Chapter 6) found that there was some stability with regard to the traditional obligations of donors in aid and development funding, although clear decreases were noted in particular by the UK, which dropped official development assistance (ODA) funding below the 0.7% gross national product, an almost moral or iconic position the UK has held since 2013. However, by mid-2021, the UK had noted its commitment to return to 0.7% gross national income (GNI), when 'fiscal conditions permit' (UK Government, 2021). The European Union's (EU) response to the pandemic within its borders, as well as globally, has been to *expand* its budgetary expenditure. Along with significant increases in expenditure, the EU collectively committed to providing ODA of 0.7% of GNI within the 2030 Agenda (European Commission, 2021). However, according to OECD estimates, the scope and complexity of global needs have increased dramatically during the COVID-19 pandemic.

The MSC report (2020) argues that from the political economy perspective, responses to the pandemic and differentiated impacts reflect 'normal' conditions globally. In their words,

> wealthier states' pandemic responses are a continuation of a pre-pandemic behavior: one of underinvestment in the safety and well-being of the world's most vulnerable places.
>
> *(n.p.)*

The recognition of effective capacity of various nation states in sub-Saharan Africa to have demonstrated a more effective public health response challenges the political economy of global governance and health in many ways. This narrative runs alongside a more contentious narrative whereby the capacity of African states to absorb vaccine donations and get them into arms is widely questioned, due to supply chain issues all the way through to the vaccination sites. Yet closer examination highlights issues with vaccine distribution through COVAX, including issues with shelf life, advance notice of arrivals, as well as more structural domestic issues. A continuation of the 'capacity' discourse is used alongside the locus of vaccine production debates.

The issue of a Trade and Intellectual Property Agreement (TRIPS) waiver was raised by South Africa and India early in the pandemic (October 2020) and is supported in the World Trade Organization (WTO) by more than 100 countries. The proposed waiver on intellectual property (IP) rights is to overcome barriers to universal and affordable access to vaccines, as well as other essential medical technology for treatment and testing. In essence, it would allow countries to produce their own COVID-19 vaccines. In what has been termed '*fractiously stalemated talks at the World Trade Organization*' (Beattie, 2022, p. 1), the issue of the waiver has diverged into an ideological stalemate, with some retreating to selected firmly entranced ideological positions around the moral imperative, not just to help the 'less fortunate' but also the moral imperative to act in solidarity, to be '*part of the group*' (Thambisetty, 2021, n.p.). The alternate view is of IP as 'property', which is to be protected and valued.

Current debates feature the spectre of *Moderna* (vaccine manufacturer) announcing its own plant in South Africa and *BioNTech* developing 'mobile' manufacturing facilities for Africa (Beattie, 2022), retaining IP in the process, and thus presumably full profits. In response to the lack of movement on TRIPS waiver and lack of progress on getting vaccines accessible across the continent, South African scientists, collaborating with WHO, are in early stages of developing mRNA vaccine as an alternative to Moderna vaccine (Meyer, 2022). The debate on IP is argued by some to be a diversion, yet the relationship between the Global South and the Global North in the WTO is inevitably biased by the liberalisation of trade that framed the WTO at its inception (or emergence from the ashes of the General Agreements on Trades and Tariffs (GATT) depending on one's perspective). Becker (2021) notes that the claims of the Global North are predominantly upheld under the TRIPS to enforce copyrights. Of particular relevance to this debate is the position of the then new Director General of the WTO in May 2021, Ngozi Okonjo-Iweala, the first woman and the first African to hold this position. Her take on this issue was to condemn vaccine nationalism and protectionism and move towards cooperation in treatment and vaccine development, not through TRIPS waivers, but the promotion of multilateralism in exchange of ideas and the promotion of licensing agreements. By December 2021, talks between the US, the EU (seen as the main blocker of the TRIPS waiver), South Africa, and India were still stalled around details, and Dr Okonjo-Iweala highlighted what she termed '*an orchestrated effort to block success on the issue*' (Blenkinsop, 2021).

The primacy or apparent alignment with neoliberalism through private-sector interests and nationalism is a recurring theme across a political economy assessment of responses to COVID-19. We, therefore, turn now to notions of crisis, nationalism, and neoliberalism.

From crisis to mega-crisis: nationalism and COVID-19 as a political economy imperative

In the broadest term, *pandemic* is often denoted as a *crisis*. However, in political economy terms, a deeper delve is warranted. Crises are caused by actual or supposed dangers and are usually exceedingly disruptive incidents, which, in political economy terms, may question the legitimacies of authorities, governments, and supranational organisations, as much as the values and norms of the existing world order (Brecher and James 2019), thereby increasing political and economic uncertainties, with the potential to change the settings within which political economy of a rules-based world order is framed and upheld. Such changes are often initiated by political, economic, societal, and cultural shocks, which are beyond the control of any authority and may subsequently lead to structural indeterminacy of the national and international political economy (see Jakupec, Chapter 6).

COVID-19 pandemic encompasses all the above-mentioned criteria. Thus, the dangers of the pandemic have already prompted a succession of sequential crisis in health, politics, economics, and others such as foreign and humanitarian aid. The pandemic is now endangering the existing Western political economy structure by enforcing nationalist values and norms.

The politicisation of COVID-19 pandemic as a crisis is however not limited to national levels. Based on the above discussion, it could be argued that COVID-19 pandemic is equally applicable to the multilateral scene. That is, as the COVID-19 pandemic spread globally, and the science community raced against time to find a vaccine, the WHO regime to combat pandemics faced significant political pressure. As Kelly and McGlasson (this volume, Chapter 7) note, the US had strong political interactions with WHO, from Trump's withdrawal to reinstatement under Biden, yet not without criticism from the Biden administration. Other powerful WHO members simply ignored its role in coordinating the collection and dissemination of information, distribution of medical equipment, and allocation of resources globally to countries and regions that needed it most (Buranyi, 2020). Two schools of thought can be identified. One subscribes to the theory that WHO has yielded to nationalist intimidation amongst its membership and thus failed to protect (neo-)liberal rules-based world order of which it is an integral part. The other school of thought contends that WHO was seemingly reluctant to exercise its authority. From either viewpoint, the COVID-19 pandemic response from the key multilateral institution in global health, as a health crisis spiralled out of control and became a mega-crisis, created a multifaceted interplay of health, humanitarian, political, and economic crises. Thus, in comparison to a *crisis*, a *mega-crisis* is more severe and greater in complexity (Yew-Cho Yen and Salmon, 2017).

To explain, being a *mega-crisis*, the COVID-19 pandemic is different from other recent *crises* such as the Global Financial Crisis (GFC), the European Sovereign Debt Crisis (ESDC), the European Refugee Crisis, or the SARS-CoV-1 crisis. The first two crises were mainly economic crises; the third one was mainly a political crisis, fuelled by political discord amongst EU member states; and the last was a health crisis. The global community's reactions to these four crises required dealing with each crisis within its problem confines. For example, the SARS-CoV-1 crisis did not become a political or an economic crisis. It was dealt with as a health crisis. In contrast, COVID-19 pandemic was turned into a combined political and economic crisis. This leads to a potential partial destabilisation of the (neo-)liberal rules-based world order, caused by the rise of vaccine nationalism and the weaponisation of vaccine production and dissemination on the global stage.

However, even the most cursory review of mainstream literature discussing COVID-19 pandemic as a crisis in relation to foreign aid locates political economy as central to the analysis. In essence, the economic analysis of the COVID-19 mega-crisis in foreign aid is rather a side theme, embedded in mitigation of the economic fallout, the role of monetary policy, and health-output trade-off (Baldwin and Weder di Mauro, 2020; Faria e Castro, 2021; OECD, 2020). In the foreign aid realm, the prevailing discourse of the mainstream academic community rather focuses on political economic issues of the COVID-19 pandemic.

This is somewhat speculative, but it is instructive to recall some basic historical factors. From the WHO declaration, on 11 March 2020, that COVID-19 is a pandemic, two phenomena emerged. One was global recognition, by multilateral organisations and governments, that it would be impossible to prevent the worldwide spread of the pandemic. Second, the recognition by political powers that the pandemic constitutes a worldwide danger not only to health but also to economic well-being and political stability (Legrain, 2020). It was the last-mentioned factor that was seen by social and political scientists as a catalyst for an increasingly politically divided world due to a rise of nationalism (cf. Bieber 2022; Schertzer and Woods, 2020).

As noted above, the original, perhaps naïve, focus on COVID-19 as a health crisis soon gave way to broader concerns. It did not take long to realise at all political levels that COVID-19 pandemic caused not only a health crisis and humanitarian crisis but also an associated economic and a political crisis. Each of these crises posed a different problem for national governments and relevant multilateral development aid organisations. Only slowly did the governments and multilateral development aid organisations recognise that the world and its rules-based world order are being confronted from an array of interconnected crises. Attempting to contain this pandemic with many faces, the MSC's (2020) 'polypandemic', governments, and multilateral organisations politicised and weaponised vaccine production, allocation, and distribution, which turned the health crisis into a political economy crisis. Thus, the response by governments to the COVID-19 pandemic impacted through the imposition of various restrictive measures negatively on the economy. In turn, the combined impact of economic downturns, restrictive measures such as lockdowns, border closures, and limited movement of goods became politicised. In parallel, there emerged an anti-vaccination movement – mainly in developed economies – which provided a platform for fringe right-wing illiberal and national populist political parties.

One of the most striking aspects of the COVID-19 pandemic was the misinformation and political positioning that occurred at all levels of politics within and without the nation state. For example, Tanzania's president actively denied the existence of COVID-19. Even the then US President Donald Trump was spreading misinformation about the virus and potential cures. At the same time, Venezuela, feeling the effects of the pandemic as its health sector disintegrated, developed a gap between the haves and the have-nots of alarming proportions, exacerbating what was already a humanitarian crisis. Due to the combination of economic and political factors, an unprecedented political economy crisis emerged, which has put people's trust in their governments and the rules-based world order to the test, by questioning their legitimacy. In short, the COVID-19 pandemic became politicised in a context of nationalism.

COVID-19 as a catalyst for nationalism

Much of the discourse concerning nationalism in the preceding chapters is positioned within an ideological perspective of political economy. From this vantage point, nationalism is based on nation states – in shorthand, a territorial group of people with common societal norms and values and autonomy in determining and regulating its own political, economic, social, and cultural affairs. In line with this notion, the rationale for self-determination in world politics is given. Thus, nationalism is built on the foundations of anarchic states and stands in opposition to anarchic supranational organisations. In a contemporary context, it is important to note that COVID-19 pandemic emerged at a political point when nationalism was experiencing a renaissance (Schertzer and Woods, 2020), further supporting the unambiguous political economy aspects of the pandemic.

Nationalism has gained political traction in many developed countries, since the GFC and ESDC, including the US, India, and European countries such as Hungary, Poland, and UK. Over the past two decades, nationalism was fuelled by illiberalism, and at the same time, it provided a basis for populism. With the onset of the COVID-19 pandemic, nationalism gained further political economy traction in the form of 'COVID-19 nationalism'. Thus, it could be argued that COVID-19 pandemic as a mega-crisis is a catalyst for nationalism. This raises the question: to which extent will nationalism as a political ideology and movement expand due to the COVID-19 pandemic as a crisis? As the COVID-19 pandemic progressed rapidly in Europe, the US, and other countries and regions, a significant number of nation states across all continents closed their borders, hoarded much-needed vaccines, and resorted to playing blame games. From its beginnings, COVID-19 as a mega-crisis emerged, with health crisis spawning emergence of associated crises, humanitarian, political, economic, social, and cultural crisis, all rolled into one, consisting of health nationalism, economic nationalism, and a political nationalism. A fleeting review of the academic literature provides an answer, namely that a crisis often leads to the resurgence of nationalism (Wang, 2021). COVID-19 as a mega-crisis (Bildt, 2020) expanded nationalism.

But this is only one side of the coin. There is also some evidence that the COVID-19 pandemic as a crisis has also enhanced the significance of regional solidarity and has supported and reinforced a cross-national regional and multilateral cooperation under an umbrella of multilateral organisations (UNCTAD, 2020). While COVID-19 is a lost opportunity for multilateralism, it has renewed recognition of the desirability of multilateral action. However, the COVID-19 pandemic as seen from a multilateral perspective is in direct ideological contrast with the nationalist perspective. In other words, the former is very much couched in the ideology of neoliberalism, and thus, this crisis may indeed provide a space for the further demise of neoliberalism.

Nationalism versus multilateralism

Against the background and notwithstanding the co-existence of multilateralism built on the neoliberal ideology and nationalism underpinned by illiberalism and populism, the COVID-19 mega-crisis has enabled the national populist agenda to gain further traction in response to the pandemic in Europe, the US, and beyond (cf. Pevehouse, 2020). To explain, in many developed countries, especially in Europe, segments of the population seem to consider the COVID-19 crisis as a consequence of neoliberalism, perceived as a driving force for globalisation with free movement of people, goods, and services. Neoliberal globalisation, so the nationalist argument goes, turned life in nation states upside down with the advent and rapid spread of COVID-19. The nationalist arguments against neoliberal multilateralism are simple. First, a response to COVID-19 pandemic is best facilitated by ensuring a differentiation between the national population and populations from other nations. Second, nationalism accentuates practical effects of national membership, which includes individual rights and obligations. The latter refers to the submission of individuals to the national political agenda. Third, there is a requirement to adhere to political self-determination and self-reliance on combatting COVID-19 pandemic, independent from other nations, regional alliances, and multilateral organisations (Chikvaidze, 2020; Knight, 2020; Sakwa, 2020).

This reconfirms to a certain degree the argument that COVID-19 pandemic has, in specific political and economic arenas, become a catalyst for nationalism. On the one hand, nationalism establishes indifference towards the need of other nations and the functions of multilateral organisations in the fight against COVID-19 pandemic especially with reference to the needs of low- and middle-income countries. On the other hand, nationalism facilitates the uniting of the population in a nation state and bond them to their homeland. It is obvious by now that nationalism by its own definition rejects the legitimacy of neoliberal multilateral organisations and, at the same time, is leading to institutional exhaustion.

Institutional exhaustion and legitimation crisis

There have been repeated warnings about further global pandemics following the 2009 H1N1 pandemic and the 2014 Ebola outbreak, including Bill Gates' 2017 warning of a pandemic that could kill up to 30 million people (Lee, 2017). To date, official records indicate that some 6 million people have died from COVID-19, but a recent report in *Nature* (Adam, 2022) suggests that unreported deaths or those who died having tested positive for COVID-19 may mean that the death toll is significantly higher than the official figure. COVID-19 was an exogenous event to the extent that the global community was unprepared for it.

With the benefit of hindsight, global preparedness for a pandemic may have deployed vaccine manufacturing capabilities throughout the major regions of the world. However, the institutions that would deliver such a capability were already suffering from a legitimation crisis that, by the time the pandemic struck, were exhausted in that they could no longer perform the function they were designed for. The concept of institutional fatigue, or institutional exhaustion, frames debates on relative weakness of international institutions (de Percy, Chapter 12; Kortunov, this volume, Chapter 2). Drawing on weakened institutions to address global crisis, in the face of their 'exhaustion', requires potentially diverse approaches, including a focus on coincidence of interests rather than a common set of values, or ideology, embedded in the 'western' multilateral system. Value pluralism is argued by Kortunov (this volume, Chapter 2) as essential for 21st-century multilateralism. The links between shared interests or values are, of course, at the heart of some of the soft power debates. The pursuit of cultural and political values and foreign policies that lie at the heart of Nyes' (1990) soft power analysis has become synonymous with vaccine nationalism.

World order, soft power, and diplomacy in an age of crisis

There is a series of intense pain points globally, nationally, and locally that have challenged responses to COVID-19, in terms of vaccines, tests, treatment, and control. Although Western rules-based world order institutions have enjoyed a significant amount of legitimation, in terms of their role in global governance over time, they have lost significant ground, through disruptors, and in terms of their own failures to achieve significant impact on health globally. China's response to the pandemic was coordinated and focused on restricting the spread of the virus. Hong Kong, however, which retains some remnants of its British-supervised political culture, is at the time of writing one of the largest COVID-19 hotspots in China, with Beijing to consider implementing the mainland's strict COVID-19 measures to contain the virus. While the US floundered as some individuals prioritised their individual rights over collective health and safety measures, the ability of the world's oldest liberal democracy appeared to be stumbling. Vaccine nationalism, linked to internal domestic political, economic, and health imperatives, derailed multilateral responses particularly in the context of vaccines (Kelly and McGlasson, this volume, Chapter 7).

Meanwhile, the WHO was confronted by its own crisis of legitimacy through the discourse of its capability to provide neutral, unhindered global response and the public display of no confidence by Trump's US government. This position was deliberately and overtly addressed with the election of Biden, but the legitimacy of the WHO is an ongoing discourse. The political affiliations of these multilateral agencies receive attention, with the relationship between China and WHO at the centre of a spat, with Donald Trump famously labelling the WHO as a 'puppet of China' and levelling a number of critiques that have been challenged (see, for example, BBC reality-check team (2021)). Whether COVAX would have been less undermined if the WHO were not subject to dispute is unknown, but COVAX as a multilateral response sits within the overarching aid and development architecture that is challenged by non-traditional donors, shifting global powers and disruptors. The influence of Western power holders within the Bretton Woods institutions and the UN is not discussed in a similar vein but taken for granted as the natural order of things, in response to the post–World War II world order architecture and powers, which turns the debate towards the notion of the world order.

There is significant focus on the new bipolarity of the world order. However, this is a potentially overtly simplistic argument, if one considers disruptors (as discussed in Jakupec *et al.*, Chapter 1). The disruptors also embed moves towards popularism and illiberalism – which also comes within the framework of nationalism. A general trend in literature is of heading towards or standing firmly in a new bipolar world and a resulting bipolar 'rules-based' world order or potentially a non-rules-based order. This assumes multipolarity is either uncertain or future state. If this US–China bipolarity stands, there may be a new neoliberal world order or other, or a world order that has a different format and rules and that is much more eclectic. Specially China is not heading towards a similar rules-based world order. Arguably, the 'West' is almost incapable of conceptualising a world order that is not rules based, nor ordered, nor made in the image of the existing world order.

What does such a scenario mean? As far as foreign aid is concerned, countries may align themselves or seek aid from alternative sources, rules based or other. This is the case now, but to link to economic and ideologically based decisions would be a speculative progression. Returning to economic nationalism, the level of fiscal spending in OECD countries and concurrent reductions in traditional aid donor commitments has opened further alterative spaces for 'non-traditional' donors – especially China – to provide leadership on global issues, including but not limited to well-timed international development aid. The soft power implications of such trends are widely recognised (Kelly and McGlasson, this volume, Chapter 7). The rules-based world order has failed to address COVID pandemic in any meaningful way – it has resulted in a deepening of the issues of nationalism and self-interest, with a focus on bilateral arrangements that are based on soft power objectives rather than global solidarity. The legitimation crisis that has embroiled the WHO and COVAX, as well as other institutions, also begs a reflection on the ongoing capacity of these institutions to respond. The concept of soft power is typically based on the idea that other nation states gravitate towards the nation state with the most admirable moral, political, industrial, scientific, and cultural leadership and ideas and outputs. Such 'soft' power is derived from the gravitational force created when other nation states attempt to emulate the soft power leader, whether in terms of 'ways of doing' or the consumption of leisure products such as movies and entertainment. To be sure, and in the absence of an alternative power, the US was a leader in this space in much the same way that the Roman Empire's cosmopolitanism facilitated the replication of the Roman way of life over a period of centuries. Like the Roman Empire, however, the US' occasionally tenuous grip on soft power was further challenged by emerging vaccine nationalism that gripped developed nations and left developing nations out on a limb. China and Russia quickly filled the soft power vacuum where scientific and industrial power that morphed into vaccine diplomacy displaced moral, political, and cultural power out of necessity.

Great power rivalry amid the pandemic exposed many of the pre-existing fault lines in the rules-based world order that originated with the Bretton Woods conference of 1944. While there are some continuities in the Bretton Woods world order that outlasted the Cold War, embraced neoliberalism, survived global terrorism and the GFC, and resulted in a largely coherent, rules-based, and relatively peaceful global economic system, COVID-19 appears to be the straw that broke the camel's back. Throughout this volume, the contributors have used a variety of terms, neoliberal, US led, rules-based, to describe the world order that existed when the COVID-19 pandemic began. What emerged from the research presented in this volume is that, at the beginning of the COVID-19 pandemic, the world order was facing a legitimacy crisis from within, with the US in particular (but soon followed by its allies) challenging the nature of the rules-based multilateral system, not just in foreign aid and development but also in trade, security, and economic policies, and carbon emissions strategies, addressing refugees, and human rights. As nation states turned further inward, the retreat from globalisation left vacuums in the multilateral systems that had existed, for the most part, for several generations.

Conclusions

The increased emphasis on donor self-interest, even in the face of a global health emergency, is not new to the pandemic context. Rather, COVID has accelerated this pre-existing trend, observable since the 2008 GFC. A *British Medical Journal* opinion piece described COVID vaccines' distribution as '*crumbs from the rich person's table*' and the broader charity model as 'a *catastrophic failure*' (Benton *et al.*, 2021, para. 1).

It has, therefore, been argued that the current pandemic reveals that global health policies are still insufficiently oriented towards human rights standards, equity, and the social and political determinants of health and that this has a particular impact on the situation of structurally marginalised people not only in the Global South but also in the Global North (Meisterhans, this volume, Chapter 4).

There is a tendency for authors to flag that if there is no way to order a global response to a pandemic, then we will never be able to tackle climate change, which appears disingenuous. Alternative perceptions include the argument that we can or must build back better at the international level, addressing national interests and policies that erode global solidarity. The need for the Global South to take a much harder stand against their role as essentially pawns in a power game played with vaccines is strengthened by the experiences of fighting infectious diseases, in the failures of many 'northern' countries to control the pandemic, which took hold in dramatic fashion across the globe.

While there is plenty of evidence to suggest that the changes brought about by COVID-19 will cement a further shift in the geopolitical world order, especially with Russia commencing military operations against Ukraine at the time of writing, common explanations that have been touted by some scholars oversimplify what has become a much more fragmented world. In the earlier era of globalisation, one might be forgiven for imagining a world where aid and development would soon be replaced by capitalism's promise of prosperity. One might also be forgiven for characterising contemporary forms of aid and development, especially China's Belt and Road Initiative, as a form of debt-trap diplomacy that would ultimately lead to war between the US and China as foretold by Thucydides' Trap. But as this volume demonstrates, the geopolitics of multilateralism and the system of foreign aid and development that continues to evolve alongside global human society are increasingly complex and contested. This volume does not provide simple, comprehensible explanations in uncertain times with such memification providing little explanatory power. Indeed, if anything, the diversity of views and cases presented in this volume proves that simple, comprehensible explanations of how any future system funds and coordinates foreign aid and development are entirely unhelpful in understanding the realities that we, as a species, now face. The evolving context of foreign aid, and global solidarity, through regional or multilateral contexts is never more necessary but never more challenged.

References

Abidoye, B., Felix, J., Kapto, S. and Patterson, L. (2021). *Leaving No One Behind: Impact of COVID-19 on the Sustainable Development Goals (SDGs).* New York and Denver, CO: United Nations Development Programme and Frederick S. Pardee Center for International Futures.

Adam, D. (2022). The pandemic's true death toll: millions more than official counts. *Nature* (18 January 2022). https://www.nature.com/articles/d41586-022-00104-8

Baldwin, R. and Weder di Mauro, B. (2020). *Mitigating the COVID Economic Crisis: Act Fast and Do Whatever It Takesa.* VoxEU.org. Washington, DC: CEPR Press.

BBC Reality Check Team (2021). Coronavirus: what are President Trump's charges against the WHO? *BBC News.* https://www.bbc.com/news/world-us-canada-52294623

Beattie, A. (2022). A Covid vaccine breakthrough bypasses the stale debate on patent waivers. *Financial Times* (17 February 2022). https://www.ft.com/content/27fada1a-1dcb-492c-a5ef-9d88a1d91b49

Becker, D. (2021). The global south in the World Trade Organization: an interview with Douglas Becker. 6 April 2021, Glimpse from the Globe website: https://www.glimpsefromtheglobe.com/topics/politics-and-governance/the-global-south-in-the-world-trade-organization-an-interview-with-douglas-becker/

Benton, A., Majumder, M. and Yamey, G. (2021). The global health security agenda rewards rich nations for their selfish behaviour. *BMJOpinion.* https://blogs.bmj.com/bmj/2021/08/20/the-global-health-security-agenda-rewards-rich-nations-for-their-selfish-behaviour/

Bieber, F. (2022). Global nationalism in times of the COVID-19 pandemic. *Nationalities Papers,* Vol. 50 (1), pp. 13–25.

Bildt, C. (2020). Covid-19: the crisis we didn't have to have. *The Strategist* (21 May 2020). https://www.aspistrategist.org.au/covid-19-the-crisis-we-didnt-have-to-have/

Blenkinsop, R. (2021). WTO chief says vaccine answer close, but facing effort to block it. *Reuters.* https://www.reuters.com/business/healthcare-pharmaceuticals/exclusive-wto-chief-says-vaccine-answer-close-facing-effort-block-it-2021-12-16/

Brecher, M. and James, P. (2019). *Crisis and Change in World Politics.* Milton Park, Oxfordshire: Routledge.

Buranyi, S. (2020). The WHO v coronavirus: why it can't handle the pandemic. *The Guardian* (10th April 2020). https://www.theguardian.com/news/2020/apr/10/world-health-organization-who-v-coronavirus-why-it-cant-handle-pandemic

Chikvaidze, D. (2020). Multilateralism: its past, present and future. *Cadmus,* Vol. 4 (2). pp. 127–133.

European Commission (2021). International development aid. Website: https://ec.europa.eu/info/business-economy-euro/economic-and-fiscal-policy-coordination/international-economic-relations/international-development-aid_en

Faria e Castro, M. (2021). Fiscal policy during a pandemic, Federal Reserve Bank of St. Louis. Working Paper 2020-006. https://doi.org/10.20955/wp.2020.006

Knight, R. (2020). Multilateralism vs nationalism in race to provide vaccine. *University Global News* (26 September 2020). https://www.universityworldnews.com/post.php?story=20200922133458856

Lee, B.Y. (2017). Bill Gates warns of epidemic that could kill over 30 million people. *Forbes* (19 February 2017) https://www.forbes.com/sites/brucelee/2017/02/19/bill-gates-warns-of-epidemic-that-will-kill-over-30-million-people/?sh=1996db0b282f

Legrain, P. (2020). The coronavirus is killing globalization as we know it. *Foreign Policy* (March 12, online).

Meyer, D. (2022). Moderna wouldn't share its vaccine technology, so South Africa and the WHO made a COVID jab based on it anyway. *Fortune.* https://fortune.com/2022/02/04/south-africa-afrigen-moderna-covid-vaccine-mrna-who-hotez-corbevax/

MSC (2020). *Polypandemic. Munich Security Report Special Edition on Development, Fragility, and Conflict in the Era of Covid-19.* Munich: Munich Security Conference. November 2020.

National Intelligence Council (2021). *Global Trends 2040: A More Contested World. Global Trends*, 7th Edition, Washington, DC: Office of the Director of national Intelligence.

Nye, J.S. (1990). Soft power. *Foreign Policy*, (80), 153–171.

OECD (2020). *The Impact of the Coronavirus (COVID-19) Crisis on Development Finance*. Paris: OECD. https://oecd.org/coronavirus/policy-responses/the-impact-of-the-coronavirus-covid-19-crisis-on-development-finance-9de00b3b/

Pevehouse, J.C.W. (2020). The COVID-19 pandemic, international cooperation, and populism. *The IO Foundation* (December 2020), pp. E191–E212. https://www.cambridge.org/core/services/aop-cambridge-core/content/view/D38BD179B976E06E6627E11B10F125B3/S0020818320000399a.pdf/the-covid-19-pandemic-international-cooperation-and-populism.pdf

Sakwa, R. (2020). Multilateralism and nationalism in an era of disruption: the great pandemic and international politics. *Journal of International Analytics*, Vol. 11(3), pp. 129–150. https://doi.org/10.46272/2587-8476-2020-11-3-129-150

Schertzer, R., and Woods, E.T. (2020). *How Nationalism Can Be a Force for Good in the Struggle against Covid-19*. LSE: Phelan USA Centre. https://blogs.lse.ac.uk/usappblog/2020/04/09/how-nationalism-can- be-a-force-for-good-in-the-struggle-against-covid-19/

Thambisetty, S. (2021). Opposition to the TRIPS waiver: dispatches from the frontline. *BLOGS@LSE*. https://blogs.lse.ac.uk/politicsandpolicy/trips-waiver-one-year-on/

UK Government (2021). Government sets out conditions for returning to 0.7% aid target, Press Release, *Gov.uk*, Westminster. https://www.gov.uk/government/news/government-sets-out-conditions-for-returning-to-07-aid-target#:~:text=The%20Government%20has%20today%20set,ODA)%20as%20the%20economy%20recovers.&text=The%20Government%20is%20committed%20to,Income%20(GNI)%20on%20ODA.

UNCTAD (2020). South-South Cooperation at the time of COVID-19: Building Solidarity among Developing Countries. https://unctad.org/system/files/official-document/gdsinf2020d4_en.pdf

Wang, Z. (2021). From crisis to nationalism? The conditioned effects of the COVID-19 crisis on neo-nationalism in Europe. *Chinese Political Science Review*, Vol. 6(1), pp. 20–39. doi: 10.1007/s41111-020-00169-8

WHO (2022). *Social Determinants of Health*. Health Topics online. Rome: World Health Organisation. https://www.who.int/health-topics/social-determinants-of-health#tab=tab_1

Yew-Cho Yen, V. and Salmon, C.T. (2017). Further explication of mega-crisis concept and feasible responses. https://pdfs.semanticscholar.org/b060/b2bb834ad30f44533f5654464685c8cdc423.pdf

INDEX